Lake Erie
and
Lake St. Clair
Handbook

Lake Erie
and
Lake St. Clair

Handbook

Edited by

STANLEY J. BOLSENGA

and

CHARLES E. HERDENDORF

WAYNE STATE UNIVERSITY PRESS   DETROIT

GREAT LAKES BOOKS

A complete listing of the books in this series can be found at the back of this volume

Philip P. Mason, Editor
Walter P. Reuther Library, Wayne State University

Dr. Charles K. Hyde, Associate Editor
Department of History, Wayne State University

Copyright © 1993 by Wayne State University Press, Detroit, Michigan 48202. All rights are reserved. No part of this book may be reproduced without formal permission. Manufactured in the United States of America.
99 98 97 96 95 94 93   5 4 3 2 1

Library of Congress Cataloging-in-Publication Data

Lake Erie and Lake St. Clair handbook / edited by Stanley J. Bolsenga and
    Charles E. Herdendorf.
          p. cm. -- (Great Lakes books)
      Includes bibliographical references (p.   ) and index.
      ISBN 0-8143-2486-X (alk. paper).-- ISBN 0-8143-2470-3 (pbk. : alk. paper)
          1. Limnology--Erie, Lake. 2. Limnology--Saint Clair, Lake (Mich. and Ont.).
      3. Natural history--Erie, Lake. 4. Natural history--Saint Clair, Lake (Mich. and
      Ont.). I. Bolsenga, S.J. II. Herdendorf, Charles E. III. Title: Lake Erie and
      Lake Saint Clair handbook. IV. Series.
      GB1627.G83L33 1993
      551.48'2'097712--dc20
                                                                    93-10208
                                                                    CIP
Text Designer: Cathy Darnell
Cover Designer: Mary Primeau

The cover shows a computer-generated image of the Lake Erie and Lake St. Clair region (center left), Lake Ontario (upper right), and a portion of Lake Huron (upper left) constructed by Professor S.I. Outcalt of the University of Michigan using National Oceanic and Atmospheric Administration 30-second, digital, medium resolution, point topography data. Shoreline detail is generalized due to the lack of detail in the original data set combined with the lack of marked elevation increase in the low sloping shoreline areas (for example, Point Pelee does not appear). A data set with increased resolution, using the same computer software, would have accurately portrayed these subtle differences in elevation. However, the combination of shadow and color coded elevations provides a striking overall view of the geologic setting and topography of the land area surrounding the lakes. Note, for example, the transition from the folded Appalachians in the southeast to the glaciated interior lowlands in the northwest. The Niagara escarpment appears prominently to the north of the eastern portion of Lake Erie.

Contents

Contents

Contents

PREFACE AND ACKNOWLEDGEMENTS

This book addresses the wonders of Lake Erie and Lake St. Clair. It is written for all who love and want to know more about the scenic beauty and natural heritage of this international region. More than merely a description, the material in this book presents the scientific reasons for features we see and the phenomena we experience here. Although the manuscript has been used extensively as a reference source, this book is not intended to be a scientific treatise; rather, it promotes an understandable explanation of the fascinating realm known to the early French missionaries as the "Sweetwater Seas."

Lake Erie and its adjoining waterways, including Lake St. Clair, and the Detroit and Niagara Rivers are the subjects for this book. Lake Erie is the most southerly of the Great Lakes, and, therefore, the first to form as the glacial ice sheets began to recede from the region over 12,000 years ago. Also, Lake Erie has had a dramatic environmental history that shows a progression from one of the most productive large lakes in the world in the late 1800s to one of the most polluted in the mid-1900s to today, where it has recovered much of its former glory. The editors of this book have attempted to present a comprehensive view of the environmental quality and natural features of Lake Erie, Lake St. Clair and their environs. We hope the following chapters will enhance your enjoyment and appreciation of this magnificent body of water.

Numerous individuals and two scientific organizations have contributed to the successful completion of this book. Overall authorship and scientific editorial responsibility are by Stanley Bolsenga and Charles Herdendorf. Subject area contributors are as follows:

Chapter 1. The Introduction
Stanley Bolsenga and Charles Herdendorf

Chapter 2. The Lithosphere
Charles Herdendorf

Chapter 3. The Atmosphere
Stanley Bolsenga and Bonnie James

Chapter 4. The Hydrosphere
Stanley Bolsenga and Theodore Ladewski

Chapter 5. The Biosphere
Charles Herdendorf (Lake Ecology and Wetlands)
Laura Fay (Water Chemistry)
Jeffrey Reutter (Fishes)
Sandra Schuessler (Birds)

Kurt Knebusch prepared material on the recreational resources of the region. Technical editing was provided by Cathy Darnell, Carolyn Greco, and Kurt Knebusch. Illustrations were prepared by Suzanne Abbati and Dick James. Design and electronic production by Cathy Darnell.

Scientific review was provided by several individuals including: Raymond Assel, Eugene Aubert, Keith Bedford, Alfred Beeton, Gerald Bell, John Bennett, Paul Liu, Gerald Miller, Frank Quinn, James Saylor, and David Schwab.

The editors are indebted to the Great Lakes Environmental Research Laboratory (GLERL), National Oceanic and Atmospheric Administration and the Center for Lake Erie Area Research (CLEAR) - Ohio Sea Grant College Program, The Ohio State University for supporting this undertaking, and to our colleagues for their contributions.

Stanley J. Bolsenga
Ann Arbor, Michigan

Charles E. Herdendorf
Huron, Ohio

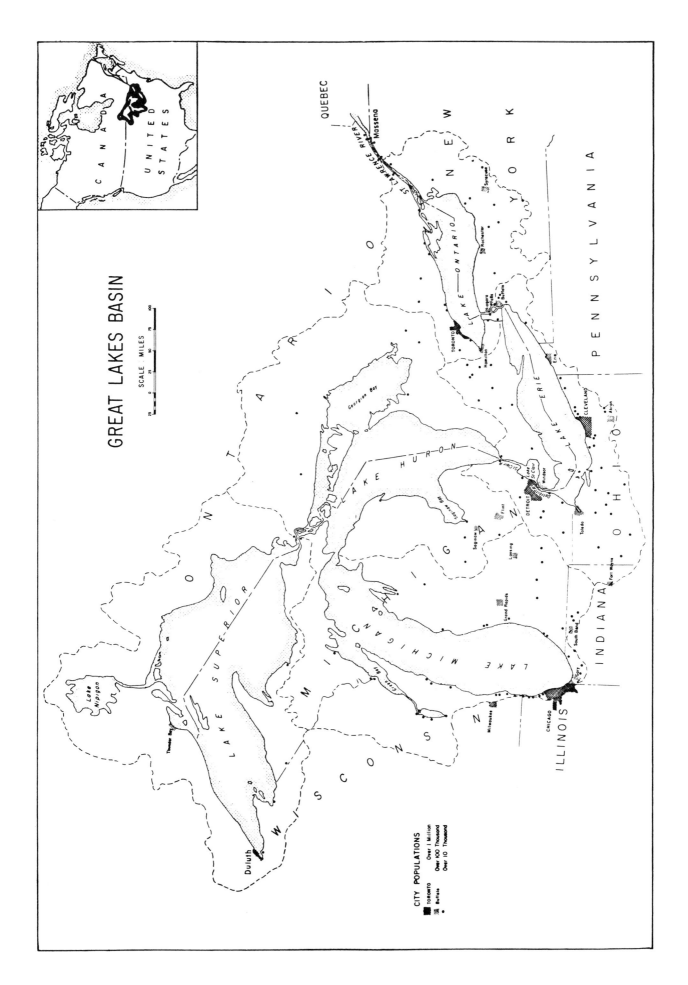

Figure 1.1. Great Lakes of North America.

Chapter 1

Introduction

The Great Lakes system represents the world's largest fresh water resource (Figure 1.1). It is an area that is heavily used for a variety of water related activities. Water is provided for drinking and industrial use, a valuable fishery is contained in the lakes, the lakes constitute a major transportation route, they are a source of hydropower, and they serve as a focal point for recreation.

Lakes Erie and St. Clair are truly two of the remarkable lakes of the Great Lakes system. Some widely known and little known facts are listed below.

- Between Port Huron and Buffalo only three bridges connect Canada and the United States: the Blue Water Bridge between Port Huron and Sarnia, the Ambassador Bridge between Detroit and Windsor, and the Peace Bridge between Buffalo and Fort Erie.

- Lakes Erie and St. Clair are the shallowest in the Great Lakes system.

- Each day over 11 million people get their drinking water from Lake Erie.

- The treachery of Lake Erie has claimed over 500 ships since the launching of the Griffin in 1679.

Harry M. Ross, in his charming 1949 book, described Lake Erie as the busiest, most traveled, and most important lake in the world. While this description emphasizes the commercial importance of the lake, its importance to the people of the region extends far beyond these narrow boundaries. This book will highlight the diverse natural features, and, therefore, opportunities available to visitors and those who choose to dwell along Lake Erie's shores. Most importantly, the recreational, educational, and esthetic features of this region provide unique possibilities for personal growth and family enjoyment.

Historically, this has not always been the busy body of water described by Mr. Ross. Early French trappers used the Ottawa River system as a route between the St. Lawrence River and the upper Great Lakes. Largely because of this and the ferocity of the Iroquois Indians occupying the south, Lake Erie was the last of the Great Lakes to be discovered by Europeans. The Frenchman Louis Jolliet is the first to have recorded seeing Lake Erie in 1669. In 1679, on a trip across the lake, the famous explorer La Salle may have stopped at Middle Bass Island.

Rene Robert Cavalier and Father Louis Hennepin, his Jesuit companion, built a 60-ton wooden sailing ship on the banks of the Niagara River in the winter of 1678-79 and launched her in the spring. The ship was built with the intention of sailing the lakes above the falls at Niagara for the purpose of obtaining furs by bartering with the Indians along the shores. The furs would be eventually marketed in Europe. On August 7, 1679, the Griffin started her voyage with 34 men aboard, sailing up the Niagara River as the first ship to sail onto the broad waters of Lake Erie. La Salle's party crossed Lake Erie in 3 days; en route they discovered the Lake Erie Islands. In her 1953 book on Ohio history, Grace Goulder Izant gives the following account of that discovery:

> "Out of the lake's mist a patch of green appeared. Land at
> last! The good ship Griffin, with the mythical monster—half
> lion, half eagle—on its prow, nosed into a cove. La Salle and
> Father Hennepin leaped from her deck and soon discovered
> that they had stopped at an island, one of the twenty dropped
> across Lake Erie like stepping stones to Canada."

The Griffin then sailed up the Detroit River, through Lakes St. Clair and Huron, and anchored in Green Bay on Lake Michigan on September 3. Here, La Salle found an abundance of valuable furs, loaded the Griffin for the return trip, and ordered the ship's pilot and five sailors to spread her sails for Lake Erie. La Salle, Father Hennepin, and the other members of the party remained on the shores of Lake Michigan to explore the wilderness and await the return of the Griffin in the spring. On September 28, 1679, the Griffin weighed anchor. The following week the lakes were swept by gales. The Griffin was never seen again, and it is believed that she perished with all hands in the storm.

The succession of ownership and habitation of Lake Erie's shores is rather confusing due to conflicting reports and lack of accurate records. Reports show much of the land simultaneously claimed by the French, British, Americans (including several states), and the Indians. After the War of 1812, there was still some confusion as to which islands in Lake Erie were Canadian and which were American. A definitive boundary was not set until 1913 when the International Waterways Commission established the boundary as a series of straight lines determined in reference to fixed objects.

Archeological excavations on Kelleys Island indicate occupation as early as 3000 B.C. Inscription Rock tells the story of Erie Indians, after whom the lake was named, and pictures the final annihilation of the tribe by the Iroquois. It is thought that none of the other islands served as permanent residences for any Indian tribe; rather, they were used for hunting grounds and resting points for travel across the lake. The Ottawa Indians frequented the area until 1831 and are the subject and source of many legends about Catawba Island.

A large part of northern Ohio and Pennsylvania was granted to Connecticut in 1662 by Charles II of England. In 1763, Connecticut deeded 500,000 acres to the people who had been burned out during the Revolutionary War and it became known as the Firelands. Another tract including most of the islands, was sold to the Connecticut Land Company. All but 3,000,000 acres along the lakeshore were relinquished by Connecticut in 1786 when Congress designated the Northwest Territory. After Ohio gained statehood in 1803 and the Fort Industry Treaty of 1805, which rescinded all Indian claims to the south shore of Lake Erie, settlement of the northern part of the state accelerated.

In the early nineteenth century, the whole of the Great Lakes basin supported fewer than 300,000 people. The basin has since been transformed from a hunting ground of the Indians to the industrial heartland of North America. Today, over 30 million people live along the Great Lakes, a hundredfold increase in population in less than 200 years. Understandably, much of the natural character of the region has changed in the last two centuries, and perhaps Lake Erie has changed the most. However, beautiful natural areas and fascinating flora and fauna still abound in its waters and along its shores. Let this book be your guide to discovering them.

The information in this book describes the conditions, processes, and natural features of the coastal and offshore waters of Lakes Erie and St. Clair. The geographical area covered includes Lakes Erie and St. Clair, and the St. Clair, Detroit, and Niagara Rivers (Figure 1.2) extending from Sarnia, Ontario to Niagara-on-the-Lake, New York. Subject areas covered include natural features and processes, meteorological conditions, lake and river conditions, and biotic character.

The following chapter in this book describes the **LITHOSPHERE** or solid earth surrounding or under the lakes and rivers covered in our subject area. Information is presented on the geology of the lake, such as descriptions of the glacial process which formed the lake, and the resulting deposits and features that are currently visible. Descriptions and maps of the shoreline topography and bathymetry (the shape of the lake's bottom) are included. Information is also contained on the beaches and bottom sediments of the lake. After perusing this chapter, the reader should be able to more easily understand and appreciate many of the natural features of the area including facts such as:

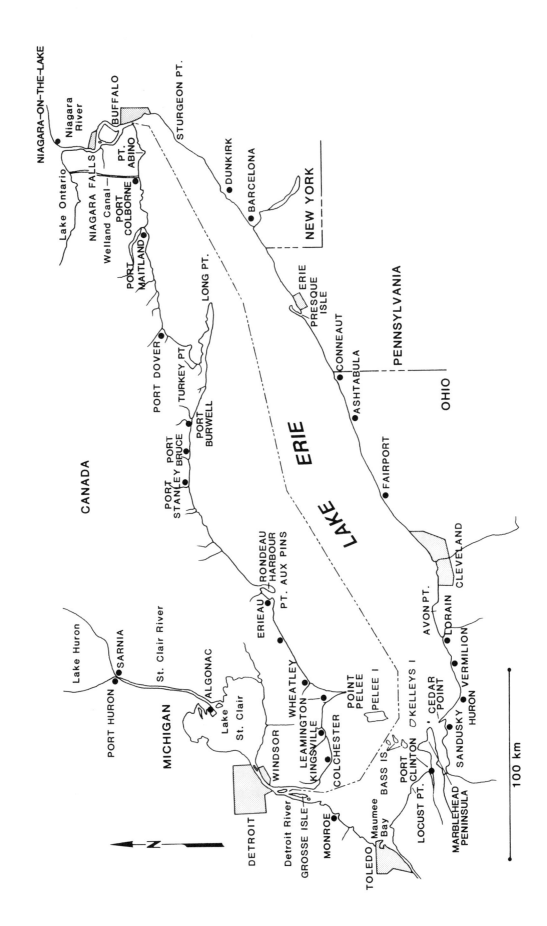

Figure 1.2. Lakes Erie and St. Clair and their connecting waterways.

- Geologically, Lake Erie was the first of the Great Lakes formed.

- The largest sandstone quarry in the world is located at Amherst, Ohio within Lake Erie's coastal zone.

- Massive salt mines are located under Lake Erie at Cleveland and Fairport and under the Detroit River at Detroit and Windsor.

- A large percentage of the sand and gravel needed for the construction industry is produced in the Lake Erie area.

- Long Point sandspit has been naturally built 20 miles out into Lake Erie by alongshore currents. Interestingly enough, this spit is being built into the deepest part of the lake.

- The world-famous glacial grooves on Kelleys Island are 300 feet long, 15 feet deep, and abound with Devonian fossils. The fossils are remains of marine organisms that lived in a warm, shallow sea on a coral reef, 350 million years ago.

In the chapter on the **ATMOSPHERE**, the variations in air temperatures for each season of the year are shown using a variety of charts, tables, and graphs. Precipitation amounts for different times of the year and different places in the region are described. Variations in wind speed and direction are also included. Meteorological parameters which can help or hinder recreation, such as fog and sunshine, are detailed. A section on severe weather dealing with items such as tornadoes, hail, and lightning is included. After reading this chapter, one will be able to easily understand many of the interesting phenomena pertaining to the meteorology of the region including facts such as:

- The climate of Lake Erie's shoreline is greatly affected by the Lake's influence on weather systems which usually move from west to east across the lake.

- Snow belts east of Cleveland are the result of moisture laden air moving over the land from the lake.

- The islands, situated in the midst of the western end of Lake Erie, have slightly less rainfall than the surrounding mainland on a yearly basis.

The chapter on the **HYDROSPHERE** deals with lake and river conditions. The march of the water temperature cycle throughout the year is described including the reason for changes and the magnitude of expected changes. General current patterns in the lakes and the meteorological and astronomical forces which make them occur are discussed. Through a series of charts, the formation, growth, and decay of the ice cover is shown. The levels of the Great lakes are always a topic of conversation for shoreline property owners. The variability of these fluctuations are described in detail. Characteristics and climatology of waves are included. Rapid water level changes peculiar to Lake Erie due to winds of proper direction and duration are fully covered. After reading this chapter the reader should be more thoroughly versed on Lake Erie area limnological conditions. Facts such as those listed below will seem more common and easily understandable.

- Lake Erie is noted for its severe storms and high waves—as high as 12 feet at Marblehead, Ohio.

- Extreme wind-induced water level changes occur on both Lake Erie and St. Clair, sometimes causing great damage to shoreline property.

- Lake Erie is the warmest of the Great Lakes.

- Lake Erie is more often completely covered by ice than any of the Great Lakes. Lake St. Clair normally has a 100% ice cover throughout most of the winter.

- Annually, the western basin freezes from shore to shore providing recreational ice fishing, snowmobiling, and ice boating

The chapter of the **BIOSPHERE** includes segments on ecology, fish, birds, wild game, and wetlands. The fish of Lakes Erie and St. Clair are described in the **Lake Ecology** section as well as other members of the aquatic food web such as phytoplankton and zooplankton. The **Flora and Fauna** section describes various species of wildlife and their habitats; included are waterfowl, upland birds, and wetland and upland mammals. Twenty-one sites throughout the region where opportunities for birdwatching are available are also described. The **Coastal Wetlands** section discusses the origins of the various types of wetlands, their value, plants and animals, and detailed information about specific wetlands areas. After reading the chapter on the Biosphere, the reader will likely appreciate and have a greater understanding of wildlife and their habits in the Lake Erie area including facts such as:

- Over 100 square miles (270 km^2) of coastal marshes fringe western Lake Erie and Lake St. Clair.

- The only National Estuarine Sanctuary on the Great Lakes is located at the mouth of Old Woman Creek near Huron, Ohio, the southernmost point on the Great lakes.

- Over 100 species of fish are found in Lake Erie.

- Each year Ohio sport fishermen spend over 13 million hours to catch 25 million fish from Lake Erie.

- More fish are produced each year for human consumption from Lake Erie than from the other four Great Lakes combined.

- Half of all the fish caught in Lake Erie are taken from the western basin, and half of those are caught in Sandusky Bay.

- Thousands of herons and egrets nest on the rocky islands of Lake Erie and daily fly over 10 miles to feed in the mainland marshes.

- Over 300 species of birds have been observed in the island archipelago in Lake Erie.

- Two major migration flyways cross at the western end of Lake Erie.

- Lake Erie and Lake St. Clair wetlands produce more furbearers than the rest of the Great lakes combined.

Taken together these four spheres—Lithosphere, Atmosphere, Hydrosphere, and Biosphere—comprise all the natural history and environmental processes of the Lake Erie region. This book attempts to present each in an easily understood way that will add to the appreciation of the natural features and phenomenon by both visitors and those dwelling along the lake. References and a glossary are additional sources of information to define technical terms and to assist in the location of material on a specific topic.

Chapter 2

Lithosphere –
The Solid Earth

The lithosphere is the solid portion of the earth, as contrasted with the atmosphere and hydrosphere. It is the earth's crust which contains the basins that hold Lake Erie and Lake St. Clair. Geologically, the basin which contains Lake Erie was formed in the recent past, but some of the rocky outcrops along the shore are nearly 500 million years old. The landforms we see today in the Lake Erie region are the product of a complex series of events and processes, many of which are still active. This chapter will explore (1) landforms of the shore, that branch of geology known as physiography, or more specifically coastal geomorphology, and (2) the shape of the lake basin, a field of study called morphometry. The materials of which these features are formed are discussed in sections on bedrock geology and glacial geology. The latter topic also addresses the events of the last million years which created the Great Lakes and shaped the entire region. The most recent surface materials are the lake sediments and beach deposits. These deposits are continually in flux under the influence of waves, currents, and other coastal processes. Each geologic process has created its own set of features and in some cases this has resulted in the concentration of mineral deposits.

Physiography

The physiography of a region embodies all its landforms and topography. The Lake Erie basin lies in the Central Lowlands Physiographic Province, near where the lowlands wedge out between the Appalachian Plateau and Laurentian Upland (Figure 2.1). The boundary between the

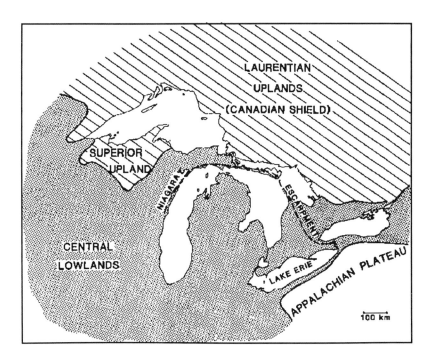

Figure 2.1. Physiographic map of the Great Lakes region.

Central Lowlands and the Appalachian Plateau is a sharp rise of 200 to 300 ft (60 to 90 m) in elevation, known as the Portage Escarpment (Lobeck, 1939). As illustrated in Figure 2.2, from Cleveland eastward this escarpment parallels and lies less than 5 mi (8 km) from the lake shore. At Cleveland the escarpment turns southward across central Ohio. The southeastern part of the Lake Erie drainage basin extends less than 30 mi (50 km) into the Appalachian Plateau.

The portion of the Central Lowlands adjacent to Lake Erie is called the Lake Plain and for the most part is comprised of the very flat former lake bottom. East of Cleveland the Lake Plain is narrow and lies between the Portage Escarpment and the present lake shore (Figure 2.2). West of Cleveland it widens quickly and in western Ohio is more than 50 mi (80 km) wide. The Lake Plain narrows again in Michigan to about 20 mi (30 km) wide. In Canada, it is 20 to 30 mi (30 to 50 km) wide, but is not so well defined because of the complexity of glacial features. The Lake Plain is characteristically low and comprised of poorly drained silt and clay soils. Occasional sandy ridges mark former beaches and bars deposited in ancient lakes. Beyond the Lake Plain lies the Till Plain. This gently rolling country results from glacial debris deposited as the ice sheets receded to the north.

Most of the streams entering Lake Erie originate either within or just outside the boundaries of the Lake Plain. The valleys are generally narrow and winding with steep to vertical walls. These shapes indicate that most of the valleys are in a youthful stage of maturity, having been

Figure 2.2.
Physiographic map of
the Lake Erie region.

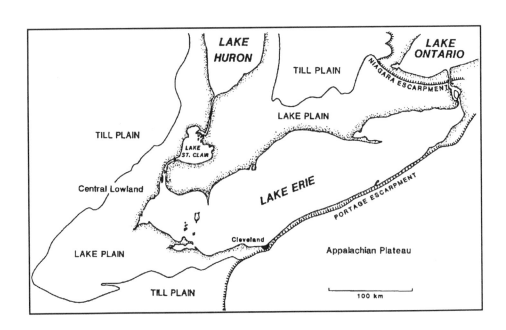

cut rapidly since the Ice Age in a flat region, which stands high relative to Lake Erie. Figure 2.3 illustrates the dissection of the Lake Plain by streams which has taken place on the north shore of the lake.

The landscape of the Lake Erie basin is characterized by thousands of square miles of flat terrain. This is interrupted only by occasional ancient beach ridges and the relatively steep valley walls of many of the major tributaries. Even these features are subdued in the western part of the basin. The terrain is less monotonous along the south shore from Cleveland eastward, where the basin reaches into the Appalachian uplands and rolling hills. Here, and in the northern part of the drainage basin near Waterloo, Ontario, the hills rise to elevations over 1,000 ft (300 m) above sea level (Figure 2.4).

Soils in the extensive flatlands of the Lake Erie basin are characteristically dominated by poorly drained and relatively impervious clays, derived from old lake sediments and glacial drift (Figure 2.5). These soils are fertile, and because of this, much of the area has been artificially drained and cultivated. The uplands along the southeast edge of the basin are naturally well-drained, rock-derived, and less fertile. The ancient beach ridges surrounding the basin are extensively used for highways and farming, and residential development.

Figure 2.3. Stream dissection of Lake Erie's north coast in the vicinity of Port Stanley, Ontario (after Chapman and Putnam, 1966).

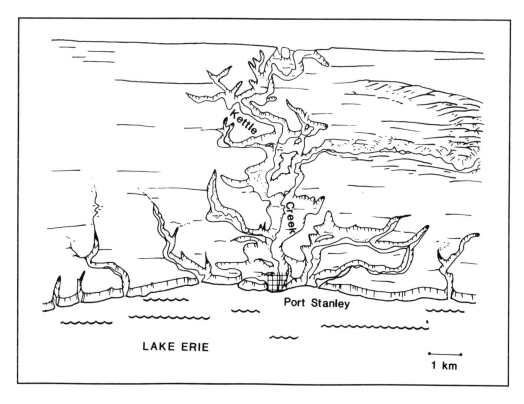

Figure 2.4. Topographic relief map of the Lake Erie region (after Sly, 1976).

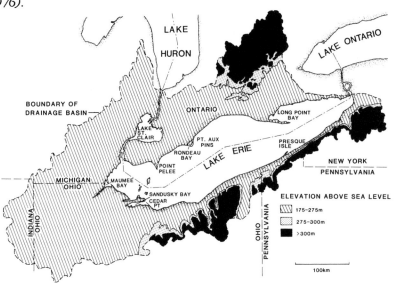

Figure 2.5. Surface geology map of the Lake Erie region.

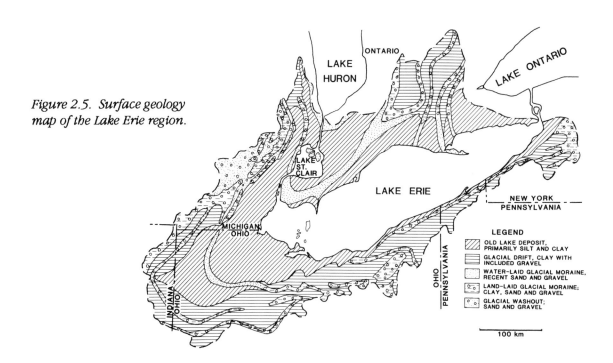

Streams entering Lake Erie generally have a low gradient. They carry large silt loads where they traverse easily-eroded clay flatlands and smaller loads in the rocky hilly areas. Excluding the Detroit River, a connecting channel to the upper Great Lakes, only the Maumee River in Ohio and the Grand River in Ontario supply significant quantities of water to Lake Erie. Figure 2.6 shows that all other tributaries deliver less than 100 cfs (30 m³/sec) to the lake.

The morphometry of a lake or river is its shape and depth statistics, and is usually expressed as a series of dimensions (Table 2.1). Such information is useful in understanding how a lake was formed and how it responds to environmental stress. Lake Erie, Lake St. Clair, the Detroit River, and the Niagara River each have their own distinct characteristics.

Lake Erie

Lake Erie is geologically the oldest of the Saint Lawrence Great Lakes and by far the shallowest. Its entire water mass lies above sea level, which is not true for the other four Great Lakes (Figure 2.7). It has the smallest volume of water with the shortest water retention time. The water temperatures of Lake Erie have the widest seasonal fluctuations of

Figure 2.6. Mean tributary flow into Lakes Erie and St. Clair.

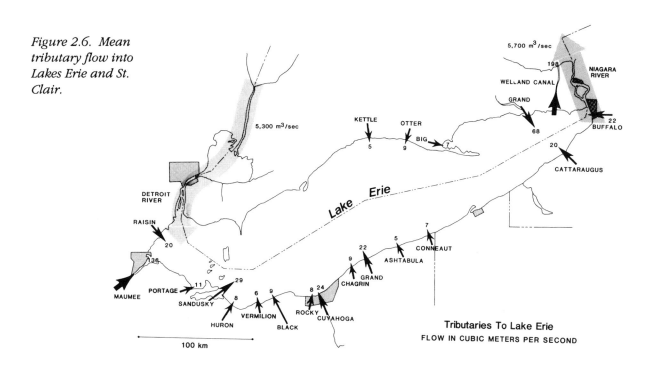

Table 2.1. Morphometry of the Lake Erie basins.

Dimension	Western Basin	Central Basin	Eastern Basin	Entire Lake
Maximum length (km)	80	212	137	388
Maximum breadth (km)	64	92	76	92
Maximum depth (m)	18.9	25.6	64.0	64.0
Mean depth (m)	7.4	18.5	24.4	18.9
Area (km²)	3,284	16,138	6,235	25,657
Volume (km³)	25	305	154	484
Shoreline length (km)	445	520	437	1,402
Percent of area (%)	12.8	62.9	24.3	100
Percent of volume (%)	5.1	63.0	31.9	100
Percent of shoreline (%)	31.7	37.1	31.2	100
Development of volume (ratio)[1]	1.2	2.2	1.1	0.9
Development of shoreline (ratio)[2]	2.3	1.3	1.7	2.1
Water storage capacity (days)	51	635	322	1,008
Drainage basin land area (km²)	37.000	15,000	6,800	58,800
Mean elevation (m)	173.86	173.86	173.86	173.86
Highest monthly mean elevation (m)	174.58	174.58	174.58	174.58
Lowest monthly mean elevation (m)	172.97	172.97	172.97	172.97
Mean tributary inflow (m³/sec)	5,300	200	200	5,700
Mean outflow (m³/sec)	5,300	5,500	5,700	5,700
Highest mean monthly outflow (m³/sec	6,600	6,900	7,200	7,200
Lowest mean monthly outflow (m³/sec)	3,100	3,200	3,300	3,300
Longitudinal axis bearing	N 67°W	N 67°E	N 67°E	N 67°E

1. **Development of volume** is the ratio of the volume of the lake to that of a cone of basal area equal to area of the lake and a height equal to the maximum depth of the lake.

2. **Development of shoreline** is the ratio of the length of the shoreline to the length of the circumference of a circle of area equal to that of the lake.

any of the Great Lakes, and it is the only lake that typically freezes from shore to shore. In comparison to the other Great Lakes, Lake Erie is also the southernmost, warmest, most turbid, most biologically productive, and most eutrophic of all.

Lake Erie lies between 41° 21'N and 42° 50'N latitude, and 78° 50'W to 83° 30'W longitude. It is a relatively narrow lake, with its long axis oriented west southwest-east northeast. This axis parallels the prevailing wind direction which causes the lake to react violently to storms, with

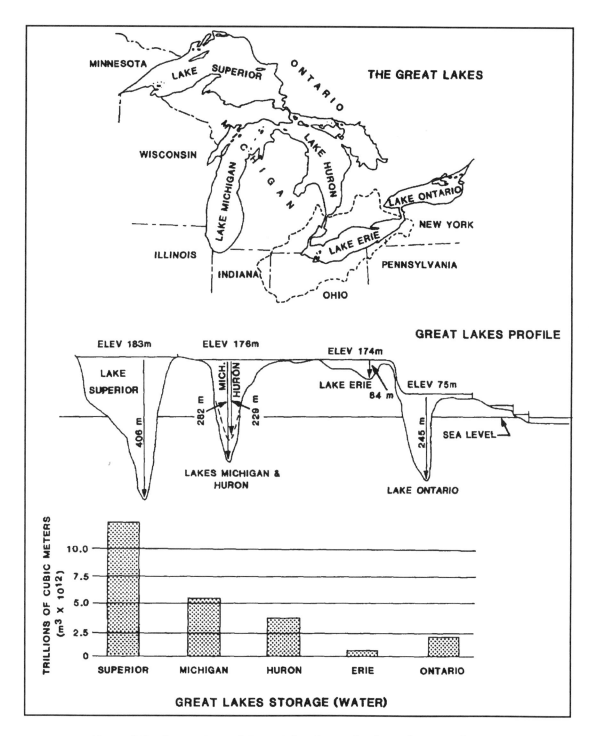

Figure 2.7. Comparison of Great Lakes shape, depth, and water volume.

high waves and wide fluctuations in water level. Lake Erie is approximately 240 mi (388 km) long and 57 mi (92 km) wide, with a mean depth of 62 ft (19 m). The water covers an area of 9,906 mi² (25,657 km²), and has a volume of 116 mi³ (484 km³). Lake Erie's three major physiographic divisions: western, central, and eastern basins are shown by the depth contours (bathymetry) in Figure 2.8. The differences in depth of these three basins are also illustrated in the cross-section on Figure 2.9.

Western Basin. This basin lies west of a line from the tip of Cedar Point, Ohio, northward to Point Pelee, Ontario. It is the smallest and shallowest basin with most of the bottom at depths between 25 and 35 ft (8 and 11 m). In contrast with the other basins, a number of bedrock islands and shoals—locally called "reefs"—are situated in the western basin (Table 2.2) and form a partial divide between it and the central basin. Figure 2.10 depicts the major islands and reefs in the Ohio portion of western Lake Erie. The bottom is flat except for the steep-sided islands and shoals. The deepest sounding is nearly 62 ft (19 m) in a depression north of Starve Island Reef. The western basin possesses only 12.8% of the area and 5.1% of the volume of Lake Erie.

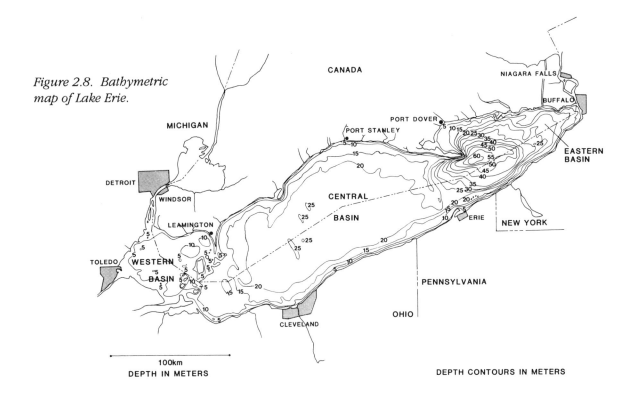

Figure 2.8. Bathymetric map of Lake Erie.

Figure 2.9. Longitudinal cross section of Lake Erie.

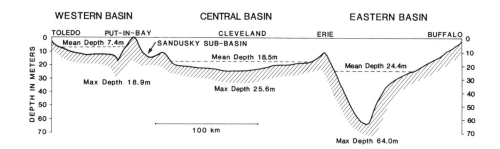

Central Basin. This basin is separated from the western basin by a chain of islands and Point Pelee, and from the eastern basin by a relatively shallow sand and gravel bar between Erie, Pennsylvania, and the base of Long Point, Ontario. The central basin has an average depth of 61 ft (19 m) and a maximum depth of 84 ft (26 m). Except for the rising slopes of a low bar of glacial origin extending south-southeast from Point Pelee, Ontario, the bottom of the central basin is extremely flat. This basin is the largest, containing 62.9% of the lake's area and 63.0% of its volume.

Eastern Basin. This basin is relatively deep and bowl-shaped. A considerable area lies below 100 ft (30 m). The deepest sounding, 210 ft (64 m), is located about 8 mi (13 km) east-southeast of the tip of Long Point, Ontario. This basin comprises 24.3% of the lake's area and 31.9% of its volume.

Lake St. Clair

Lake St. Clair is located between the St. Clair River and Detroit River (Figure 2.11) in a broad, flat valley that is broken only by three glacial moraines running transverse to the axis of the valley. The heart-shaped lake is fed with water from Lake Huron via the St. Clair River. Outflow from the lake leaves via the Detroit River into Lake Erie. At the northeastern portion of the lake is an extensive delta system which is the largest within the Great Lakes. Figure 2.12 illustrates the numerous distributary channels which carry St. Clair River flow through the delta.

Although its delta is immense, Lake St. Clair is by far the smallest lake in the Great Lakes system. It has a total area of only 28,400 mi² (1,114 km²) and a drainage basin area of 48,000 mi² (12,430 km²). It is the only lake in the system with such a large drainage basin-to-lake surface ratio (11:1). The other Great Lakes average 2:1. The mean depth of the lake is only 10 ft (3 m), with a maximum natural depth of 21 ft (6.4 m) and a maximum depth along a dredged shipping channel of 27 ft (8 m).

Table 2.2. Islands and Major Reefs of Lake Erie.

Ohio Islands	Area (km²)	Shore Length (km)
Kelleys	11.32	18.3
South Bass	6.35	17.2
Middle Bass	3.29	12.4
North Bass	2.85	8.4
Johnson	1.17	5.3
West Sister	0.31	2.1
Rattlesnake	0.26	2.6
Sugar	0.13	1.4
Green	0.08	1.3
Ballast	0.05	1.1
Mouse	0.03	0.8
Gibraltar	0.02	0.8
Starve	<0.01	0.3
Buckeye	<0.01	0.2
Rattles	<0.01	0.1
Lost Ballast	<0.01	<0.1
Gull	<0.01	<0.1
Ontario Islands		
Pelee	42.70	37.2
Middle	0.42	2.6
Middle Sister	0.25	1.7
East Sister	0.23	1.9
Hen	0.07	0.7
North Harbor	0.03	0.3
Big Chicken	<0.01	<0.1
Little Chicken	<0.01	<0.1
TOTAL	**69.56**	**116.7**

Ohio Reefs and Shoals	Area (km²)	Least Depth (m)	Maximum Depth (m)
West Reef	5.31	1.2	3.0
Niagara Reef	2.49	0.9	6.0
Gull Island Shoal	2.05	0.0	6.0
Kelleys Island Shoal	1.92	0.6	7.5
Scott Point Shoal	1.48	3.0	6.4
Middle Harbor Reef	1.40	0.3	4.5
Toussaint Reef	1.23	0.9	3.3
Locust Point Reef	0.93	1.5	4.0
Round Reef	0.88	2.1	4.0
Mouse Island Reef	0.85	2.7	6.0
Crib Reef	0.85	0.6	4.5
Little Pickerel Reef	0.72	4.6	6.7
Starve Island Reef	0.67	2.1	6.0
Cone Reef	0.67	3.0	6.0
Lakeside Reef	0.05	3.7	6.0
TOTAL	**21.50**	**MEAN 1.8**	**MEAN 5.3**

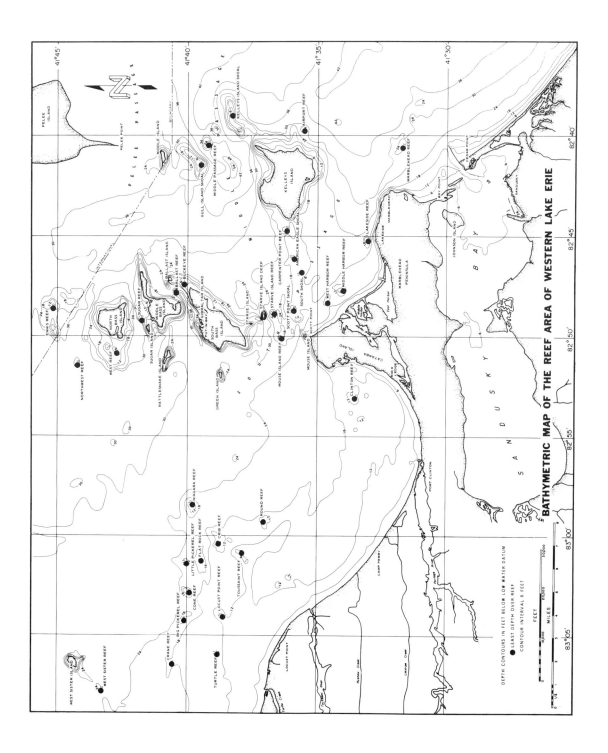

Figure 2.10. Bathymetric map of the southern islands area in western Lake Erie (after Herdendorf and Braidech, 1972).

Figure 2.11. Map of Lake St. Clair and its connecting waterways.

The Michigan portion of the delta has been largely urbanized, whereas the Ontario portion is set aside as Walpole Indian Reservation and is comprised mainly of natural wetlands. These marshes show distinctive plant zonation relating to the strata and heights of the delta (Raphael and Jaworski, 1982). Most of the water entering the lake (98%) comes directly from Lake Huron. Thus, the state of the water in Lake Huron is the predominant influence on the quality of the water in Lake St. Clair. Similarly, sedimentation rates in Lake St. Clair are directly related to the amount of wave energy that breaks on the beaches and cliffs of Lake Huron (Duane, 1969). Lake St. Clair is a sink for particles and particle associated chemical pollutants that enter the lake via the St. Clair River and the tributary streams.

This small lake is an important link in the St. Lawrence Seaway. Because the lake is so shallow, a shipping channel must be periodically dredged to assure bottom clearance for large ships. Fortunately, the shallow depth, coupled with a relatively short fetch -- a maximum of 67 mi (42 km)—inhibits the development of very strong waves. Thus shoreline features are reasonably stable because of the small rates of shore erosion. When waves develop, most of their energy is dissipated before they reach the shore, because the gentle slope of the bottom causes the waves to break well offshore.

Detroit River

The Detroit River forms a strait, 31 mi (50 km) long, connecting Lake St. Clair and Lake Erie (Figure 2.11). The terrain through which the river

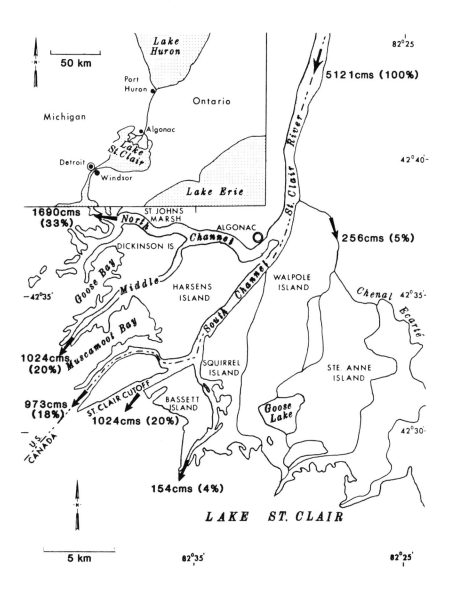

Figure 2.12. St. Clair delta map showing distributary channels. Average discharge per second (cms) and flow distribution in percent (%) are indicated for each of the main channels.

flows is relatively flat and broken only by the River Rouge on the Michigan side and the Canard River and Turkey Creek on the Ontario side. The upper half of the Detroit River has steep banks, a width of less than 0.6 mi (1 km), depths to 50 ft (15 m), and two sizable islands at its head, Belle Isle and Peach Island. The lower half of the river has gently sloping banks, a width of 3.7 mi (6 km) at its mouth, and depths generally less than 33 ft (10 m). The mouth contains several small islands and one major island, Grosse Ile. At the mouth, the depth is only 10 ft (3 m), except in the dredged navigation channels. The average flow of the Detroit River is 187,000 cfs (5,300 m³/sec) which generates a strong current, but not so strong that freighters and pleasure craft cannot traverse the channels. The constant movement of bulk cargo (iron ore, coal, cement, grain, and stone) and manufactured products from domestic and overseas ports makes this river one of the busiest waterways in the world, even though it freezes each winter.

Niagara River

Forming the boundary between New York and Ontario, the Niagara is also a short river connecting Lake Erie to Lake Ontario across the Niagara Escarpment (Figure 2.13). In a distance of 32 mi (51 km) its waters drop 326 ft (99 m) from the level of Lake Erie to the level of Lake

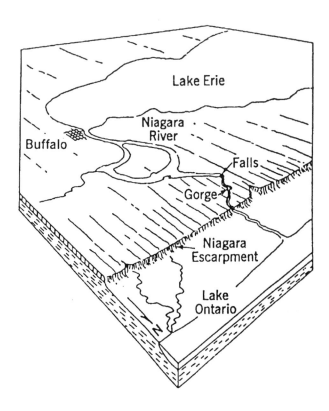

Figure 2.13. Diagrams of the Niagara River illustrating the gorge cut into the rocks of the Niagara Escarpment (after Strahler, 1971).

Ontario. Approximately half of this plummet occurs at Niagara Falls. Here, the brink and the steep-sided gorge below the falls are among the most scenic vistas in the Great Lakes region.

Starting at Buffalo, New York, the upper 10 mi (16 km) is a broad, relatively quiet river in a valley only 25 ft (8 m) deep. At this point, it separates into two arms which enclose Grand Island and several smaller islands. Below these islands the river is over 1.5 mi (2.5 km) wide, but narrows to 1 mi (1.5 km) at the rapids above the falls. Here the river is again divided, this time by Goat Island so that there are two falls, the American, which is 1,000 ft (300 m) in width and drops 165 ft (50 m), and the Canadian or Horseshoe falls which drops 158 ft (48 m). The rim of the latter is about 2,600 ft (800 m) in length and is strongly arched upstream. The curved shape is due to rapid erosion in the center of the falls, amounting to about 3.5 ft (1.1 m) per year (Chapman and Putnam, 1966).

The Niagara River plunges over the brink of the falls into a gorge that is between 1,000 to 1,300 ft (300 to 400 m) wide. The gorge extends northwards for 6 mi (10 km) to the edge of the escarpment. Within the narrower ravine cut into the escarpment, the river enters the lowland plain at Queenston, Ontario. From here to Lake Ontario the river flows more quietly in a channel only 0.5 mi (0.3 km) wide.

Early geologists believed that the Niagara gorge was entirely the result of postglacial cutting and thus, the length of its channel divided by its present erosion rate would yield a convenient measure of the time since the last glacier covered the region (Leverett and Taylor, 1915). It is now known that part of it is the result of the re-excavation of a previously eroded gorge, a still-buried portion of which extends from the whirlpool to St. David's, Ontario (Chapman and Putnam, 1966). The rapids above the falls are also believed to be the result of uncovering of an old valley. In addition, it is likely that the volume of water in the Niagara River has varied greatly in the past millennia, hence the rate of recession at the brink of the falls has not been constant.

The Niagara is a splendid example of a river gorge produced by the retreat of a waterfall. The steep sides and great depth are produced by the undermining of soft shale beneath the hard dolomite (Lockport Formation) of the cap-rock (Figure 2.14). The effects of early valley cutting, before the falls had migrated so far upstream, can be seen in the flat area of Niagara Falls Park on the Ontario side of the river.

This river serves as the outlet for Lake Erie, draining four of the five Great Lakes—an area of 263,378 mi^2 (682,148 km^2). Average flow of the river is 202,000 cfs (5,700 m³/sec). Because of the relatively uniform rate of flow throughout the year, it is among the world's most dependable sources of water power for hydroelectric plants on both sides of the river.

Currents have been measured as high as 9 mi/hr (4 km/sec) at the Peace Bridge between Buffalo and Fort Erie, Ontario. The rate of flow of the Niagara River water depends on the height of Lake Erie at Buffalo. The water level fluctuates significantly depending on wind direction and intensity. A prolonged westerly gale over Lake Erie produces a substantial increase in flow of the Niagara River. Conversely, a strong northeast wind drops the river flow by holding water in the lake. Wind-caused variations up to 8 ft (2.4 m) can occur in the course of a few hours, but average seasonal variation in lake level is only 1.2 ft (0.4 m). The maximum flow record for the Niagara River (256,000 cfs or 7,240 m³/sec

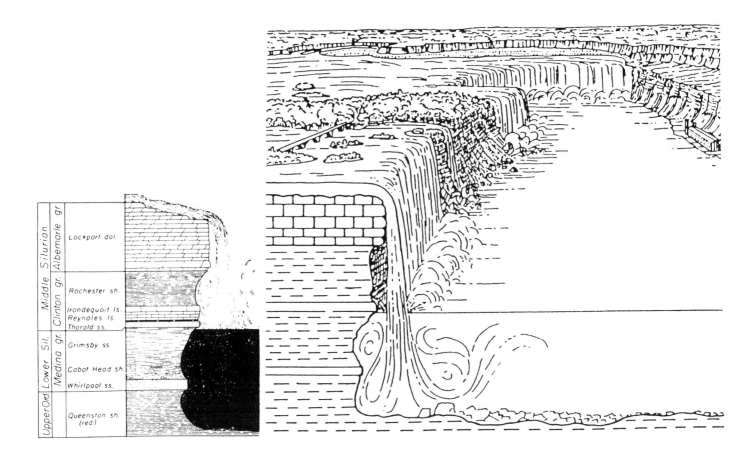

Figure 2.14. Cross-sectional diagram of Niagara Falls showing the cap-rock of Lockport dolomite and the underlying weak shales and sandstones which have been eroded to form the Maid-of-the-Mist plunge pool (after Strahler, 1971).

in 1929) is only slightly less than twice the minimum record (129,000 cfs or 3,650 m³/sec in 1936). This 2:1 fluctuation is very small in comparison with the seasonal differences most of the world's great rivers undergo. These may range from 20 to 30 times the minimum rate. For example, the Mississippi River ratio is 25:1, while the Columbia River ratio is 35:1.

Bedrock Geology

Lake Erie

The bedrock of the Lake Erie Region was formed during the middle portion of the Paleozoic Era, that span of time from 300 to 500 million years ago (Table 2.3). Geologists have named 62 bedrock formations that crop out in the states and province which surround Lake Erie. Figure 2.15 shows the distribution of the various rock types in the Great Lakes Region. The varying depths of Lake Erie's three basins are attributed to differential erosion of the bedrock by preglacial streams, glaciers, and post-glacial lake processes (Carman, 1946). This erosion is largely in response to the hardness and structure of the underlying formations. As we have already seen, Lake Ontario is separated from Lake Erie by resistant Silurian limestones and dolomites of the Niagara Escarpment (Figures 2.15 and 2.16). However, the central and eastern basins of Lake Erie are underlain by nonresistant shale, shaly limestone, and shaly sandstone of the Upper Devonian Age, which dip gently to the southeast. Inland along the south shore, eastward from Cleveland, the Portage Escarpment, composed largely of Mississippian sandstone, rises 300 ft (100 m) above the level of the lake and forms the northwest front of the Appalachian Plateau (Figure 2.2 and 2.4).

An outcrop belt of Devonian shales swings inland between Cleveland and Sandusky and continues southward through central Ohio (Figure 2.17) in response to the structural pattern of the bedrock. The shallow western basin is underlain by Silurian and Devonian limestones and dolomites (Figure 2.18) on the northward plunging end of the Findlay Arch of the Cincinnati Anticline. Glacial erosion had relatively slight effects on these resistant rocks other than to form impressive grooves such as those found on Kelleys Island and the Bass Islands. The glacial scour was probably controlled by the pre-glacial stream valleys, resulting in the shallow basin and the island chains.

The bedrock in the islands area of western Lake Erie is sedimentary in origin and was deposited as lime muds in shallow, warm Silurian and Devonian seas, which covered the region from 410 to 375 million years ago. Figure 2.19 shows the various marine beds that were deposited in Late Silurian time. The halite (rock salt) deposits in the vicinity of Cleveland are currently being mined 2,300 ft (700 m) below the lake

Table 2.3. *Geologic time scale in millions of years ago.*

TIME	ERA	PERIOD	EPOCH
	CENOZOIC	QUATERNARY	PLEISTOCENE
		TERTIARY	PLIOCENE
			MIOCENE
			OLIGOCENE
50			EOCENE
			PALEOCENE
100	MESOZOIC	CRETACEOUS	UPPER LOWER
150		JURASSIC	UPPER MIDDLE LOWER
200		TRIASSIC	UPPER MIDDLE LOWER
250	PALEOZOIC	PERMIAN	UPPER MIDDLE LOWER
300		PENNSYLVANIAN*	
350		MISSISSIPPIAN*	
		DEVONIAN*	UPPER MIDDLE LOWER
400		SILURIAN*	
450		ORDOVICIAN*	UPPER MIDDLE LOWER
500 550		CAMBRIAN	UPPER MIDDLE LOWER

MILLIONS OF YEARS

*Ages of the rocks exposed around Lake Erie.

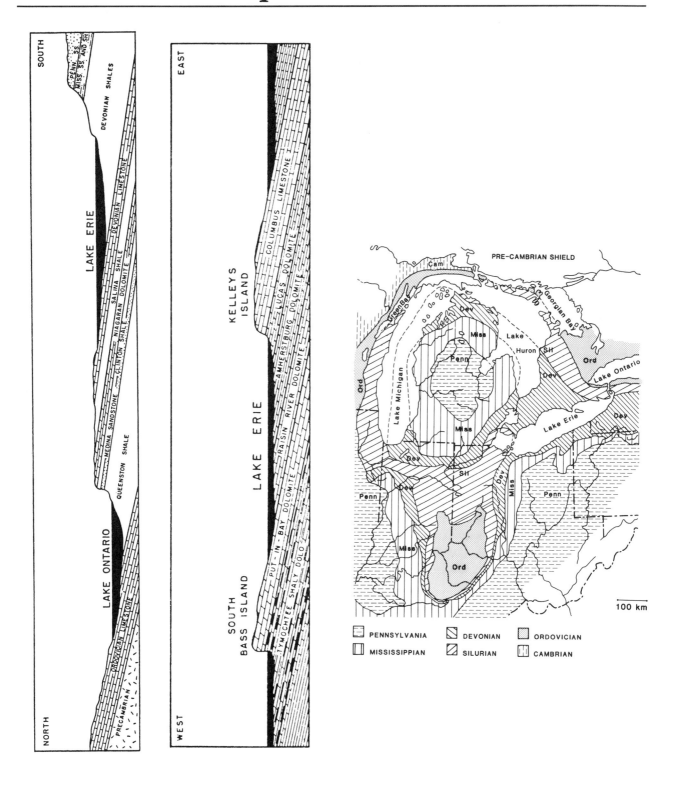

Figure 2.15. Geologic map of the Great Lakes region and geologic cross-sections of Lake Erie and Lake Ontario (after Carman, 1946; Hough, 1958; Hunt, 1974).

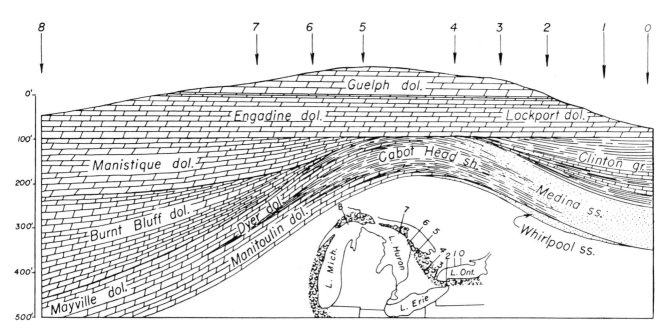

Figure 2.16. Stratigraphic section of the Silurian bedrock formations along the Niagara Escarpment (after Dunbar, 1960).

Figure 2.17. Structural features of the bedrock in the central Great Lakes region (after Carman, 1946).

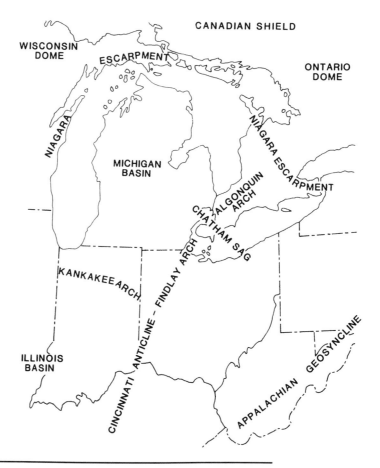

LEGEND FOR GEOLOGIC MAP

ONTARIO

System	Formation	Symbol	Lithology
Devonian	Hamilton	Dha	Shale
Devonian	Delaware	Dd	Limestone
Devonian	Columbus	Dc	Limestone
Devonian	Detroit River	Ddr	Dolomite
Silurian	River Raisin	Srr	Dolomite

MICHIGAN

System	Formation	Symbol	Lithology
Mississippian	Coldwater	Mc	Shale
Mississippian	Berea	Mbe	Sandstone
Devonian	Antrim	Dat	Shale
Devonian	Ten Mile Creek	Dt	Dolomite
Devonian	Silica		Shale
Devonian	Dundee	Ddd	Limestone
Devonian	Anderdon	Ddr	Limestone
Devonian	Lucas		Dolomite
Devonian	Amherstburg		Dolomite
Devonian	Sylvania	Ds	Sandstone
Silurian	River Raisin	Srr	Dolomite
Silurian	Put-in-Bay	Sp	Dolomite
Silurian	Tymochtee	St	Dolomite
Silurian	Greenfield	Sg	Dolomite

OHIO

System	Formation	Symbol	Lithology
Mississippian	Berea	Mbe	Sandstone
Mississippian	Bedford	Mbd	Shale
Devonian	Cleveland	Dcl	Shale
Devonian	Huron	Dh	Shale
Devonian	Prout	Dp	Limestone
Devonian	Plum Brook	Dpb	Shale
Devonian	Delaware	Dd	Limestone
Devonian	Columbus	Dc	Limestone
Devonian	Lucas	Dl	Dolomite
Devonian	Amherstburg	Dah	Dolomite
Silurian	River Raisin	Srr	Dolomite
Silurian	Put-in-Bay	Sp	Dolomite
Silurian	Tymochtee	St	Dolomite
Silurian	Greenfield	Sg	Dolomite
Silurian	Lockport	Sl	Dolomite

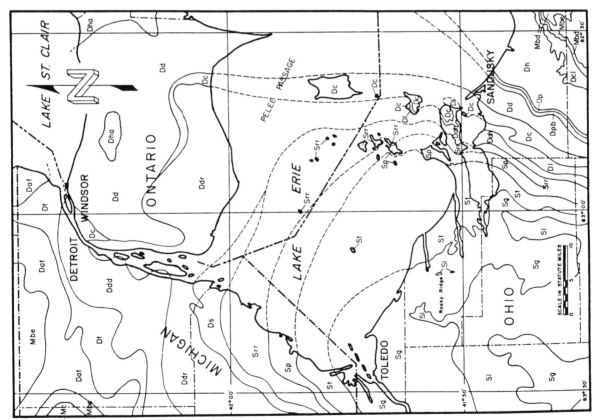

Figure 2.18. Geologic map of western Lake Erie showing plunging nose of the Findlay Arch and the resulting island cuestas (after Carman, 1946; Herdendorf and Braidech, 1972).

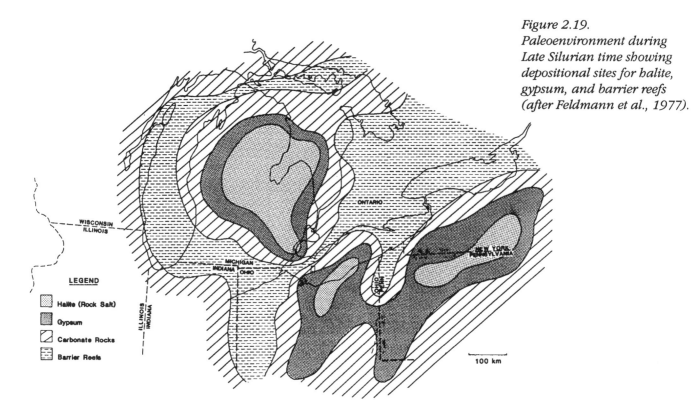

Figure 2.19.
Paleoenvironment during
Late Silurian time showing
depositional sites for halite,
gypsum, and barrier reefs
(after Feldmann et al., 1977).

bottom. The existence of evaporite beds such as halite and gypsum
indicate that several isolated basins occurred at this time. Enclosed by
barrier reefs, the waters were repeatedly evaporated to form the massive
salt deposits. The warm, clear conditions of the Devonian sea can be
inferred from the abundant fossil corals and other invertebrates found in
the rocks on Kelleys and Johnson islands. Figure 2.20 is a reconstruction
of the marine animals in the Middle Devonian sea. The abandoned
limestone quarries in Kelleys Island State Park are excellent sites for
fossil collecting and have yielded over 70 species of marine organisms
(Figure 2.21).

While the shallow Devonian sea occupied the islands area, the
Appalachian Mountains were being built to the east. Recent studies of
plate tectonics (Bird and Dewey, 1970; Kennett, 1982) indicate that the
collision of the northwest coast of Africa and that of eastern North
America caused the sediments in the Appalachian geosyncline to be
folded into a formidable mountain chain. Erosion of these newly formed
mountains resulted in the deposition of shales and sandstones which
cover the limestones in central and eastern Lake Erie (Figure 2.22).

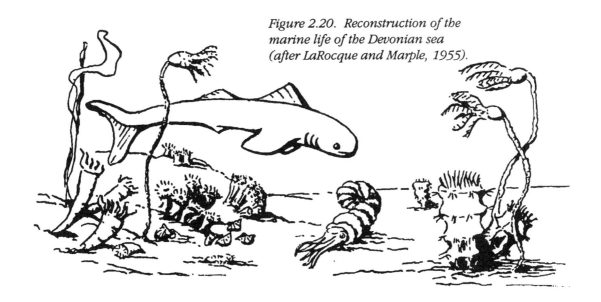

Figure 2.20. Reconstruction of the marine life of the Devonian sea (after LaRocque and Marple, 1955).

Much of the south shore of central Lake Erie is a wave-cut bluff composed of hard, black shale (Ohio Formation) of the Upper Devonian Age. Bluff heights are 65 to 80 ft (20 to 24 m) east of Cleveland where shale and siltstone outcrop near lake level and only form the basal bluff structure when present. Bedrock, however, does form much of the lake bottom to 1 mi (1.6 km) offshore intermittently from Vermilion, Ohio to Erie, Pennsylvania. Eastward from Erie, the south shore bluffs reach elevations up to 100 ft (31 m) above the lake. The basal section is composed of gentle, southeastward-dipping, thick-bedded shales and siltstone with occasional interbedded limestones of the Canadaway Formation and other Upper Devonian shale formations. The rock surface in the bluffs generally lies within 50 ft (15 m) of the lake level. Unconsolidated deposits composed of gray, glacial till, overlain with light brown lacustrine silt and sand, mantle the rock surface and form the upper portion of the lake cliffs.

To a greater extent than along the south shore, the bedrock is responsible for numerous irregular headlands and shoals which characterize the Ontario shore of the eastern basin. A thin mantle of till, 3 to 10 ft (1 to 3 m) thick, covers the bedrock and in places, particularly between rocky headlands such as Point Abino and Port Maitland, is buried beneath extensive sand dunes. To the west, the Ontario shore of the central basin is characterized by vertical bluffs rising up to 125 ft (38 m) above lake level (Figure 2.3). Throughout this reach of shoreline, the bedrock surface is over 50 ft (15 m) below lake level. Here the bluffs

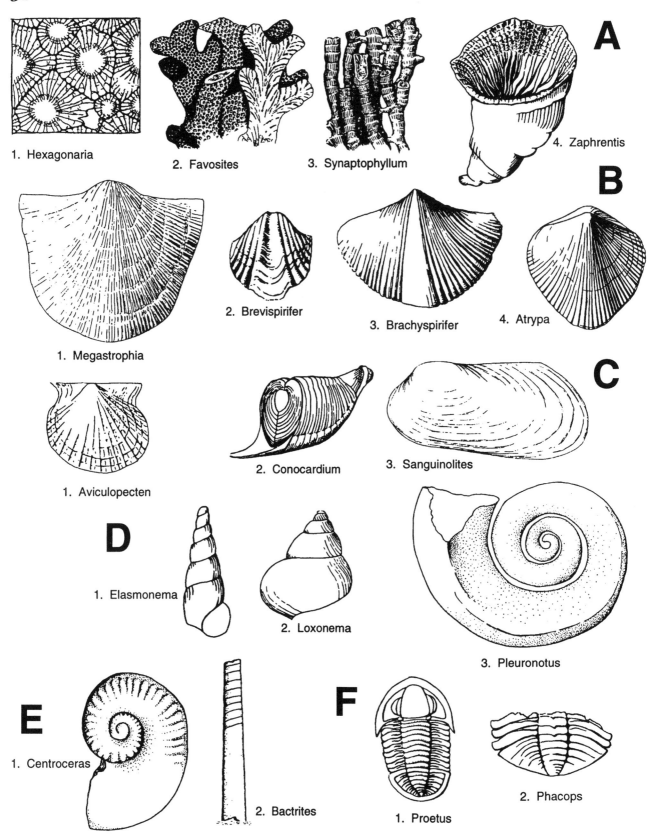

1. Hexagonaria

2. Favosites

3. Synaptophyllum

4. Zaphrentis

A

1. Megastrophia

2. Brevispirifer

3. Brachyspirifer

4. Atrypa

B

1. Aviculopecten

2. Conocardium

3. Sanguinolites

C

D

1. Elasmonema

2. Loxonema

3. Pleuronotus

E

1. Centroceras

2. Bactrites

F

1. Proetus

2. Phacops

Figure 2.21. Common Middle Devonian fossils from the Lake Erie Islands: A) corals, B) brachiopods, C) pelecypods, D) gastropods, E) cephalopods, and F) trilobites (after LaRocque and Marple, 1955).

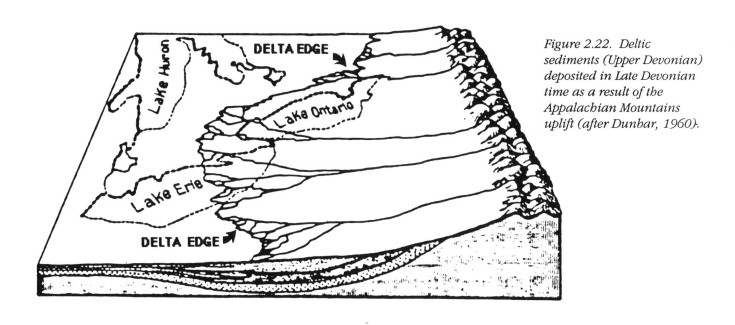

Figure 2.22. Deltic sediments (Upper Devonian) deposited in Late Devonian time as a result of the Appalachian Mountains uplift (after Dunbar, 1960).

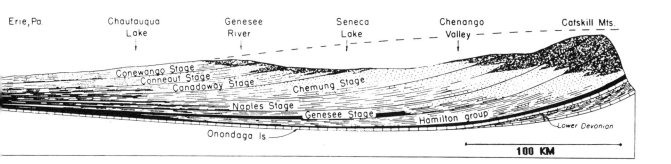

are composed of two till sheets overlain with lake-deposited silt and sand. A few miles east of the 20-mi (32-km) long sand spit known as Long Point, lacustrine sands constitute the entire bluff and provide material for dunes rising 175 ft (53 m) above the lake.

Following the deposition of the black Devonian shales, during the Mississippian and Pennsylvanian periods, new deltas were built from the north into the shallow mid-continent sea where Lake Erie is now located (Figure 2.23). Sandstones and shales were deposited inland from what is now the lake's south shore to form the red beds of the Bedford Shale, the ridge-forming strata of the Berea Sandstone and the "pudding stone" quartz pebbles of the Sharon Conglomerate. Each of these formations has been quarried for building materials. When deeply buried beneath a cap-rock, the sandy beds of these formations are excellent aquifers and reservoirs for gas and oil.

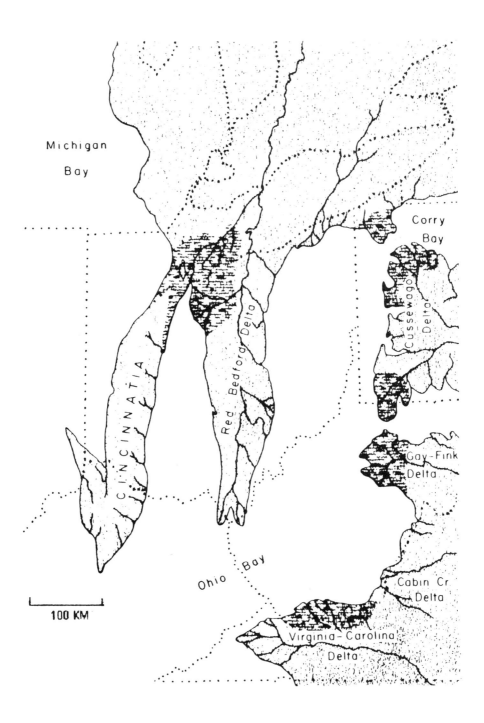

Figure 2.23. Paleogeography of the Lake Erie region during the Mississippian Period showing the deposition of the Bedford Shale and the peninsula formed by the Cincinnati Anticline (after Pepper et al., 1954).

A long period of erosion ensued following the deposition of the Upper Paleozoic rock and little is known of the geologic processes for over 250 million years. Here, the geologic record stops until the glacial deposits of the Pleistocene Epoch. But before we discuss the Ice Age, let's explore the rocks of the Lake Erie islands in more detail.

Lake Erie Islands

Bedrock Structure. The dominant structural feature of the bedrock underlying western Lake Erie is the Findlay Arch (Figure 2.17). The nearly north-south axis of this arch passes through the island region and then plunges gently to the north. Studies of the structure of Precambrian—or basement—rock of Ohio indicate that the crest of the arch lies a few kilometers east of West Sister Island (Hubbard, 1932). As a consequence of the alignment of the arch, the overlying Paleozoic bedrock dips to the east at approximately 20 to 40 ft/mi (4 to 8 m/km) in the Bass-Kelleys islands area (Figure 2.24). For this reason, oldest rocks are exposed on West Sister Island and successively younger formations

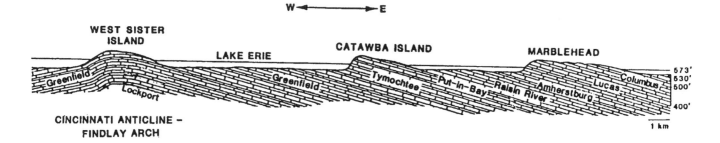

Generalized Section of Silurian Rocks in Western Lake Erie

System	Series	Formation	Thickness	Outcrop Locations
UPPER SILURIAN	Bass Island Group	Raisin River Dolomite	40-60'	Bass Islands Marblehead
		Put-In-Bay Dolomite	40-60'	South Bass Island Catawba Island
	Salina Group	Tymochtee Dolomite	125-175'	South Bass Island Catawba Island
		Greenfield Dolomite	75-125'	West Sister Island Benton Twp., Ottawa Co.
	Niagara Group	Lockport Dolomite	50-80'	Benton Twp., Ottawa Co.

Figure 2.24. Geological cross-sections between Marblehead-Catawba Island-West Sister Island showing dipping bedrock strata on the flanks of the Findlay Arch (after Carman, 1946).

Table 2.4. *Description of bedrock formations exposed in the islands region. Source: Herdendorf and Braidech (1972).*

System	Group	Formation	Thicknesses	Description
DEVONIAN		Delaware	11	Limestone, dark-to bluish-gray, thin-bedded; calcareous shale partings; nodular chert; exposed in vicinity of Sandusky, Ohio.
		Columbus	13	Limestone, light-gray to buff, moderately thin- to massive-bedded, very fossiliferous; locally changing to dolomite; exposed on Pelee Is., Kelleys Is., Marblehead, and SW of Sandusky.
	Detroit River	Lucas	9-23	Dolomite, gray to drab, thin- to massive-bedded, relatively nonresistant; carbonaceous parting between layers; exposed in western part of Kelleys Island, on Marblehead, and southwest of Sandusky.
		Amherstburg	20-25	Dolomite, drab to brown, massive bedded, relatively non-resistant; exposed on shore near Lakeside.
SILURIAN	Bass Islands	Raisin River	12-20	Dolomite, blue-gray to drab, thin-bedded to shaly, argillaceous; exposed on Bass Islands and on Marblehead peninsula between Lakeside and Catawba.
		Put-in-Bay	10-20	Dolomite, gray-to-drab, medium-bedded, brecciated, rough-textured, crystalline; irregular, knobby, weathered surface; exposed on South Bass Island, Green Island and Catawba Island.
	Salina	Tymochtee	170	Dolomite, dark, bluish-gray to brown, thin-bedded to shaly; calcareous shale partings in upper beds; containing gypsum and anhydrite; uppermost 5 m exposed on S. Bass Is., Catawba and W. Sister Is.
		Greenfield	35	Dolomite, light-drab to yellowish-brown, thin- to massive-bedded; generally dense and hard but some layers granular or vesicular; exposed at Rocky Ridge in Ottawa County, Ohio.
	Lockport	Guelph	60-135	Dolomite, white, light-gray, or bluish-gray, massive-bedded, crystalline; open and porous in texture; exposed in southwest Ottawa County, Ohio.

crop out to the east along the flank of the arch (Figure 2.18). Table 2.4 contains descriptions of the bedrock formations in the islands area.

The islands and reefs are arranged in three north-south belts, or chains (Figure 2.10). The most westerly belt lies north of Locust Point and includes approximately 12 reefs and West Sister Island. The middle belt extends from Catawba Island through the Bass and Sister islands, and includes 14 reefs and 10 islands. The easterly belt encompasses Johnson Island, Marblehead Peninsula, Kelleys Island, Middle Island, and Pelee Island, and about seven reefs and shoals. This arrangement and the cuesta shape of the islands are controlled by the structure and relative resistance of the underlying bedrock. The major islands and reefs in western Lake Erie are listed in Table 2.2.

The bedrock exposed on West Sister Island and on the reefs in the vicinity of Locust Point as far east as Niagara Reef is the lower portion of the Tymochtee dolomite (Figure 2.18). This formation is highly variable in its resistance to weathering, a factor that may explain the lack of bedrock reefs between Niagara Reef and the Bass Islands.

The reefs consist of submarine bedrock exposures and associated rock rubble and gravel. The topography of the reef tops varies from rugged surfaces caused by bedrock pinnacles and large boulders to smooth slabs of nearly horizontally-bedded rock. In places, the exposed bedrock has the appearance of low stairs with the "steps" dipping slightly to the east, from the fringe of the reefs to its crest. Bedrock formations that form the reefs are carbonate rock which contain many solution cavities. Most of the reefs are conical in shape and elongated— as are many of the islands—in a northeast-southwest direction. Two factors appear to have influenced this elongation: (1) vertical joint systems in the bedrock which are oriented parallel to the elongation, and (2) general alignment with the major trends of glacial ice movement as deduced from grooves found on the major islands. The bathymetric map of Gull Island Shoal, north of Kelleys Island, illustrates the rugged topography of the reef area (Figure 2.25).

The middle and eastern belts of bedrock islands (Catawba-Bass and Johnson-Kelleys) are characterized by high elevations and cliffs at their western shorelines. Elevations generally decrease eastward resulting in shelving rock along the eastern shorelines. The resulting topographic form is that of a cuesta, or asymmetrical ridge, where the gentle slope agrees with the dips of resistant beds and the steeper slope is an eroding cliff maintained partly by the undercutting of less resistant rocks. Because West Sister Island lies on the west flank of the Findlay Arch, the dip of the strata is also to the west. This has resulted in the develop-

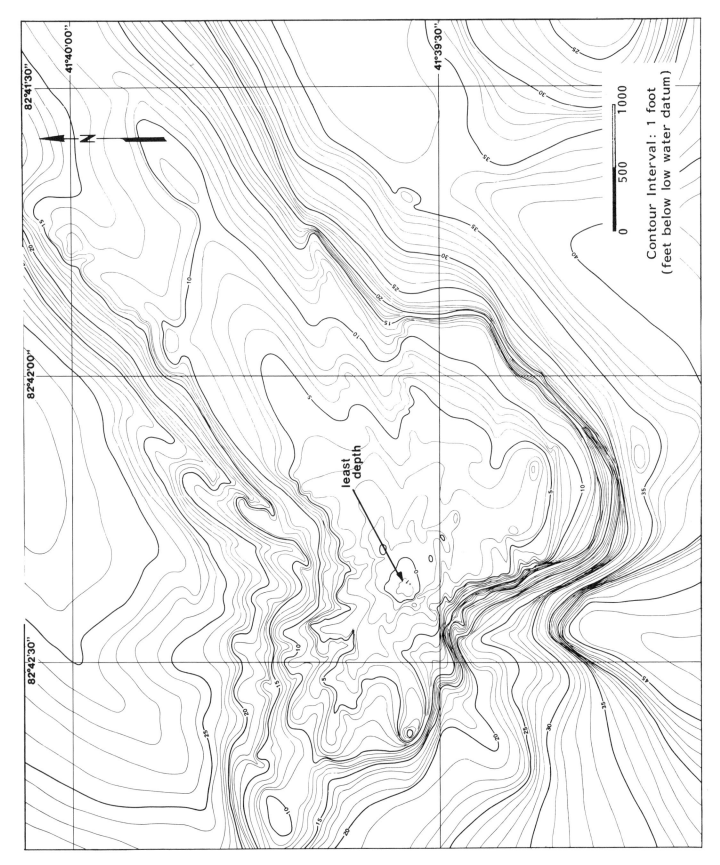

Figure 2.25. Bathymetric map of Gull Island shoal illustrating the northeast longation typical of many of the reefs and islands in western Lake Erie (after Herdendorf and Braidech, 1972).

ment of a cuesta with its steep cliff on the east side of the island, the opposite of those formed on the more easterly islands.

A band of resistant dolomites of the Bass Island Group underlies Catawba and the Bass Islands. The Put-in-Bay dolomite of this group is responsible for most of the rugged features of the shoreline. The Tymochtee Formation, which underlies the Put-in-Bay dolomite at the base of the cliffs, is more readily eroded by waves and results in the undermining of the rock above, which falls away in large blocks, forming nearly vertical walls. The shoreline of Catawba Island from Rock Ledge to West Harbor is 10 km (6 mi) long and consists of an alternation of rocky headlands and glacial bluffs. The dolomite headlands rise to 70 ft (21 m) above lake level, whereas the glacial till is much less resistant to erosion and has been cut back into coves and indentations along the coast. Pebble and cobble beaches have formed locally in the coves. The 4 mi (6 km) of shore from West Harbor to Lakeside are low and bordered by sandy beaches. The beaches lie on marsh deposits which formed in the shallow bay between Catawba Island and Marblehead Peninsula. The underlying material is glacial till and lacustrine clay. An extensive sand deposit has accumulated in the East Harbor area and low sand dunes have formed behind the beach.

Resistant lower beds of the Columbus Limestone are responsible for the easterly chain of bedrock highs, including Johnson and Kelleys islands. Between South Bass Island and Kelleys Island three formations are less resistant than the Put-in-Bay dolomite and the Columbus Limestone, which explains the depression between the islands.

The Marblehead Peninsula shore arcs for 4 mi (6 km) from Lakeside to the base of Bay Point and is lined with limestone and dolomite bluffs, which are generally less than 20 ft (6 m) above lake level. Sections of the shore are composed of thin-bedded rock which yields to wave attack; elsewhere the rock is massively bedded and more resistant to erosion. Glacial till commonly caps the bluffs. The narrow pebble beaches which line the shore at the base of the bluffs have been largely derived from the bedrock. Bay Point extends southward from Marblehead Peninsula for 2 mi (3 km) into Sandusky Bay. This point is a compound spit that is growing from sand contributed by littoral currents moving along Cedar Point and around the end of the Sandusky Harbor jetty. Johnson Island, lying in Sandusky Bay adjacent to Bay Point, is composed of low limestone and glacial till shores. The shore is bordered by discontinuous cobble beaches.

Caves and Sinkholes

Western Lake Erie's islands, including Catawba and Marblehead, possess a rather unusual cave and sinkhole topography. The carbonate bedrock of these islands is soluble in weak, naturally-occurring acids, such as carbonic acids and various organic acids. These acids have slowly dissolved portions of the rock, producing caves, sinkholes, and other solution features. This process has taken place for millions of years, starting soon after the time when the islands were created.

Most of the caves are the result of solution and then the collapse of the surrounding and overlying rock into the void. The exact origin of the caves and sinkhole features has been a matter of speculation. The most widely accepted theory (Verber and Stansbery, 1953) states that the structure of the rock materials combined with their mineral composition and contact with water has resulted in cave and sinkhole formation (Figure 2.26). Specifically, the Put-in-Bay dolomite is underlain by the Tymochtee Formation which contains lenses or pockets of anhydrite gypsum. At some time in the past, water filtered down through the surface materials, the Put-in-Bay dolomite, and eventually into the Tymochtee anhydrite gypsum. Anhydrite gypsum has the property of swelling in contact with moisture. Hydration increases the volume from 33 to 63%. The drastic increase of volume exerted a pressure of approximately 1 ton/in² (1600 tons/m²) on the surrounding materials. Such pressure caused a doming of the overlying Put-in-Bay rock structure. Later, the gypsum was dissolved away by solution leaving a large, unsupported subterranean cavern. Eventually, the roof of the cavern collapsed, forming crescent-shaped caves and caverns around the perimeter. The collapse generally formed large shallow circular depressions on the land surface and created small caves around the margins of these collapse features.

In areas of Catawba and Marblehead, the lenses of anhydrite may have been thinner and less extensive producing only a slight doming and eventually resulting in the formation of a sinkhole rather than a cave. The lower levels of many of the caves, formed either by solution or collapse, are now flooded by water coming in from the lake along cracks and solution openings. Perry's Cave on South Bass Island and Crystal Rock Cave on the south shore of Sandusky Bay near Castalia are the only caves of this type open to the public.

Crystal Cave is quite different and is the most unusual cave on South Bass Island because of its mineral deposits. The walls are completely covered to a thickness of 48 in (60 cm) with blue celestite crystals ($SrSO^4$). These are very large, usually ranging from 8 to 15 in (20 to 38

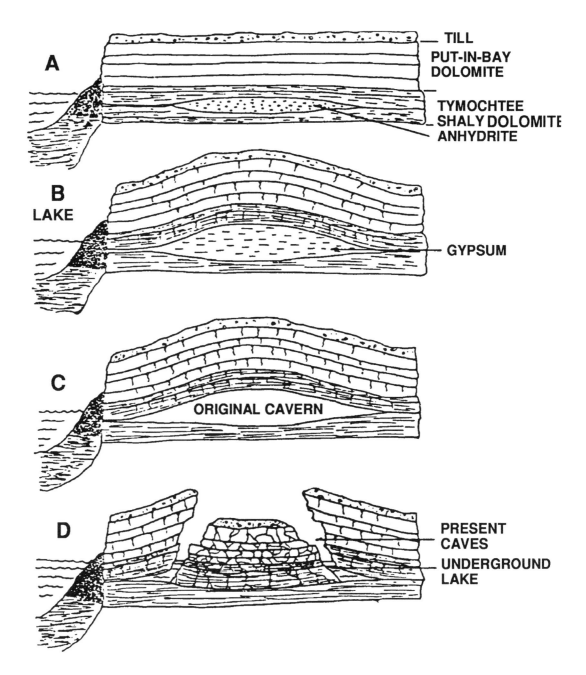

Figure 2.26. Explanation of cave and sinkhole formation in the islands area of Lake Erie: (A) cross-section showing original anhydrite bed, (B) uplifting of overlying strata by hydration into gypsum, (C) cavern left by gypsum solutioning, and (D) collapse of overlying strata and formation of sinkholes and new peripheral caves (after Verber and Stansbery, 1953).

cm) in length and have a tabular shape. The appearance of the interior of this cave is that of an immense geode. This cave was discovered by Gustav Heineman in 1891 while digging a water well. The cave is about 30 ft (9 m) below ground level and consists of two small connected rooms. It had an original height of about 3 ft (1 m); crystals removed from the floor when the cave was deepened were sold to fireworks manufacturers for their strontium. Crystal Cave is also open to the public during summer months.

Lake St. Clair and Detroit River

The Lake St. Clair-Detroit River system is underlain by Middle and Upper Devonian and by lower Mississippian rocks (Figure 2.18). The oldest rocks are the dolomites of the Detroit River formations and the limestone of the Dundee Formation, found near the mouth of the Detroit River. From here the rocks are successively younger in a northwest direction through Lake St. Clair and the St. Clair River valley. Traveling north the character of the bedrock changes from carbonates to black shale (Antrim and Kettle Point formations) and eventually to sandstones (Marshall and Port Lambton formations) near the head of the St. Clair River. Because of the thick mantle of glacial debris and delta sediments, few of these bedrock formations are visible near the waterways. Along much of the St. Clair River valley and Lake St. Clair, the bedrock surface lies at elevations less than 450 ft (137 m) above sea level. Because Lake St. Clair lies at an elevation of about 575 ft (175 m) and is less than 25 ft (8 m) deep, the bedrock is buried by more than 100 ft (30 m) of glacial till and recent lake sediment. Near the mouth of the Detroit River the bedrock surface rises to an elevation of 550 ft (168 m) and is covered by a thin veneer of more recent lacustrine (lake) deposits.

Niagara River

The bedrock geology of the Niagara River and Falls is comparatively simple, and consists of gently dipping layers of shale, limestone, dolomite, and sandstone. The ages of the rocks vary from 400 million years for the Queenston Shale (Ordovician Period) at the bottom of the gorge, to 325 million years for the Lockport dolomite (Silurian Period), which is the upper stratum forming the rim of the 320 ft (98 m) deep gorge and the lip of the 166 ft (51 m) high Falls. As we have seen, the reason for the Falls is the topographic feature known as the Niagara Escarpment (Figure 2.14). This escarpment is rather like the cuestas of the Bass Islands in form, but dips in a more southerly direction at the Falls. It is the product of erosion, the work of flowing water over hundreds of millions of years. The two bedrock units mentioned above may be readily recognized by visitors. The Queenston shale is distinctively reddish-brown and occurs in the northern part of the Niagara gorge and along the banks of the Niagara River below the escarpment. The Lockport dolomite is whitish-gray throughout its course, and forms the brink of the Falls. Dolomite is similar to limestone ($CaCO^3$), except that it also contains a significant amount of magnesium ($CaMgCO^3$). Another formation, the Guelph dolomite is also noteworthy. It is exposed above the brink of Niagara Falls, forming the upper rapids. The Guelph is characterized by peculiar fossil fauna of gastropods, hingeless brachiopods, and a large clam (Megalomus) which is shaped like a cow's hoof. Between the Lockport and Queenston rocks lie layers of other sedimentary rocks—sandstones, limestones, and more shale and dolomite. As illustrated in Figure 2.14, these underlying beds are weak in comparison with the resistant dolomite which forms the cap. If it were not for this sequence of beds, Niagara Falls would not have the grandeur that it exhibits today.

Glacial Geology

Glacial Erosion and Deposition

Geologically speaking, the last glacier retreated from the Lake Erie basin in very recent times—less than 12,000 years ago. The glacial story starts much earlier, though. About a million years ago, the first ice sheets invaded the Lake Erie region from the northeast. Geologists refer to this segment of the earth's history as the Pleistocene Epoch, or Ice Age. As the ice overrode the resistant limestone which now forms the brink of Niagara Falls, it dug deeply into the softer Devonian shales of western New York. The ice front was obstructed by the steeply rising Portage Escarpment which lies a few miles inland of the present south shore of the lake between Buffalo and Cleveland (Figure 2.2). Thus, the glacier was deflected to the west along the outcrop of the soft shale. These shales were scoured to form the deep bottom of the narrow eastern basin (Figures 2.8 and 2.9). Farther west, where the width of the shale belt is greater, glacial erosion resulted in the broader—but shallower—central basin. The western basin owes its islands, reefs, and shallowness to the tough Devonian and Silurian limestones and dolomites which resisted glacial scour.

During the long period between the deposition of Paleozoic sediments in the region and the first glacier advance—approximately 250 million years—an extensive river drainage system cut into the rocks. Several theories have been put forth on how this river system developed and what the drainage pattern looked like just prior to glaciation. The most plausible shows a divide running roughly east-west through the mid-portions of Ohio and Indiana (Figure 2.27). South of this divide a

Figure 2.27. Preglacial drainage divides in the southern Great Lakes Region (after Thornbury, 1965).

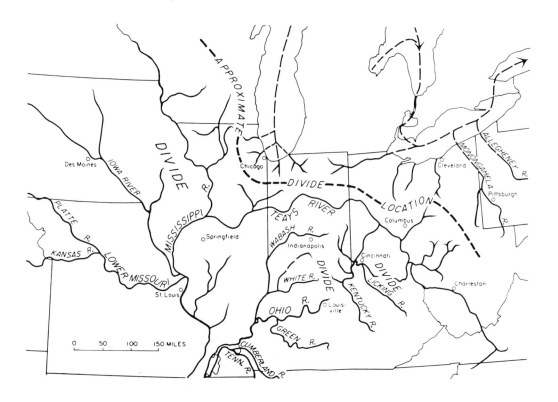

major river system (Teays River) drained westward and into the preglacial Mississippi River (Figure 2.28), while to the north of the divide, drainage was through the basin which now holds Lake Erie (Figure 2.29) and northeast along the ancestral St. Lawrence River valley. Figure 2.30 shows the many valleys of this drainage pattern that were buried by glacial debris

The preglacial topography of the Lake Erie basin has been inferred from recent test borings and seismic measurements of the sediments overlying the bedrock surface (Figure 2.31). Hobson et al. (1969) and Herdendorf and Braidech (1972) discovered a trellis-shaped stream pattern formed in the islands area (Figure 2.32). The islands and reefs were probably hills between the trellis streams. The match between the preglacial drainage pattern inland from the shore and that pattern found offshore (Figure 2.32) is exceptionally good which adds confirmation to the early work of Spencer. The main-trunk stream apparently entered the present lake basin from the northwest and exited in the vicinity of the Niagara River.

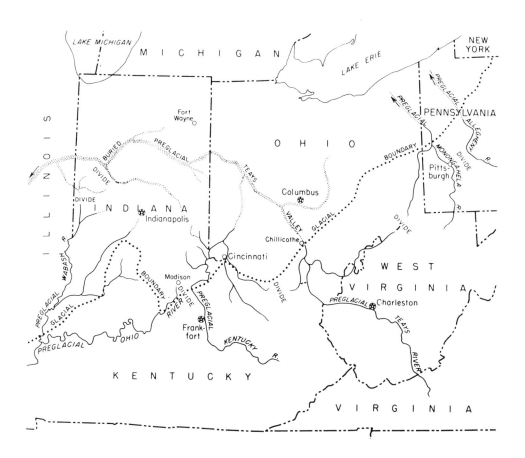

Figure 2.28. Preglacial Teays River drainage system in relation to the glacial boundary south of Lake Erie (after Thornbury, 1965).

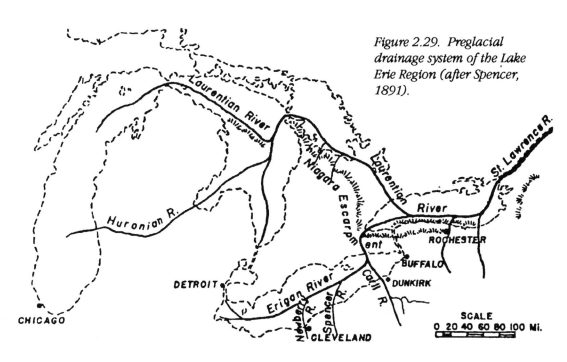

Figure 2.29. Preglacial drainage system of the Lake Erie Region (after Spencer, 1891).

48

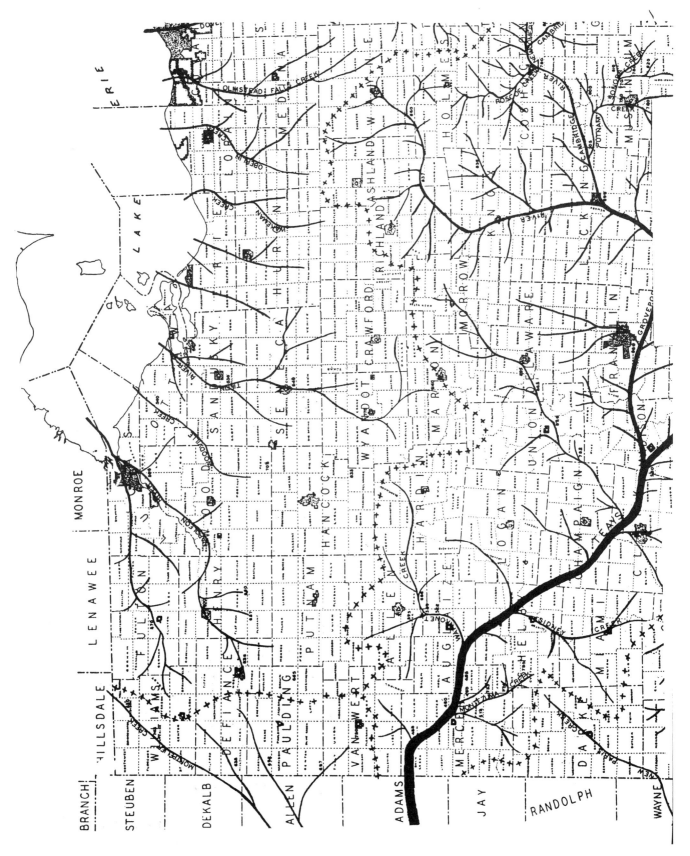

Figure 2.30. Preglacial drainage system in northwestern Ohio during the Teays River Stage as inferred from well logs (after Stout et al., 1943).

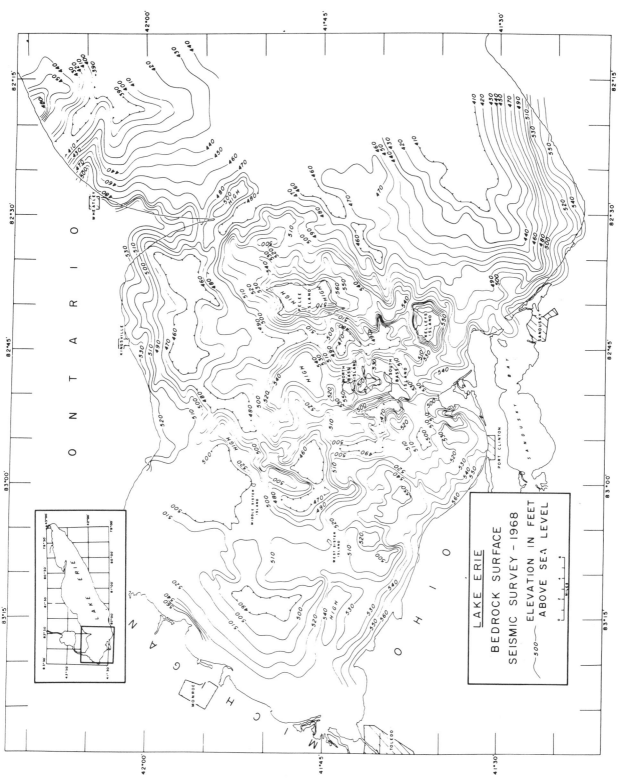

Figure 2.31. Preglacial topography (bedrock surface) of western Lake Erie as inferred from seismic records and test borings (after Hobson et al., 1969).

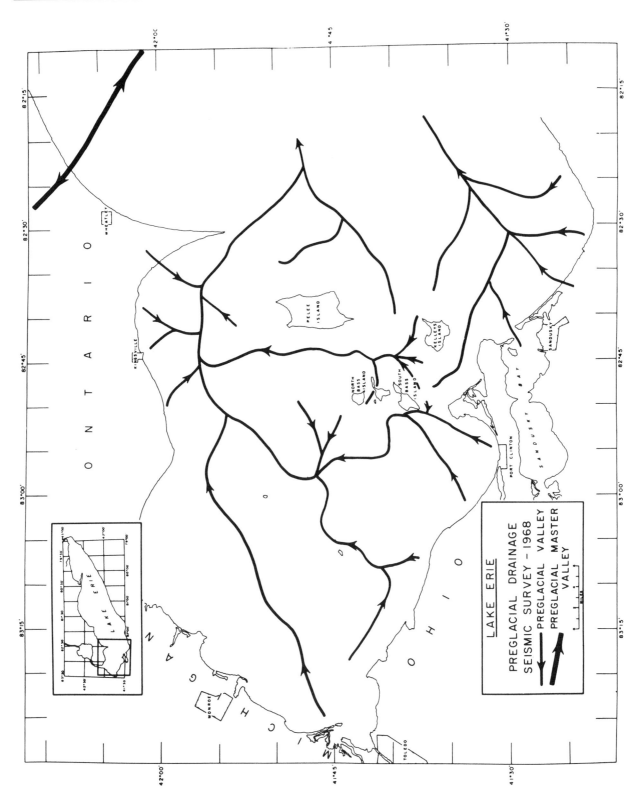

Figure 2.32. Preglacial drainage pattern in western Lake Erie as inferred from the bedrock surface topography (after Hobson et al., 1969).

The Pleistocene glaciers followed these preglacial valleys, scouring them deeper and smoothing their meanders as they moved southwest (Figure 2.33). The end result was much broader and deeper stream valleys. Since the retreat of the last glacier, over 100 ft (30 m) of sediment have been deposited in many of the glaciated valleys to give the current Lake Erie a much smoother and flatter bottom than it had when water first filled the basin. As the ice sheets paused in their advance or retreat, ridges known as moraines were built up of rock debris at the ice margins (Figure 2.34). The debris, often called glacial till, is composed of a heterogeneous mixture of rock fragments ranging in size from clay to boulders (Figure 2.35). A chronology of the glacial deposits in the Lake Erie Region is given in Table 2.5 and their geographic distribution is shown in Figure 2.36. In places, end moraines were deposited in such a way as to dam the natural drainage and thereby form large lakes in the scoured depressions (Flint, 1971; Goldthwait et al., 1961; White, 1969). Lake Erie is the remnant of such a lake, which at its highest stage was 230 ft (70 m) above the present level of the lake. As the ice retreated, new outlets (Figure 2.37) were uncovered and several lake stages were formed at successively lower levels.

Glacial Lake Stages

The chronology of the lake stages in Lake Erie tells a fascinating story of glacial action, movements of the earth's crust, and erosion by the lake waters to form the lake we see today. Noted researchers including Leverett and Taylor (1915), Hough (1958 and 1963), Hartley (1960), and Forsyth (1971) have contributed materially to our knowledge of the sequence of events which have taken place during the evolution of Lake Erie. The story begins nearly 15,000 years ago when the last Pleistocene glacier, known as the Wisconsin ice sheet, was forming the Fort Wayne Moraine in northwestern Ohio, northeastern Indiana and southwestern Michigan. A series of glacial lakes occupied the basin before modern Lake Erie had its birth less than 5,000 years ago.

Low, continuous, sandy ridges within a few kilometers of the lake shore, in southeastern Michigan, northern Ohio, and northeastern Pennsylvania, are the most conspicuous reminders of the former glacial lakes. These abandoned beaches have long been used by the people living near Lake Erie. Numerous east-west roads follow these ridges and many early homes were built on them. As we have seen, each ridge represents an ancient beach, formed along the shore of former lakes which once occupied the Lake Erie basin at elevations much higher than the present lake. Because these former lakes (Maumee, Arkona, Whittlesey, Warren, Wayne, Grassmere, and Lundy) each had a different outline and each stood at a different elevation, each stage is marked by a separate

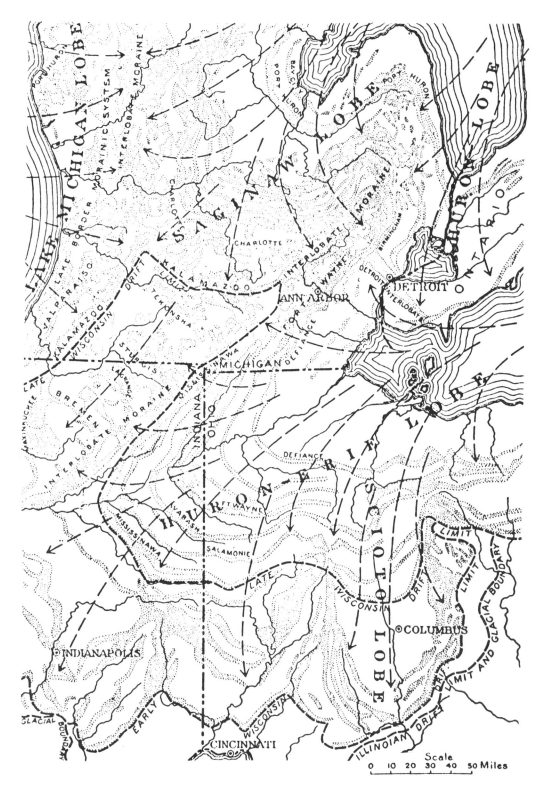

Figure 2.33. Positions of the Wisconsin glacier ice fronts in the Lake Erie region at various stages of advance and the directions of ice movement (after Leverett and Taylor, 1915; Fenneman, 1938).

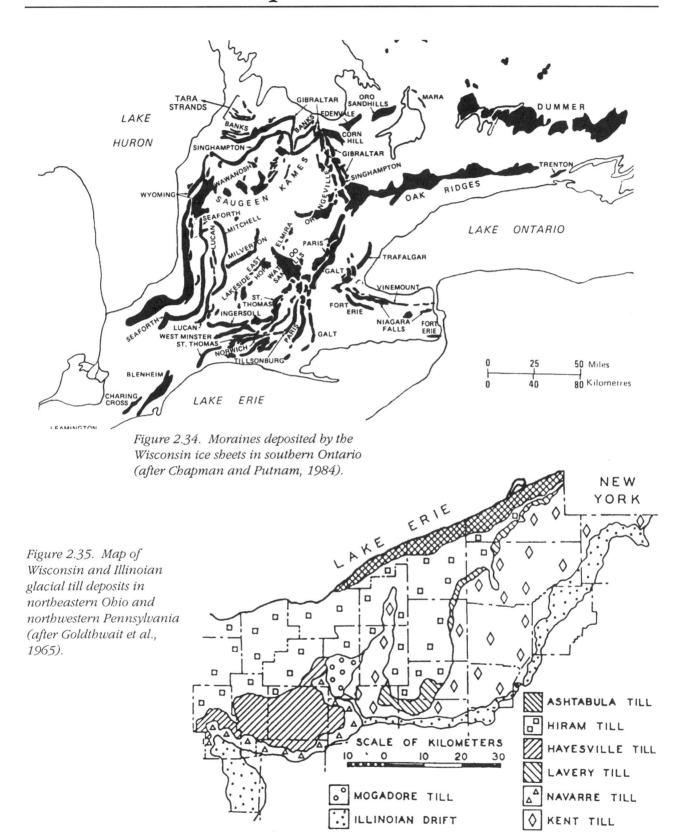

Figure 2.34. Moraines deposited by the Wisconsin ice sheets in southern Ontario (after Chapman and Putnam, 1984).

Figure 2.35. Map of Wisconsin and Illinoian glacial till deposits in northeastern Ohio and northwestern Pennsylvania (after Goldthwait et al., 1965).

Table 2.5. Quaternary time scale for the Lake Erie region. Sources: Terasmae and Dreimanis (1976), Goldthwait et al. (1965), Flint (1971), and Nilsson (1983).

Time Unit and Activity	Age (years ago)
HOLOCENE EPOCH (= RECENT)	0-10,000
PLEISTOCENE EPOCH (= ICE AGE)	10,000-1,000,000
Wisconsin Glaciation	10,000-75,000
Late Wisconsin Stage (= Mankato-Cary-Tazewell)	10,000-25,000
Valders Till	12,000
Port Huron Moraine/Cary Till	13,000
Waterdown Moraine	
Ashtabula/Halton Till	
Paris Moraine	
Lake Border Moraine	13,500
Hiram/Wentworth Till	
St. Thomas Moraine	
Defiance Moraine	14,000
Port Stanley Drift	
Fort Wayne Moraine	14,500
Powell Moraine	
Cuba Moraine	20,000
Catfish Creek Till	
Kent/Navarre Till	22,000
Middle Wisconsin Stage (= Iowan-Farmdale?)	25,000-55,000
Gahanna Drift	40,000
Magadore/Millbrook Till	42,000
Southwold Drift	43,000
Port Talbot II Beds	47,000
Dunwich Till	51,000
Early Wisconsin Stage	55,000-75,000
Port Talbot I Beds	56,000
Titusville Till	58,000
Bradtville/Sunnybrook Till	62,000
Sangamon Interglaciation	~75,000-150,000
Don Beds	
Illinoian Glaciation	~150,000-200,000
York/Mapledale Till	
Yarmouth Interglaciation	~200,000-500,000
Soil	
Kansan Glaciation	~500,000-700,000
Slippery Rock Till	
Aftonian Interglaciation	~700,000-900,000
Nebraskan Glaciation	~900,000-1,000,000
Till	

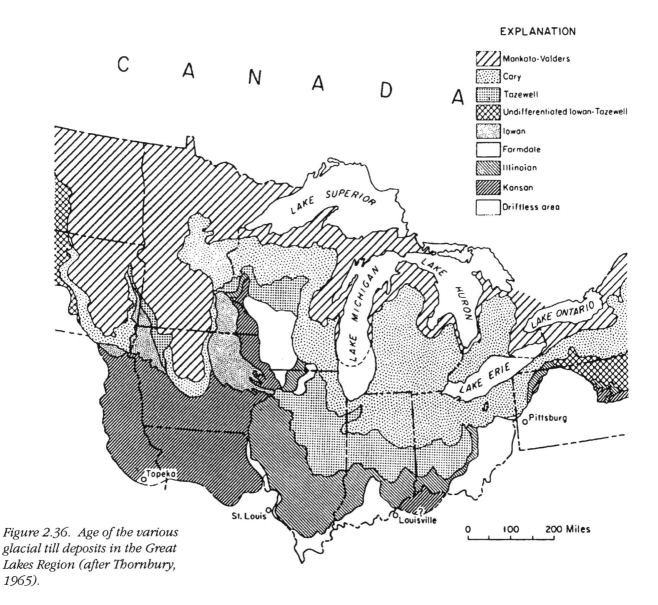

EXPLANATION

- Mankato-Valders
- Cary
- Tazewell
- Undifferentiated Iowan-Tazewell
- Iowan
- Farmdale
- Illinoian
- Kansan
- Driftless area

C   A   N   A   D   A

LAKE SUPERIOR

LAKE MICHIGAN

LAKE HURON

LAKE ONTARIO

LAKE ERIE

o Pittsburg

o Topeka

St. Louis o

o Louisville

0   100   200 Miles

Figure 2.36. Age of the various glacial till deposits in the Great Lakes Region (after Thornbury, 1965).

set of beaches at a characteristic elevation. Beaches formed by a slowly rising water level are much more pronounced than those which have been totally submerged by a higher level. Figure 2.55 (page 2-62) differentiates these two types. Because submergence permits the erosion of former beaches by waves and alongshore (littoral) currents, only three former beaches are easily recognizable, Maumee, Whittlesey, and Warren. At several places in northcentral Ohio where the former lake shore was rocky (such as Amherst, Berlin Heights, and Castalia), spectacular cliff features resembling sea caves, arches, and stacks can be seen by those hardy enough to hike through the bush.

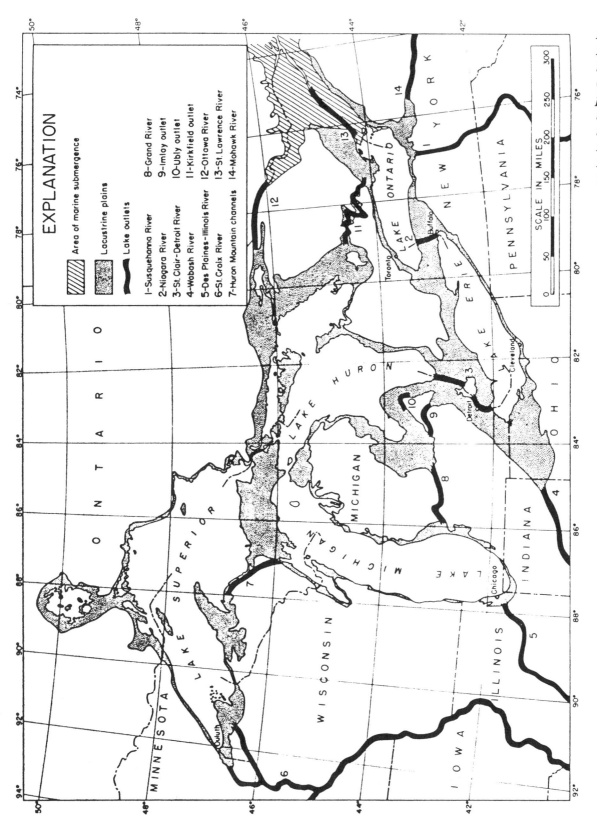

Figure 2.37 Former glacial lakes (lacustrine plains) and their outlets in the Great Lakes Region (after Leverett and Taylor 1915).

EXPLANATION

Area of marine submergence

Lacustrine plains

Lake outlets

1-Susquehanna River
2-Niagara River
3-St. Clair - Detroit River
4-Wabash River
5-Des Plaines - Illinois River
6-St Croix River
7-Huron Mountain channels
8-Grand River
9-Imlay outlet
10-Ubly outlet
11-Kirkfield outlet
12-Ottawa River
13-St. Lawrence River
14-Mohawk River

SCALE IN MILES

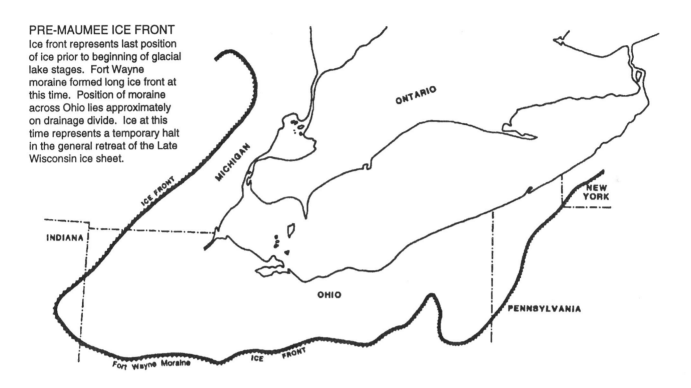

Ice front represents last position of ice prior to beginning of glacial lake stages. Fort Wayne moraine formed long ice front at this time. Position of moraine across Ohio lies approximately on drainage divide. Ice at this time represents a temporary halt in the general retreat of the Late Wisconsin ice sheet.

Figure 2.38. Pre-Lake Maumee glacial ice front (adapted from Leverett and Taylor, 1915).

Highest Lake Maumee (Maumee I). The highest stage of Lake Maumee, surface elevation 800-810 ft (244-247 m) above sea level, was formed when the ice front retreated from the Fort Wayne Moraine (Figure 2.38) and occupied the position of the Defiance Moraine. Drainage was westward through the Fort Wayne outlet into the Wabash River. Figure 2.39 shows the extent of Lake Maumee I and the inferred location of the glacial ice front at that time. Thus, this lake extended as far southwest as the present city of Fort Wayne, Indiana and drained via the Wabash (Figure 2.40) and Mississippi rivers to the Gulf of Mexico.

Lowest Lake Maumee (Maumee II). The second and lowest stage of Lake Maumee, 760 ft (232 m), resulted from ice retreat in Michigan opening the Grand River outlet (Figure 2.37). During this stage (Figure 2.41), bottom deposits in Lake Erie indicate that the ice front stood between Avon Point, Ohio and Point Pelee, Ontario. The ice probably

HIGHEST LAKE MAUMEE
Ice front at time of Highest Lake Maumee
occupied position of Defiance Moraine and
lake occupied area between Defiance and Ft.
Wayne moraines draining into Wabash River.
It is possible that ice had retreated previously
and then re-advanced to the Defiance
moraine so that original Highest Maumee may
have been somewhat larger than shown. Ice
at this time represents a temporary halt in
general retreat of Late Wisconsin ice sheet.
Maximum water depth of Highest Lake
Maumee about 30 m (100 ft.).

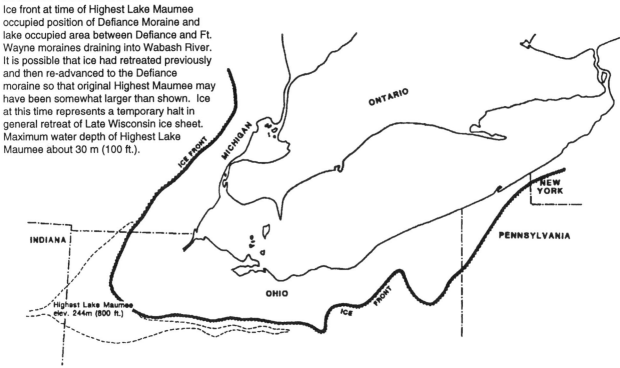

*Figure 2.39. Highest Lake Maumee (Maumee I)
shoreline and Wisconsin glacier ice front
(adapted from Leverett and Taylor, 1915).*

stood just off the present shore from Avon Point east to Cleveland. At
Cleveland, it apparently reached across the present shore to the Portage
Escarpment.

Another lobe of ice apparently stood in the western basin of Lake
Erie at the same time, the front extending from Point Pelee south-
southwest to Kelleys Island, then west to Catawba Point. It then curved
southwestward toward Port Clinton and northwestward to Niagara Reef,
and then occupied a curved position, convex southward and touching
the present Michigan shore in the vicinity of Stony Point, Michigan.

Middle Lake Maumee (Maumee III). Advance of the ice in Michigan closed off the outlet of Lake Maumee II and raised the level to 780-
790 ft (238-241 m). Waters then discharged through both the Imlay
Channel in Michigan and through the Fort Wayne outlet again (Figure
2.37). The ice in the Erie basin had retreated to the vicinity of Erie,

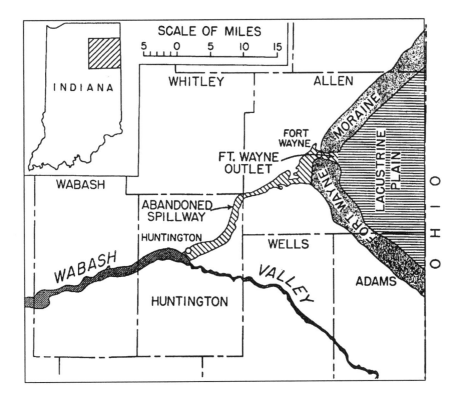

Figure 2.40. Lacustrine plain formed by Lake Maumee I adjacent to the Fort Wayne Moraine and the abandoned outlet spillway to the Wabash River (after Thornbury, 1965).

LOWEST LAKE MAUMEE

The second or lowest stage of Lake Maumee occurred when ice retreated from the Defiance moraine and opened a lower outlet near Imlay, Michigan draining westward into Grand River. Position of ice front marked by sand and gravel covered till ridges in Lake Erie. Lowest Maumee beaches formed approximately along Ft. Wayne and Defiance moraines. Beach along south shore ends at Cleveland. Maximum water depth of Lowest Lake Maumee near 76 m (250 ft.).

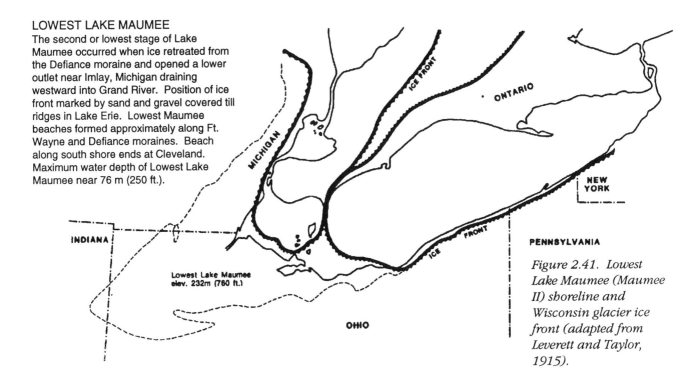

Figure 2.41. Lowest Lake Maumee (Maumee II) shoreline and Wisconsin glacier ice front (adapted from Leverett and Taylor, 1915).

MIDDLE LAKE MAUMEE
A slight advance of the ice front in Michigan raised the outlet raising the waters of the Lowest Maumee stage to the level of Middle Lake Maumee. The Huron and Erie glacial lobes retreated to approximate positions shown. The massive bar northwest of Erie, Pennsylvania marks the position of the ice front at this time. Ice position again shows a temporary halt in the general retreat of the Late Wisconsin ice front. South shore of Middle Lake Maumee ended near Girard, Pennsylvania. Maximum water depth of Middle Lake Maumee near 100 m (330 ft.)

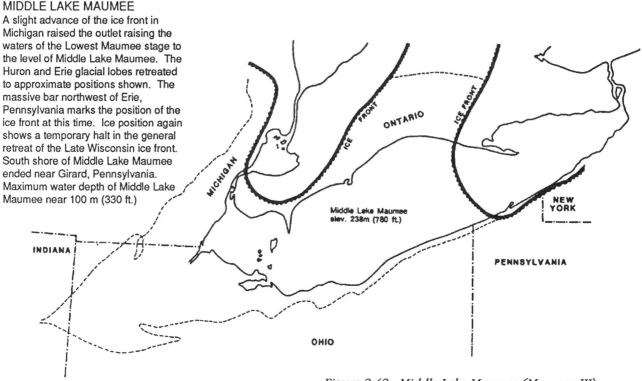

Figure 2.42. Middle Lake Maumee (Maumee III) shoreline and Wisconsin glacier ice front (adapted from Leverett and Taylor, 1915).

Pennsylvania (Figure 2.42). A very wide sand and gravel bar extends across Lake Erie from Erie, Pennsylvania to Long Point, Ontario. The ice front apparently occupied the position of this bar at this time during most of the ensuing lake stages. Coverage of such a large area by sand and gravel indicates the occurrence of a major frontal moraine system in this region.

Lake Arkona. Following the last stage of Lake Maumee, the ice again retreated in Michigan allowing water to flow into Saginaw Bay and lowering the level in three substages to 710 ft, then to 700 ft, and finally to 695 ft (216 to 213 and to 212 m) by minor ice movements and Grand River outlet downcutting in the Saginaw Bay area. During this stage the ice apparently retreated beyond the eastern basin of Lake Erie, since the Arkona beach extends to the eastern end of the present lake (Figure 2.43). General ice retreat throughout the Great Lakes Region brought an end to the Arkona stage. Some researchers, including Hough (1963), believe that the ice may have retreated far enough at this time to un-

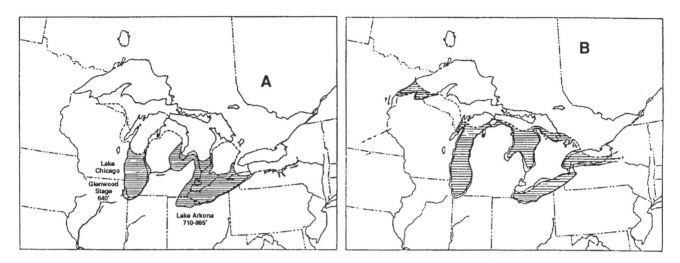

Figure 2.43. Late Wisconsin glacier ice front and glacial lakes' shorelines during (A) Lake Arkona stage and (B) Lake Ypsilanti low stage (after Hough, 1963).

LAKE WHITTLESEY

Lake Whittlesey was formed by ice advance after retreat had ended Arkona stage. Ice advance was major and has been called the Port Huron substage. Ice front as shown represents position of the Port Huron moraine. Bar north of Erie, Pennsylvania marks ice border in Lake Erie. Former drainage was dammed and drainage was transferred to the Ubly channel in Michigan. Lake Whittlesey is marked by strongest beach system in Erie Basin. Lake Whittlesey south shore end near east end of Lake Erie. Maximum Lake Whittlesey water depth near 88 m (290 ft.).

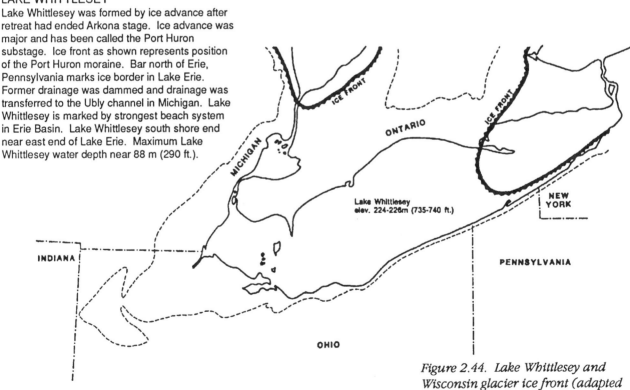

Figure 2.44. Lake Whittlesey and Wisconsin glacier ice front (adapted from Leverett and Taylor, 1915).

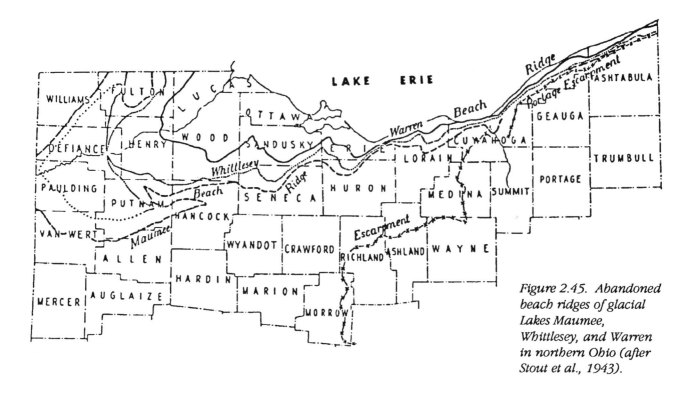

Figure 2.45. Abandoned beach ridges of glacial Lakes Maumee, Whittlesey, and Warren in northern Ohio (after Stout et al., 1943).

cover outlets to the east lowering the level in the Erie basin an unknown amount, possibly below the present level of Lake Erie. This low stage has been named Lake Ypsilanti.

Lake Whittlesey. The next lake stage, following the Lake Ypsilanti stage, stood at 735 to 740 ft (224 to 226 m) above sea level. This stage was created by ice damming the drainage and transferring outflow to the Ubly Channel in Michigan. This is known as the Lake Whittlesey stage (Figure 2.44) and is marked by the most pronounced abandoned beach ridges in the Lake Erie basin (Figure 2.45). During Whittlesey time the ice front apparently occupied the position of the Port Huron Moraine, which was built at this time. The ice front in the Erie basin probably again laid along the ridge from Erie to Long Point, Ontario.

Because Lake Whittlesey existed for a comparatively long period, the ice front probably retained approximately the same position for an equal length of time. If so, it appears that the Port Huron Moraine could have been built at the same time merely by a pause in the general retreat of the ice. It also appears that the major portion of the ridge from Erie, Pennsylvania across Lake Erie to Long Point, Ontario formed at this time.

LAKE WARREN

The ice front at this stage has retreated so far northward that Lake Chicago occupies the southern half of the Lake Michigan basin and some adjoining territory. The waters in front of the Huron and Ontario lobes are united and form Lake Warren. These waters have united near the front of the ice with the Finger Lakes to the east and Lake Saginaw to the west. Their drainage is westward across the southern peninsula of Michigan by way of the present valley of the Grand River. Maximum Lake Warren water depth about 70 m (230 ft.).

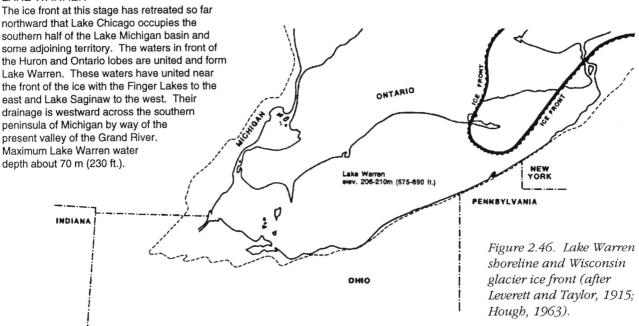

Figure 2.46. Lake Warren shoreline and Wisconsin glacier ice front (after Leverett and Taylor, 1915; Hough, 1963).

Before the end of Lake Whittlesey, the ice retreated somewhat in the eastern basin of Lake Erie but did not leave the basin entirely. This accounts for weak beach development east of Dunkirk, New York. Hough (1963) describes a possible low water stage following Lake Whittlesey which drained to the east, but this may fall between sub-stages of Lake Warren.

Lake Warren and Lake Wayne. Ice retreat in Michigan closed the Lake Whittlesey stage and lowered the level to the highest Lake Warren (Figure 2.46) stage at 690 ft (210 m). However, ice still occupied the eastern basin of Lake Erie at this time with the ice front again along the moraine from Erie to Long Point. Ice retreat in the Saginaw Bay area lowered the level to 682 ft (208 m). Discharge during both levels was down the Grand River (Figure 2.37). A short time later a lowest Warren (675 ft or 206 m) may have occurred due to minor ice retreat and outlet down-cutting.

General ice retreat from the Great Lakes area occurred after the lowest Warren stage and another low water stage followed in the Lake Erie basin, the evidence of which is the buried St. David Gorge of the

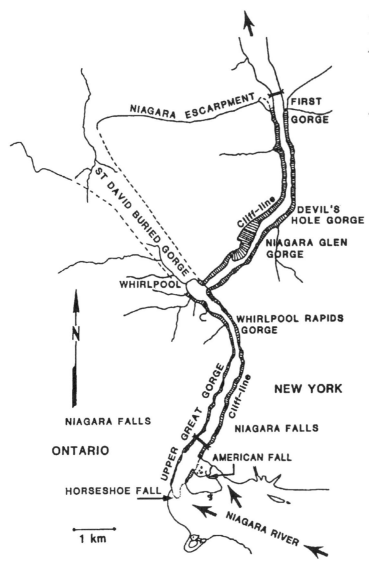

Figure 2.47. Buried St. David Gorge which was probably excavated by drainage from an early low water stage in the Lake Erie basin and later filled with glacial drift by a readvance of the ice front (after Nilsson, 1983).

Niagara River (Figure 2.47). Following the retreat of ice from the Port Huron Moraine, there was a general re-advance, but ice apparently did not progress as far southward as the moraine. Although the ice never invaded the Lake Erie basin again, it did re-advance to the Niagara Falls area and the land south of Lake Ontario. At this time, the water in the Lake Erie basin was again raised to the lowest Warren level at 675 ft (206 m) after a pause at the Lake Wayne level of 660 ft (200 m). Lake Wayne probably drained through the Mohawk River to the east (Figure 2.37). Ice damming of that outlet caused the Warren waters to again discharge through the Grand River outlet.

Lake Warren was the latest stage in the Erie basin to produce conspicuous beach features (Figure 2.45). Water apparently stood at this level for a considerable length of time.

Lake Grassmere and Lake Lundy. The end of Lake Warren was brought about by ice retreat, probably from the New York and Michigan areas, lowering the level to the Grassmere stage at 640 ft (195 m) and then to the Lundy stage at 620 ft (189 m). Some investigators believe the drainage continued eastward during these stages, while others contend that drainage was westward into the Lake Huron basin. Both the Lake Grassmere and Lake Lundy stages (Figure 2.48) were brief as evidenced by weak and discontinuous beach features.

Early Lake Erie. The ice front was located near the eastern end of the basin during the Lake Lundy stage. When the ice retreated, it brought the Lake Lundy stage to a close and lowered the level to a low Early Lake Erie stage which drained for the first time through the present Niagara River gorge (Figure 2.49). This initiated the Early Lake Algonquin stage (605 ft or 184 m) in the Lake Huron and Lake Michigan basins and drainage into Lake Erie (Figure 2.50). The ice continued its retreat

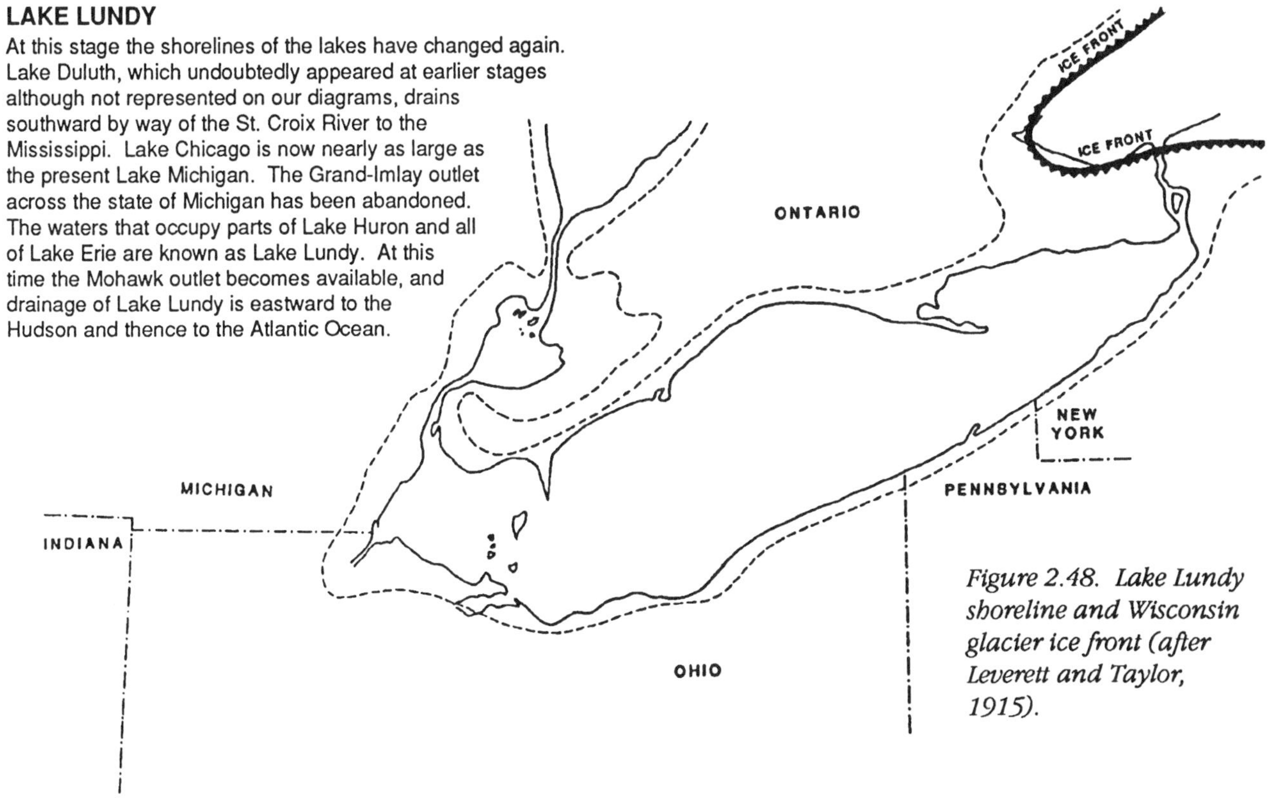
LAKE LUNDY
At this stage the shorelines of the lakes have changed again. Lake Duluth, which undoubtedly appeared at earlier stages although not represented on our diagrams, drains southward by way of the St. Croix River to the Mississippi. Lake Chicago is now nearly as large as the present Lake Michigan. The Grand-Imlay outlet across the state of Michigan has been abandoned. The waters that occupy parts of Lake Huron and all of Lake Erie are known as Lake Lundy. At this time the Mohawk outlet becomes available, and drainage of Lake Lundy is eastward to the Hudson and thence to the Atlantic Ocean.
ICE FRONT
ICE FRONT
ONTARIO
NEW YORK
PENNSYLVANIA
MICHIGAN
INDIANA
OHIO

Figure 2.48. Lake Lundy shoreline and Wisconsin glacier ice front (after Leverett and Taylor, 1915).

EARLY LAKE ERIE

Early Lake Erie originated when the glacial ice retreated sufficiently in the Ontario basin to allow water in that basin to fall below the Niagara sill. Ice also retreated between the Huron and Ontario basins opening the Kirkfield outlet shortly after the beginning of Early Lake Erie so that upper lakes no longer drained into Erie. At this time Early Lake Erie stood at its lowest level, near 149 m (490 ft.) above sea level. Ice then advanced to block the Kirkfield outlet, raising the level in the Huron and Michigan basins to Main Algonquin level at 184 m (605 ft.) above sea level, draining out both the Chicago and Port Huron outlets, probably raising the Erie level slightly. Ice retreat ended Lake Algonquin and Erie remained fairly stable while upper lakes underwent a series of successively lower stages, none of which drained into Erie. Lowest stages of upper lakes drained through Ottawa River. Uplift of Ottawa outlet began raising the level and uplift of Niagara sill, ending Early Lake Erie, is probably correlative.

Figure 2.49. Early Lake Erie shoreline (after Hartley, 1960)

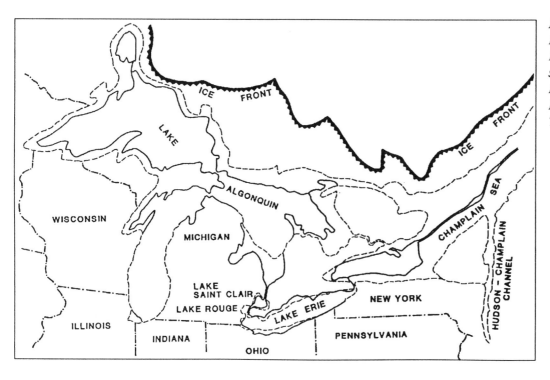

Figure 2.50. Early Lake Erie and Lake Algonquin stages in the Great Lakes basin (after Leverett and Taylor, 1915).

until the Kirkfield outlet (Figure 2.37) to Lake Ontario was opened, lowering the level in the Huron and Michigan basins and stopping their drainage into Lake Erie. Later, a slight re-advance of the ice dammed the Kirkfield outlet raising the Huron and Michigan waters to the Lake Algonquin stage (605 ft or 184 m), again discharging into Lake Erie.

Another ice retreat finally ended the Lake Algonquin stage by uncovering a lower outlet, probably the old Kirkfield outlet. The drainage from the upper lakes to the Erie basin was again lost. The upper lakes then went through a series of successively lower stages until the North Bay-Ottawa River outlet (Figure 2.37, outlet no. 12) was opened to the St. Lawrence embayment of the Atlantic Ocean to create the lowest Lake Chippewa and Lake Stanley stages in the Lake Michigan and Lake Huron basins. From this time on, the level in the Michigan and Huron basins was controlled by uplift of the North Bay - Ottawa River outlet (Figure 2.37). This period of gradually rising levels lasted until the Lake Nipissing stage in the Huron basin. Water was again transferred to the Erie basin and this flow has remained until the present.

During the period between the Early Lake Algonquin and the Lake Stanley stages in the Huron basin, Lake Erie probably remained at a fairly constant level (Figure 2.51) of about 470 to 490 ft (143 to 149 m).

Figure 2.51. Chronology of lake levels and stages in the Huron and Erie basins for the past 12,000 years (after Dorr and Eschman, 1970; Hartley, 1960).

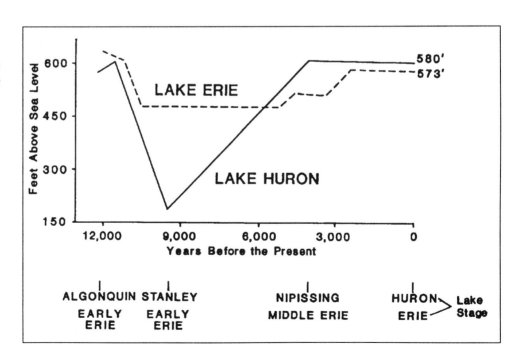

Since Early Lake Algonquin time, the level in the Erie basin has been controlled by uplift of the Niagara sill (elevation of the bedrock at the head of the Niagara River).

The Early Lake Erie stage was confined mainly to the eastern basin east of Erie, Pennsylvania, but a very shallow lake may have existed as far west as Avon Point, Ohio. Drainage into the eastern basin was by way of a channel about 6 mi (10 km) off the present shore northwest of Erie, Pennsylvania. This channel still exists but is filled to some degree with sediment. Field evidence for this low stage of Lake Erie is presented in Figure 2.52.

Middle Lake Erie. As illustrated in Figure 2.51, uplift of the Niagara sill ended the Early Lake Erie stage and the water rose gradually to an elevation of about 525 ft (160 m). It remained long enough to create beach features now found on the lake bottom. This stage, called Middle

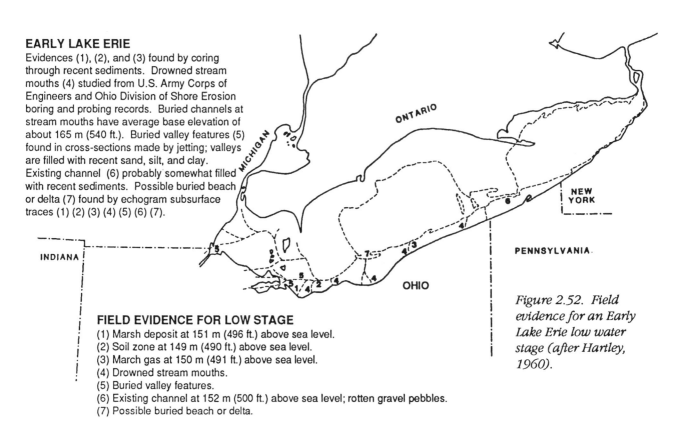

EARLY LAKE ERIE

Evidences (1), (2), and (3) found by coring through recent sediments. Drowned stream mouths (4) studied from U.S. Army Corps of Engineers and Ohio Division of Shore Erosion boring and probing records. Buried channels at stream mouths have average base elevation of about 165 m (540 ft.). Buried valley features (5) found in cross-sections made by jetting; valleys are filled with recent sand, silt, and clay. Existing channel (6) probably somewhat filled with recent sediments. Possible buried beach or delta (7) found by echogram subsurface traces (1) (2) (3) (4) (5) (6) (7).

FIELD EVIDENCE FOR LOW STAGE
(1) Marsh deposit at 151 m (496 ft.) above sea level.
(2) Soil zone at 149 m (490 ft.) above sea level.
(3) March gas at 150 m (491 ft.) above sea level.
(4) Drowned stream mouths.
(5) Buried valley features.
(6) Existing channel at 152 m (500 ft.) above sea level; rotten gravel pebbles.
(7) Possible buried beach or delta.

Figure 2.52. Field evidence for an Early Lake Erie low water stage (after Hartley, 1960).

MIDDLE LAKE ERIE

Middle Lake Erie was probably created by a rising water level, caused by uptilting of the outlet at Niagara Falls. It appears to have halted at this elevation long enough to have created extensive and well-developed beach features. Beach ridges, now expressed as massive bars, were built over wide areas, especially south from Point Pelee, south of Pointe aux Pins, Long Point, along central section of south shore, and on the morainic ridge south of Long Point. Bay at southwest end of lake probably averaged less than 6 m (20 ft.) in depth, central portion probably 15 to 18 m (50 to 60 ft.), east end up to 60 m (200 ft.). Uplife of Niagara Falls ended Middle Lake Erie; levels in Huron and Michigan basins were rising but still draining through Ottawa River.

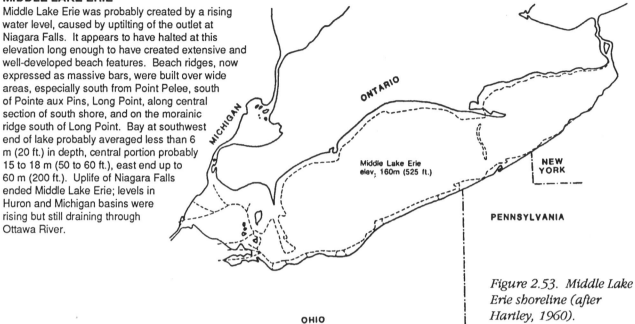

Figure 2.53. Middle Lake Erie shoreline (after Hartley, 1960).

Lake Erie (Figure 2.53), actually was a static phase in a rising level created either by a pause in uplift or a balance between uplift and downcutting of the outlet.

Middle Lake Erie probably extended as far west as Kelleys Island, being very shallow west of the Lorain-Vermilion morainic sand and gravel bar. This bar and the bar from Erie, Pennsylvania to Long Point were beaches at that time.

Highest Lake Erie (Modern Lake Erie). Uplift of the Niagara sill ended the Middle Lake Erie stage and the level rose gradually to its present elevation of 572 ft (174 m). Figure 2.54 illustrates the original shoreline of Lake Erie when it reached its present level approximately 4,000 years ago. Shore processes of erosion and accretion have modified the shore significantly since that time. Crustal uplift continues today, but only at a very slow rate (less than 0.1 ft or 3 cm per century).

It is doubtful that drainage into Lake Erie from the upper lakes has affected its level to a great degree; the variation in level caused by the drainage transfers during the Lake Algonquin and Lake Nipissing stages

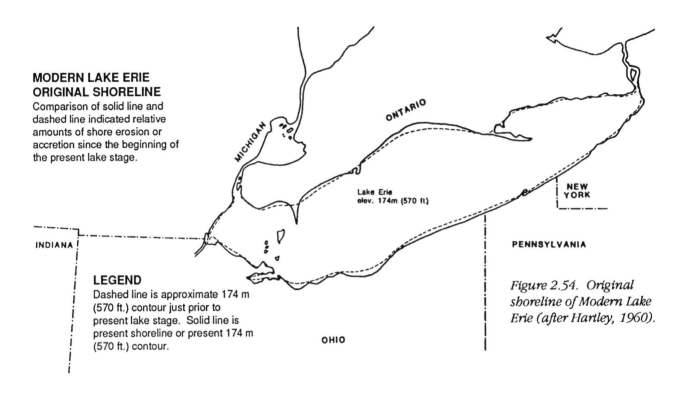

**MODERN LAKE ERIE
ORIGINAL SHORELINE**
Comparison of solid line and
dashed line indicated relative
amounts of shore erosion or
accretion since the beginning of
the present lake stage.

LEGEND
Dashed line is approximate 174 m
(570 ft.) contour just prior to
present lake stage. Solid line is
present shoreline or present 174 m
(570 ft.) contour.

*Figure 2.54. Original
shoreline of Modern Lake
Erie (after Hartley, 1960).*

was probably less than 10 ft (3 m). The Niagara River has the capacity
to dampen the effect of greatly varying lake input.

The foregoing sequence of events from Lake Maumee to Lake Lundy
occurred in a brief 2,000 year span from 14,000 to 12,000 years ago
(Table 2.6). Figure 2.55 summarizes the rather complicated series of lake
stages. When the last glacier retreated from the vicinity of Buffalo, a
new drainage outlet became available through the Niagara River. However, the new outlet was as much as 100 ft (30 m) lower than at present
because the land surface had been depressed by the weight of glacial ice
which was approximately 1.2 mi (2 km) thick.

This new and very low outlet caused a massive flood of water to exit
the lake basin toward the east, resulting in the draining of the western
end of the lake and the formation of separate, shallow lakes in the
central and eastern portions of the lake basin. During this low lake
stage (12,000 to 4,000 years ago), much of the western basin was dry
and exposed to erosion, which greatly altered and reshaped the bottom
surface. The Niagara outlet gradually rebounded to its present elevation,

Table 2.6. *Glacial lake stages of the Lake Erie basin. Sources: Leverett and Taylor (1915), Hough (1963), Herdendorf and Braidech (1972).*

Lake Stage	Age (years ago)	Elevation (meters)	Reason for Change in Level	Outlet
Erie (modern)	4,300	174	Isostatic uplift to the north	Niagara River
Erie (middle)		160	Pause in isostatic uplift	Niagara River
Erie (early)	12,200	150-143	Continued ice retreat	Niagara River
Lundy		195-190	Erosion of outlet and continued ice retreat	
Grassmere		195	Retreat of ice	Mohawk River or Lake Huron basin
Wayne		200	Advance of ice	Mohawk River, NY
Low water stage		<150?	Extensive retreat of ice	Niagara River (?)
Warren		210-206	Continued ice advance (Valders Drift) and erosion of outlet	Grand River, MI
Whittlesey	13,000	224	Readvance of ice Port Huron Moraine	Ubly Channel Grand River, MI
Low water stage (Lake Ypsilanti)		<150?	Extensive retreat of ice	Niagara River (?)
Arkona		217-212	Retreat of ice and erosion of outlet	Grand River, MI
Maumee III		238	Readvance of ice, Lake Border Moraine	Imlay Channel, MI Wabash River, IN
Maumee II		232	Continued ice retreat	Imlay Channel, Grand River, MI
Maumee I	14,000	244	Formation of first major lake stage in depression between ice at Defiance Moraine and Fort Wayne Moraine	Wabash River, IN

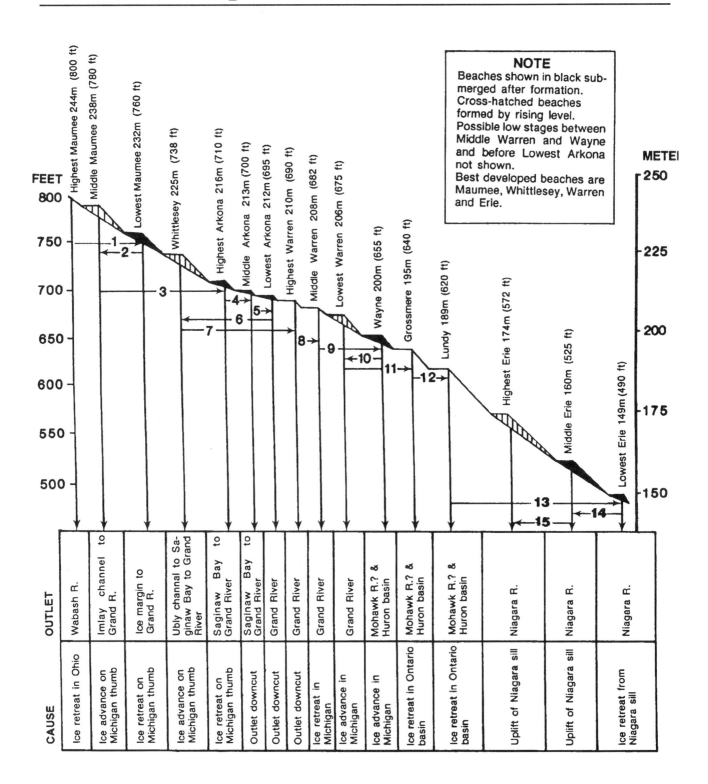

Figure 2.55. Sequence of glacial lake stages and beach ridges in the Lake Erie basin (after Leverett and Taylor, 1915; Hough, 1958 and 1963; Hartley, 1960).

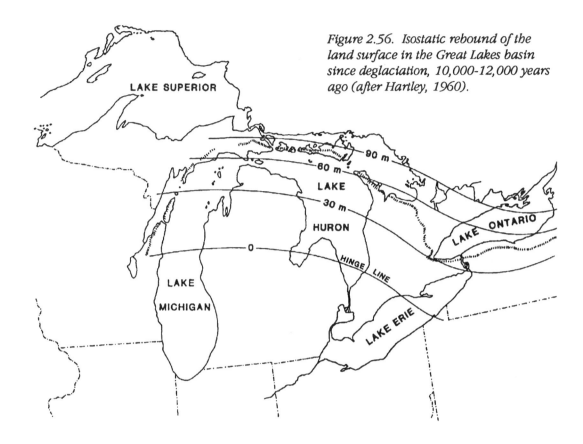

Figure 2.56. Isostatic rebound of the land surface in the Great Lakes basin since deglaciation, 10,000-12,000 years ago (after Hartley, 1960).

and Lake Erie correspondingly rose from this low elevation of 470 ft (140 m) to its present level. Figure 2.56 illustrates the amount of isostatic rebound that has taken place in the Great Lakes basin since the deglaciation. As the lake rose, waves and currents cut into the lake bottom, locally excavating the glacial deposits and exposing some of the shallowly buried bedrock. The exposed bedrock now forms the islands, reefs, and rocky shorelines of the lake. Also during the low lake stage, tributary valleys were deeply entrenched. When the lake eventually rose, these rivers' mouths were drowned forming the excellent estuarine harbors along the south shore (Brant and Herdendorf, 1972).

Lake St. Clair and Detroit River

As noted earlier, during many of the glacial lake stages, a strait connected the waters in the Lake Huron and Lake Erie basins. This strait occupied the area or route of the present St. Clair-Detroit River valley. The floor of this strait was wide and flat with a few low ridges that ran transverse to the axis of the strait. These ridges, or moraines, were left by the glaciers that scoured the river valley and the lake basin. Except where the rivers have cut through them, these moraines remain nearly as they were when left by the glaciers. As lake waters fell with the recession of the glaciers, the strait grew narrower to form a large river. Eventually, water levels fell to their present elevation and the St. Clair and Detroit Rivers were established in the lowest confines of the valley. Lake St. Clair formed as a large pool between these rivers. Sediments eroded from fresh shorelines of the upper lakes were carried south by the St. Clair River and deposited in the quiet waters of Lake St. Clair to form the massive delta we see today (Figure 2.57).

Niagara River

As we have seen, glaciation played an important role in the geological history of the Niagara Frontier. This process formed the basins of the present Great Lakes, controlled the level of the preceding lakes, and

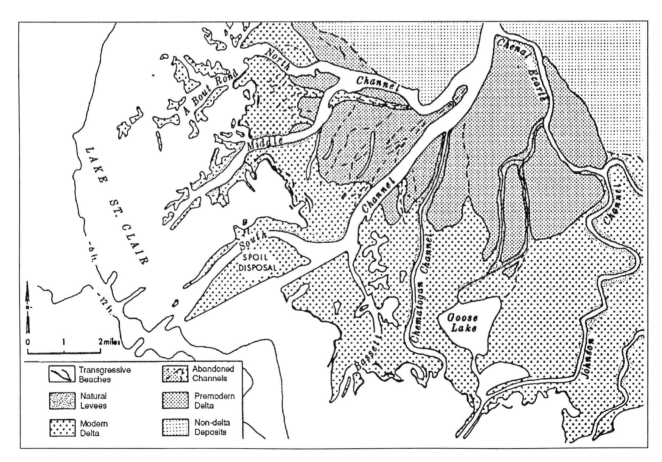

Figure 2.57. Depositional features and landforms of the St. Clair Delta (after Raphael and Jaworski, 1982).

influenced the drainage patterns which now funnel water from the entire system over Niagara Falls into Lake Ontario. Following a 27 mi (43 km) course established about 12,000 years ago, the Niagara River has cut a deep trench into the Niagara Escarpment, exposing 400,000 years of geological history. At the whirlpool below the Falls, St. David Gorge once carried the flow of higher lake stages, but it is now buried under debris left by a re-advance of the glacier (Figure 2.47). The downcutting of Niagara Falls continues today, with Horseshoe Falls retreating at a rate of 2 to 5 ft/yr (0.6 to 1.5 m/yr) and the American Falls at less than 1 ft/yr (0.3 m/yr).

Lake Sediments and Beach Deposits

Lake Erie

The bottom deposits of Lake Erie consist of silt and clay muds, sand and gravel, peat, compact glacio-lacustrine clays, glacial till, shoals of limestone and dolomite bedrock and rubble, shale bedrock shelves, and erratic cobbles and boulders composed chiefly of igneous and metamorphic rocks. The distribution of bottom sediments is closely related to the bottom topography (Figure 2.58). The broad, flat areas of the western and central basins, and the deep areas of the eastern basin have mud bottoms. Midlake bars, nearshore slopes, and beaches are comprised mostly of sand and gravel or glacial till. Rock is exposed in the shoals of western Lake Erie and along the south shore of the central basin and both shores of the eastern basin. Figure 2.59 illustrates two

Figure 2.58. Lake Erie bottom surface sediments (after Lewis and Herdendorf, 1974).

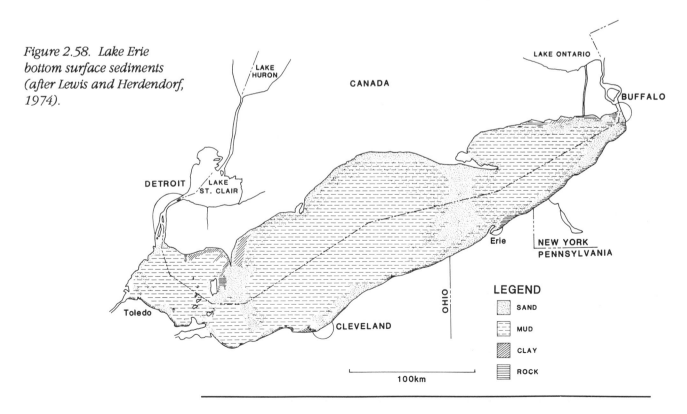

LEGEND

▦	SAND
▦	MUD
▨	CLAY
▤	ROCK

100km

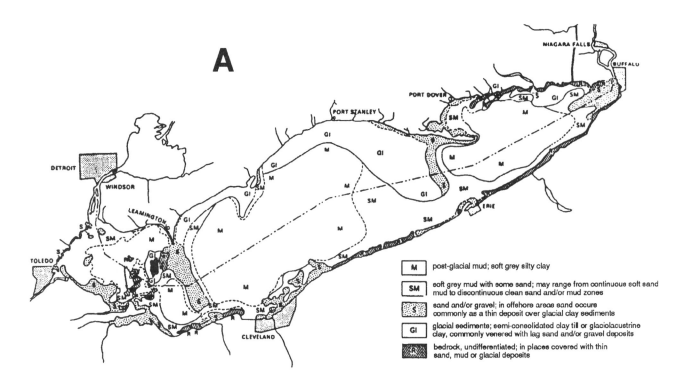

Figure 2.59. *Comparison of Lake Erie sediment distribution maps (A) sediment type and (B) mean grain size in phi units (-log² particle diameter in mm). Note the high correlation between the mud bottom and large (<8) phi numbers, and the sandbed and low (<3) phi numbers (after Thomas et al., 1976).*

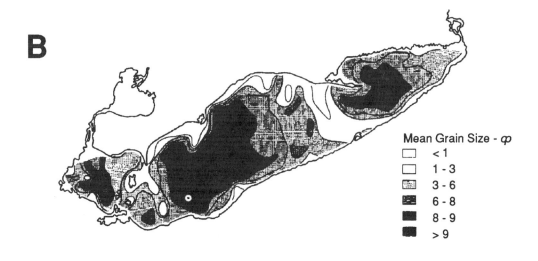

techniques used by geologists to display the type and size of the material which composes the bottom sediments. Sediment type names refer to grain sizes. For example, gravel includes all sediment particles greater than 2 mm in diameter, sand ranges from 2 mm to 63 microns, silt from 63-4 microns, and clay consists of the very fine material less than 4 microns in size. The above classification is known as the Wentworth Scale.

In general, sand is limited along the shoreline, but extensive dunes have been formed at several places, notably at the base and southwestern side of Long Point, Point Abino, and Sturgeon Point, all in eastern Lake Erie. These dunes were formed presumably under the influence of the prevailing southwest winds. Littoral currents have concentrated sand spits, baymouth bars, and harbor breakwalls at places such as Point Pelee (Figure 2.60), Pointe Aux Pins, and Long Point, Ontario; North Cape, Michigan; Magee Marsh (Figure 2.61), East Harbor, Cedar Point, Vermilion Harbor, and Fairport Harbor, Ohio; Presque Isle, Pennsylvania (Figure 2.62); and Hanford Bay, New York.

The bottom sediments of the eastern basin of Lake Erie are mostly silt and clay muds bounded by relatively steep slopes of sand and gravel or rock. The massive spits at Presque Isle and Long Point are the largest accumulation of beach sand in Lake Erie. Bedrock is exposed in a narrow strip along most of the shoreline, with black shale on the south shore and fossiliferous gray limestone on the north shore.

Figure 2.60. Accumulation of sand deposits at the Point Pelee spit. The sand spit has been built on a glacial moraine. Marshes have developed between the east spit and west spit, which resulted in the accumulation of peat near the center of the spit (Coakley, 1972).

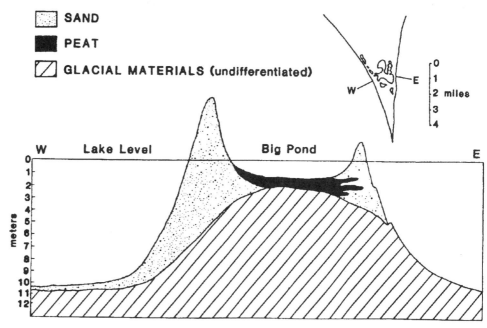

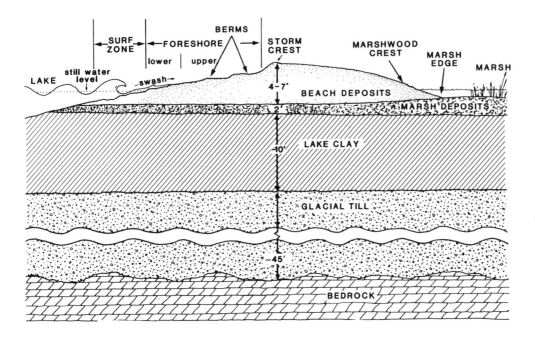

Figure 2.61. Cross-section of barrier sand spit formed between Lake Erie and Magee Marsh, Ohio (courtesy U.S. Fish and Wildlife Service).

Figure 2.62. Presque Isle sand spit on the south shore of Lake Erie provides a sheltered harbor for Erie, Pennsylvania.

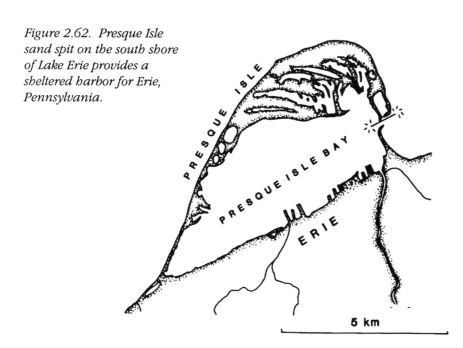

The bottom surface material of the Ohio portion of central Lake Erie consists of silt and clay (77%), sand and gravel (22%), and shoal bedrock (1%). The unconsolidated material appears to have been derived mainly from glacial deposits and till and occurs near the south shore, particularly eastward from Cleveland. Extensive glacial clay deposits are exposed along the north shore of the basin. Large quantities of sand and gravel occur north of Vermilion, nearshore from Cleveland to Fairport, and midlake off Ashtabula and Conneaut. Commercial sand and gravel dredging areas have been designated on both sides of the international boundary on a low morainal ridge between Vermilion and Point Pelee and on the bar between Erie, Pennsylvania, and Long Point, Ontario. Ohio has also assigned another dredging area 5 mi (8 km) northwest of Fairport in an ancient delta deposit from Grand River when its mouth was in the vicinity of Mentor Marsh (Figure 2.63).

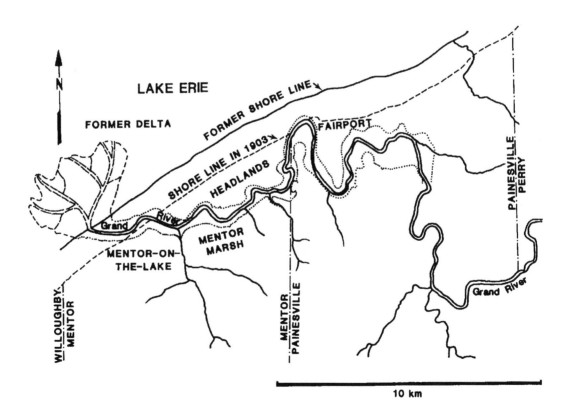

Figure 2.63. Course of ancient Grand River (during low stage of Early Lake Erie) showing deltaic sand deposit near Fairport, Ohio (Gault, 1957).

The bottom deposits of the Ohio portion of western Lake Erie are composed mainly of mud (58%), semifluid silt- and clay-sized material (Verber 1957; Hartley 1961). Sand (17%), mixtures of mud and sand (12%), mixtures of sand, gravel, and coarser material (7%), glacio-lacustrine clay (3%), and limestone/dolomite bedrock (3%) account for the remaining bottom material. Peat and plant detritus occur in isolated areas along the low, marshy shores. Sand concentration in Maumee Bay and near the entrance to Sandusky Bay are sites of commercial dredging. The surface bottom sediments in the islands area are depicted in Figure 2.64. The rocky and coarse bottom deposits associated with the islands are apparent from this map.

Test borings into the subsurface bottom deposits in the vicinity of the Lake Erie islands show a predominance of lake deposited material with only a thin veneer of glacial till overlying bedrock (Figure 2.65). Pregla-cial buried valleys are indicated by bedrock topography, which in places has 200 ft (60 m) of relief. Some borings also indicate the possibility of interglacial or postglacial buried valleys and lower lake stages. Beach deposits and peat have been found 35 to 80 ft (11 to 24 m) below the present lake level, buried under more recent deep-water sediments. A radiocarbon date of 6,550 YBP (years before present) was obtained for a sample of oak wood buried 23 ft (7 m) below the lake bottom (Herden-dorf and Braidech, 1972). This date permits the calculation of a sedi-mentation rate of 0.35 ft/century (10.6 cm/century). A deep boring in the central basin 30 mi (48 km) north of Cleveland (water depth of 84 ft or 26 m) yielded soft, gray-brown clay that became stiffer downward. At 111 ft (34 m) of bottom penetration, impenetrable rock or hard glacial till was reached. Seismic reflection surveys have revealed a maximum unconsolidated sediment thickness of 275 ft (84 m) in the central basin and 130 ft (40 m) in the western basin (Hobson et al., 1969). Test borings in the central basin have also yielded evidence of a lower lake stage (Figure 2.65).

Fine-grained sediments, such as silt-clay muds, have an affinity for agricultural and industrial pollutants, particularly toxic metals. In Lake Erie, lead, nickel, copper, silver, vanadium, zinc, cadmium, chromium, and mercury have elevated concentration levels in the sediments off-shore from the major tributaries, especially the Detroit River (Kemp et al., 1976). Figure 2.66 is a distribution map of mercury concentrations in the surface sediment showing exceptionally high values in western Lake Erie adjacent to the mouth of this river. Sediment cores taken here in 1971 yielded surface mercury values up to 3.8 ppm (3,800 ppb) with considerably lower levels only 1 ft (30 cm) below the sediment-water interface (Figure 2.67).

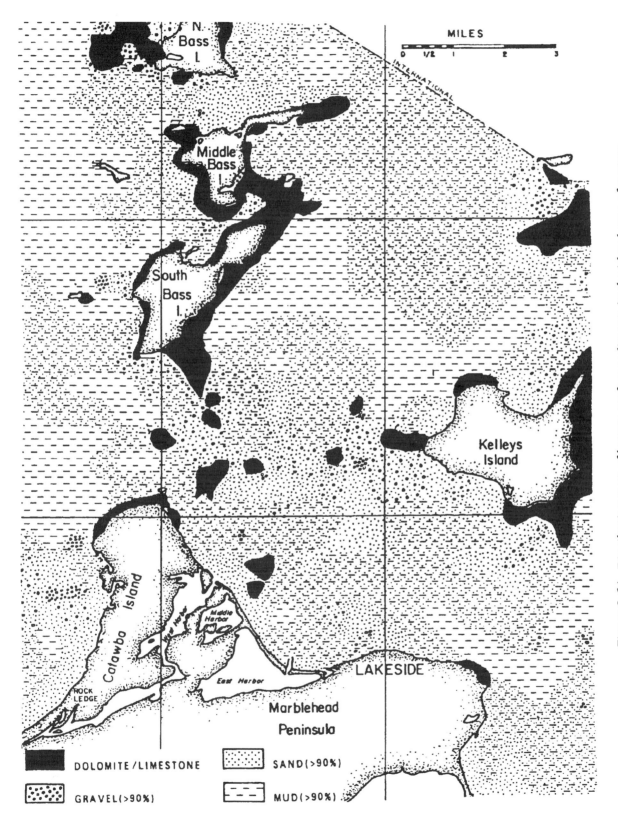

Figure 2.64. *Distribution map of bottom surface sediments in the island area of western Lake Erie (after Hartley, 1961; Herdendorf, 1968; Herdendorf and Braidech, 1972).*

DOLOMITE/LIMESTONE

GRAVEL(>90%)

SAND(>90%)

MUD(>90%)

A

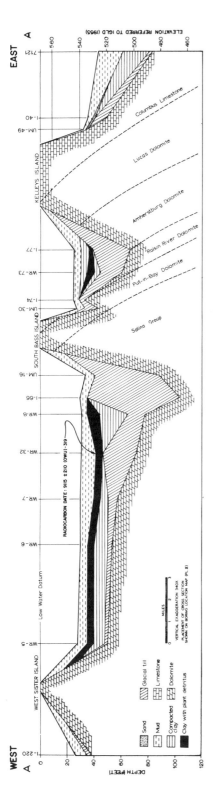

Figure 2.65. Subsurface bottom deposits in Lake Erie (A) western basin and (B) central basin (after Lewis and Herdendorf, 1974; Herdendorf and Braidech, 1972).

The high surface values were attributed to waste discharges of elemental mercury from chlor-alkali plants on the Detroit and St. Clair rivers which operated during the period 1950-1972. Hazardous concentrations of mercury in fish of Lake St. Clair and western Lake Erie was a major contaminant problem in the early 1970s. In 1977, several years after these plants diminished operation the area was again cored. Analyses showed that recent deposits were covering the highly contaminated sediment with a thin layer of new material which had mercury concentrations approaching background levels (Wilson and Walters, 1978).

Fortunately, the levels of total mercury in walleye (*Stizostedion vitreum*) collected from Lake St. Clair have likewise declined from over 2 ug/g in 1970 to 0.5 ug/g in 1980. In western Lake Erie, 1968 levels of mercury were 0.84 ug/g as compared to only 0.31 ug/g in 1976. The U.S. Department of Agriculture considers fish tissue with mercury concentrations under 0.5 ug/g to be safe for human consumption. The rapid environmental response subsequent to the cessation of the point source discharges is attributed to rapid flushing of the St. Clair-Detroit River system and the high load of suspended sediment delivered to western Lake Erie which absorbs metals and traps them in the bottom sediments.

Recent sedimentation in Lake Erie can be attributed to two primary sources: suspended solids from inflowing streams, and bluff material contributed by shore erosion (Figure 2.68). Approximately four million tons of clay, silt, and sand are transported annually to Lake Erie from its tributaries. Shore erosion of glacial till and lacustrine clay bluffs is an acute problem at many locations along the shoreline, accounting for another eight million tons. Maximum shore erosion, based on volume of material removed, occurs along the north

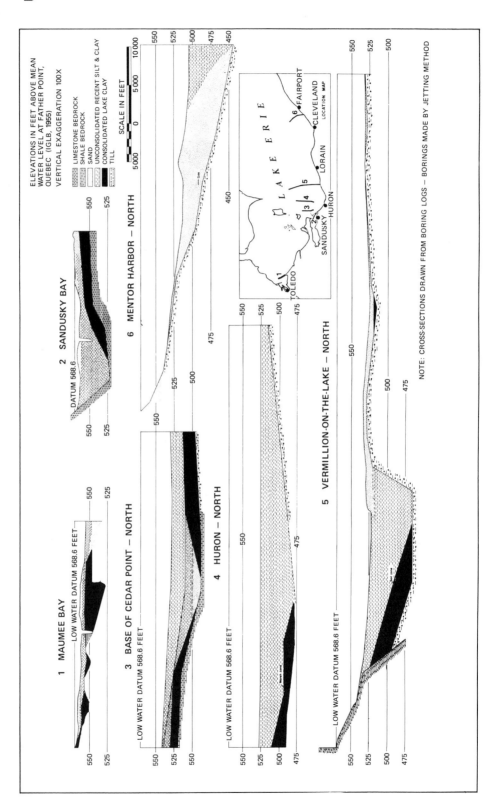

Figure 2.65. Subsurface bottom deposits in Lake Erie (A) western basin and (B) central basin (after Lewis and Herdendorf, 1974; Herdendorf and Braidech, 1972).

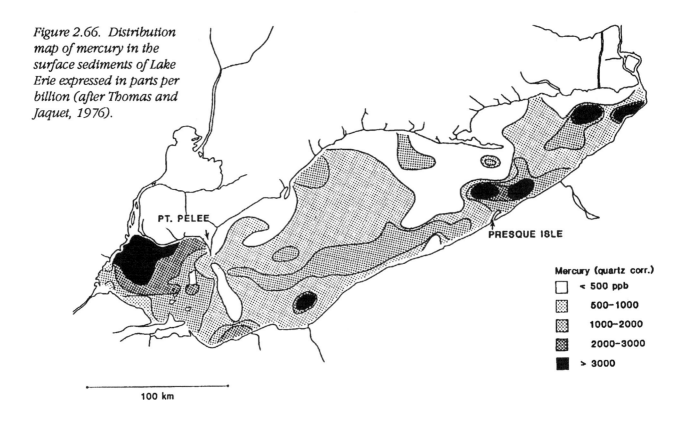

Figure 2.66. Distribution map of mercury in the surface sediments of Lake Erie expressed in parts per billion (after Thomas and Jaquet, 1976).

PT. PELEE

PRESQUE ISLE

Mercury (quartz corr.)

☐ < 500 ppb

▦ 500-1000

▦ 1000-2000

▦ 2000-3000

■ > 3000

100 km

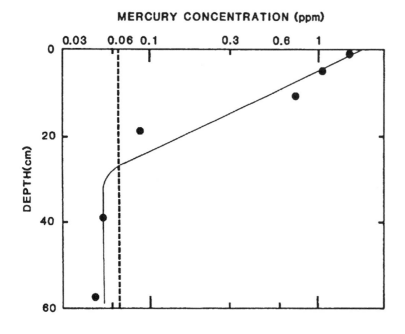

MERCURY CONCENTRATION (ppm)

DEPTH(cm)

Figure 2.67. Mercury concentration in sediment core from western Lake Erie near mouth of Detroit River (after Walters et al., 1974). Note mercury-enriched surface zone overlying sediment having natural background mercury levels (dashed line).

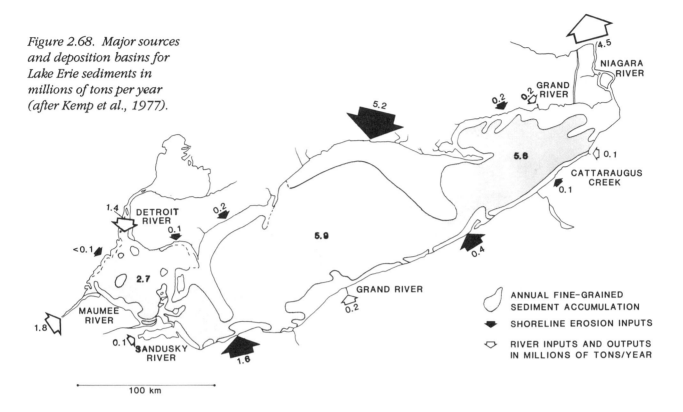

Figure 2.68. Major sources and deposition basins for Lake Erie sediments in millions of tons per year (after Kemp et al., 1977).

shore of the central basin between Port Stanley and the base of Long Point, although the low-lying south shore of Maumee Bay has experienced the maximum rate of shore recession—as high as 20 ft (6 m) per year (Herdendorf, 1975). Estimates of erosion rates for the Ohio shoreline indicate that about 10,000 yd³ of bluff material erode per mile of shore (12,000 m³/km) each year. Extended for the entire shore of the lake, 8,500,000 yd³ (6,500,000 m³) of sediment are contributed to the lake each year, which would equate to a thickness of 0.01 in (0.25 mm) if spread uniformly over the lake bottom. As might be expected however, sedimentation is not uniform at the bottom. Figure 2.69 illustrates the various rates of sedimentation, from all sources, at 47 stations throughout the lake. The maximum rate, 6300 g/m²/yr, occurs in western Lake Erie. This equates to a thickness of about 1-2 cm. This high sedimentation rate requires regular maintenance dredging of the navigational channels in western Lake Erie. Due to differences in sediment resuspension rates associated with bathymetry and water circulation, the eastern basin of Lake Erie has the highest net annual sediment accumulation rate.

Lake St. Clair

Sediments that enter Lake St. Clair via the St. Clair River are largely derived from the shores of Lake Huron and to a much lesser extent from

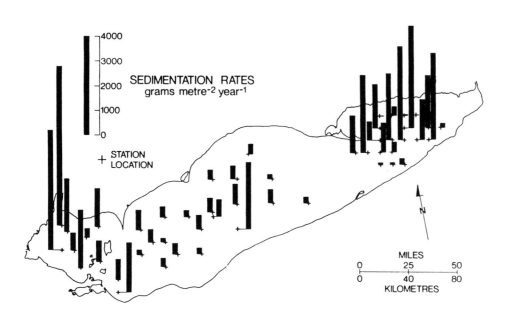

SEDIMENTATION RATES
grams metre⁻² year⁻¹

*Figure 2.69.
Distribution map of
modern sedimentation
rates in Lake Erie (after
Kemp et al., 1977).*

the river banks. Most of these sediments come from glacial moraines and ancient lake beaches, thus the amount of sediments that reach Lake St. Clair is dependent on the energy of the waves breaking on the shores of Lake Huron. Because the grain size of the sediment carried to the St. Clair River is largely sand, most of the sediment is carried along the river bottom as bed load rather than entrained in the water as suspended load. The river currents are generally not able to suspend particles larger than fine sand.

Most of the sediment that reaches Lake St. Clair is deposited along the delta structure at the north end of the lake (Figure 2.57). Much of this material is laid down at the mouths of the distributary channels, forming bars. During high lake levels, water flows over the levees through crevasses. Material is carried into the interdistributary bays via these crevasses and deposited at right angles to the distributary flow. Eventually, these sediments will fill the interdistributary bays as the delta grows (Raphael and Jaworski, 1982). Figure 2.70 illustrates the infilling of Goose Bay and Muscamoot Bay by this process.

Test borings indicated that the St. Clair Delta is growing much slower now than it did during its early history and that the sediments now being delivered to it are finer than the coarse sands of the premodern delta. Figure 2.71 shows the massive size of the premodern delta in compari-

Figure 2.70. Landforms of Dickinson Island, St. Clair Delta. Note infilling of interdistributary bay by sediment carried through crevasses during high water (after Raphael and Jaworski, 1982).

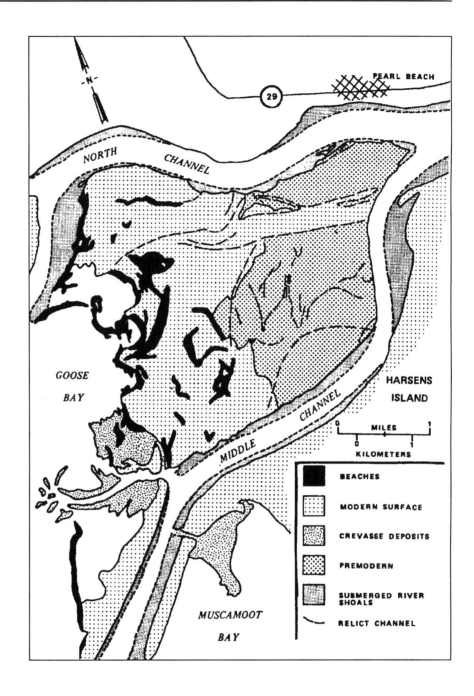

son to the modern deposits of silty sand. Because of the present low sedimentation rate in Lake St. Clair, there has been very little recent growth of the delta structure. Two factors greatly influence this low sedimentation. First, because of the large grain size, most of the material is carried as bed load, reducing the overall sedimentation. Second, much of the bed load carried to the distributary channels of the St. Clair

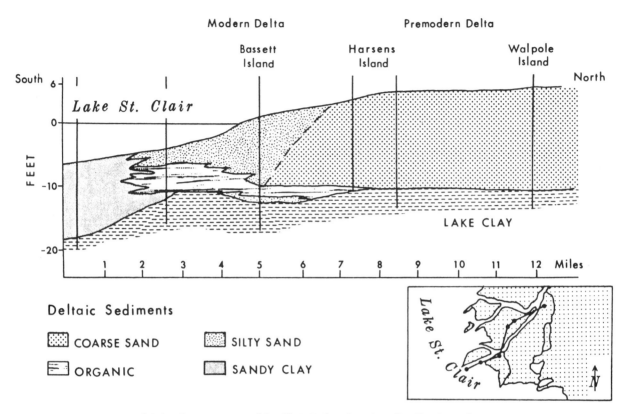

Figure 2.71. Cross-section of St. Clair Delta showing distribution of modern and premodern sediments (after Raphael and Jaworski, 1982).

River is dredged and removed from the area for navigation purposes. The only periods of increased sedimentation are during the spring when high water flows carry more sediment and intrude the crevasses to deposit material in the inter-distributary bays. Beyond the delta most of the surface bottom sediments in Lake St. Clair are silt and clay with some fine sand.

Coastal Processes

The geologic features of the Lake Erie coast are closely intertwined with the physical processes of the lake. Currents, waves, and water level fluctuations all markedly influence the development of the coastal landforms.

Shore Erosion

The record high water levels in Lake Erie of 1952, again during 1972-1973 and once again in 1985 (Figure 2.72), have contributed greatly to

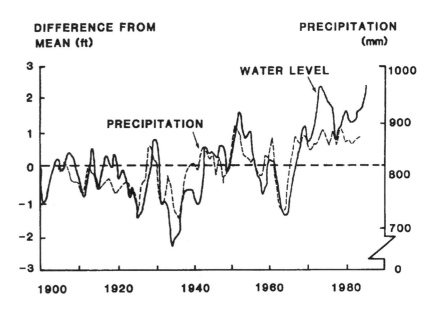

Figure 2.72. Lake Erie water levels from 1900-1985. Note close correlations between Lake Erie levels and precipitation in the Great Lakes basin.

increased erosion of the shores. The narrow beaches fronting the shore bluffs of the islands have been submerged exposing the bluffs to direct wave attack and erosion by alongshore currents. Severe storms have resulted in profound changes in shoreline configuration and disruption of man's use of the coastal zone. Most of Lake Erie's shores are characterized by easily eroded banks of glacial till and lacustrine sediments (Figure 2.73-A), while lesser reaches are composed of resistant bedrock bluffs. The shore of western Lake Erie consists of low banks of lake clay which were originally fronted by barrier spits and islands (Figure 2.73-B). Many of these sand barriers have been seriously eroded and are now protected by rip-rap bulkheads. The bluffs of the central basin are more typically till, capped by lake clay and sand, which rise to 75 ft (23 m) above lake level on the south shore and over 150 ft (46 m) above lake level on the north shore. Resistant limestone and dolomite crops out only in 30-ft (9-m) cliffs along the Ohio shore between Port Clinton and Sandusky, on all of the western Lake Erie islands, and in low headlands along much of the Ontario shore of eastern Lake Erie. Shale bedrock forms erosion-resistant, nearly vertical bluffs, 20 to 50 ft (6 to 15 m) high between Vermilion and Cleveland and from Erie to Buffalo. The susceptibility of the coast to shore erosion is illustrated in Figure 2.74.

All of the islands are rockbound and are undergoing very slow erosion by scour from waves and currents. However, during the recent

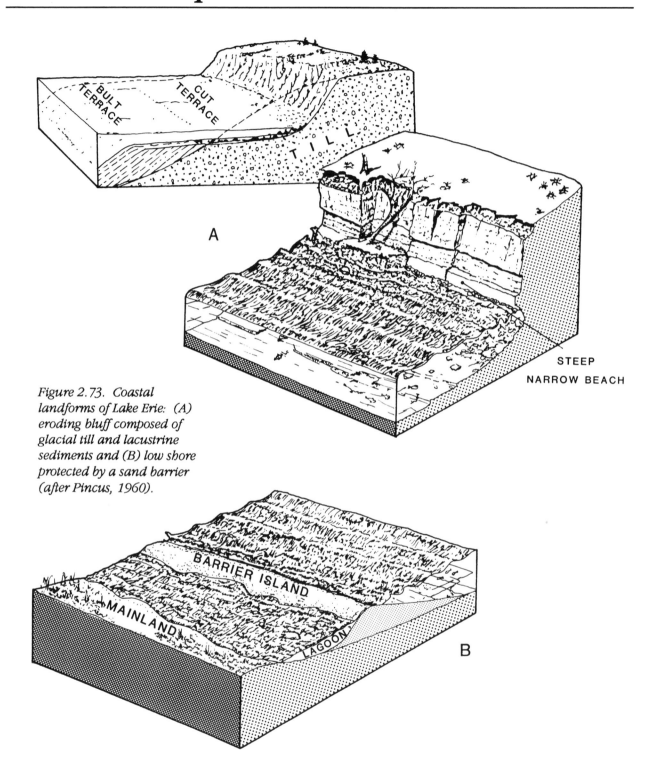

Figure 2.73. Coastal landforms of Lake Erie: (A) eroding bluff composed of glacial till and lacustrine sediments and (B) low shore protected by a sand barrier (after Pincus, 1960).

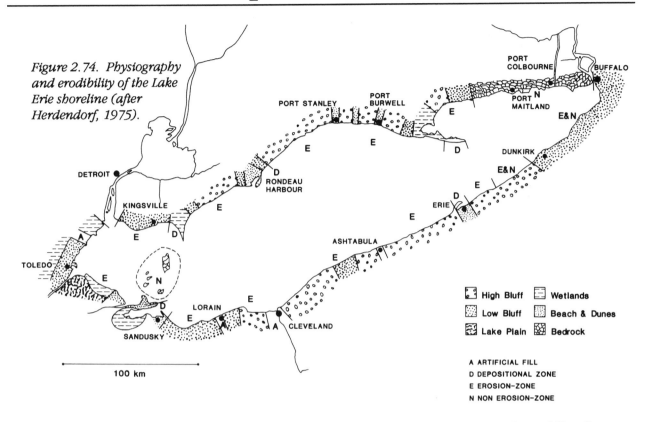

Figure 2.74. Physiography and erodibility of the Lake Erie shoreline (after Herdendorf, 1975).

High Bluff   Wetlands

Low Bluff   Beach & Dunes

Lake Plain   Bedrock

A ARTIFICIAL FILL
D DEPOSITIONAL ZONE
E EROSION-ZONE
N NON EROSION-ZONE

100 km

period of high water, many large blocks of dolomite have fallen from high cliffs of several of the islands. This problem became particularly acute at the south point of South Bass Island in 1976 and necessitated the relocation of the U.S. Coast Guard navigation light tower which was in danger of falling into the lake. The highest incidence of erosion appears to take place in the spring and fall. Ground water seeping into cracks and joints in the rocks freezes, expands, and tends to split the rock from the cliffs, a process known as frost wedging. This process, coupled with frequent and severe storms in the spring and fall, has resulted in many offshore blocks of dolomite which ring the west shores of several of the islands.

The low western shores of the lake have experienced another problem during the high water period—flooding. Several homes and cottages have been destroyed or severely damaged during northeastern storms which caused the lake to inundate the shores. This problem has heightened in the past decade (1980s) as the lake has risen to record high water levels (Figure 2.72).

Alongshore Currents

As waves approach the shoreline, the water level rises at the shore and the excess water escapes as alongshore currents. These currents can be particularly rapid (up to 4 ft/sec or 1.2 m/sec) when waves approach the shore at angles other than perpendicular and can result in the transport of beach materials as large as cobbles and boulders. The currents are important agents of erosion, transportation, and deposition of sediments along the shoreline. Figure 2.75 depicts the generalized direction of littoral drift (transported sediments—mainly sand) along the coast. The direction of the drift is usually governed by the direction of the waves as they impinge on the shoreline, generating alongshore currents downwind. Thus, wind patterns strongly influence beach development. The progressive northeastward migration of Presque Isle (Figure 2.76) is an excellent example of littoral drift process.

Alongshore currents also produce excellent beaches. The best example in western Lake Erie is on Pelee Island. Fish Point, a spit at the southern tip of the island, contains the largest deposit of sand in the island region (Figure 2.10). It is likely that the bulk of the sand has come from glacial moraine deposits of sand and gravel lying east and west of the island. Converging southerly, currents along the east and west sides of the island have built the nearly 2-mi-long (3.2-km) spit.

In the north bay of Kelleys Island at the State Park, accretion of sand has formed a bayhead beach, the largest sand deposit in the Ohio

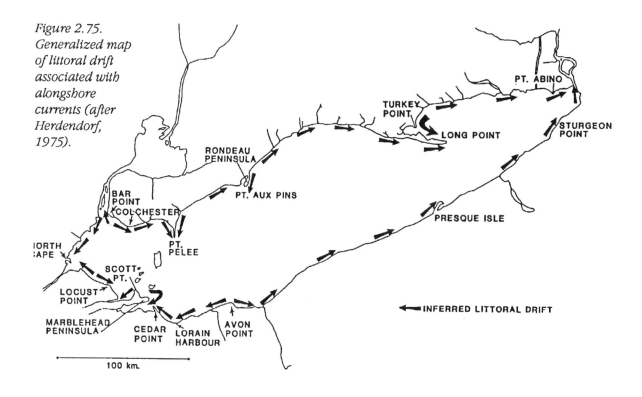

Figure 2.75. Generalized map of littoral drift associated with alongshore currents (after Herdendorf, 1975).

100 km.

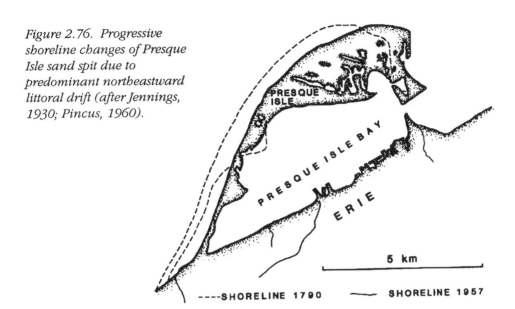

Figure 2.76. Progressive shoreline changes of Presque Isle sand spit due to predominant northeastward littoral drift (after Jennings, 1930; Pincus, 1960).

islands (Figure 2.10). The sand and gravel is mainly derived from erosion of the low glacial till banks of the bay's shore. Rattlesnake, Green and West Sister islands have pebble bars extending eastward from their eastern shores. The bars were probably formed by strong eastward-moving currents along the north and south shores of the islands. Sand and gravel beaches occur in small pockets on Middle Bass and South Bass islands. The beaches are thin and are either residual material from the underlying till or are deposits trapped between the bedrock headlands. Wave and current action is vigorous throughout the islands region.

Mineral Resources

The mineral resources of the Lake Erie basin are few in number but are significant to the region's economy. Mineral deposits within the basin, but unrelated to the lake processes, include (1) limestone and dolomite, (2) sandstone, (3) shale and glacial clay, (4) gypsum, (5) salt and brines, and (6) gas and oil. Minerals directly related to Lake Erie are (1) sand and gravel from beach, dune, and bottom deposits, (2) lake clay, (3) peat, marl, and bog ores, and (4) water itself.

Bedrock Quarries

Limestone and dolomite are extensively quarried in northwestern Ohio and southeastern Michigan. Once used as dimension stone for building construction, today these rocks are crushed for a variety of engineering and agricultural purposes including rip-rap for shore protection works. One of the largest sandstone quarries in the world is located near Amherst, Ohio. Originally used to make grinding stones for grist mills and blocks for harbor breakwaters, this sandstone is now largely used as a decorative stone on buildings or crushed for road bed material. Shale and glacial clay are quarried at a number of locations around the lake for brickmaking and other clay products. Gypsum ($CaSO_4 \cdot 2H_2O$) is mined and quarried at two locations on Marblehead Peninsula near Port Clinton, Ohio. This soft, white rock taken from Silurian beds (Figure 2.19) is used to manufacture wallboard and other plaster products.

Salt

Salt mines are located at Cleveland, Fairport, and along the Detroit River. Halite, or rock salt ($NaCl$), is extracted from deeply buried Silurian evaporite beds (Figure 2.19). The International Salt Company, on Whiskey Island in Cleveland, and Morton Salt Company at the mouth of the Grand River in Fairport Harbor, extract over two million tons of salt from beneath Lake Erie each year.

The mine at Fairport was opened in June 1956 and has a capacity of 12,000 tons per day. It is considered to be one of the world's biggest and deepest salt mines, extending to a depth of 2,025 ft (617 m). The producing horizon is in the Salina Formation of Silurian age and is about 22 ft (6.7 m) thick. The mining technique employed is the "room-and-pillar" method, providing for the excavation of large "rooms" and the retention of blocks or "pillars" of salt between the rooms, which serve as a natural support for the mine. By this technique, approximately 50% of the salt in the mine will remain untouched. Eventually, a system of tunnels will provide a 5 mi (8 km) subterranean network extending under Lake Erie. Estimated reserves of salt exceed 200 million tons, or an equivalent of nearly 200 years of production at the present rate. Full production capacity of the mine is between 300 to 500 tons per hour.

The Cleveland mine was opened in 1962 after considerable difficulty in grouting a 88 ft (27 m) thickness of Oriskany Sandstone at 1,300 ft (400 m) below ground level. Estimates indicate that water flows of 20,000 gal/min (1.3 m³/sec) could have been expected in the shaft if the grouting program had not been carried out. The production horizon is also in the Salina Formation but the updip location of the mine requires only 1,816-ft (554 m) shafts to reach the producing zone. Similar mining techniques to those used at Fairport are employed in the Cleveland mine. The rooms are 17 ft (5.2 m) high and 45 ft (13.7 m) wide. The production hoist, with two, 20-ton-capacity skips in balance, can deliver salt from the mine to the surface at a rate of 700 tons per hour. Salt extraction takes place in the vicinity of the harbor breakwall.

Gas and Oil

Over 1,500 offshore gas wells have been drilled during the past 30 years in the Canadian waters of Lake Erie. Approximately 60% of the wells were successful. Canadian gas production in the Long Point Bay area is found at a depth of about 1,200 ft (370 m) in the Clinton formation (Silurian) and additional gas is believed to be present in deeper formations. Annually 4 billion ft^3 (370 million m^3) of gas are produced from beneath the Canadian waters and prospects for reserves under the United States side of Lake Erie are considered good.

Sand and Gravel

Sand and gravel have many commercial and construction purposes, one of the most important being aggregate in concrete. Because Lake Erie contains valuable deposits of these resources, Ohio has taken steps to regulate their extraction. The Shore Erosion Act of 1955 provides for leases and permits for persons desiring to remove sand, gravel, stone, gas and oil, and other minerals from and under the bed of Lake Erie. The royalties derived from the sale of minerals on and below the lake bottom are used for the protection of Lake Erie shores from erosion, for planning and construction of recreational facilities, and to support lake research.

Guided by this legislation, Ohio has established six commercial sand and gravel dredging areas in Lake Erie (Figure 2.77). Two are located in Maumee Bay one on either side of the Toledo navigation channel (Figure 2.78-A), one is northwest of the Sandusky channel off Cedar Point, two are at areas 6 and 12 mi (10 and 20 km) offshore between Lorain and Vermilion (Figure 2.78-B), and the last is 5 mi (8 km) offshore near Fairport Harbor. Several companies presently extract over 650,000 yd^3 (500,000 m^3) of sand and gravel from the bed of Lake Erie annually. Pennsylvania has designated a large offshore area on the Northwest Bar (Norfolk Moraine) for commercial sand extraction. This bar extends from Erie, Pennsylvania to Long Point, Ontario. Ontario has also opened this deposit to sand dredging, as well as an area opposite the Vermilion, Ohio area which extends northward to Point Pelee.

The origins of the Lake Erie commercial sand deposits are quite different. The Toledo and Sandusky deposits (Figure 2.79) were likely formed by alongshore currents when the lake stood at a lower stage, while the Fairport sand was deposited as a delta at the former mouth of

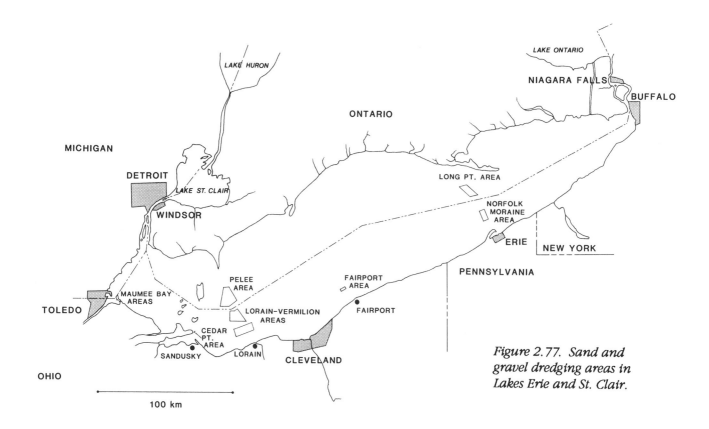

Figure 2.77. Sand and gravel dredging areas in Lakes Erie and St. Clair.

the Grand River near Mentor Headlands, and also when the lake was at a lower stage (Figure 2.63). All of the other deposits were once glacial ridges or moraines. Waves and currents have since concentrated sand and gravel on the surface of these features. The Lake Erie dredging sites have been wisely selected well offshore where extraction does not adversely effect the supply of beach-building material in the littoral zone, or disrupt nearshore-spawning fish species.

Peat, Marl, and Bog Ore

Peat is found locally along the lake shore and in the vicinity of the abandoned glacial lake ridges where paludal (swampy environment) conditions have existed. The broad, level topography near the lake and the irregular lake shore favor the development of marshes. The lower courses of the streams are usually sluggish and, before the advent of harbor dredging, were commonly clogged with vegetation. In general, such accumulations of plant debris are shallow and of little commercial significance. Marsh areas in Lucas, Ottawa, Erie, and Lake counties contain the majority of the peat deposits associated with Lake Erie. Peat has been utilized in the past, to a limited extent, as a low grade fuel. It is

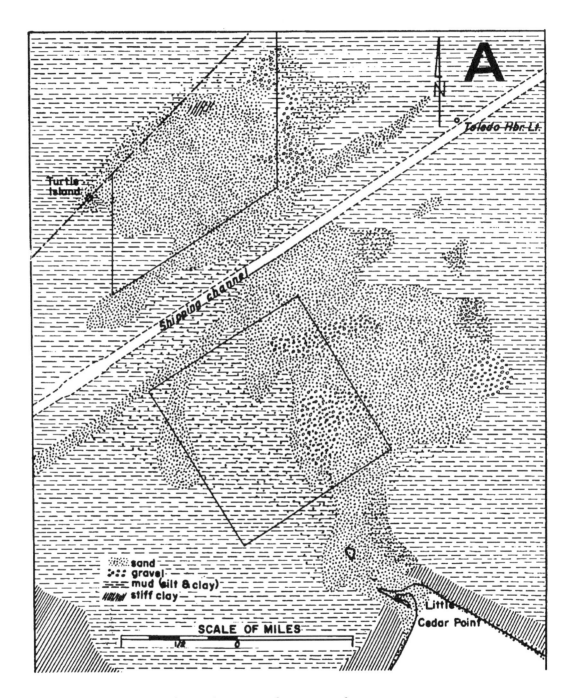

Figure 2.78. Bottom surface sediments in the vicinity of Lake Erie sand and gravel dredging areas: (A) Maumee Bay areas and (b) Lorain-Vermilion areas, and (C) Fairport area (after Ohio Department of Natural Resources, 1960).

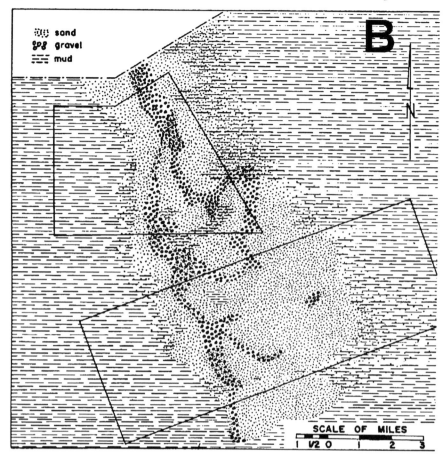

*Figure 2.78 (Continued).
Bottom surface sediments in
the vicinity of Lake Erie sand
and gravel dredging areas:
(A) Maumee Bay areas and
(B) Lorain-Vermilion areas,
and (C) Fairport area (after
Ohio Department of Natural
Resources, 1960).*

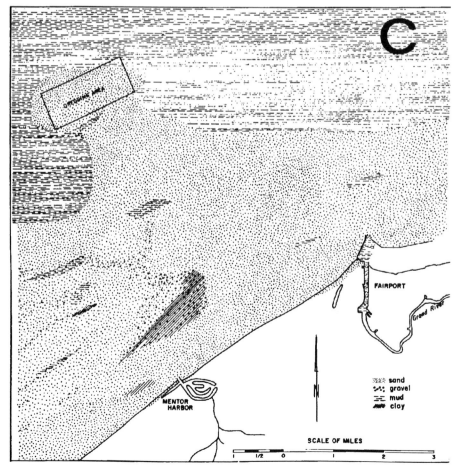

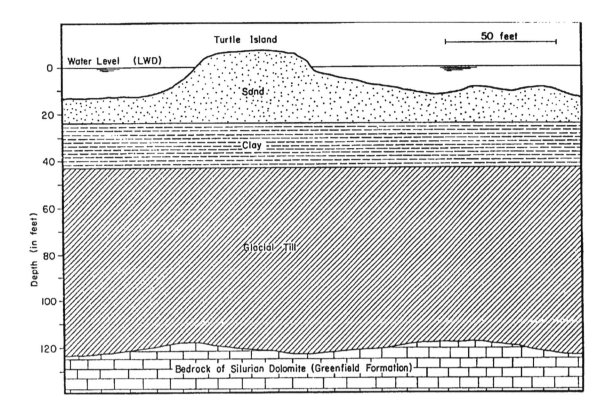

Figure 2.79. Geologic cross-section of Maumee Bay sand deposit showing the remnant of a sand spit (Turtle Island) which at one time extended across Maumee Bay when Lake Erie stood at a lower elevation (after Cooper and Herdendorf, 1977).

now used extensively for humidity control in greenhouses, for adding acidity to soils, for a moisture and mineral retention agent in fertilizers, and for a packing filler.

Marl is a mixture of clay material and calcium carbonate in varying proportions. Marl is also found in shallow lakes and marshy areas and is usually overlain by peat deposits. Marl forms by the incorporation of calcium carbonate, which is precipitated from the water by aquatic life, into the lacustrine bottom sediments. The most notable deposit of marl in the vicinity of Lake Erie is found near Castalia in Erie County, Ohio. A marshy prairie of over 3,500 acres (1,400 ha) extends north and west toward Sandusky Bay. Spring water, highly charged with lime, has given rise to this extensive marl deposit which in the past was used on a large scale to produce Portland cement. Travertine or calcareous tufa are also associated with the Castalia marl beds.

Bog iron ores are formed by precipitation in springs and in the surface waters of swamps and marshes. The iron is derived initially from the bedrock (commonly the Bedford and Ohio shales) through the action of organic acids which cause the iron to be carried in a reduced state as a solution of ferrous bicarbonate. Bog ore is later precipitated as ferrous or ferric carbonate or hydroxite, depending upon the local conditions. These ores are found as scattered nodules or thin layers, 1 to 2 ft (30 to 61 cm) thick, up to several hectares in extent. Bog ores have been found along the abandoned beach ridges from west of Vermilion to Pennsylvania. Bog iron ore deposits were used extensively during the early 1800s. At least 12 smelting operations were located along the lake shore during this period. These bog ores are not utilized today but remain as potential resources because of their high manganese and phosphorus contents.

Water

The most basic natural resource of the lake is water. Lake Erie contains more than 100,000 billion gallons (380 billion m^3) of water. In Ohio, nearly 2.7 billion gallons (10.2 million m^3) of water per day are withdrawn from Lake Erie for municipal and industrial use. Approximately 70% of this amount is used for cooling in manufacturing processes. Nearly 15% is used for public water supply and the remaining 5% is used as process water in manufacturing. Non-withdrawal water uses include navigation (Figure 2.80), recreation, commercial and sport fishing, and waste disposal.

As we have seen, the Lake Erie Region is endowed with abundant natural features, some like as Niagara Falls are famous world-wide. Many can be seen from the main transportation arteries, but a few fascinating areas are remote and accessible only to the more adventuresome. As a guide, Table 2.7 is presented as a list of some of the geologic features of special interest. The general locations of these features are indicated on Figure 2.81.

Natural Features of Special Interest

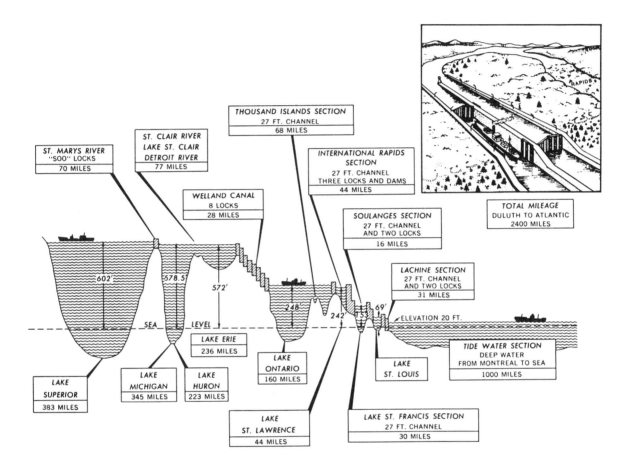

Figure 2.80. Lock and canal system on the St. Lawrence Seaway. Once the ship enters the lock, the lower gate is closed and the lock is flooded; when the water level reaches that of the upper canal, the upper gate is opened and the ship can proceed into the canal (courtesy U.S. Army Corps of Engineers and St. Lawrence Seaway Development Corportation).

Table 2.7.   *Geologic features of special interest in the Lake Erie region.*

Natural Features	Map No.
1. St. Clair River/Lake - Detroit River	
a. Headwater (Port Huron)	1
b. St.Clair Delta	2
c. River Islands (Belle Isle, Grosse Ile)	3
2. Lake Erie Estuaries	
a. Maumee River Estuary	4
b. Sandusky Bay Estuary	5
c. Old Woman Creek National Estuarine Sanctuary	6
3. Limestone and Dolomite Cliffs of Lake Erie Islands	
a. Catawba Island	7
b. South Bass Island	8
c. Gibraltar Island	9
d. Kelleys Island	10
4. Glacial Grooves	
a. Kelleys Island	10
b. Gibraltar Island	9
c. West Sister Island	11
5. Sand Spits and Barrier Beaches	
a. North Cape	12
b. Marblehead Peninsula	13
c. Cedar Point	14
d. Presque Isle	15
e. Long Point	16
f. Rondeau (Pt. Aux Pins)	17
g. Point Pelee/Fish Point	18
6. Shale Cliffs of Central and Eastern Lake Erie	
a. Ohio	19
b. Pennsylvania	20
c. New York	21
7. Limestone Platform	
a. Marblehead Peninsula	13
b. Fort Erie	22
8. Sand Dunes and Beaches	
a. Point Abino	23
b. Sturgeon Point	24
c. Hanford Bay	25
d. Fairport	26
e. Monroe	27

Table 2.7.   Geologic features of special interest in the Lake Erie region (Continued).

Natural Features	Map No.
9. Glacial Till and Lacustrine Sediment Shorelines	
a. Port Stanley	28
b. Ashtabula	29
c. Conneaut	30
d. Kingsville	31
10. Niagara River	
a. Falls and Gorge	32
b. Whirlpool	33
c. Escarpment	34
11. Modern and Historic Marshes	
a. Black Swamp (Toledo)	4
b. Coastal Wetlands (Bass Islands, Point Mouillee)	8,35
c. Diked Marshes (Port Clinton)	36
12. Abandoned Shorlines of Glacial Lakes	
a. Castalia	37
b. Berlin Heights	38
c. Amherst	39
d. Vermilion	40
e. Erie	20
13. Mineral Deposits	
a. Salt Mines (Cleveland, Windsor, Fairport)	41,42,26
b. Gypsum Mines and Quarries (Port Clinton)	36
c. Sand and Gravel Quarries (Castalia)	37
d. Clay Quarries (Vermilion)	40
e. Limestone Quarries (Sandusky)	14
f. Sandstone Quarries (Amherst)	39
14. Devonian Fossils	
a. Kelleys Island	10
b. Marblehead Peninsula	13
c. Sandusky	14
15. Blue Holes, Caves and Sinkholes	
a. Castalia	37
b. South Bass Island	8
c. Catawba Island	7

Location map of natural features shown on Figure 2.84

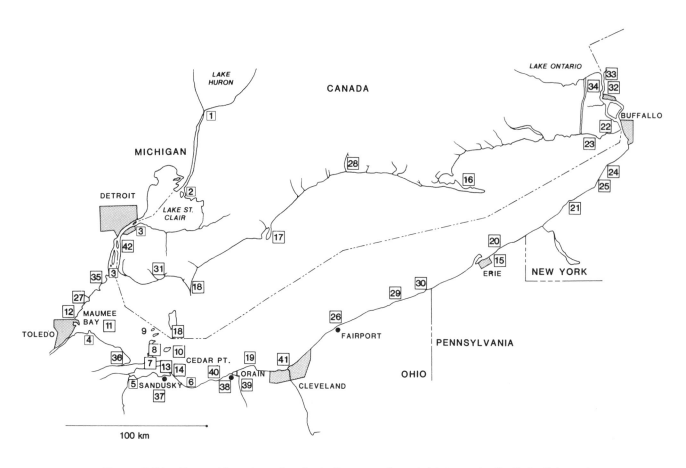

Figure 2.81. General location of geologic features of special interest in the Lake Erie region.

Chapter 3

Atmosphere –
The Air

Weather, the state of the atmosphere with respect to its effects upon life and human activities is popularly thought of in terms of temperature, humidity, precipitation, cloudiness, wind, visibility, and storms. As distinguished from climate, weather consists of short-term (minutes to months) variations in the atmosphere. The climate of a specified area is represented by the statistical collective of its weather conditions over a period of time, usually decades. The atmosphere has a variety of phenomena of different intensity and size or dimensions in space (horizontal and vertical) and time, and which influence the weather at a particular location. These phenomena grow, dissipate, and move across your town, state, or Lakes Erie and St. Clair and are associated with changes in the wind, atmospheric pressure, temperature, humidity, cloudiness, and precipitation. Atmospheric phenomena include cyclones (also referred to as lows), anticyclones (also referred to as highs), thunderstorms, tornados, hurricanes, sea breezes, and squall lines. The characteristic scales of common atmospheric phenomena are shown in Table 3.1. The characteristic space scale refers to the horizontal dimensions relative to the earth's surface of these phenomena. For example, the tornado is less than 6/10 mi (1 km) across its destructive swath, while the cyclone, a phenomena of significantly less severity, has a space scale of approximately 620 mi (1,000 km). The time scale refers to the life of the phenomenon—the time period from formation to dissipation. For example, the tornado lasts only minutes, while the cyclone lasts days. The wind speed amplitude gives a typical maximum wind speed associated with these phenomena and gives an indication of the severity or force of these phenomena impacting upon a person, a structure, or a boat.

Phenomenon	Space Scale	Time Scale	Occurrence	Wind Speed Amplitude
Large-scale Disturbance	1000-8000 km	2-10 days	continuous	10-20 m/sec
Cyclone (or low) and Anticyclone (or high)	200-1500 km	18 hr-5 days	frequent	20-30 m/sec
Hurricane	100-1000 km	1-10 days	occasional	50 m/sec or greater
Squall Line	40-200 km	3-24 hrs	occasional	20-50 m/sec
Sea and Lake Breeze	5-40 km	3-24 hrs	frequent	10 m/sec
Thunderstorm	2-12 km	45 min-6 hrs	occasional	20-50 m/sec
Convective Cloud	0.2-5 km	5 min-1 hr	occasional	1-10 m/sec

Table 3.1. Characteristic scale of atmospheric phenomena (from Jacobs, Pandolfo, and Aubert, 1968).

All phenomena do not occur with equal frequency at different locations on the earth or during the different seasons of the year. All of the weather phenomena listed in Table 3.1 are not of equal importance to Lakes Erie and St. Clair. For example, only in extremely rare occasions does the hurricane influence the Lake Erie region. All of these phenomena influence not only the daily or hourly changes in the wind of Lake Erie, but also the temperature, the clouds, the precipitation, etc.

The Lake Erie area is influenced by three main air mass types— maritime tropical (mT), continental polar (cP), and maritime polar (mP) (Figure 3.1). Air masses are vast, widespread bodies of air with nearly uniform temperature and humidity. They are formed when a large body of air remains over a certain area for an extended period of time and thus, acquires the characteristics of that region, be it cold, hot, wet, or dry.

An mT air mass is composed of warm, moist air which flows north from the Gulf of Mexico. This moist air is the major precipitation-maker for the Lake Erie region. Cold, dry air from Canada makes up the cP air mass and is typically responsible for the cool, dry relief in summer and the cold winds in winter. If, in the winter, this air mass originates in the far north, it can send a cold, biting blast of air over the area. When this happens, the air mass is often referred to as Arctic air. The third air mass, the mP air, originates over the North Pacific Ocean. Though "maritime" usually implies moist air, by the time the mP air mass has traveled up and over the Rocky Mountains it has released most of its moisture in the form of precipitation and arrives at Lake Erie as a dry, moderately cool body of air. When these three different air masses collide, Lake Erie's weather undergoes drastic changes.

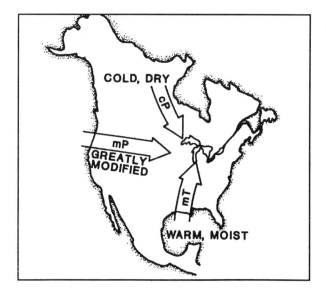

Figure 3.1. The three air masses influencing the weather of the Lake Erie area (from Eichenlaub, 1979).

As the cold, dry air of the cP air mass extends southward and encounters mT air, a "front" develops. Front is the name given to a boundary between two contrasting air masses. The polar front which affects the Lake Erie region usually separates continental polar and maritime tropical air masses.

When the contrasting cold and warm air masses meet, they tend to create turbulent, rotating spirals of air called "lows" and "highs." A "low" is an area with lesser air pressure around which the air spins upward in a counterclockwise direction. These often form along the polar front boundary and their energy supplies are fed by the air mass contrasts across the front. A "high" is a shortened expression for a region of high atmospheric pressure where the air circles and spirals downward from above (in a clockwise direction). Highs and lows generally journey from west to east in an alternating pattern. Highs and lows each have distinct weather characteristics. Highs, with their downward spiraling air flows, suppress cloud formation and precipitation processes and, therefore, are usually associated with good weather (clear, sunny skies). Lows are normally associated with bad weather (precipitation, high winds) since the air in these areas is spiraling upward, causing it to expand (lesser air pressure above it), cool from the expansion, and condense moisture. This causes clouds to form and, if atmospheric conditions are correct, condensation may lead to precipitation.

Since the low ushers in foul weather such as clouds and precipitation, it deserves further discussion. When low pressure systems travel over the Lake Erie area, they generally follow climatic storm tracks with a similar sequence each time: first a warm front, then a warm sector, and last a cold front. The warm front is the forward boundary of the warm, moist air. Here the warm air has overridden the cold air. The warm sector is the moist, unstable region of the low pressure system where severe weather tends to develop. Lastly, the cold front passes over with cooler air felt at the ground; west and northwest winds typically increase at this time as the cold air replaces the warm air, abruptly and with gustiness. As the entire low passes over, the good weather of a high approaches, since lows and highs generally travel in alternating pairs. Hence, the weather Lake Erie experiences is largely due to its mid-latitude position relative to the preferred tracks of cyclones and anticyclones.

Lake Erie, though the shallowest of the Great Lakes, is still a colossal water reservoir with 19,906 mi^2 (51,557 km^2) of surface area. Such an enormous amount of water is capable of imposing "lake effect" modifications on the smaller scale atmospheric phenomena over the lake and nearshore land area. Temperatures are moderated, humidities are increased and decreased, cloud and fog patterns are altered, rain and snowfall are enhanced, and wind flow is modified.

Any early-June Lake Erie swimmers know that the water is usually very chilly despite the fact that the air temperature might have reached 75°-80°F (24°-27°C). In fall, the water feels warm to the touch even though the air may feel quite brisk. It is clear that land and water absorb and release heat very differently. Water does not respond to heat changes as rapidly as land does. It always progresses through a more moderate temperature change. Therefore, Lake Erie moderates the temperature of the air that blows across it. In spring, when the land is warming up quickly, the lake is still providing a cooling effect downwind. In late fall and early winter, when the land is cold, Lake Erie provides a warming effect downwind, preventing the temperatures from dropping drastically in some areas.

The lake has a tremendous influence on the humidity of the area. Every year Lake Erie loses, on the average, 3 ft (1 m) of water from its entire surface area due to evaporation. This tremendous release of moisture due to the sun's heating increases the amount of water vapor contained in the air and, thus, the humidity. Each year the humidity over the Great Lakes averages about 10-15% more than that of inland areas. Over the Lake Erie area, air moisture is at its lowest in December-January and its highest in July-August. Graphs displaying different degrees of comfort for different temperature/humidity combinations show that during January the area is too cold and dry for the utmost comfort. In July, the Lake Erie area is too hot and humid. During the transition months, however, the region provides ample exceptional weather days with moderate temperatures and mild humidities.

Lake Erie's ability to retain heat more efficiently than the surrounding land is a major factor in determining the cloud cover over the area. The region is one of the cloudiest in all of the U.S., especially during winter. The polar front frequently passes through the area during winter, and the passage of lows and highs are common. The larger number of fronts increases the amount of cloud cover during this time of year. During spring and early summer, however, when Lake Erie is colder than the land, air blowing across the lake cools and sinks, suppressing cloud formation.

Lake Erie has an averaging effect on monthly precipitation rates. Over the entire Lake Erie region, precipitation averages 2-3 in (5-8 cm) each month with slightly more over the western sector. A comparison of precipitation amounts directly over the lake to those over land shows, for most of the year, that the lake receives more precipitation. In April-

July, however, the land receives more precipitation. Lake Erie's annual snowfall is marked by a high degree of variability. A dramatic effect of the lake is to increase the snowfall along the lee shore. The "snowbelt area" to the east and south of Lake Erie extends from Buffalo to the northeast corner of Ohio. During early winter, the lake, which loses its heat more slowly than the land, maintains a warmer temperature. Air blowing over the lake is heated and acquires additional moisture. As it moves onshore to the east and south of the lake, it is lifted by the terrain and releases this extra moisture as snow. Average annual snowfall amounts in the snowbelt areas are about 120 in (305 cm), whereas annual snowfall amounts in the rest of the Lake Erie region are only 20-30 in (51-76 cm) a year.

Surface winds across Lake Erie predominantly blow out of the south to west directions (S-SW-W) mainly because of the dominant flow of the prevailing westerlies. Wind speeds are greatest during late winter/early spring due to the more intense cyclonic storms during these seasons. Spring and winter also show the highest occurrences of gusting conditions. One of the most well known lake effects on winds occurs on a smaller scale during summer. The diurnal contrast in temperatures between land and lake creates what are known as lake/land breezes. These refreshing winds blow from the lake during the day, providing cool relief to those onshore.

Lake Erie has the reputation of being the stormiest of all the Great Lakes. This region is noted for its sudden late afternoon thunderstorms in summer. Lake Erie's location near the polar front and cyclonic storm tracks is the primary factor. In the following sections of this chapter, each of these weather elements is analyzed in detail.

Temperature

Temperature plays a major role in determining the relative desirability of any form of recreation. It also exerts a large influence on other climatic factors such as precipitation and evaporation. Generally, temperatures decrease northeastward from the southwestern corner of the Lake Erie region. The highest average monthly temperatures occur over the area during July, while the coldest temperatures occur during January and February. Extremes range from -20° to 100°F (-29° to 38°C).

Analyzing monthly and seasonal temperature changes in the Lake Erie area would be a simple task if these were based only on the latitude of a particular location. However, Lake Erie waters have a drastic effect on temperature trends of the nearby land area. The air temperatures over cities or rural land areas are often very different from air temperatures over nearby lake waters (Figure 3.2, for example). Figures 3.3 and

Figure 3.2. Average air versus lake temperatures (°F) at Cleveland, Ohio.

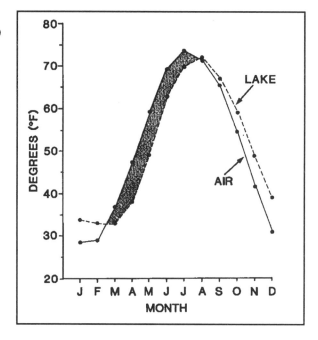

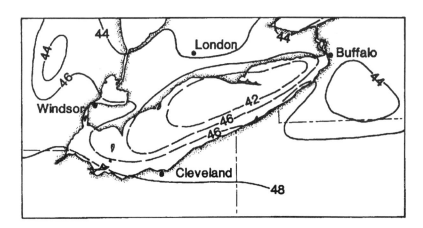

Figure 3.3. A comparison of average air temperatures (°F) over land and average surface water temperatures (°F) of the Lakes Erie and St. Clair region for the month of April (after Phillips and McCulloch, 1972)

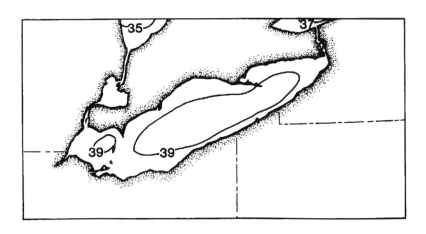

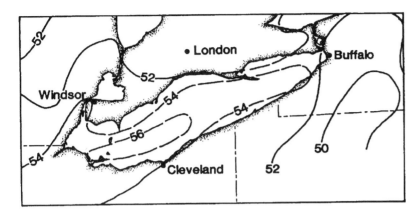

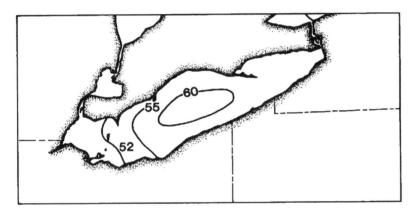

Figure 3.4. A comparison of average air temperatures (°F) over land and average surface water temperatures (°F) of the Lakes Erie and St. Clair region for the month of October (after Phillips and McCulloch, 1972).

3.4 compare land and lake surface temperatures for a representative month of each transitional season, spring and fall. Note that in April when the sun begins to warm the region, the waters of Lake Erie tend to heat up less than the surrounding land, thus showing colder temperatures. In fall, however, when the opposite transition occurs, the land cools more quickly than the water. The reasons why the water responds less rapidly to heating and cooling are as follows:

Transparency. Water, unlike land, is fairly transparent to incoming solar radiation; heat energy penetrates to significant depths and is dispersed rather than confined mostly to the surface layers as with land.

Evaporation. More evaporation takes place from the water surface. When evaporation occurs, a surface cools because heat energy is required to change liquid into vapor. This evaporational cooling of the water slows any warming processes that occur (note: condensation, the opposite of evaporation, slows any cooling process).

Heat Capacity. More heat is required to produce a similar temperature change in water than land. In addition, Lake Erie has a large volume, and the heating from the sun absorbed in the surface layer of the lake is mixed throughout much of this volume.

Mixing. Mixing is expressed by a numerical value called thermal conductivity. Thermal conductivity provides an idea of the efficiency with which a body transfers heat. If water is absolutely still and the land surface is totally made up of dry sand, for example, thermal conductivities are 0.0015 and 0.0013, respectively. These values show that there is little difference in the ability to transfer heat. The water in Lake Erie, however, is constantly in motion. With water in motion, thermal conductivity increases to approximately 50, showing that heat transfer is much more effective. Therefore, in this case the heat transport, or mixing, within Lake Erie is thousands of times more effective than in its surrounding land. This large amount of mixing is the primary reason for Lake Erie's slower response to heating and cooling.

The end result of these four properties is a "lake effect" on the air temperature patterns over the Lake Erie region. Generally, the role of this "lake effect" is one of moderation; the lake waters tend to decrease the range of air temperatures over the water and nearshore area during all seasons. Lake Erie's influence in moderating these air temperatures can clearly be seen from the average daily range of temperatures in the basin (Figures 3.5-3.8). In January, the greatest daily temperature range, 24°F (13°C), over the entire Great Lakes region occurs 50-100 mi (80-160 km) to the northeast and northwest of Lake Superior. Areas nearer to the Great Lakes, such as the Lake Erie area, have smaller temperature ranges as shown in the Figure. In April, the average range between the highest daytime and the lowest nighttime temperatures in the Lake Erie area varies from 14° to 24°F (-10° to -4°C), with the range becoming larger away from the lakeshore. Differences between day and night temperatures are greater in summer than in winter as evidenced by Figure 3.7 for July. The small temperature ranges near Lake Erie show the moderating effect and can be compared to the much larger range inland. The moderating effect of Lake Erie can still be seen in October. The greatest temperature ranges in an area close to the Lake Erie region occur in the Adirondack and Allegheny Mountains.

The contrast between land heating and water heating plays a major role in setting the trends in seasonal temperature patterns. The lake causes cooler temperatures along its shore in summer and warmer temperatures in winter as seen in the average daily air temperatures by month (Figures 3.9-3.12), as well as in the maximum and minimum temperatures (Figures 3.13-3.20). The lake begins its cooling effect on

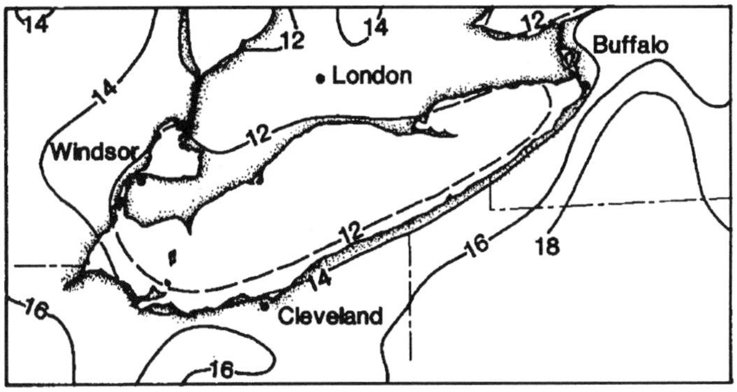

Figure 3.5. Average daily range of January air temperatures (°F) in the Lakes Erie and St. Clair region, 1931-60 (after Phillips and McCulloch, 1972).

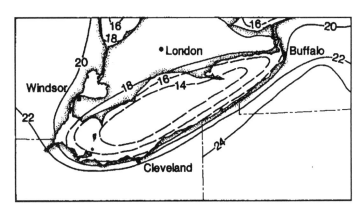

Figure 3.6. Average daily range of April air temperatures (°F) in the Lakes Erie and St. Clair region (after Phillips and McCulloch, 1972).

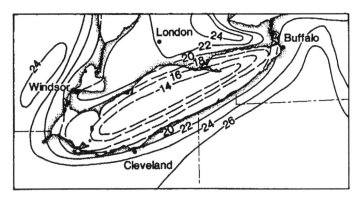

Figure 3.7. Average daily range of July air temperatures (°F) in the Lakes Erie and St. Clair region (after Phillips and McCulloch,, 1972).

Figure 3.8. Average daily range of October air temperatures (°F) in the Lakes Erie and St. Clair region (after Phillips and McCulloch, 1972).

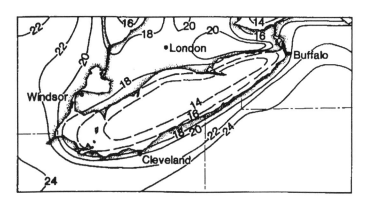

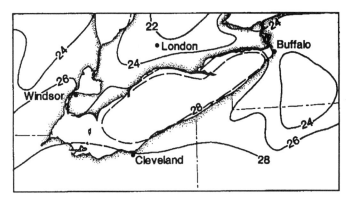

Figure 3.9. Long-term average daily January air temperatures (°F) for the Lakes Erie and St. Clair region (after Phillips and McCulloch, 1972).

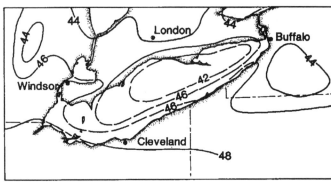

Figure 3.10. Long-term average daily April air temperatures (°F) for the Lakes Erie and St. Clair region (after Phillips and McCulloch, 1972).

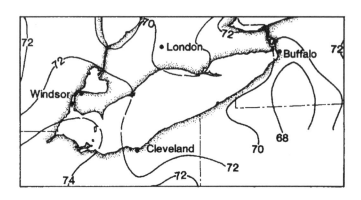

Figure 3.11. Long-term average daily July air temperatures (°F) for the Lakes Erie and St. Clair region (after Phillips and McCulloch, 1972).

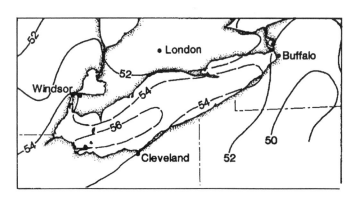

Figure 3.12. Long-term average daily October air temperatures (°F) for the Lakes Erie and St. Clair region (after Phillips and McCulloch, 1972).

Figure 3.13. Long-term average daily maximum January air temperatures (°F) for the Lakes Erie and St. Clair region (after Phillips and McCulloch, 1972).

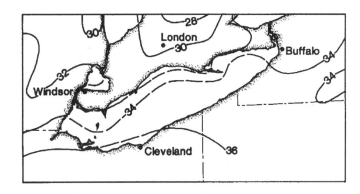

Figure 3.14. Long-term average daily maximum April air temperatures (°F) for the Lakes Erie and St. Clair region (after Phillips and McCulloch, 1972).

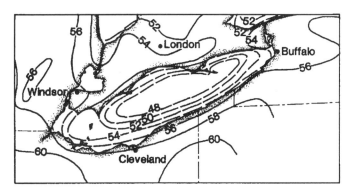

Figure 3.15. Long-term average daily maximum July air temperatures (°F) for the Lakes Erie and St. Clair region (after Phillips and McCulloch, 1972).

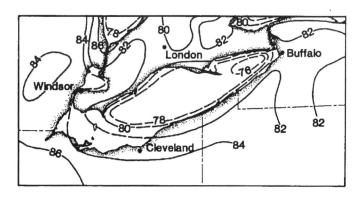

Figure 3.16. Long-term average daily maximum October air temperatures (°F) for the Lakes Erie and St. Clair region (after Phillips and McCulloch, 1972).

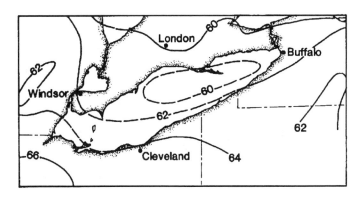

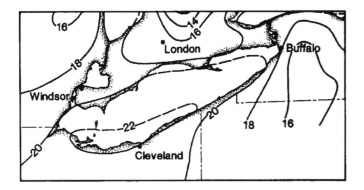

Figure 3.17. Long-term average daily minimum January air temperatures (°F) for the Lakes Erie and St. Clair region (after Phillips and McCulloch, 1972).

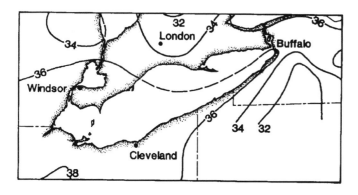

Figure 3.18. Long-term average daily minimum April air temperatures (°F) for the Lakes Erie and St. Clair region (after Phillips and McCulloch, 1972).

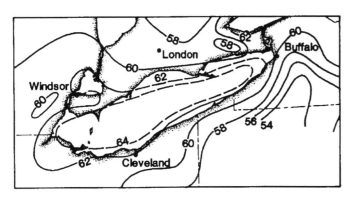

Figure 3.19. Long-term average daily minimum July air temperatures (°F) for the Lakes Erie and St. Clair region (after Phillips and McCulloch, 1972).

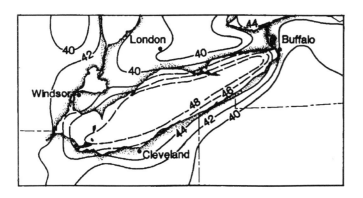

Figure 3.20. Long-term average daily minimum October air temperatures (°F) for the Lakes Erie and St. Clair region (after Phillips and McCulloch, 1972).

the eastern shoreline in springtime, with the peak cooling around June. As summer proceeds, however, the cooling lessens so that by early fall, as the land is cooling more quickly than the water (because of the four water properties discussed earlier), the air moving over the warmer lake heats up and sends a warming breeze to the eastern shoreline areas. By December-January, the maximum warming is evident. This warming effect then diminishes as Lake Erie freezes. By February, when Lake Erie attains its maximum ice cover (see section on ice), we see negligible warming from the lake, and land/lake temperatures are nearly the same. By early spring, the cooling effect of the lake on the land begins again as the entire cycle repeats.

Table 3.2 shows the percentage probability that daily mean temperatures will equal or exceed a given temperature during a particular month for several United States and Canadian stations arranged alphabetically (data from an unpublished report by S. J. Bolsenga). As an example, in London, Ontario, daily mean temperatures in March historically equaled or exceeded freezing about 37% of the time and never equaled or exceeded 50°F (10°C). One should always keep in mind, however, that all of these figures should be used as a general guide to obtain a better idea of expected temperatures at a particular location; lower or higher temperatures can always occur either nearby or even at the same location. These figures are based on data from the historical period of record; new records can—and usually do—occur!

Precipitation

Over the Lake Erie area, rain and snowfall are the most frequent forms of precipitation, although others, such as hail, may also occur. Precipitation is abundant but not excessive; Lake Erie's mean annual precipitation total falls in the middle of the United States range. Figure 3.21 shows the Lake Erie area with a mean annual precipitation range of 30-45 in (76-114 cm). (Snowfall is included in equivalent amounts of water in this total.) In comparison, the mean annual precipitation ranges from near zero in some desert areas along the coast of Chile, to 39 ft (12 m) on the slopes of Mount Waialeale, Kauai, HI.

Lake Erie has an impact on the precipitation over its own surface and over the surrounding land. One evident feature is the lack of variation of average monthly precipitation over the entire Lake Erie region as compared to a more continental area. Figure 3.22 compares precipitation between New York and Minnesota, which has a more continental regime. This chart indicates that the seasonal variation of Minnesota's precipitation is much greater than that of New York. Both states receive nearly the same amount of precipitation when totaled for the year, but the distribution by month is dramatically different.

Table 3.2. Percent probability that temperatures will equal or exceed -5°C (23°F), 0°C (32°F), 5°C (41°F), 10°C (50°F), 15°C (59°F), or 20°C (68°F) for Monroe, MI, (a); Port Huron, MI, (b); Allegany State Park, NY, (c); Buffalo, NY, (d); Jamestown, NY, (e); Lewiston, NY, (f); Bowling Green, OH, (g); Chardon, OH, (h); Cleveland, OH, (i); Hiram, OH, (j); Norwalk, OH, (k); Oberlin, OH, (l); Plymouth, OH, (m); Sandusky, OH, (n); Tiffin, OH, (o); Toledo, OH, (p); Corry, PA, (q); Erie, PA, (r); Greenville, PA, (s); Meadville, PA, (t); Warren, PA, (u); Centralia, ONT, (v); Leamington, ONT, (w); London, ONT, (x); Port Dover, ONT, (y); St. Thomas, ONT, (z); and Windsor, ONT, (aa).

(a) Monroe, MI
Probability

Temperature Greater Than	JAN	FEB	MAR	APR	MAY	JUN	JUL	AUG	SEP	OCT	NOV	DEC
-5	81.2	93.8	100.0	100.0	100.0	100.0	100.0	100.0	100.0	100.0	100.0	93.8
0	0.0	18.8	87.5	100.0	100.0	100.0	100.0	100.0	100.0	100.0	100.0	37.5
5	0.0	0.0	0.0	100.0	100.0	100.0	100.0	100.0	100.0	100.0	75.0	0.0
10	0.0	0.0	0.0	31.2	100.0	100.0	100.0	100.0	100.0	100.0	0.0	0.0
15	0.0	0.0	0.0	0.0	43.8	100.0	100.0	100.0	100.0	6.2	0.0	0.0
20	0.0	0.0	0.0	0.0	0.0	81.2	100.0	100.0	12.5	0.0	0.0	0.0
25	0.0	0.0	0.0	0.0	0.0	0.0	6.2	0.0	0.0	0.0	0.0	0.0

(b) Port Huron, MI
Probability

Temperature Greater Than	JAN	FEB	MAR	APR	MAY	JUN	JUL	AUG	SEP	OCT	NOV	DEC
-5	62.5	81.2	100.0	100.0	100.0	100.0	100.0	100.0	100.0	100.0	100.0	93.8
0	0.0	6.2	81.2	100.0	100.0	100.0	100.0	100.0	100.0	100.0	100.0	43.8
5	0.0	0.0	0.0	93.3	100.0	100.0	100.0	100.0	100.0	100.0	81.2	0.0
10	0.0	0.0	0.0	0.0	100.0	100.0	100.0	100.0	100.0	93.8	0.0	0.0
15	0.0	0.0	0.0	0.0	31.2	100.0	100.0	100.0	100.0	6.2	0.0	0.0
20	0.0	0.0	0.0	0.0	0.0	60.0	100.0	93.8	6.2	0.0	0.0	0.0
25	0.0	0.0	0.0	0.0	0.0	0.0	6.2	6.2	0.0	0.0	0.0	0.0

(c) Allegheny State Park, NY
Probability

Temperature Greater Than	JAN	FEB	MAR	APR	MAY	JUN	JUL	AUG	SEP	OCT	NOV	DEC
-5	50.0	75.0	93.8	100.0	100.0	100.0	100.0	100.0	100.0	100.0	100.0	81.2
0	0.0	6.2	75.0	100.0	100.0	100.0	100.0	100.0	100.0	100.0	100.0	25.0
5	0.0	0.0	0.0	100.0	93.8	100.0	100.0	100.0	100.0	100.0	12.5	0.0
10	0.0	0.0	0.0	12.5	87.5	100.0	100.0	100.0	100.0	46.7	0.0	0.0
15	0.0	0.0	0.0	0.0	18.8	100.0	100.0	100.0	62.5	0.0	0.0	0.0
20	0.0	0.0	0.0	0.0	0.0	0.0	31.2	12.5	0.0	0.0	0.0	0.0

(d) Buffalo, NY
Probability

Temperature Greater Than	JAN	FEB	MAR	APR	MAY	JUN	JUL	AUG	SEP	OCT	NOV	DEC
-5	69.0	82.8	100.0	100.0	100.0	100.0	100.0	100.0	100.0	100.0	100.0	93.1
0	6.9	6.9	58.6	100.0	100.0	100.0	100.0	100.0	100.0	100.0	100.0	37.9
5	0.0	0.0	6.9	82.8	100.0	100.0	100.0	100.0	100.0	100.0	44.8	0.0
10	0.0	0.0	0.0	3.4	100.0	100.0	100.0	100.0	100.0	72.4	0.0	0.0
15	0.0	0.0	0.0	0.0	20.7	100.0	100.0	100.0	86.2	3.4	0.0	0.0
20	0.0	0.0	0.0	0.0	0.0	10.3	96.6	72.4	3.4	0.0	0.0	0.0

Table 3.2 (Continued).

(e) Jamestown, NY
Probability

Temperature Greater Than	JAN	FEB	MAR	APR	MAY	JUN	JUL	AUG	SEP	OCT	NOV	DEC
-5	60.0	66.7	100.0	100.0	100.0	100.0	100.0	100.0	100.0	100.0	100.0	93.3
0	6.7	20.0	80.0	100.0	100.0	100.0	100.0	100.0	100.0	100.0	100.0	40.0
5	0.0	0.0	0.0	93.3	100.0	100.0	100.0	100.0	100.0	100.0	33.3	6.7
10	0.0	0.0	0.0	20.0	93.3	100.0	100.0	100.0	100.0	66.7	0.0	0.0
15	0.0	0.0	0.0	0.0	26.7	100.0	100.0	100.0	71.4	0.0	0.0	0.0
20	0.0	0.0	0.0	0.0	0.0	26.7	78.6	46.7	0.0	0.0	0.0	0.0

(f) Lewiston, OH
Probability

Temperature Greater Than	JAN	FEB	MAR	APR	MAY	JUN	JUL	AUG	SEP	OCT	NOV	DEC
-5	81.2	93.8	100.0	100.0	100.0	100.0	100.0	100.0	100.0	100.0	100.0	100.0
0	12.5	12.5	87.5	100.0	100.0	100.0	100.0	100.0	100.0	100.0	100.0	53.3
5	0.0	0.0	0.0	100.0	100.0	100.0	100.0	100.0	100.0	100.0	75.0	0.0
10	0.0	0.0	0.0	6.2	100.0	100.0	100.0	100.0	100.0	93.8	0.0	0.0
15	0.0	0.0	0.0	0.0	31.2	100.0	100.0	100.0	100.0	6.2	0.0	0.0
\20	0.0	0.0	0.0	0.0	0.0	56.2	93.8	93.8	12.5	0.0	0.0	0.0
25	0.0	0.0	0.0	0.0	0.0	0.0	6.2	0.0	0.0	0.0	0.0	0.0

(g) Bowling Green, OH
Probability

Temperature Greater Than	JAN	FEB	MAR	APR	MAY	JUN	JUL	AUG	SEP	OCT	NOV	DEC
-5	87.5	93.8	100.0	100.0	100.0	100.0	100.0	100.0	100.0	100.0	100.0	87.5
0	12.5	31.2	87.5	100.0	100.0	100.0	100.0	100.0	100.0	100.0	100.0	43.8
5	0.0	0.0	12.5	100.0	100.0	100.0	100.0	100.0	100.0	100.0	75.0	0.0
10	0.0	0.0	0.0	68.8	100.0	100.0	100.0	100.0	100.0	93.8	0.0	0.0
15	0.0	0.0	0.0	0.0	62.5	100.0	100.0	100.0	100.0	6.2	0.0	0.0
20	0.0	0.0	0.0	0.0	0.0	93.8	100.0	100.0	18.8	0.0	0.0	0.0
0.0	0.0	0.0	0.0	0.0	0.0	6.2	6.2	0.0	0.0	0.0	0.0	0.0

(h) Chardon, OH
Probability

Temperature Greater Than	JAN	FEB	MAR	APR	MAY	JUN	JUL	AUG	SEP	OCT	NOV	DEC
-5	62.5	87.5	100.0	100.0	100.0	100.0	100.0	100.0	100.0	100.0	100.0	87.5
0	0.0	12.5	87.5	100.0	100.0	100.0	100.0	100.0	100.0	100.0	100.0	43.8
5	0.0	0.0	0.0	100.0	100.0	100.0	100.0	100.0	100.0	100.0	62.5	0.0
10	0.0	0.0	0.0	18.8	100.0	100.0	100.0	100.0	100.0	81.2	0.0	0.0
15	0.0	0.0	0.0	0.0	37.5	100.0	100.0	100.0	93.8	6.2	0.0	0.0
20	0.0	0.0	0.0	0.0	0.0	37.5	93.8	62.5	6.2	0.0	0.0	0.0

(i) Cleveland Airport, OH
Probability

Temperature Greater Than	JAN	FEB	MAR	APR	MAY	JUN	JUL	AUG	SEP	OCT	NOV	DEC
-5	82.8	93.1	100.0	100.0	100.0	100.0	100.0	100.0	100.0	100.0	100.0	96.4
0	27.6	24.1	82.8	100.0	100.0	100.0	100.0	100.0	100.0	100.0	100.0	50.0
5	0.0	0.0	10.3	100.0	100.0	100.0	100.0	100.0	100.0	100.0	75.9	0.0

Table 3.2 (Continued).

(i) Cleveland Airport, OH (Continued)
Probability

Temperature Greater Than	JAN	FEB	MAR	APR	MAY	JUN	JUL	AUG	SEP	OCT	NOV	DEC
10	0.0	0.0	0.0	37.9	100.0	100.0	100.0	100.0	100.0	93.1	0.0	0.0
15	0.0	0.0	0.0	0.0	55.2	100.0	100.0	100.0	100.0	10.3	0.0	0.0
20	0.0	0.0	0.0	0.0	0.0	62.1	96.6	93.1	6.9	0.0	0.0	0.0
25	0.0	0.0	0.0	0.0	0.0	0.0	6.9	3.4	0.0	0.0	0.0	0.0

(j) Hiram, OH
Probability

Temperature Greater Than	JAN	FEB	MAR	APR	MAY	JUN	JUL	AUG	SEP	OCT	NOV	DEC
-5	73.3	85.7	100.0	100.0	100.0	100.0	100.0	100.0	100.0	100.0	100.0	86.7
0	6.7	28.6	93.8	100.0	100.0	100.0	100.0	100.0	100.0	100.0	100.0	53.3
5	0.0	0.0	0.0	100.0	100.0	100.0	100.0	100.0	100.0	100.0	75.0	0.0
10	0.0	0.0	0.0	31.2	100.0	100.0	100.0	100.0	100.0	87.5	0.0	0.0
15	0.0	0.0	0.0	0.0	33.3	100.0	100.0	100.0	93.3	6.2	0.0	0.0
20	0.0	0.0	0.0	0.0	0.0	43.8	100.0	80.0	6.7	0.0	0.0	0.0

(k) Norwalk, OH
Probability

Temperature Greater Than	JAN	FEB	MAR	APR	MAY	JUN	JUL	AUG	SEP	OCT	NOV	DEC
-5	75.0	93.3	100.0	100.0	100.0	100.0	100.0	100.0	100.0	100.0	100.0	81.2
0	18.8	26.7	86.7	100.0	100.0	100.0	100.0	100.0	100.0	100.0	100.0	56.2
5	0.0	0.0	0.0	100.0	100.0	100.0	100.0	100.0	100.0	100.0	81.2	0.0
10	0.0	0.0	0.0	53.8	100.0	100.0	100.0	100.0	100.0	87.5	0.0	0.0
15	0.0	0.0	0.0	0.0	40.0	100.0	100.0	100.0	100.0	6.2	0.0	0.0
20	0.0	0.0	0.0	0.0	0.0	66.7	100.0	93.3	13.3	0.0	0.0	0.0

(l) Oberlin, OH
Probability

Temperature Greater Than	JAN	FEB	MAR	APR	MAY	JUN	JUL	AUG	SEP	OCT	NOV	DEC
-5	75.0	87.5	100.0	100.0	100.0	100.0	100.0	100.0	100.0	100.0	100.0	87.5
0	12.5	25.0	87.5	100.0	100.0	100.0	100.0	100.0	100.0	100.0	100.0	43.8
5	0.0	0.0	0.0	100.0	100.0	100.0	100.0	100.0	100.0	100.0	68.8	0.0
10	0.0	0.0	0.0	25.0	100.0	100.0	100.0	100.0	100.0	68.8	0.0	0.0
15	0.0	0.0	0.0	0.0	43.8	100.0	100.0	100.0	93.8	6.2	0.0	0.0
20	0.0	0.0	0.0	0.0	0.0	56.2	100.0	81.2	6.2	0.0	0.0	0.0

(m) Plymouth, OH
Probability

Temperature Greater Than	JAN	FEB	MAR	APR	MAY	JUN	JUL	AUG	SEP	OCT	NOV	DEC
-5	80.0	86.7	100.0	100.0	100.0	100.0	100.0	100.0	100.0	100.0	100.0	86.7
0	13.1	33.3	93.3	100.0	100.0	100.0	100.0	100.0	100.0	100.0	100.0	46.7
5	0.0	0.0	6.7	100.0	100.0	100.0	100.0	100.0	100.0	100.0	68.8	0.0
10	0.0	0.0	0.0	53.3	100.0	100.0	100.0	100.0	100.0	81.2	0.0	0.0
15	0.0	0.0	0.0	0.0	40.0	100.0	100.0	100.0	100.0	6.2	0.0	0.0
20	0.0	0.0	0.0	0.0	0.0	73.3	100.0	81.2	10.0	0.0	0.0	0.0
25	0.0	0.0	0.0	0.0	0.0	0.0	6.7	0.0	0.0	0.0	0.0	0.0

Table 3.2 (Continued).

(n) Sandusky, OH
Probability

Temperature Greater Than	JAN	FEB	MAR	APR	MAY	JUN	JUL	AUG	SEP	OCT	NOV	DEC
-5	81.5	86.3	100.0	100.0	100.0	100.0	100.0	100.0	100.0	100.0	100.0	96.
0	25.9	25.9	92.6	100.0	100.0	100.0	100.0	100.0	100.0	100.0	100.0	53.
5	0.0	0.0	14.8	100.0	100.0	100.0	100.0	100.0	100.0	100.0	69.2	0.0
10	0.0	0.0	0.0	44.4	100.0	100.0	100.0	100.0	100.0	100.0	0.0	0.0
15	0.0	0.0	0.0	0.0	59.3	100.0	100.0	100.0	100.0	15.4	0.0	0.0
20	0.0	0.0	0.0	0.0	0.0	88.9	100.0	100.0	25.9	0.0	0.0	0.0
25	0.0	0.0	0.0	0.0	0.0	0.0	11.1	11.1	0.0	0.0	0.0	0.0

(o) Tiffin, OH
Probability

Temperature Greater Than	JAN	FEB	MAR	APR	MAY	JUN	JUL	AUG	SEP	OCT	NOV	DEC
-5	93.8	93.8	100.0	100.0	100.0	100.0	100.0	100.0	100.0	100.0	100.0	87.5
0	12.5	31.2	87.5	100.0	100.0	100.0	100.0	100.0	100.0	100.0	100.0	43.8
5	0.0	0.0	18.8	100.0	100.0	100.0	100.0	100.0	100.0	100.0	75.0	0.0
10	0.0	0.0	0.0	68.8	100.0	100.0	100.0	100.0	100.0	93.8	0.0	0.0
15	0.0	0.0	0.0	0.0	68.8	100.0	100.0	100.0	100.0	12.5	0.0	0.0
20	0.0	0.0	0.0	0.0	0.0	81.2	100.0	93.8	25.0	0.0	0.0	0.0
25	0.0	0.0	0.0	0.0	0.0	0.0	12.5	0.0	0.0	0.0	0.0	0.0

(p) Toledo, OH
Probability

Temperature Greater Than	JAN	FEB	MAR	APR	MAY	JUN	JUL	AUG	SEP	OCT	NOV	DEC
-5	72.4	89.7	100.0	100.0	100.0	100.0	100.0	100.0	100.0	100.0	100.0	82.8
0	6.9	13.8	75.9	100.0	100.0	100.0	100.0	100.0	100.0	100.0	100.0	41.4
5	0.0	0.0	10.3	100.0	100.0	100.0	100.0	100.0	100.0	100.0	41.4	3.4
10	0.0	0.0	0.0	24.1	100.0	100.0	100.0	100.0	100.0	79.3	0.0	3.4
15	0.0	0.0	0.0	0.0	51.7	100.0	100.0	100.0	100.0	6.9	0.0	0.0
20	0.0	0.0	0.0	0.0	0.0	69.0	100.0	86.2	6.9	0.0	0.0	0.0
25	0.0	0.0	0.0	0.0	0.0	0.0	6.9	3.4	0.0	0.0	0.0	0.0

(q) Corry, PA
Probability

Temperature Greater Than	JAN	FEB	MAR	APR	MAY	JUN	JUL	AUG	SEP	OCT	NOV	DEC
-5	53.3	75.0	93.8	100.0	100.0	100.0	100.0	100.0	100.0	100.0	100.0	81.2
0	0.0	6.2	81.2	100.0	100.0	100.0	100.0	100.0	100.0	100.0	100.0	37.5
5	0.0	0.0	0.0	93.8	100.0	100.0	100.0	100.0	100.0	100.0	37.5	0.0
10	0.0	0.0	0.0	18.8	93.8	100.0	100.0	100.0	100.0	62.5	0.0	0.0
15	0.0	0.0	0.0	0.0	25.0	100.0	100.0	100.0	68.8	0.0	0.0	0.0
20	0.0	0.0	0.0	0.0	0.0	20.0	62.5	37.5	0.0	0.0	0.0	0.0

(r) Erie, PA
Probability

Temperature Greater Than	JAN	FEB	MAR	APR	MAY	JUN	JUL	AUG	SEP	OCT	NOV	DEC
-5	87.1	93.5	100.0	100.0	100.0	100.0	100.0	100.0	100.0	100.0	100.0	100.0
0	22.6	9.7	74.2	100.0	100.0	100.0	100.0	100.0	100.0	100.0	100.0	58.1

Table 3.2. (Continued)

(r) Erie, PA (Continued)
Probability

Temperature Greater Than	JAN	FEB	MAR	APR	MAY	JUN	JUL	AUG	SEP	OCT	NOV	DEC
5	0.0	0.0	6.5	93.5	100.0	100.0	100.0	100.0	100.0	100.0	67.7	0.0
10	0.0	0.0	0.0	16.1	96.8	100.0	100.0	100.0	100.0	90.3	0.0	0.0
15	0.0	0.0	0.0	0.0	29.0	100.0	100.0	100.0	100.0	9.7	0.0	0.0
20	0.0	0.0	0.0	0.0	0.0	25.8	93.5	80.6	3.2	0.0	0.0	0.0

(s) Greenville, PA
Probability

Temperature Greater Than	JAN	FEB	MAR	APR	MAY	JUN	JUL	AUG	SEP	OCT	NOV	DEC
-5	87.5	87.5	100.0	100.0	100.0	100.0	100.0	100.0	100.0	100.0	100.0	93.8
0	12.5	24.0	93.8	100.0	100.0	100.0	100.0	100.0	100.0	100.0	100.0	50.0
5	0.0	0.0	0.0	100.0	100.0	100.0	100.0	100.0	100.0	100.0	68.8	0.0
10	0.0	0.0	0.0	43.8	100.0	100.0	100.0	100.0	100.0	87.5	0.0	0.0
15	0.0	0.0	0.0	0.0	43.8	100.0	100.0	100.0	100.0	0.0	0.0	0.0
20	0.0	0.0	0.0	0.0	0.0	62.5	100.0	81.2	18.8	0.0	0.0	0.0

(t) Meadville, PA
Probability

Temperature Greater Than	JAN	FEB	MAR	APR	MAY	JUN	JUL	AUG	SEP	OCT	NOV	DEC
-5	62.5	75.0	93.8	100.0	100.0	100.0	100.0	100.0	100.0	100.0	100.0	81.2
0	0.0	0.0	81.2	100.0	100.0	100.0	100.0	100.0	100.0	100.0	100.0	31.2
5	0.0	0.0	0.0	100.0	100.0	100.0	100.0	100.0	100.0	100.0	31.2	0.0
10	0.0	0.0	0.0	6.2	100.0	100.0	100.0	100.0	100.0	56.2	0.0	0.0
15	0.0	0.0	0.0	0.0	20.0	100.0	100.0	100.0	68.8	0.0	0.0	0.0
20	0.0	0.0	0.0	0.0	0.0	6.2	62.5	25.0	0.0	0.0	0.0	0.0

(u) Warren, PA
Probability

Temperature Greater Than	JAN	FEB	MAR	APR	MAY	JUN	JUL	AUG	SEP	OCT	NOV	DEC
-5	75.0	87.5	100.0	100.0	100.0	100.0	100.0	100.0	100.0	100.0	100.0	87.5
0	6.2	12.5	87.5	100.0	100.0	100.0	100.0	100.0	100.0	100.0	100.0	50.0
5	0.0	0.0	0.0	100.0	100.0	100.0	100.0	100.0	100.0	100.0	50.0	0.0
10	0.0	0.0	0.0	18.8	100.0	100.0	100.0	100.0	100.0	62.5	0.0	0.0
15	0.0	0.0	0.0	0.0	37.5	100.0	100.0	100.0	75.0	0.0	0.0	0.0
20	0.0	0.0	0.0	0.0	0.0	25.0	81.2	50.0	0.0	0.0	0.0	0.0

(v) Centralia, Ontario
Probability

Temperature Greater Than	JAN	FEB	MAR	APR	MAY	JUN	JUL	AUG	SEP	OCT	NOV	DEC
-10	100.0	95.5	100.0	100.0	100.0	100.0	100.0	100.0	100.0	100.0	100.0	100.0
-5	50.0	60.0	94.4	100.0	100.0	100.0	100.0	100.0	100.0	100.0	100.0	84.2
0	0.0	0.0	50.0	100.0	100.0	100.0	100.0	100.0	100.0	100.0	94.7	5.3
5	0.0	0.0	0.0	75.0	100.0	100.0	100.0	100.0	100.0	100.0	21.1	0.0
10	0.0	0.0	0.0	0.0	95.0	100.0	100.0	100.0	100.0	63.2	0.0	0.0
15	0.0	0.0	0.0	0.0	5.0	100.0	100.0	100.0	78.9	0.0	0.0	0.0
20	0.0	0.0	0.0	0.0	0.0	10.0	70.0	45.0	0.0	0.0	0.0	0.0

Table 3.2. (Continued)

(w) Leamington, Ontario Probability

Temperature Greater Than	JAN	FEB	MAR	APR	MAY	JUN	JUL	AUG	SEP	OCT	NOV	DEC
-5	67.7	83.9	100.0	100.0	100.0	100.0	100.0	100.0	100.0	100.0	100.0	93.5
0	0.0	3.2	67.7	100.0	100.0	100.0	100.0	100.0	100.0	100.0	100.0	35.5
5	0.0	0.0	6.5	96.8	100.0	100.0	100.0	100.0	100.0	100.0	38.7	0.0
10	0.0	0.0	0.0	9.7	100.0	100.0	100.0	100.0	100.0	83.9	0.0	0.0
15	0.0	0.0	0.0	0.0	29.0	100.0	100.0	100.0	100.0	6.5	0.0	0.0
20	0.0	0.0	0.0	0.0	0.0	41.9	100.0	93.5	3.2	0.0	0.0	0.0

(x) London, Ontario Probability

Temperature Greater Than	JAN	FEB	MAR	APR	MAY	JUN	JUL	AUG	SEP	OCT	NOV	DEC
-10	96.8	96.8	100.0	100.0	100.0	100.0	100.0	100.0	100.0	100.0	100.0	100.0
-5	41.9	51.6	96.7	100.0	100.0	100.0	100.0	100.0	100.0	100.0	100.0	77.4
0	0.0	0.0	36.7	100.0	100.0	100.0	100.0	100.0	100.0	100.0	96.8	0.0
10	0.0	0.0	0.0	3.2	90.3	100.0	100.0	100.0	100.0	48.4	0.0	0.0
15	0.0	0.0	0.0	0.0	3.2	100.0	100.0	100.0	61.3	0.0	0.0	0.0
20	0.0	0.0	0.0	0.0	0.0	6.5	77.4	41.9	0.0	0.0	0.0	0.0

(y) Port Dover, Ontario Probability

Temperature Greater Than	JAN	FEB	MAR	APR	MAY	JUN	JUL	AUG	SEP	OCT	NOV	DEC
-5	58.1	74.2	100.0	100.0	100.0	100.0	100.0	100.0	100.0	100.0	100.0	93.5
0	0.0	0.0	56.7	100.0	100.0	100.0	100.0	100.0	100.0	100.0	100.0	29.0
5	0.0	0.0	6.7	74.2	100.0	100.0	100.0	100.0	100.0	100.0	29.0	0.0
10	0.0	0.0	0.0	0.0	90.3	100.0	100.0	100.0	100.0	64.5	0.0	0.0
15	0.0	0.0	0.0	0.0	3.2	100.0	100.0	100.0	80.6	0.0	0.0	0.0
20	0.0	0.0	0.0	0.0	0.0	6.5	61.3	38.7	0.0	0.0	0.0	0.0

(z) St. Thomas, Ontario Probability

Temperature Greater Than	JAN	FEB	MAR	APR	MAY	JUN	JUL	AUG	SEP	OCT	NOV	DEC
-10	100.0	100.0	100.0	100.0	100.0	100.0	100.0	96.8	100.0	100.0	100.0	100.0
-5	56.7	71.0	96.7	100.0	100.0	100.0	100.0	96.8	100.0	100.0	100.0	83.9
0	3.3	0.0	53.3	100.0	100.0	100.0	100.0	96.8	100.0	100.0	100.0	12.9
5	0.0	0.0	6.7	80.6	100.0	100.0	100.0	96.8	100.0	100.0	12.9	0.0
10	0.0	0.0	0.0	3.2	93.5	100.0	100.0	96.8	100.0	58.1	0.0	0.0
15	0.0	0.0	0.0	0.0	6.5	100.0	100.0	96.8	71.0	0.0	0.0	0.0
20	0.0	0.0	0.0	0.0	0.0	6.5	71.0	32.3	0.0	0.0	0.0	0.0

(aa) Windsor, Ontario Probability

Temperature Greater Than	JAN	FEB	MAR	APR	MAY	JUN	JUL	AUG	SEP	OCT	NOV	DEC
-5	66.7	77.8	100.0	100.0	100.0	100.0	100.0	100.0	100.0	100.0	100.0	92.9
0	0.0	3.7	73.1	100.0	100.0	100.0	100.0	100.0	100.0	100.0	100.0	28.6
5	0.0	0.0	7.7	96.3	100.0	100.0	100.0	100.0	100.0	100.0	35.7	0.0
10	0.0	0.0	0.0	14.8	100.0	100.0	100.0	100.0	100.0	75.0	0.0	0.0
15	0.0	0.0	0.0	0.0	37.0	100.0	100.0	100.0	100.0	7.1	0.0	0.0
20	0.0	0.0	0.0	0.0	0.0	51.9	100.0	82.1	0.0	0.0	0.0	0.0

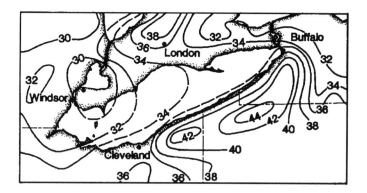

Figure 3.21. The average annual precipitation (in inches) over the Lake Erie area (after Phillips and McCulloch, 1972).

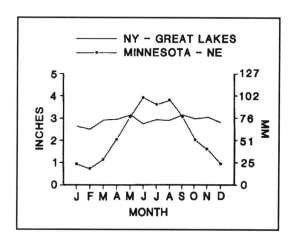

Figure 3.22. Average monthly precipitation for Minnesota and New York (from Eichenlaub, 1979).

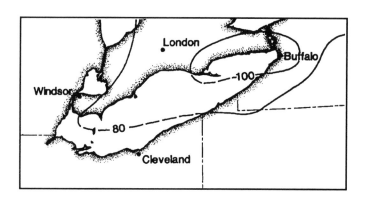

Figure 3.23. Winter precipitation as a percentage of summer precipitation for the Great Lakes basin (from Phillips and McCulloch, 1972).

Minnesota's precipitation reaches a sharp peak during summer and then falls below that of New York during spring, fall, and winter. New York, conversely, experiences between 2 and 3 in (5-7.5 cm) of precipitation every month of the year. Figure 3.23 shows the evenness of monthly precipitation around Lake Erie in another way by displaying winter precipitation as a percentage of the total summer precipitation. Continental areas to the north and west of Lake Superior experience winter precipitation that is only 20-40% of that during the summertime. On the other hand, the Lake Erie region receives 60-80% of the summer precipitation total during winter, with the Buffalo area having approximately the same precipitation amounts in summer as in winter. Figures 3.24-3.27 display mean monthly precipitation totals by season, each chart representing the middle month of a particular season. The charts indicate that during each season, the leeward side of the lake receives slightly more precipitation and that seasonal precipitation around Lake Erie is generally even.

A number of studies have been conducted on many of the Great Lakes to determine the differences between precipitation amounts on the lake and on the land. None of the most recent studies, based on data from islands in the western parts of the lake and perimeter stations in the same area, show clear seasonal differences between lake and land precipitation (Table 3.3). It can be stated that on a general basis the lake stations received about 4-5% less precipitation than the land. Larger seasonal differences have been observed in other studies in other lakes, but the investigators have usually stated that measurement errors are often greater than the lake vs. land differences observed. Wilson and Pollock (1981) confirm this in a report on a study over Lake Ontario:

> Thus, during the year about half of all the precipitation days are significantly affected by the lake, suppressing overlake precipitation during the warm season and initiating precipitation activity during the cold season. These are, however, days when the precipitation is relatively light and scattered. The overall effect of the lake on seasonal or yearly precipitation totals is, therefore, not as impressive as one might expect from observations of the day-to-day precipitation patterns.

For the Lake Erie study shown in Table 3.3, Derecki (1975) states:

> Thus, derived precipitation ratios do not confirm the theoretical spring-summer reduction and fall-winter increase in the overwater precipitation.

Another factor affecting precipitation around Lake Erie is topography. To the east of the lake, the land becomes increasingly hilly. Large

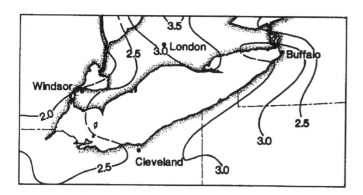

Figure 3.24. Average January precipitation (in inches) over the Lakes Erie and St. Clair area (from Phillips and McCulloch,, 1972).

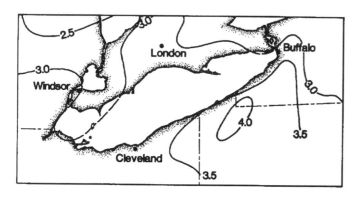

Figure 3.25. Average April precipitation (in inches) over the Lakes Erie and St. Clair area (from Phillips and McCulloch, 1972).

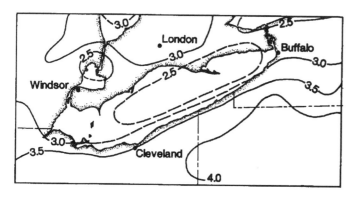

Figure 3.26. Average July precipitation (in inches) over the Lakes Erie and St. Clair area (from Phillips and McCulloch, 1972).

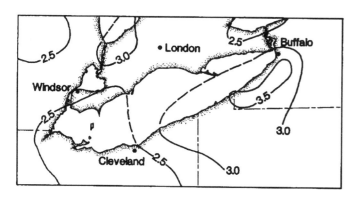

Figure 3.27. Average October precipitation (in inches) over the Lakes Erie and St. Clair area (from Phillips and McCulloch, 1972).

	Quinn (1971)[1] 22-42 years of data Rp	Derecki (1975)[2] 36 years of data Rp
January	1.02	1.03
February	0.88	0.90
March	0.97	0.94
April	1.06	1.03
May	1.04	0.99
June	0.87	0.92
July	0.88	0.95
August	1.00	1.00
September	0.95	0.91
October	0.90	0.91
November	0.96	0.94
December	0.89	0.94
ANNUAL	0.95	0.96

Table 3.3. Lake Erie overwater/ overland precipitation analysis. Rp is overwater divided by overland values.

LAKE: (1) 2 island stations: Put-in-Bay and Pelee
(2) 2 island stations: Put-in-Bay and Pelee

LAND: (1) 2 perimeter stations: Sandusky, OH, and Leamington, ONT.
(2) 5 perimeter stations: Monroe, MI; Toledo, OH; Sandusky, OH; Cleveland, OH; and Leamington, ONT.

topographical obstructions have an important effect on precipitation. When moist air reaches hilly terrain, it usually is forced to rise over it. This upward motion causes the air mass to expand and cool. Colder air retains less water. Therefore, as the air rises and cools, it is forced to release its excess moisture in the form of precipitation. As the moist air from Lake Erie travels eastward (in general, weather travels from west to east) into these hilly areas, it begins to rise, cool, and precipitate its excess water.

One of the most notable characteristics of snowfall in the Lake Erie area is the high variability of snow depth from year to year. Migratory low pressure weather systems, which spawn a great deal of the snowfall, and the extent of ice cover over the lakes are important controls in determining the amount of snow in any given area. If Lake Erie is not extensively covered with ice, air moving over the lake has the opportunity to collect vast amounts of moisture, which is often subsequently deposited on the lee shorelines as snow. "Lake-effect" snow is familiar to many. During a lake-effect storm which occurred on November 18, 1930, there were 48 in (122 cm) of snowfall at Orchard Park, New York, (about 15 mi [24 km] south of Buffalo), 6 in (15 cm) south of Buffalo, and no snow north of Buffalo, while the sun was shining brightly at nearby Lockport, New York. In another storm on December 14-18, 1945, the Buffalo airport measured 37 in (94 cm) of snow that had fallen while there were estimated falls of 70 in (178 cm) just a few miles to the south. Some authors have estimated that typical "lake-effect" snows account for 40-55% of all heavy snows reported at Buffalo.

Perhaps the best general description of a lake-effect snowfall is given by M.K. Thomas in an article published in 1964:

> Lake-effect snow is produced when cold Arctic air moves across a relatively warm lake. This usually happens after a low pressure area has moved eastward across the lakes and cold air rushes southward and eastward behind the cold front. With the proper temperature difference, wind speed and wind direction "snow cells" may be formed. The production of snowfall may begin over the lake and is most certainly intensified as the cell extends over the shoreline and inland over hills and mountains. The local pattern of air flow and the location of the lake-effect snowfall areas are dependent upon the orientation of the weather system. When the Arctic air flow is from the north, the areas most affected are the south and southeast shores of the lakes, while when the air flow is from the west and southwest, it is the eastern ends of the lower Great Lakes (Lakes Erie and Ontario) that receive an abundance of lake-effect snow.

The total average annual snowfall in the Lake Erie region varies from the extreme highs of 120 in (305 cm) in the Erie, Pennsylvania, and Buffalo, New York, areas to much lower amounts (20-30 in [51-76 cm]) in the northern and western portions of the region. Figures 3.28-3.30 show the average snowfall for the Lake Erie area in November, January, and March. In general, the snowfall amounts increase slightly from November to January and decrease from January to March. A possible reason for this is that the lake is free of ice early in the year allowing much moisture to escape into the air, which subsequently precipitates as snow at the shoreline. After ice forms, the lack of available moisture cuts down on the snowfall.

The amount of snowfall over a given period is often far different from the depth of snow on the ground. This is due to reasons such as present or future temperatures, wind speed and direction, soil temperatures, and so on.

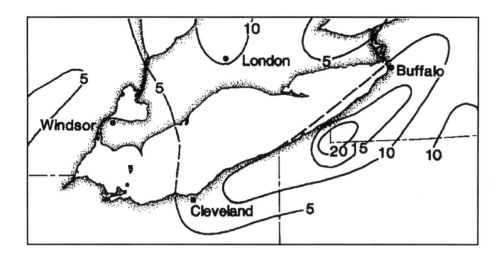

Figure 3.28. Average November snowfall (in inches), (after Phillips and McCulloch, 1972).

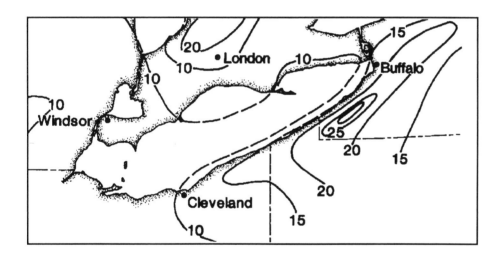

Figure 3.29. Average January snowfall (in inches), (after Phillips and McCulloch, 1972).

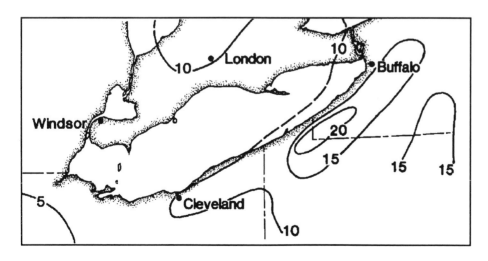

Figure 3.30. Average March snowfall (in inches), (after Phillips and McCulloch, 1972).

Snowfall and snow depth affect activity in different ways. Snow depth is important to skiers; snowfall and snow depth are important to motorists. It is very important to keep in mind that both snowfall and snow depth may vary greatly over a small geographic area (as opposed to temperature, for example). Snow measurements are taken at a single location, but in Figures 3.28-3.30 a few measurements are used to represent a much larger geographic area. The charts, tables, and graphs in this section are constructed from data collected over a number of years and averaged. This technique makes them representative of average conditions in the region. Actual conditions at a site on a given day can differ greatly from the averages.

Snow depth probability is defined as the percentage of time the snow depth equals or exceeds selected levels. For example, if the depth were 10 in (25 cm) only once during a 20-year period, the probability is 5% for a depth level of 10 in (1 divided by 20 = 0.05 x 100 = 5%). Probability diagrams computed for stations in the Lake Erie/Lake St. Clair region are shown in Figures 3.31-3.40. Probability values from which the diagrams are drawn are for the last day of each month.

The London, Ontario, diagram (Figure 3.37) is used here to illustrate the use of the graphs. Snow depth at the end of February at London equals or exceeds 30, 10, and 5 in (76, 25, and 13 cm) about 0%, 10%, and 27% of the time, respectively, and the ground is free of snow 13% of the time. Thus, probability of a snow depth greater than (>) zero is 87%. The average snow depth (2 in [5 cm]) may be estimated from the graphs by tracing a horizontal line across the y-axis at the 50% probability level and a vertical line for the time period of interest (February in this case). The intersection at those two lines is the average snow depth for that particular time.

Snow depth probability at the end of January at stations circling Lake Erie with depths greater than or equal to 5 in (13 cm) and greater than or equal to 10 in (25 cm) is shown in Figure 3.41. In comparison to the other Great Lakes, snow depths of the Lake Erie basin are quite low. In the Lake Erie region in January, snow depth probability varies from 0% (Cleveland, Ohio; Toledo, Ohio; Detroit, Michigan) to 14% (London, Ontario) for a 10-in (25-cm) depth and from 8% (Cleveland, Ohio) to 55% (London, Ontario) for a 5-in (13-cm) depth. Probability values are higher in the southeastern portion of the region (Buffalo, New York; Erie, Pennsylvania) than in the southwestern portion (Cleveland, Ohio; Toledo, Ohio; Detroit, Michigan). This is most likely due to lake-effect snowfall. December and February probability ranges for the Lakes Erie and St. Clair area are shown in Table 3.4.

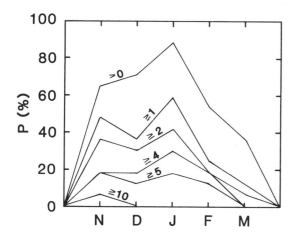

Figure 3.31. Snow depth probability (%) for the last day of each month (October-April) for Akron, Ohio (from Bolsenga, 1967a).

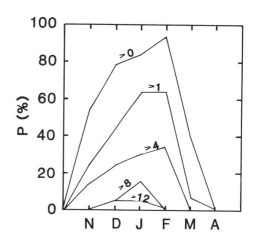

Figure 3.32. Snow depth probability (%) for the last day of each month (October-April) for Buffalo, New York (from Bolsenga, 1967a).

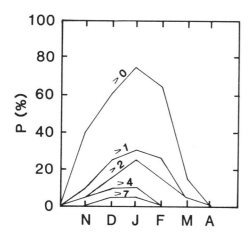

Figure 3.33. Snow depth probability (%) for the last day of each month (October-April) for Cleveland, Ohio (from Bolsenga, 1967a).

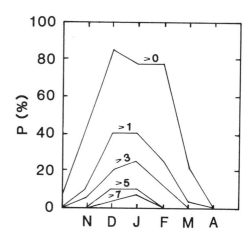

Figure 3.34. Snow depth probability (%) for the last day of each month (October-April) for Detroit, Michigan (from Bolsenga, 1967a).

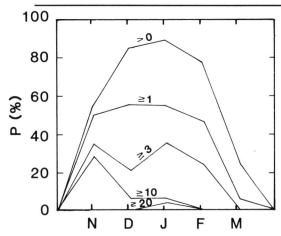

Figure 3.35. Snow depth probability (%) for the last day of each month (October-April) for Erie, Pennsylvania (from Bolsenga, 1967a).

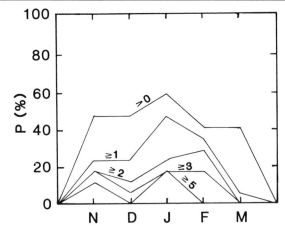

Figure 3.36. Snow depth probability (%) for the last day of each month (October-April) for Findlay, Ohio (from Bolsenga,, 1967a).

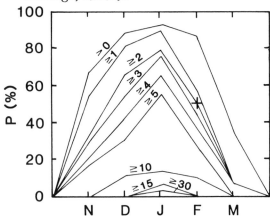

Figure 3.37. Snow depth probability (%) for the last day of each month (October-April) for London, Ontario (from Bolsenga, 1967a).

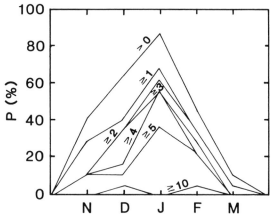

Figure 3.38. Snow depth probability (%) for the last day of each month (October-April) for Port Huron, Michigan (from Bolsenga, 1967a).

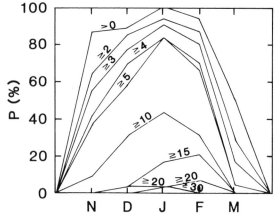

Figure 3.39. Snow depth probability (%) for the last day of each month (October-April) forStratford, Ontario (from Bolsenga, 1967a).

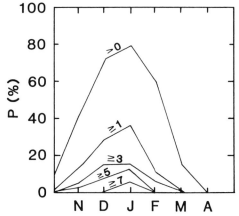

Figure 3.40. Snow depth probability (%) for the last day of each month (October-April) for Toledo, Ohio (from Bolsenga, 1967a).

Figure 3.41. Snow depth probability (%) at the end of January at six stations in the Lake Erie area (from Bolsenga, 1967b).

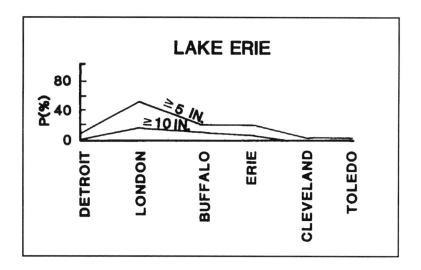

Month	Depth (greater than or equal to specified level)	High P (%) Station	Low P (%) Station
December	5 in (12.7 cm)	31 (London, ONT)	7 (Cleveland, OH; Toledo, OH)
	10 in (25.4 cm)	12 (London, ONT)	0 (Cleveland, OH; Detroit, MI; Toledo, OH)
February	5 in (12.7 cm)	27 (London,ONT)	0 (Cleveland, OH; Detroit, MI; Toledo, OH)
	10 in (25.4 cm)	10 (London, ONT)	0 (Buffalo, NY; Cleveland, OH; Detroit, MI; Erie, PA; Toledo, OH)

Table 3.4. December and February snow depth (in inches [centimeters]) probability (p) ranges for the Lakes Erie and St. Clair area (from Bolsenga, 1967b).

A meteorological equation, the geostrophic wind equation, and atmospheric phenomena, as labeled in Table 3.1 of the introduction to this chapter, perhaps best and most accurately describe air in motion—the wind. Geostrophic wind results when a balance is achieved between the pressure gradient and Coriolis forces. Both wind direction and velocity are determined primarily by this alignment of the pressure gradient—the rate and direction of pressure change. The pressure gradient is also defined as the maximum rate of change of pressure between two reference points of the same elevation. Winds are stronger when pressure gradients are larger. Air will flow from areas of high to low pressure at a velocity proportional to the pressure gradient. In the absence of the earth's rotation, pressure differences would be equalized by flow from high to low pressure areas. However, rotation of the earth creates the Coriolis force, which, in the northern hemisphere, deflects the air to the right. The Coriolis force varies from zero at the equator to its maximum at the pole. At levels above 2,000 ft (610 m), the pressure gradient force and the Coriolis force are nearly balanced. At lower levels, the Coriolis force is reduced since friction due to surface irregularities reduces the wind velocity, and the Coriolis effect is partly a function of velocity. Finally, each of the atmospheric phenomena previously discussed has an effect on the velocity of the wind. For example, large-scale disturbances give preferred orientation to storm tracks.

When compared to annual average wind speeds in different parts of the United States, the wind speeds of the Lake Erie region are moderate. Average annual wind speeds in the Lake Erie area range from 8-10 mph (3.6-4.5 m/sec), which falls near the middle of the national range of approximately 5-16 mph (2.2-7.2 m/sec). On a yearly basis, the prevailing wind direction in the Lake Erie region is from the southwest quadrant (S-SW-W).

How does the wind direction and speed change from season to season? Figures 3.42-3.45 show these wind parameters for four different months, each the mid-month for a particular season. In the Lake Erie area, in every season, winds from the S-SW-W (the third quadrant) predominate. (Longer bars in these directions mean more occurrences of wind from those directions.) The direction of the prevailing wind becomes more variable during spring and fall as indicated by the bars, which become more equal in length, with the prevailing direction showing less dominance on the April and October charts. A strong westerly component of the winds is shown during winter, while during summer and fall a southerly direction is more frequent.

Winds

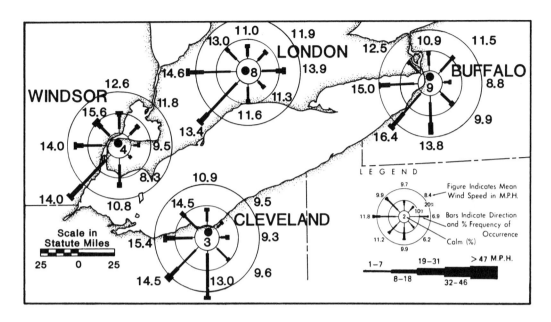

Figure 3.42. Wind roses for Lake Erie area stations in January (after Phillips and McCulloch, 1972).

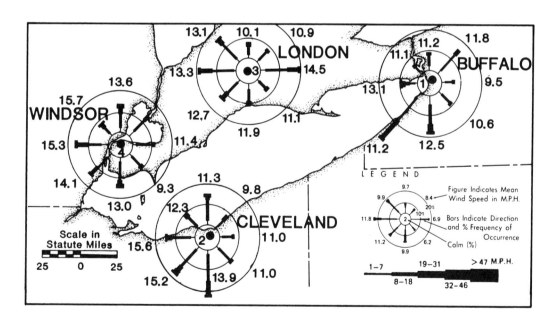

Figure 3.43. Wind roses for Lake Erie area stations in April (after Phillips and McCulloch, 1972).

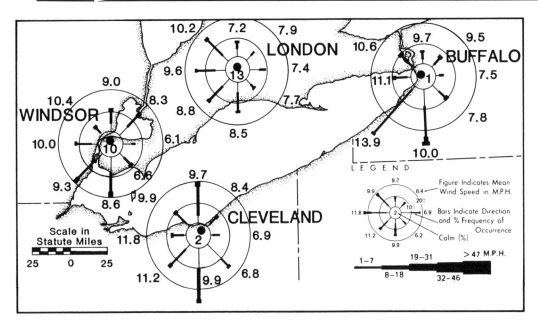

Figure 3.44. Wind roses for Lake Erie area stations in July (after Phillips and McCulloch, 1972).

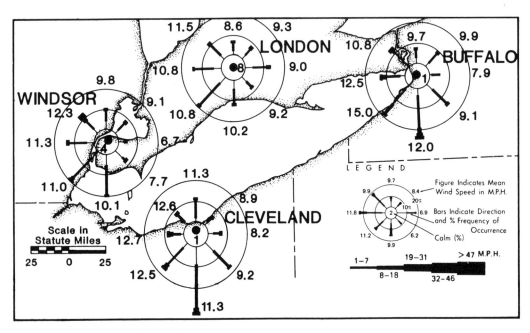

Figure 3.45. Wind roses for Lake Erie area stations in October (after Phillips and McCulloch, 1972).

Figure 3.46 was created by taking the wind speed in all directions for four cities in the Lakes Erie and St. Clair area and averaging them to determine an overall monthly wind speed for each city. A dramatic decline in wind speed is noticeable as summer approaches and an increase is evident toward fall. During spring/summer, Lake Erie (because it is shallow) warms up quickly and soon the temperature difference between land and lake is minimal. As the temperature differential decreases, so does the wind speed. The opposite holds true for fall as the land quickly cools and the lake initially lags behind. A comparison of wind speed and direction shows that summer winds are generally more variable in direction, while winter winds tend to be more variable in speed.

The previous discussion has examined large-scale wind patterns. Equally important are small-scale, local winds. One of these is the lake and land breeze. During periods of light winds in summer, cool surface winds often flow off the lake onto the shore during the day (the lake breeze) and in the opposite direction during the evening (the land breeze) (Figure 3.47). Since the shoreline is generally a favorite recreational area during the summertime and most outings occur during the day, these cooling breezes from the lake are usually welcomed.

Figure 3.46. Monthly average wind speed for four cities in the Lake Erie area.

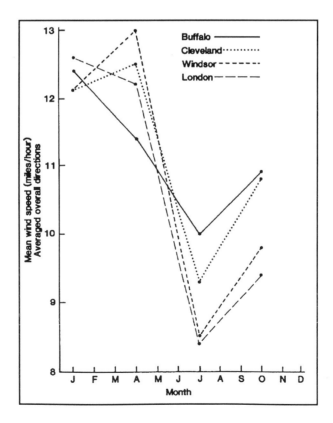

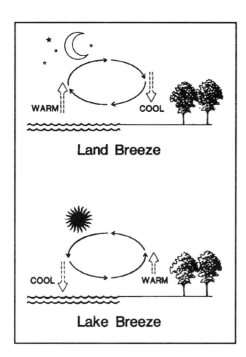

Figure 3.47. Relative warming and cooling of the lake and land surface, the air masses above them, and the associated air circulation.

What causes these lake and land breezes? The key is differential heating. In summer during the heat of the day, the land warms. Since the lake does not warm as fast as the land, it stays at a lower temperature than its shoreline. The heated air over the shoreline rises and the cooler, heavier air over the lake moves under the rising land air to replace it. It is this local circulation of air between land and lake that sets up the lake breeze. At night the situation is the opposite. During evening hours, the land surface cools more rapidly than the lake surface. Therefore, at night, the lake is warmer than the land along its shoreline and the air over the lake tends to rise. The air over the cooler land tends to sink, however, and this sets up a circulation pattern which is exactly opposite that of the lake breeze. At night, the cooler land air moves in under the rising lake air and a land breeze occurs. Figure 3.48 compares temperatures between an inland location and a shoreline station on Lake Huron during three different months. The stations are not in the Lake Erie region, but serve to illustrate a phenomenon which occurs throughout the lakes. During June, the lake and land breezes take effect. An inland city becomes hotter than a shoreline city during the day and cooler at night. The cooling effect of the lake breeze begins in mid- to late morning and lasts until sunset. In March and September, (early spring and early fall) the lake/land breeze circulations are not as common due to stronger prevailing winds associated with larger scale

Figure 3.48. Lake breeze effects in air temperature near the shore. Average hourly temperatures for Douglas Point and Paisley, Ontario, for March, June, and September (from Pond, 1964).

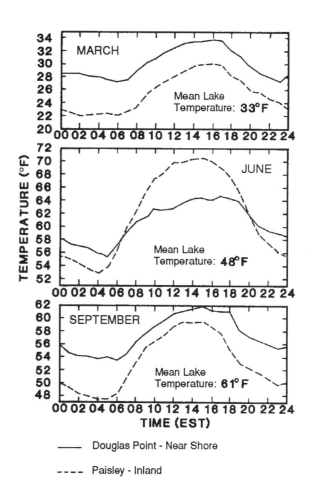

circulation phenomena and a significant difference in the daily average air temperature over the lake and land.

The lake breeze also modifies the humidity along Lake Erie's shore-line. The pleasant, cool, temperatures brought in from the lake during the day are accompanied by a not-so-pleasant humidity increase. Sometimes a fog layer may even penetrate the immediate shoreline. Frequently, an increase in cloud cover also accompanies the lake breeze. During summer days, air flowing from Lake Erie will eventually meet a wall of very warm land air. The boundary where the differing air masses meet is called the lake-breeze front. According to Eichenlaub (1979), this front may penetrate inland anywhere from several blocks to over approximately 25 mi (40 km). When the incoming lake breeze meets with the warm, rising air above the land, moist air is lifted and clouds form. Occasionally, a line of rain showers will develop from this cloud

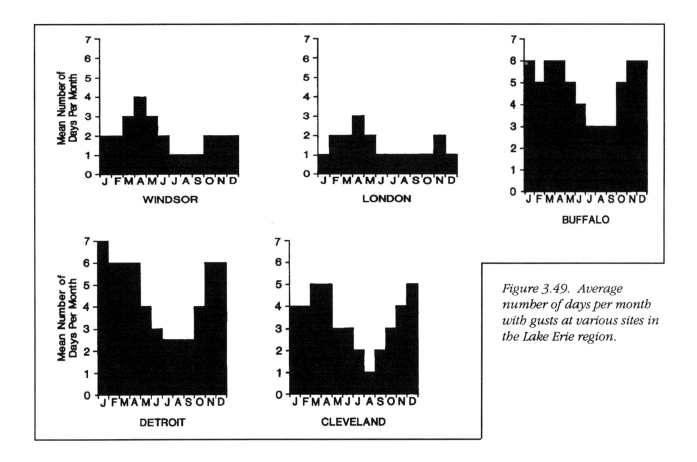

Figure 3.49. Average number of days per month with gusts at various sites in the Lake Erie region.

band. In the Detroit metropolitan area, some evidence exists that the lake breeze front which pushes westward from Lake St. Clair may be at least partially responsible for the occurrence of some excessively heavy rains over the northwestern suburbs of the city (Eichenlaub, 1979).

There are many aspects of air motion that, when systematically observed, provide useful information for recreation. Some are of special importance to boaters. For example, a guide to determining surface wind direction changes is to watch onshore smoke plumes. These provide visual observations of wind direction changes which may foretell changing weather conditions. The movements of high clouds reveal upper wind patterns. Watching surface wind directions and comparing them to upper-air winds provides valuable clues to weather changes.

Figure 3.49 shows the number of gusts that occur, on the average, each month at several sites around Lake Erie. The charts display a definite drop in the number of days with gusts during summer at all locations. Winter and spring, however, show an increase in gust occurrences. These results make sense when we compare them with our previous findings from Figures 3.42-3.45, which gave seasonal wind speeds around the Lake Erie region. Those figures indicated that during summer, the winds were the weakest. Therefore, they have less chance of producing these short, forceful bursts of air. During early spring, the wind speeds were found to be at their highest, possessing a greater ability to create gusting conditions.

Wind speeds over the water can differ significantly from wind speeds over the land. Overall, water is a much smoother surface than land, since land has many obstacles which may slow wind. In the evening, under light wind conditions on land, the winds over the lake may have speeds 2 to 2-1/2 times greater than those over the land. As the wind over the land increases in speed, the difference between land and lake speeds will diminish, though the differences are always likely to be significant. In fall, when the air temperature is cold relative to the water temperature, the overwater wind speed can be 50% greater than the overland wind speed. In spring, when the air temperature is warm relative to the water temperature, the overwater wind speed can be 20% less than the overland wind speed. Another general rule of thumb that may be helpful is that when approaching or leaving the land, wind direction shifts are around 15° because of the different frictional aspects between land and water surfaces. Again, flags, smoke plumes, etc. may give good estimates of this change.

Obstructions, such as hills, cliffs, or even tall buildings in the path of a prevailing wind will often generate a confused chaotic wind pattern to the lee of the obstacle. A general rule is that obstacles will influence the wind velocity over a distance of 5-6 times the height of the obstruction. Another wind phenomenon to be aware of has been termed the "funneling effect." On or near rivers, such as the Detroit or Niagara Rivers or other narrowing areas, the wind sometimes increases in speed and drastically changes direction. It is not uncommon for the funneling effect to generate as much as a 60°-80° difference in the previous wind direction (McMurray and Sillars, 1980).

A useful guide when trying to determine local wind speeds, when no instruments are available, is the Beaufort Scale. This scale, developed in the early nineteenth century by Sir Francis Beaufort, is still in general use today. Table 3.5 shows an up-to-date version of this scale. By watching the characteristics of the water and referring to this chart, an estimation of local wind speeds can be made. Wind speeds are also the most universally accepted basis for classifying coastal weather warnings. A complete list of radio stations broadcasting weather warnings is given in the Hydrosphere Chapter—Waves Section.

Beaufort Number	Knots	Miles Per Hour	Description	Effect at Sea
0	0-0.9	0-0.9	Calm	Sea like a mirror.
1	1-3	1-3	Light air	Scale-like ripples form, but without foam crests.
2	4-6	4-7	Light breeze	Small wavelets, short but more pronounced. Crests have a glassy appearance and do not break.
3	7-10	8-12	Gentle breeze	Large wavelets. Crests begin to break. Foam has glassy appearance. Perhaps scattered white horses.
4	11-16	13-18	Moderate breeze	Small waves, becoming longer. Fairly frequent white horses.
5	17-21	19-24	Fresh breeze	Moderate waves, taking a more pronounced long form. Many white horses are formed. Chance of some spray.
6	22-27	25-31	Strong breeze	Large waves begin to form. White foam crests are more extensive everywhere. Some spray.
7	28-33	25-31	Moderate gale	Sea heaps up and white foam from breaking waves begin to be blown in streaks along the direction of the wind. Spindrift begins.
8	34-40	49-46	Fresh gale	Moderately high waves of greater length. Edges of crests break into spindrift. Foam is blown in well-marked streaks along the direction of the wind.
9	41-47	47-54	Strong gale	High waves. Dense streaks of foam along the direction of the wind. Sea begins to roll. Spray may affect visiblity.
10	48-55	55-63	Whole gale and/or Storm	Very high waves with long overhanging crests. The resulting foam in great patches is blown in dense white streaks along the direction of On the whole, the surface of the sea takes a white appearance. The rolling of the sea becomes heavy and shocklike. Visibility is affected.
11	56-63	64-73	Storm and/or Violent Storm	Exceptionally high waves. Small-and medium-sized vessels might for a long time be lost to view behind the waves. The sea is completely covered with long white patches of foam lying along the direction of the wind. Everywhere, the edges of the wave crests are blown into froth. Visibility seriously affected.
12	64 or higher	74 or higher	Hurricane & Typhoon	The air is filled with foam and spray. Sea is completely white with driving spray. Visibility is very seriously affected.

Table 3.5. The Beaufort wind scale (from Kotsch, 1983).

Humidity and Dew Point Temperature

Humidity is a measure of the amount of water vapor found in the air at a given time. The most commonly used expression, relative humidity, is the amount of water vapor currently held in the air divided by the amount it is capable of holding at its particular temperature:

$$\text{Relative Humidity} = \frac{\text{Actual vapor content in air} \times 100}{\text{Vapor content the air could hold at its temperature}}$$

Relative humidity varies strongly and in the opposite direction to air temperature. Generally, when temperatures are high, relative humidities are low and vice versa. Figure 3.50 shows that relative humidities are lowest during the warmest time of day. It is difficult to detect water

Figure 3.50. Relative humidity at certain times of the day at four cities.

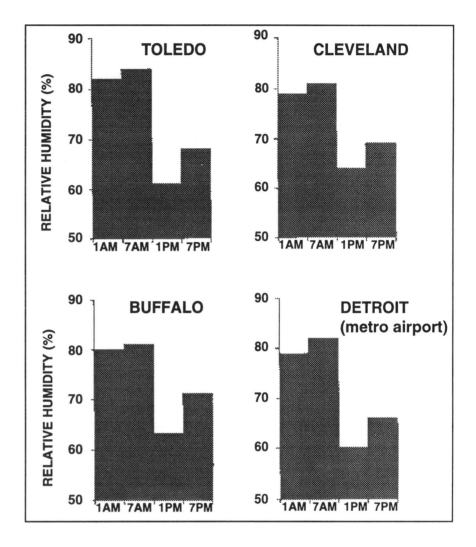

vapor changes from relative humidity. A humidity measurement that shows atmospheric water vapor changes in a more direct way is the dew point temperature.

The dew point temperature is that temperature to which a particular parcel of air must be cooled to condense its moisture (water vapor) to dew (liquid). As water vapor is cooled, it condenses—from vapor to liquid. If the air holds a great deal of moisture, it does not take much cooling to produce these liquid droplets. If the air is very dry, however, the air temperature must drop significantly before droplets form. Therefore, the dew point temperature varies directly with the humidity. Since dew point temperatures and water vapor content have this direct relationship, daily and seasonal plots of dew points also depict humidity trends.

Figure 3.51 shows that the Toledo and Buffalo areas record their highest dew point temperatures in July and August, with a steady decrease of dew point temperatures to lowest values in January and February. The high values in July and August combined with the high temperatures during these months may sometimes cause discomfort.

Comfort zones for July and January are given in Figures 3.52 and 3.53, respectively. These maps were developed using varying temperature/humidity combinations. Figure 3.52 shows that in the month of July, the Lake Erie region lies in the warm zone, slightly hotter than what is considered optimum comfort. Figure 3.53 reveals that January is thought to be colder than what is most comfortable. Although in mid- to late-summer the Lake Erie area is slightly too warm, and in winter it is slightly too cold, the transition seasons—spring and fall—provide extended periods of mild temperatures (moderated by Lake Erie) and low, comfortable humidities.

Fog

Fog consists of a visible aggregate of minute water droplets suspended in the atmosphere near the earth's surface. It is a more frequent occurrence over the entire Great Lakes area than at continental locations at similar latitudes. The effect of the enormous, nearby water source greatly enhances fog formation processes. For the beachcomber, a walk along a fog-shrouded shoreline in the early morning is very tranquil and serene. For the boater offshore, however, that same fog layer is extremely menacing because it greatly reduces visibility and hides hazards and visual aids to navigation. Since fog may sometimes pose a hazardous threat and because it forms so frequently around the Lake Erie area, it is advantageous to understand the nature of fog and details of its formation.

Fog differs from a cloud only in that the base of fog is at the earth's surface, while the base of a cloud is above the surface. Being in a fog bank is comparable to standing in the midst of a stratus cloud. Fog is composed of water droplets which range in size from 1 to 50 microns (a micron is one millionth of a meter) in diameter—compared to 1,000 microns for an average raindrop. These water droplets are so tiny that they literally hang in the air, suspended, not heavy enough to fall as precipitation.

Gaseous, invisible water vapor accounts for only a small percentage of the total gases making up the air (up to 4%), but it has dynamic effects on the overall behavior of all the weather elements, including fog. The amount of water vapor which air can hold is determined by the temperature. Cold air holds less than warm air. Fog of all types origi-

Figure 3.51. Average monthly
dew point temperatures at
Toledo, Ohio, and Buffalo, New
York.

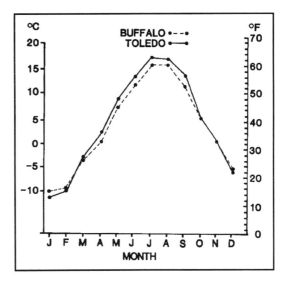

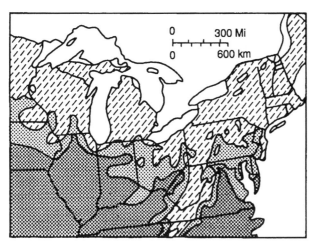

Figure 3.52. Comfort zones
for the eastern half of the
United States in July (from
Eichenlaub, 1979).
1 = Comfortable, 2 = Warm,
3 = Hot, 4 = Oppressive.

☐1 ▨2 ▦3 ▨4

Figure 3.53. Comfort zones
for the eastern half of the
United States in January
(from Eichenlaub, 1979).
1 = Very cold, 2 = Cold.

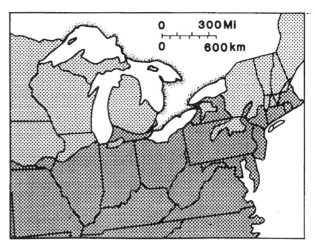

 1 ▨ 2

nates when the temperature and the dew-point of the air become identical (or nearly so), provided that sufficient condensation nuclei are present. Fog may occur from the addition of moisture (and thus elevation of the dew-point) or through the cooling of the air to its dew-point. Over Lake Erie and the adjacent land area, both mechanisms, singly or in combination, play a role in producing fog. Common fog types that occur are advection fog, steam fog, and radiation fog.

Advection fog forms when relatively warm, moist air flows over a cold surface and the air is cooled below the dew point. This fog type occurs both over the land and water. When the warm, moist air flows over a relatively cool Lake Erie, both the addition of moisture and cooling of the air occur.

Steam fog occurs when cold air drifts over relatively warm water. The addition of moisture is the key element here. Steam fog forms over Lake Erie when water vapor is added, by evaporation, to air which is much colder than the lake temperature. This can occur when cold air drifts across relatively warm water.

Radiation fog occurs over the land area when radiational cooling reduces the air temperature to or below the dew point. Thus, radiation fog is a nighttime occurrence, although it may begin to form by evening twilight and often does not dissipate until after sunrise.

Fog occurs less frequently over Lake Erie than over the adjacent Great Lakes. For example, from April through December, fog occurs over Lake Erie approximately 4% of the time (approximately 15 days) as compared to 8% (approximately 29 days) for Lake Ontario and 7% (approximately 26 days) for central Lake Huron. Table 3.6 shows that fog occurs more frequently over Lake Erie in spring as compared to fall . The higher fog frequency in spring is primarily associated with advection fog. During the spring and early summer the temperature of the lake warms up much more slowly than the temperature over the land. On occasion, warm and moist air from over the land is advected over the relatively cool lake and is cooled to the dew point. Thus, advection fog is formed.

Daylight, Sunshine, and Solar Radiation

The amount of daylight, as well as solar radiation and sunshine, is dependent on latitude and time of year. Daylight varies from a high of 15 h and 15 min on June 21, the date of the summer solstice, to 9 h and 7 min on the date of the winter solstice, December 21. The amount of daylight during the shortest part of the winter is thus only 60% of that available during the longest part of the summer.

Table 3.6. *Percentage of time of occurrence of fog (without precipitation) (National Climatic Center, 1975). Observations were taken at 6 hourly intervals (about 120 observations/ month). Observations were not taken during the winter season (January-March).*

	East Lake Erie	West Lake Erie	Average
		% of Time	
April	7	8	8
May	7	5	6
June	6	6	6
July	6	2	4
August	4	3	4
September	2	3	3
October	3	2	3
November	2	2	2
December	1	3	2

Cloud cover of various types usually persists over the Great Lakes area a significant portion of time and tends to obscure the warmth and brightness of the sun. The average January sky cover over Lakes Erie and St. Clair from sunrise to sunset (expressed in tenths of the sky covered by clouds) is eight-tenths. In April, the average sky cover over the area is about seven-tenths. The slightly decreased cloudiness is partly due to the migration of the Arctic front northward from Lake Erie across the Great Lakes basin. In direct contrast to winter conditions, average July sky cover from sunrise to sunset is about five-tenths. In fall, cloudiness increases; the mean October sky cover from sunrise to sunset is six-tenths (Phillips and McCulloch, 1972).

The number of hours of sunshine which occur during a given month are, of course, related to cloud cover conditions. In January, the average number of hours of sunshine is about 80 h in most portions of the region, and reaches 100 h in the southwestern portion. In April, the average number of hours of sunshine equals about 200 h over the entire region. In July, the average varies from 320 h over most of the region to 340 h in the southwestern portion. In October, the average number of hours of sunshine varies from 200 h in the southwestern portion to 180 h throughout the remainder of the region (Phillips and McCulloch, 1972).

Figure 3.54 shows the percentage of possible sunshine for seven stations in the area. These values are long-term averages of the percentage of time the sun actually shines, as opposed to the time the sun is above the horizon. For example, in May at Detroit, Michigan, the sun

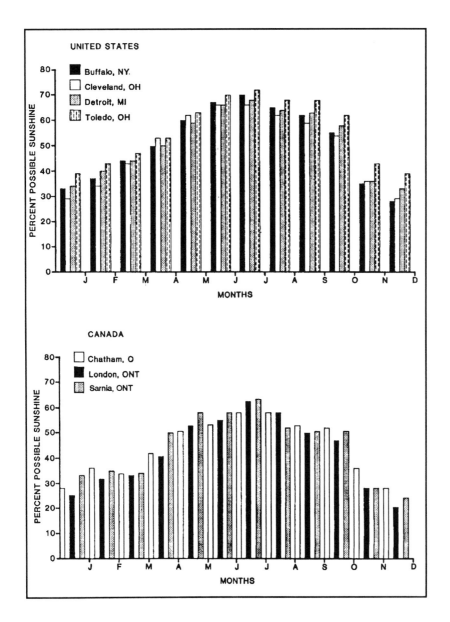

Figure 3.54. Percent possible sunshine at Lake Erie area stations.

shines 59% of the time that it's possible for it to do so. In comparison, the sunniest place on earth is the Sahara Desert. This area averages 4,300 h of sunshine a year—97% of the possible total.

Radiation from the sun is important since the sun provides about 99.97% of the heat energy required for the physical processes taking place in the earth-atmosphere system. Heat energy from the sun, for example, is responsible for warming Lake Erie's water in the spring and summer and for creating the thermocline as described in the Hydrosphere chapter. Solar radiation above the atmosphere is reduced by the

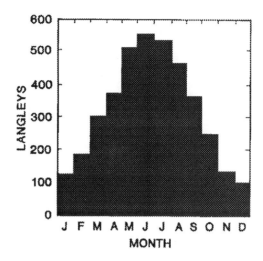

Figure 3.55. Average daily solar radiation at Cleveland, Ohio.

time it reaches the earth's surface by scattering, reflection and absorption by gas molecules, water vapor, clouds and suspended dust particles. Part of the incoming solar radiation is reflected back to the atmosphere by clouds and the surface of the earth.

The amount of solar radiation received at the earth's surface also varies from larger cities to adjacent rural areas, from higher to lower elevated areas, in areas with varying degrees of snow cover, and from areas near Lake Erie to those farther from the shore. The influence of the lake is explained by the fact that more cloud cover usually forms over the lake than over the land during autumn and winter (cold air moving over relatively warm water) and the reverse is true in late spring and summer (daytime heating of the land surfaces).

When compared with sunshine recording stations in the Lake Erie basin, solar radiation recording stations are sparse. Figure 3.55 shows the long term average of solar radiation at Cleveland, Ohio. Solar radiation is at its lowest in December and steadily increases to its maximum in June.

Clouds

What causes clouds to form? The key is cooling. One may think of cooler air as being more dense or more contracted than warm air, and therefore able to hold fewer water particles. When a parcel of air containing a certain amount of water is cooled to a lower temperature, it is able to hold less water and is forced to release some of its water content. This release is called condensation and leads to cloud formation, and possibly to subsequent precipitation.

The major cooling mechanism responsible for cloud formation is lifting. When an air parcel rises to a higher elevation in the atmosphere, it is subject to less air pressure (less air rests on top of the parcel as it goes up through the atmosphere), allowing the air parcel to expand. When air expands, it loses some of its internal heat and cools. Therefore, any process which causes lifting to occur may consequently cause cloud formation; conversely, processes that cause downward motion, and thus heating of the air, are unfavorable for cloud formation and cause cloud dissipation.

The Lake Erie area is one of the cloudiest in the U.S. The three lifting mechanisms causing such frequent cloud formation in the Lake Erie area are:

Fronts. The air moves primarily horizontal to the earth's surface. However, relatively warm air flowing along a frontal surface, e.g., a warm front associated with a cyclonic scale circulation or low, is forced to rise over the relatively cool and denser air ahead of the front.

Convection. When the sun strongly heats the surface of the earth, the air in contact with the surface warms. A buoyant or convective instability results in the air in contact with the earth relative to the air aloft. This results in cells or bubbles of upward moving air which is compensated by downward flow.

Orography. When air currents encounter obstacles (such as hills or mountains), the air is usually forced to rise up and over the obstacle.

The great amount of cloud cover over the Lake Erie region is often the result of a combination of these three lifting mechanisms. Overall, though, fronts and convection play the major role. Since the polar front and associated cyclones are much stronger during winter and the storm tracks tend to prevail directly over the Great Lakes area during this season, it is apparent why the Lake Erie area has a large amount of cloud cover during winter (Figure 3.56). The convection process is more important during the summer when heating from the sun at the latitude of Lake Erie is more intense.

In surface weather observations, the term "sky cover" is used to denote the amount of the sky that is covered but not necessarily concealed by clouds. In January, the Arctic front is located to the south of the Great Lakes bringing broken or overcast skies to the southern portion of the area including the Lake Erie region. The average January sky cover from sunrise to sunset is eight-tenths. In April, the Arctic front

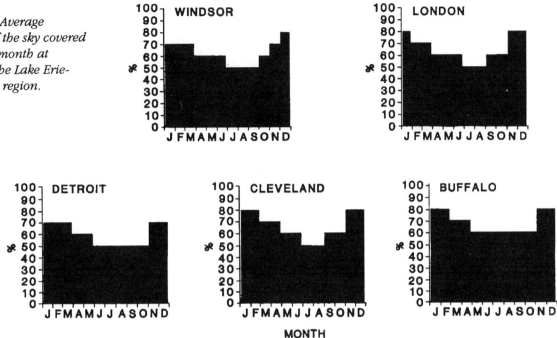

Figure 3.56. Average percentage of the sky covered by clouds by month at locations in the Lake Erie-Lake St. Clair region.

has migrated northward across the basin and the average sky cover in the region diminishes slightly to seven-tenths. In July, sky cover decreases again to five-tenths. The pattern begins to repeat itself in October when the average sky cover for the month raises to six-tenths in the Lake Erie region (Phillips and McCulloch, 1972).

Another factor which increases the cloudiness of the area is the added moisture that air masses receive as they pass over the lake. Figure 3.57 shows that in comparison to other Lake Erie area cities, Buffalo, New York, experiences the fewest days with clear skies. Buffalo, situated to the lee of Lake Erie, receives the effect of the extra moisture in the air.

Since outdoor activities typically are at their peak in the afternoon, it is beneficial to see how cloud cover amounts change for the different hours of the day. Figure 3.58 shows cloud cover amounts for four different months at London, Ontario. In every case the greatest amount of cloudiness occurs during the afternoon. July shows the greatest variation in cloudiness between daytime and nighttime. During fall and winter, the sky is cloudy over half the time, and during summer it is cloudy less than half the time. Figure 3.59 also displays monthly cloud cover, but uses only 1 p.m. readings for the different months. Again it is seen that the winter months, December, January, and February, have the

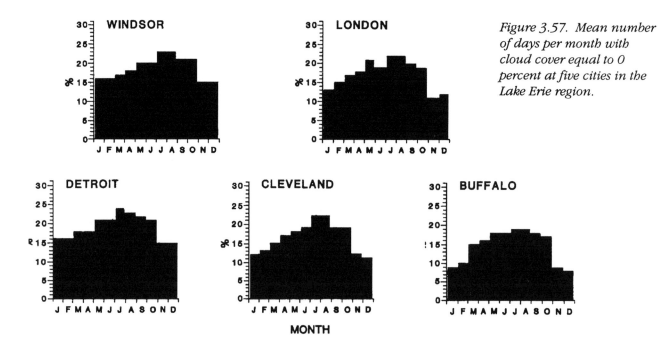

Figure 3.57. Mean number of days per month with cloud cover equal to 0 percent at five cities in the Lake Erie region.

greatest quantity of clouds in the afternoon, with February having the overall highest. July, August, and September have the fewest cloudy days. The month with the most clear sky days in the afternoon is October, and the months with the least are January and November.

Observing clouds gives valuable information concerning the possibility, type, and duration of precipitation. Clouds have a definite bearing on impending weather, and their changing patterns are effective forecasting tools. There are three items to observe: direction, height, and speed.

Direction is important when there are clouds at different altitudes. If the higher clouds are moving in a direction different from that of the lower clouds, or of the surface wind, a change in the weather may soon be coming. The height of the clouds is also a major concern. Very threatening clouds may be visible, but if they remain high and flow with the prevailing wind closer to the surface, the weather will be fair. Near the end of a period of fair weather, clouds may begin to form high in the sky. If these clouds gradually lower, precipitation is expected. Clouds are lower in the atmosphere as a warm front approaches and climb higher as a cold front approaches and the low passes by. Speed is also an important feature to note. The speed of the cloud pattern gives an idea of how quickly present weather conditions will change. Clouds

Figure 3.58. Average frequency of cloudiness (%) in (A) March, (B) July, (C) November, and (D) January in three ranges 0-2, 3-7, 8-10 tenths) for four synoptic hours at London, Ontario (from Crowe et al. 1977).

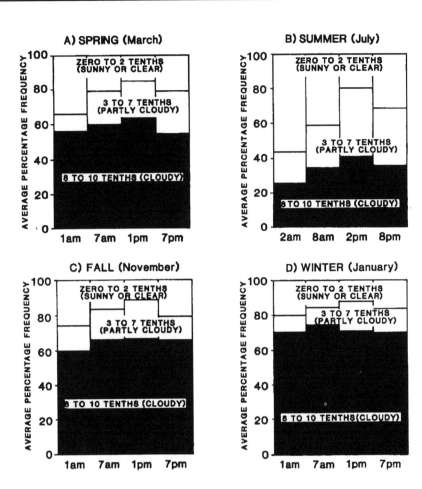

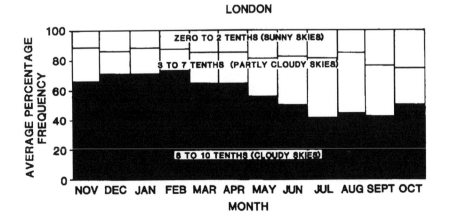

Figure 3.59. Average frequency of cloud cover (%) at London, Ontario at 1:00 p.m. in three ranges 0-2, 3-7, and 8-10 tenths (from Crowe et al. 1977).

moving leisurely across the sky imply fair conditions, whereas a rapidly traveling cloud cover signifies impending adverse weather. The interested reader can pursue this by consulting a book which describes cloud types, including photographs or drawings, and relates those cloud types to current or impending weather conditions. A number of items fitting that description are available, including Allen Watts' Instant Weather Forecasting (Dodd, Mead, New York, 1978; Lib. Cong. Card #68-9173), Vincent Schaefer and John Day's Field Guide to the Atmosphere (Houghton Mifflin, Boston, 1981; Lib. Cong. Card #80-25473), and Eric Sloane's Almanac and Weather Forecaster (Duell, Sloan and Pearce, New York, 1957; Lib. Cong. Card #68-20706).

Thunderstorms and Tornadoes

Severe Weather

The earth experiences about 44,000 thunderstorms each day. Near the base of a thunderstorm, air flows into the core at around 22 mph (10 m/sec). At 25,000 ft (7,620 m), the rapidly rising air within a thunderstorm may approach speeds of 50-60 mph (22-27 m/sec). At the upper extremes of the cloud, wind speeds may be as high as 150 mph (67 m/sec). Thunderstorms present a hazard because of the tremendous amount of energy they possess—energy that may be unleashed at any time and in many different forms. The formula for producing these thunderstorms is to mix warm air with moist air. A vertical "boost" from topography, fronts, or strong localized heating must then be added.

Hills and mountains are excellent breeding grounds for thunderstorms because they provide the proper topographic features to effectively cause incoming warm, moist air to rise. As this air encounters an obstacle such as a mountain or hill, the air tends to climb up and over it. This forced lifting motion is needed to trigger the production of towering thunderstorm clouds if conditions are correct. Areas to the lee of these obstacles usually experience dry air flowing down over the obstacle, owing to the fact that all the moisture was previously condensed out of the cloud during its ascension. Thunderstorms may also be triggered by frontal systems. Thunderheads form in the warm air that is pushed up along a frontal boundary. Along a warm front, warm air is usually lifted slower and over a broader area. Along a cold front, cold air cuts underneath the warm air and lifts it up much more abruptly. Because cold fronts provide a greater lift to the warm air, the vertical air currents, the cloud formation, and the storms are all more intense. If a localized surface region is greatly warmed by efficiently absorbing large amounts of solar radiation, the air above this region will warm quickly and soon will begin to rise. If this rising air is also moist, convective clouds and localized thunderstorms may result. Occasionally, triggering

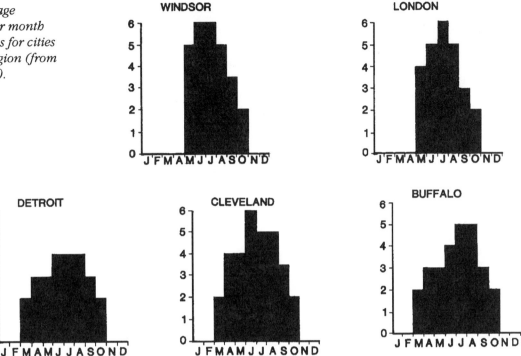

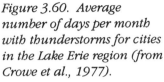

Figure 3.60. Average number of days per month with thunderstorms for cities in the Lake Erie region (from Crowe et al., 1977).

is caused by a combination of these mechanisms in an area. The result of combining any of these lifting processes can be extremely severe if the air is convectively unstable to lifting.

Lake Erie's effect on the development of thunderstorms is part of a complex situation. It is known that in winter, the Lake Erie region has more frontal activity due to the location of storm tracks over the Great Lakes region. This would increase Lake Erie's chances of producing thunderstorms. During winter, however, the land is cold, the air is dry, and Lake Erie freezes over. This suppresses upward air currents over the surface, making it less likely for thunderstorms to develop. However, in summer, both land and lake warm up and moist, unstable air more frequently occurs. Therefore, there seems to be an ongoing battle between factors increasing thunderstorm activity and those decreasing it. How, then, does Lake Erie affect storm activity overall? The Lake Erie region on the average receives 30-40 days per year with thunderstorms (Figure 3.60). This is a moderate amount in comparison to regions such as Florida.

The weather arising from thunderstorms may be particularly hazardous with respect to wind and precipitation, especially if there is no shelter close by. The best way to deal with harsh weather originating from these storms is to avoid it. Nature provides some warnings of approaching storms by changing the patterns of weather elements such as cloud cover, wind, temperature, and pressure. Watching changes in cloud cover changes greatly aids in predicting the onset of inclement weather. When harmless-looking cumulus clouds start building into dark, foreboding towering clouds, thunderstorms are a distinct possibility. For predicting the direction in which a particular storm is heading, the clouds may again be of help. Thunderstorms will normally move in the same direction as the wind 2-3 mi (3-5 km) up. By observing the direction and speed of the middle and uppermost clouds, one can obtain an estimate of the direction and speed a storm will assume. Over the Lake Erie region, thunderstorms usually come from the S-SW-W quadrant. The normal rate of approach ranges from 10-30 mph (4-13 m/sec), though many directions and speeds are possible. Since 10-30 mph (4-13 m/sec) is greater than the normal cruising speed of many boats, boaters should be especially cautious to watch clouds for signs of approaching storms in order to seek shelter in sufficient time. In general, thunderstorms are of short duration and will pass by a particular location in 30 min to 1 h. Note that the entire life of a thunderstorm or group of thunderstorms can be much longer as indicated in Table 3.1 of the Introduction to this chapter.

Surface wind patterns also herald an approaching storm. Perhaps the first effect is the air becoming very still except for a comfortable light breeze. An isolated, developing thunderstorm cloud very gently draws in air at the lower levels over an area 12-15 mi (19-24 km) across. This is what is commonly called "the calm before the storm." It occurs about half an hour before the thunderstorm enters its mature stage. During the mature and dissipating phases, a strong, cold outflow of air from the storm center occurs at the ground. These surface winds may reach 15-25 mph (7-11 m/sec). The leading edge of this downdraft may consist of gusting conditions and is sometimes referred to as the "gust front." This is the home of the most powerful and chaotic surface winds. The wind may even shift 180° as the gust front initially passes. These winds pose special hardships for boaters who must face choppy waters, gusting winds, and changing wind directions.

Very soon after the gust front passes, temperature may begin to drop rapidly in increments of 10°F (5.5°C). This phenomenon is called the "cold dome." A typical drop in temperature for the Lake Erie area during the summer would be from 85°F (29°C) before the gust front approaches to as low as 65°F (18°C) afterward. The area affected by the cooling downdraft is larger than that over which precipitation actually falls. As the storm ages and dissipates, its cooling effect also lessens.

Precipitation also begins just a few minutes after the gust front is first experienced and is heaviest within 2-3 min afterward. Precipitation usually remains heavy for at least 15 min before tapering off. The duration of moderate to heavy precipitation from a single cloud may vary from a few minutes for a weaker system to more than an hour for a large, active thunderstorm.

Some thunderstorm safety precautions:

● **Keep an eye on the weather during warm periods and during the passage of cold fronts.** When cumulus clouds begin building up and darkening, you are probably in for a thunderstorm. Check the latest weather forecast.

● **Keep calm.** At a particular location, thunderstorms are usually of short duration (less than 1 h); even squall lines normally pass within an hour or two. Be cautious, take protective action; if possible seek shelter, stay indoors, and keep informed.

● **Know what the thunderstorm is doing.** Remember that the mature stage may be marked on the ground by a sudden reversal of wind direction, a noticeable rise in wind speed, and a sharp drop in temperature. Heavy rain, hail, tornadoes, and lightning can occur only in the mature stage of the thunderstorm.

● **Conditions may favor tornado formation.** Tune in your radio or television receiver to determine whether there is a tornado watch or tornado warning for your area. A tornado watch means tornado formation is likely in the area covered by the watch. A tornado warning means one has been sighted or radar-indicated in your area. If you receive a tornado warning, seek inside shelter in a storm cellar, below ground level, or in reinforced concrete structures; stay away from windows. If you are outdoors, keep the sky under surveillance and take evasive or protective action as appropriate.

● **Lightning is a risk to life and property.** If indoors, stay away from electrical appliances while the storm is overhead. If lightning catches you outside, remember that it seeks out the easiest—not necessarily the shortest—distance between positive and negative centers.

Keep yourself lower than the nearest highly conductive object, and maintain a safe distance from it. If the object is a tree, a distance of twice its height is considered safe.

● **Thunderstorm rain may produce flash floods.** Stay out of dry creek beds during thunderstorms. If you live along a river, listen for flash-flood warnings from the National Weather Service.

With proper atmospheric conditions, an ordinary thunderstorm cloud in its mature stage may grow to severe proportions and unleash hail, lightning, and even tornadoes. What, then, leads an ordinary thunderstorm cloud to such violence? What are these "proper conditions?"

Topography, frontal passage, and intense local heating all may cause harmless cumulus clouds to build into powerful thunderheads. If any one of these lifting mechanisms gives warm, moist convectively unstable air an unusually strong lift or if the two forces combine, the thunderheads may evolve into a severe thunderstorm.

Severe thunderstorms tend to develop in an atmosphere where the upper air is cool and dry, and the air at the lower levels is warm and moist. This is exactly the atmosphere that forms when warm, moist air of maritime tropical (mT) air masses, blowing in from the Gulf of Mexico, meet the cool, dry air of the maritime polar (mP) air masses descending from the Rocky Mountains (see Introduction to this chapter). When this cool mP air meets the warm, moist mT air flowing at the surface, warm air at lower levels seeks to rise and cold air aloft seeks to sink. This ongoing struggle between the two air masses creates an ideal environment for rapid growth of severe convective storm clouds.

The internal structure of a thunderstorm cloud that produces severe weather conditions is quite different from that of an ordinary thunderstorm. The severe storm cloud must develop an internal anatomy which allows it to grow to heights above the tropopause, from 40,000 ft (12,192 m) to even 60,000 ft (18,288 m). Here the winds may reach speeds of over 100 mph (45 m/sec).

A conceptual model of a severe thunderstorm is shown in Figure 3.61. In his description of this figure, Kessler (1981) states

> Abundant low-level moisture and a conditionally unstable atmosphere triggered large storms as the air was lifted by the topography. Continued uplift triggered new cells in roughly

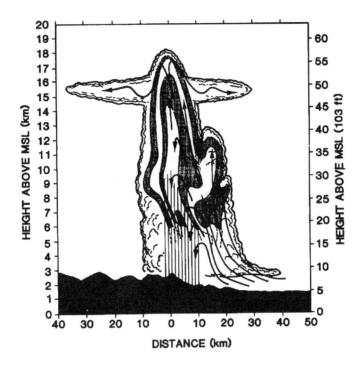

Figure 3.61. Internal structure of a severe thunderstorm cloud (from Kessler, 1981).

the same locations, thereby contributing to the stationarity of the storm system as a whole.

This storm was more intense than most which would be encountered. The intensity of the system and other physical conditions contributed to a devastating flash flood that killed 139 people and caused $35 million in property damage.

The severe thunderstorm is also responsible for the tornado. Tornadoes are funnel-shaped clouds, usually less than a mile (1.6 km) across at the surface, which generally travel out of the southwest (about 90% of the time) at speeds of approximately 30-40 mph (13-18 m/sec), with an average lifetime of 5-30 min. Tornado damage is caused by (1) the tremendous force of the spiraling winds, (2) the intense upward motion of the surface air currents, and (3) the sudden pressure difference between the air outside the tornado and that within the inner core of the tornado.

Lake Erie lies at the northeastern end of a long belt of locations with high tornado frequency extending from Texas to Illinois. This is the route that tornadoes typically tend to follow and is known as "tornado alley." Figure 3.62 shows the average number of days in each month

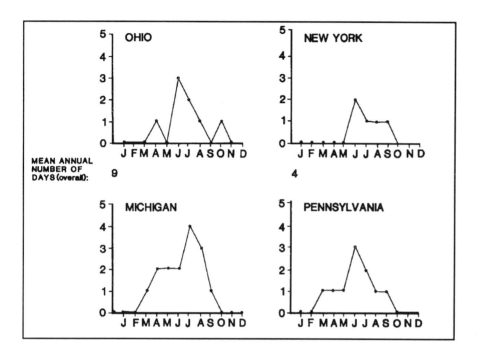

Figure 3.62. Average number of days per month with tornadoes for four states in the Lake Erie area, 1976-80.

with a tornado occurrence for four states in the Lake Erie area. June and July are the months which have the most days with tornadoes.

The surface of the earth is heated most between 4:00 and 6:00 p.m., and thunderstorm activity is at a peak at this time. It is not surprising, then, that about 25% of all tornadoes in the United States take place between 4:00 and 6:00 p.m., and 83% occur between noon and midnight.

The National Severe Storms Forecast Center in Kansas City, Missouri, issues tornado watches. Watches occur when atmospheric conditions are correct to produce severe thunderstorms and therefore possible tornado activity. Such watches are issued for large geographic areas in rectangular boxes called "watch boxes." The tornado funnel is so small in diameter, however, that usually only a very small portion of the watch box is affected. A tornado warning indicates that the direct threat of a tornado touch-down exists in a specific area. Warnings are the responsibility of the local weather service and local television and radio broadcasters. They are based on eyewitness reports or on the observation of a "hook echo" on a radar screen if the local weather station is equipped with radar. The storm is severe because the hook shows up on the screen when a separate vortex forms at the back of the thunderstorm cloud thus bringing the cloud into severe-weather-producing proportions. A problem occurs, however, in that only about half of all tornadoes come from storm clouds that display this hook shape on the radar screen since the radar must be aimed at the cloud in just the right way to see the hook shape with any clarity.

Some radios receive broadcasts of one of the hundreds of National Weather Service radio stations across the country on a continuous basis at frequencies of 162.40 to 162.55 MHz. These stations also broadcast a signal which will automatically switch on some weather radios when tornado warnings are issued.

If a tornado threat occurs, there are a few safety precautions to heed. The safest location in a tornado-stricken area is in some type of underground shelter, in a location in the shelter opposite from the approach direction of the tornado. This is usually the NE corner since about 90% of all tornadoes come out of the SW direction. The NE corner is preferable because debris carried by the funnel is likely to be hurled into the SW corner first, possibly caving it in. However, finding an underground shelter on short notice may be impossible. If there is any type of enclosure nearby, situate yourself in the NE corner of the smallest room. If you are outside with no nearby enclosure when a tornado threatens, the safest thing to do is to lie as flat as possible in the deepest depression available, such as a ditch or ravine which runs perpendicular to the path of the oncoming tornado. Automobiles offer very little protection against a tornado; it is very difficult to maneuver around a tornado funnel. Although tornadoes usually approach at a speed of 30-40 mph (13-18 m/sec), some have been known to move at 60-70 mph (27-31 m/sec).

Squall Lines

Severe thunderstorm clouds may occur as isolated clouds, as a cluster of a few clouds, or as a long, dark line of clouds commonly known as a "squall line." Very often the damage done by squall line thunderstorms far out-measures that of a single cloud or a cluster of severe storm clouds.

A squall line is a long row of very black, ominous looking thunderheads often extending hundreds of miles in length and 40-50 mi (64-80 km) in width, with an average lifespan of 12-24 h (Dabberdt, 1981). The spacing of the individual clouds that make up the line may be 10-15 mi (16-24 km) apart or may be very tightly packed. As thunderheads develop along this row, each cloud's updraft feeds on the downdrafted air from its neighbors, thus intensifying the entire line. Also, the squall

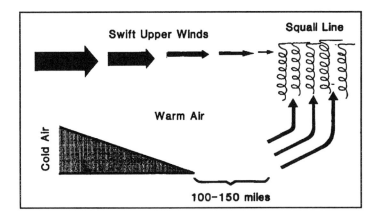

Figure 3.63. Method of squall line formation ahead of a cold front.

line establishes its own circulation, making it easier for new cells to grow downwind from the line. Usually the individual thunderheads move northward along the squall line, while the line itself moves to the east or northeast.   Squall lines are common in the Lake Erie region; the Midwest is one of three areas of the United States to claim the most occurrences of squall line thunderstorms. The other two regions are the states bordering the Gulf of Mexico and states along the mid-Atlantic coast (Whelpey, 1961).

About one-sixth of all squall lines develop directly along a cold front boundary and another one-sixth originate in large air masses not associated with any frontal activity (Dabberdt, 1981). The majority, however, precede very fast moving cold fronts by about 100-500 mi (161-804 km).

Squall lines preceding rapidly moving cold fronts tend to bring extremely severe weather. They seem to be formed by a pressure shock wave set off by the sudden vertical upward movement of warm air as an unusually forceful blast of cold air dips beneath it. Strong upper level winds, moving in the same direction as the front's advance, also play an important role. These winds put a "cap" on this rapidly rising warm air by restraining its vertical motion. Therefore, the warm air is "squeezed" ahead of the cold frontal boundary (Figure 3.63). When it finally flows into a location where it is free to ascend, it does so with almost explosive energy, creating a squall line of potent, severe thunderstorm clouds possessing enormous amounts of energy.

Lightning

Lightning forms when the tremendous updrafts in clouds shear the raindrops and carry them upward into the cloud, separating the raindrops' negative charges from their positive charges. The positive charges then cluster in certain areas of the cloud, and negative charges in other areas. The base of the cloud carries an overall negative charge. As the cloud moves over the earth's surface, the ground (which is normally negatively charged) acquires a surplus positive charge. The positive charge on the ground, recognizing a surplus of negative charge at the bottom of the cloud overhead, rushes up to the highest point of the ground, trying to connect with a companion negative charge. The surface positive charges continue to seek out negative cloud charges until all have a partner and all charges are neutralized. The air, however, keeps the positive and negative charges from each other. Compared to other environmental elements, air is a very poor conductor of electricity. It thus insulates or barricades the cloud and ground charges, serving to prevent any neutralizing flow of current. As the thunderhead becomes more powerful, the attracting force becomes stronger than the hindering force of the air. When this happens, current bursts through the air's resistance in a large surge, and negative and positive charges unite in an electrical spark—lightning.

Lightning may proceed from cloud to cloud, within a single cloud, from cloud to ground, or, where very high structures are present, from ground to cloud. The most common form of lightning—comprising over 60% of all lightning occurrences—is cloud-to-cloud. The next most common lightning is cloud-to-ground. This is the most familiar to observers and also presents the greatest danger. The typical observed cloud-to-ground strike most commonly begins as a "pilot leader" of negative charge which is too faint to be visible (Figure 3.64). The pilot leader advances downward from the cloud and sets up the initial portion of the lightning path. A sudden surge of current called a "step leader" then takes over for the pilot leader. It moves about 100 ft (30.5 m) at a time, making a jagged path to the ground, pausing and repeating the sequence until a path has been forged down to near the ground. "Streamers" extending up from the ground intercept the leader stroke and the path it has created. This completes a jagged path from the cloud to the ground, all of which remains invisible to the unaided eye. When the entire cloud-to-ground path has been constructed, a "return stroke" of positive charge surges up from the ground, illuminating the many branches of the previously invisible downward path. It is this bright light occurring along the return trip that is called lightning. The bright light associated with the return stroke is the result of atoms and molecules of air being energized by the neutralizing return current running up the lightning path. Once the return stroke has completed its upward path, secondary return strokes may occur until all charges are neutralized or the path is broken up by air currents. The entire lifetime

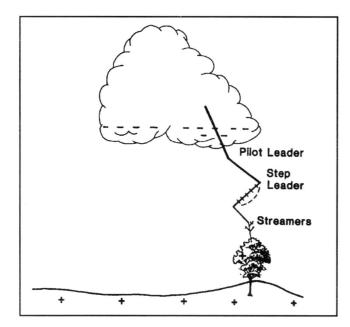

Figure 3.64. Segments of a "cloud to ground" lightning strike.

of the lightning bolt, from the pilot leader to the last return stroke, typically is less than 1 sec.

Recent statistics show that lightning kills, on the average, approximately 110 people per year in the United States. This ranks third (Kessler, 1981) as the most severe storm-related event, after thunderstorm floods (165 people per year) and tornadoes (125 people per year). Yearly damage due to lightning in the United States amounts to approximately $200 million. The Lake Erie region has a particularly high lightning-related fatality rate, with clusters around Cleveland, Ohio; Detroit, Michigan/Windsor, Ontario; and Buffalo, New York. This is probably explained by higher population levels in these areas. Over a 21-year period most fatalities occurred between June and August with an overall peak in July. Most lightning fatalities were in New York and the fewest were in Michigan. Of special concern to those who spend a great deal of time outdoors is the fact that lightning fatalities occur more frequently in open country than inside buildings. About 52% of the fatalities occur in the open, 38% indoors, and 10% under trees (Eagleman, 1983. Of the fatalities occurring in the open, 8% are on open water and 4% on golf courses.

Monthly lightning injuries for the same period do not match exactly with times and places of fatalities. Most lightning-related injuries have taken place between June and August, with the overall peak in August, however. Most of the injuries were in Michigan, and the fewest were in Ohio.

The most dangerous locations outside are under isolated trees, near wire fences, on high ground, and on open water. Safer locations outside are in ditches, valleys, or under a small tree located at a distance of at least twice the height of the nearest tall tree. If you must rely on your automobile for protection during lightning, touch only the seat. You are safe only if you do not touch the metal in your car because metal readily conducts electricity to the ground. Taller objects are most likely to be struck by lightning. An object approximately 300 ft (100 m) high located in a region such as that around Lake Erie—which has about 30 days with thunderstorms per year—may be expected to receive three lightning strikes per year. An object close to 1,000 ft (300 m) high receives approximately 10 strikes per year.

Since lightning strikes open water, it is extremely dangerous to swim during a thunderstorm. Swimmers struck by lightning are most often instantly paralyzed owing to the tremendous shock to the body. Since lightning victims carry no electrical charge—the electricity dissipates almost instantaneously—first aid should be given to the victim immediately.

A tall boat in open water is an ideal target for atmospheric discharges. Radio antennae and sailboat masts are the structures on boats most frequently hit by lightning. Lightning strikes on boats are a rare phenomenon though, and with a few safety precautions boaters can stay out of danger.

When a boat is struck by lightning, it has actually run into a streamer. As a boat passes under the thunderstorm cloud, it contacts the streamer and therefore collects the cloud's excess charge onto itself. Once this initial contact is made, surrounding thunderheads may take advantage of the situation and "dump" their excess charge.

The best way to deal with lightning strikes is to avoid them altogether, but this is not always possible. You can minimize the danger of having a vessel struck, however, by installing a grounding system on the boat. For a detailed description of such a system, a free pamphlet called "Lightning Cone of Protection" is available from:

Michigan Sea Grant
Publications Office
2200 Bonisteel Blvd.
Ann Arbor, Michigan 48109

Even if your boat is grounded correctly, you should still consider
safety precautions (Figure 3.65). Warnings of an approaching thunderstorm should be heeded well before any rain begins to fall; in many
lightning casualties, no rain was falling at the time of the strike. A
common warning system for an approaching electrical storm is an AM
radio. AM radios produce loud hissing or sizzling noises when a storm's
"electrical shadow" passes over the area.

Beneficial Lightning

It may be surprising that lightning provides an important source of
nourishment to our planet—nitrogen. The most abundant gas in the
entire atmosphere is nitrogen, and it is found in the proteins of plants
and animals, including the human body. Yet the nitrogen found in the
air does not contribute to that found in the proteins in the body; unlike
oxygen, humans cannot directly use the nitrogen in the form it is in-
haled. To eventually be used by the body, it must be altered or "broken
down." Breaking down nitrogen is not simple, however. The nitrogen
molecule requires a large blast of energy to break it apart into its individual elements.   Lightning serves as the natural source of the tremendous energy necessary to accomplish this task. When a nitrogen molecule in the air is struck by an electrical discharge, it breaks apart.
Nitrogen is then in a more usable form. Free parts of the nitrogen

---

- *Remain in the center of the cabin of a closed boat when possible.*
- *Don't go in the water or swim until the storm passes.*
- *Keep away from any metal fittings aboard the boat, particularly those which are connected to the lightning conductive (ground) system.*
- *Disconnect the major electronic equipment not being used.*
- *Don't touch the radio equipment or wiring.*
- *On small power boats, lower the radio antenna and keep a low profile below the freeboard.*

Figure 3.65. Lightning safety precautions for boaters (from Lucy et al., 1977).

molecule, the atoms, combine with oxygen and hydrogen in rainwater and form nitric acid (nitrogen fixation). Nitric acid washes into the soil, mixing with minerals to form nitrates. Nitrates are a great source of nourishment for plants. We eat fruits and vegetables, and thus finally receive the nitrogen which is so essential to the body's protein supply.

Thunder

The sounds from which the thunderstorm derives its name are caused by the tremendous current flow along the lightning path. Much of the lightning bolt's energy is used in heating the air along the path it forges to the ground. This conducting channel is typically heated to over 50,000°F (27,760°C) in less than 1 sec. The resulting hot air then expands, but air along the lightning path is heated so excessively and so suddenly that it does not get a chance to expand calmly, but does so violently. The pressure or shock waves that spread out into the atmosphere cause the sound called "thunder."

Hail

Hail is precipitation in the form of balls or irregular lumps of ice, always produced by convective clouds, nearly always thunderstorms. Thunderstorms characterized by strong updrafts, large liquid water content, large cloud-drop sizes, and great vertical height are favorable to hail formation.

The nature of hailstone formation is still being researched, but it is thought that hailstones form near the center of severe thunderstorm clouds between two vortices. Here they are trapped in tremendous up- and downdrafts and are sent on single or numerous trips above and below the freezing line of the towering thunderhead. The updrafts necessary to support large hailstones are quite powerful.

When the hailstone is below the freezing line of the hail-producing thunderhead, it develops a layer of clear ice around itself. When the hail travels upward into the frozen area of the cloud, it then acquires a "milky" ice layer from a more rapid rate of freezing. The hailstone acquires a layered appearance, somewhat like that of an onion. Splitting a hailstone may provide an idea of the number of trips it made through the storm cloud. As the hailstone gains additional layers, it becomes increasingly heavy. When it becomes too heavy for the updraft to support it, the hailstone falls to the ground.

The height to which a severe storm cloud is capable of growing is critical in determining the size of hail it may produce. Thunderstorm clouds which have grown to great vertical extent allow the hailstone to travel above the freezing line for long periods of time increasing the size of the stone. Research has shown that the height of thunderstorms that yield hailstones varies according to the location of the cloud in the United States. Clouds forming in areas where the air is warm and moist must build to greater heights to manufacture hailstones. For example, a storm cloud that reaches approximately 5 mi (8 km) in height in Alberta, Canada, has a 50% chance of producing hail. To get this same probability in Texas, a thunderhead must grow to over 10 mi (16 km) high (Eagleman, 1983).

Each year, the Lake Erie area experiences 1-4 days with hailstorms. The southern portion of the region has the highest percentage of these hailstorms, even though its yearly thunderstorm activity (approximately 30-40 storms) is uniform with that of the rest of the region. This shows that the southern Lake Erie region has slightly better atmospheric conditions for creating hail-producing thunderstorms.

An Illinois State Water Survey study on the number of thunderstorm occurrences around Lake Michigan gives valuable information about the lake's influence on hailstorms (Eichenlaub, 1979). These results can be extrapolated to the Lake Erie region with some adjustments for physical differences in the lakes. In fall, Lake Michigan increased the number of hail days by as much as 400%. This figure may seem a bit frightening, but remember that few hailstorms arise in the Lake Erie area in the first place. An increase of just one day with hailstorms, though, can be critical. One hailstorm lasting only 15-20 min can cause fatalities, injuries, and millions of dollars worth of damage. Over the United States, recent statistics indicate that hail causes fewer than five deaths per year and about $750 million per year in property damage (Kessler, 1981).

Chapter 4

Hydrosphere – The Water

The hydrosphere is defined as the water portion of the earth as distinguished from the solid part, the lithosphere, and from the gaseous outer envelope, the atmosphere. The waters of the Great Lakes are constantly moving and changing. They are sometimes inviting and sometimes threatening, but nonetheless vital to many residents of the Great Lakes basin. To others they provide endless recreational opportunities.

The information in this chapter is intended to provide the sportsman, swimmer, boater, or lake watcher with additional knowledge to further enrich his recreational experiences on the lakes.

An important feature of lakes and rivers related to their physical limnology is their bathymetry—the shape of the bottom of a body of water. Figure 4.1 shows a computerized version of Lakes Erie and St. Clair. Additional bathymetry characteristics, relating primarily to the geology of the region, are contained in the Lithosphere Chapter.

Figure 4.2 shows Lake Huron near Port Huron and Sarnia where water leaves Lake Huron and enters the first of the connecting channels, the St. Clair River. The St. Clair River is dredged for navigation purposes to a minimum depth of 27 ft (8 m) along its navigation channel. All water depths are usually stated relative to Low Water Datum (LWD). For Lake Erie, the LWD is 568.6 ft (173.3 m) above sea level, and for Lake St. Clair it is 571.7 ft (174.2 m) above sea level. This means that the 0-ft level on Lake Erie charts represents 568.6 ft (173.3 m) above sea level. In the North Channel of the St. Clair River delta, the deepest area, it is over 50 ft (15 m) deep. The water level falls a total of about 5 ft (1.5 m)

Figure 4.1. Bathymetry of Lake Erie and Lake St. Clair. The top of each box represents the bottoms of the lakes, the floor of each box represents the contour lines at lake depth.

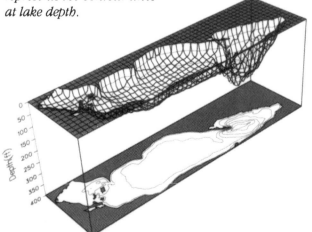

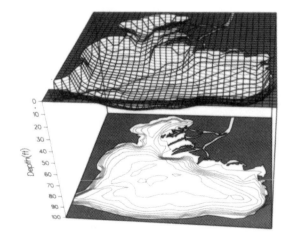

Figure 4.2. Southern Lake Huron to eastern Lake Ontario. See text to trace the flow of water through Lakes St. Clair and Erie.

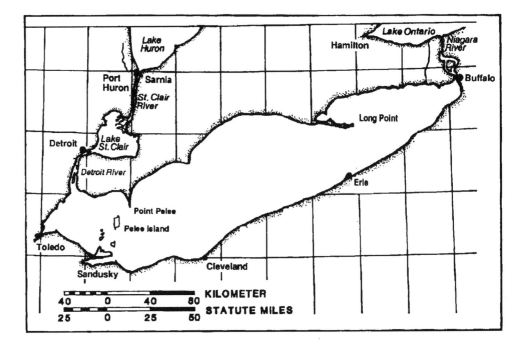

along the St. Clair River. The slope is greatest near Lake Huron and least near Lake St. Clair.

Water then enters Lake St. Clair after passing through the delta of the St. Clair River. Lake St. Clair is quite shallow, particularly near the delta. In fact, sections of the St. Clair River are almost twice as deep as the deepest points in Lake St. Clair. The average depth of Lake St. Clair is only 10 ft (3 m), and its maximum natural depth is only 23 ft (7 m). It too is dredged to 27 ft (8 m) along the navigation channel. Water leaves Lake St. Clair through the Detroit River (shipping channel dredged to a depth of 27 ft [8 m]). The water level falls about 3 ft (1 m) as it passes through the Detroit River to Lake Erie.

Water leaves the Detroit River to enter the first of three basins of Lake Erie. This first basin, the western basin, extends from the Detroit River to Point Pelee, Ontario, and is shallow, having an average depth of only 24 ft (6 m). The deepest area of substantial size is in the north and runs through the Pelee Passage, the region between Point Pelee and Pelee Island. Next, water enters the very flat central basin. The central basin is the largest basin in Lake Erie both in terms of area and volume (mean depth 60 ft [18 m]). The mean depth of the eastern basin is 80 ft (24 m) and in places it is deeper than 200 ft (60 m). It is separated from the central basin by a bar which extends from the north shore almost all the way to the south shore. Water leaves Lake Erie through the Niagara River, the last of the connecting channels between Lake Huron and Lake Ontario. The slope of the Niagara River is quite steep along most of its length. The total drop on the Niagara River is 326 ft (98 m), over half of which is at Niagara Falls.

Table 4.1 shows some characteristics of the regions just described (Coordinating Committee on Great Lakes Basin Hydraulic and Hydrologic Data, 1977).

Water Levels and the Water Budget

Water levels in the Great Lakes play a major role in our enjoyment of the lakes. High water levels often cause property damage particularly during storm periods and destroy valuable beaches. Low water levels cause problems for boaters and marina operators. Information is provided on the following pages on the water levels and the water budget (the natural factors that control the amount of water in the lake) of Lake Erie.

	Lake Erie		Lake St. Clair	
Water Volume (mi³) (km³)	116	(484)	1.0	(4.0)
Water Surface Area (mi²) (km²)				
U.S.	4,980	(12,900)	162	(420)
Canada	4,930	(12,800)	268	(694)
Maximum Depth (ft) (m)	210	(64)	21*	(6.4)
Shoreline Length (mi) (km)				
U.S.				
Mainland	431	(693)	59	(95)
Islands	43	(69)	84	(135)
Canada				
Mainland	368	(592)	71	(114)
Islands	29	(47)	43	(69)

*Deepest sounding outside dredged navigation channel which has depth of 27 ft (8.2 m).

Table 4.1. Characteristics of Lake Erie and Lake St. Clair.

```
┌─────────────────────────────────────────────────────────────┐
│                        NOAA CHARTS                          │
│                                                             │
│                Distribution Branch (N/CG33)                 │
│                 NOAA National Ocean Service                 │
│                    Riverdale, MD  20737                     │
│                                                             │
│                                                             │
│                  LAKE LEVEL BULLETINS                       │
│                                                             │
│  Department of the Army                                     │
│  Detroit District, Corps of Engineers   Department of Fisheries and Oceans │
│  Attn:  NCEED-L                          Ocean Science and Surveys │
│  P.O. Box 1027                           P.O. Box 5050      │
│  Detroit, MI  48231                      Burlington, Ontario, Canada  L7R 4A6 │
└─────────────────────────────────────────────────────────────┘
```

Table 4.2. Addresses from which additional information can be ordered.

Figure 4.3 shows the long-term average annual water levels for Lakes Erie and St. Clair. On a month-to-month basis, lake levels tend to be lowest in winter and highest in late spring or early summer (Figure 4.4). The difference between the maximum and minimum levels can be significant. A copy of an up-to-date monthly bulletin of lake levels for all of the Great Lakes may be obtained free of charge by writing to the address in Table 4.2. The lake level graphs illustrate the results of the water budget of each lake. The pieces of that budget and how they affect the water levels are discussed below.

The water budget for Lake Erie is composed of a number of factors which contribute to either the inflow, outflow, or change in the amount of water stored in the lake.   Figure 4.5 shows the breakdown of total water inputs and outputs for Lakes Erie and St. Clair. Inflow or supply factors include:

- the inflow of the Detroit River,
- the precipitation falling on the lake surface, and
- the runoff into the lake from rivers in the lake basin.

Included in the outflows are:

- the outflow through the Niagara River and the Welland Diversion,
- evaporation from the lake surface, and
- the consumptive use of water from the lake (use of water by man which is not returned to the lake).

The difference between the inflow and the outflow is the change in storage, which in turn changes lake levels. The same factors apply with

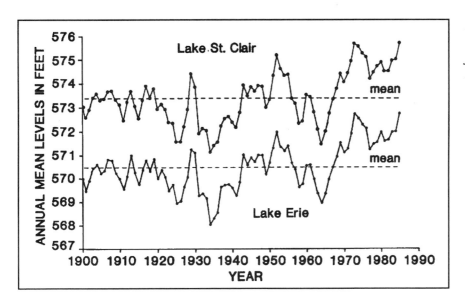

Figure 4.3. Average annual water levels from 1900 to 1984 for Lakes Erie and St. Clair (data from F.H. Quinn).

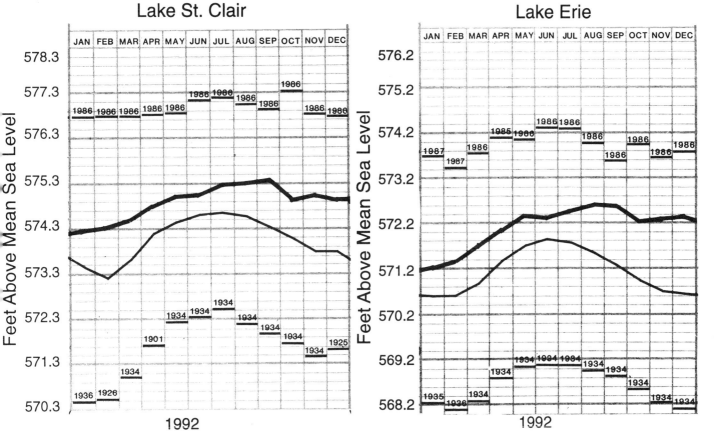

Figure 4.4. Annual water level cycle for Lakes Erie and St. Clair during 1992 (upper trace). Lower trace is the 1900-1991 average lake level. Upper and lower bars indicate record maximum and minimum water levels and their year of occurrence (from U.S. Army Corps of Engineers data).

Figure 4.5. Breakdown of total water inputs and outputs for Lakes Erie and St. Clair.

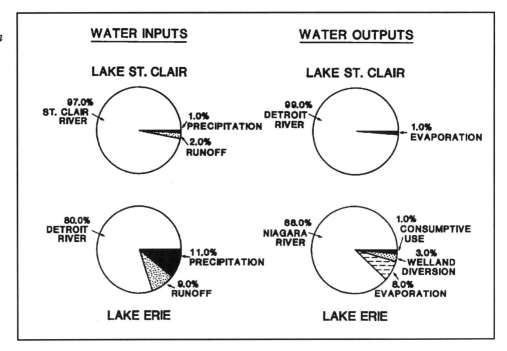

respect to Lake St. Clair except that the inflow is from the St. Clair River and the outflow through the Detroit River.

The largest terms of the water budget are the flows in the St. Clair, Detroit, and Niagara Rivers. The St. Clair River contributes 97% of all water inputs to Lake St. Clair; the Detroit River contributes 80% of all water inputs to Lake Erie. The Niagara accounts for 88% of the water outflows from Lake Erie compared with 3% for the Welland Diversion. In Lake St. Clair, the Detroit River is responsible for 99% of all water outflows.

Precipitation directly on the surface of the lake constitutes about 11% of the total water input to Lake Erie and about 1% to Lake St. Clair. Figure 4.6 shows precipitation directly on the water surface of Lake Erie on a monthly basis. Runoff, the addition of water to a lake from rivers and streams within the lake's basin, contributes 9% of the total water input to Lake Erie (Figure 4.7) and about 2% of the input to Lake St. Clair.

The largest river contributing to runoff in the Lake Erie basin is the Maumee. It alone adds 25% of the runoff to Lake Erie. The Maumee River has a large flow due to the configuration of Lake Erie's drainage basin which is largest in the southwestern corner, the Maumee River's location. Rivers on the southeast shore of Lake Erie tend to be quite

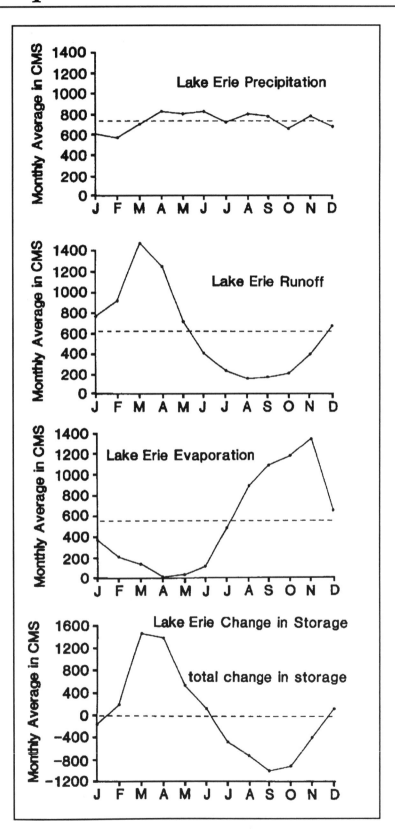

Figure 4.6. Lake Erie precipitation by months in cubic meters per second (from Quinn and Guerra, 1986). Horizontal line is the average value for the year.

Figure 4.7. Lake Erie runoff by months in cubic meters per second (from Quinn and Guerra, 1986). Horizontal line is the average value for the year.

Figure 4.8. Lake Erie evaporation by months in cubic meters per second (from Quinn and Guerra, 1986). Horizontal line is the average value for the year.

Figure 4.9. Lake Erie change in storage by months in cubic meters per second (from Quinn and Guerra, 1986). Horizontal line is the average value for the year.

small, since the drainage basin there is so narrow. North of Lake Erie, most of the land drains either into Lake St. Clair or Lake Ontario. The drainage areas of Lakes St. Clair and Erie together are about three times the surface water area of the lakes themselves. Precipitation on the watershed of the lakes contributes approximately the same amount of water into these lakes as precipitation falling directly on the surface of the lakes. If all water that fell on the watershed ran into the lakes, runoff would contribute three times as much as precipitation directly on the surface of the lakes. However, only about one-third of the water falling on the watershed makes its way to the lake. The rest is lost to the air by evaporation from the soil and by transpiration (the process by which water is lost from the leaves of plants).

The consumptive use of water is the smallest term in the water budget and amounts to about 1% of the total water output from Lake Erie (International Joint Commission, 1985). Detailed scientific studies on the consumptive use of water from Lake St. Clair have not been made. Evaporation constitutes about 8% of the total loss of water from Lake Erie and 1% of the total water loss from Lake St. Clair. Figure 4.8 shows the average monthly evaporation from Lake Erie. Due to the high spring runoff and low evaporation, storage of water in Lake Erie is highest in the spring. It is the lowest in the fall due to high evaporation and low runoff. Figure 4.9 shows the month-to-month changes in storage for Lake Erie.

Lake Erie

Water Temperature

Water temperatures are important to a wide variety of recreational and commercial users of Lake Erie. A beach outing can be ruined if it is too cold to swim, and fish activity is also influenced by the temperature of the water. The seasonal cycles of surface water temperature and average water temperature in each of the Lake Erie basins have been studied by Schertzer et al. (1987) and are illustrated in Figure 4.10 for the April through November period each year from 1967 through 1982. Data are based on 90 lakewide surveys. These curves clearly demonstrate seasonal lags in the average water temperature throughout the entire depth relative to the surface water temperature. These lags are related to the heat storage capacity of each basin. The western basin is the shallowest and heats to its maximum temperature at a faster rate in the spring than the other basins. It also cools at a faster rate in the fall primarily due to the more efficient wind-induced mixing of the water. In the spring, the warming of the deeper eastern basin lags behind the warming of the central basin. The eastern basin also retains its heat for longer periods during the fall. Comparison of the surface water tem-

Figure 4.10. Long-term mean seasonal (April-November) cycle of water surface temperature and vertically integrated temperature for Lake Erie basins (from Schertzer et al., 1987).

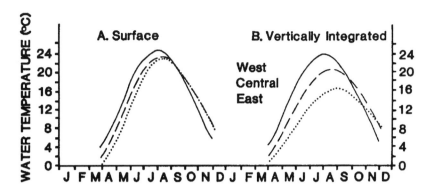

perature to temperature at different depths for the western basin reveals nearly identical values and, hence, demonstrates almost vertically mixed water throughout the year. Comparisons for the deeper basins show substantial differences in temperature for the same time periods between surface temperatures and temperatures at depth during periods where the water is stratified.

The gradient in temperature between the water surface and the lake bottom can be substantial in the summer months and varies considerably over the lake basins (Schertzer et al., 1987). Figure 4.11 shows a summary of average monthly surface water temperatures and corresponding near-bottom temperatures. Generally, surface water temperature increases progress from the shallower western basin to the east during the spring. Surface water temperatures in the summer are rather uniform over the lake, and temperature decreases quite rapidly in all portions of the lake during October and November.

The average surface water temperature and average air temperature for each month are shown in Figure 4.12. In May, the average air temperature is 57°F (13.9°C), and the average water temperature is 48°F (8.8°C). In June, the average air temperature increases to 67°F (19.4°C), and the average water temperature rises to 62°F (16.7°C). The shape of the curve is a loop since water temperature lags air temperature. Air temperature peaks in July and water temperature peaks in August. In winter, air temperatures are the lowest in January, while water temperatures are the lowest in February. For almost half of the year, the air is warmer than the surface water. In spring and fall, this temperature difference is greatest. The small cross inside the loop shows the yearly average air and surface water temperatures. The graph shows that the average annual air temperature is less than the average water temperature by about 2°F (1°C).

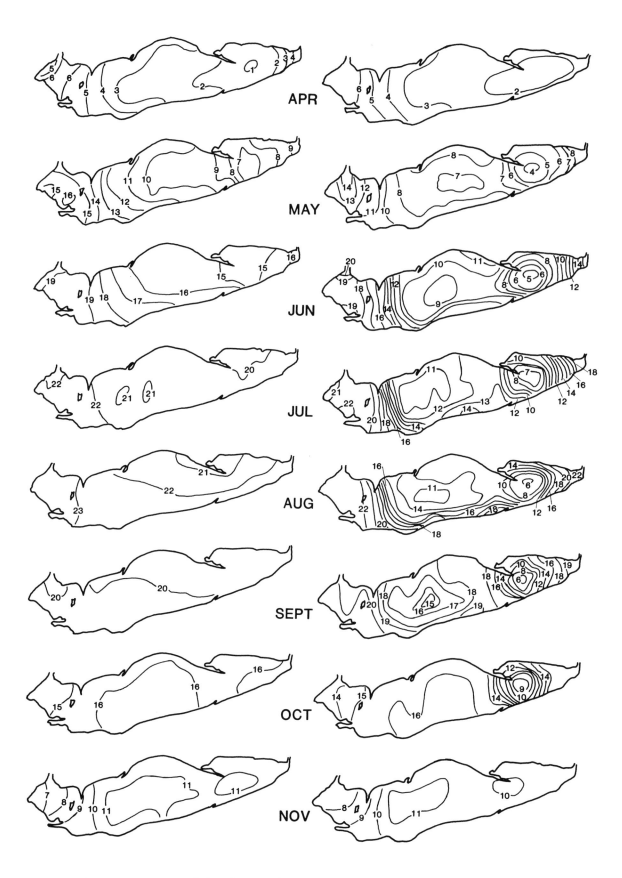

Figure 4.11. Average spatial distribution of water surface temperatures and near-bottom water temperatures based on long-term lakewide temperature surveys (from Schertzer et al., 1987).

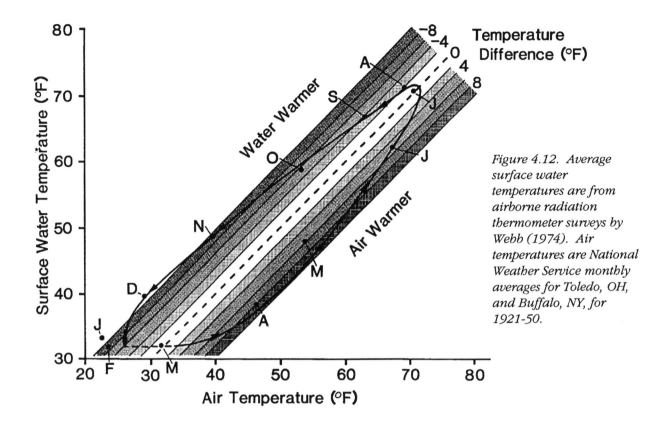

Figure 4.12. Average surface water temperatures are from airborne radiation thermometer surveys by Webb (1974). Air temperatures are National Weather Service monthly averages for Toledo, OH, and Buffalo, NY, for 1921-50.

In contrast to the general uniformity of the monthly mean surface water temperature, the spatial distribution of the mean bottom temperatures (taken within 1 m of the bottom) is more complex (Figure 4.11). The spatial distribution of mean bottom temperatures in April is similar to that of the surface. The mean temperature of the western basin is above 39°F (4°C), in contrast to the other basins (Figure 4.10). Bottom temperature values for summer are highest in the western basin while the central basin shows relatively cool bottom water, and the eastern basin has the coldest temperatures as a consequence of its greater depth; this is particularly apparent in the temperature contours in the deepest section off Long Point, Ontario (Schertzer et al., 1987).

Figure 4.13 provides examples of extreme differences between surface and near bottom temperatures using selected locations within the deeper sections of each basin. For the April-November period, the average monthly difference between surface and near-bottom temperatures is very small for the western basin. Maximum differences average approximately 16°F (9°C) for the central basin and 27°F (15°C) for the deepest location in the eastern basin (information from Schertzer et al., 1987).

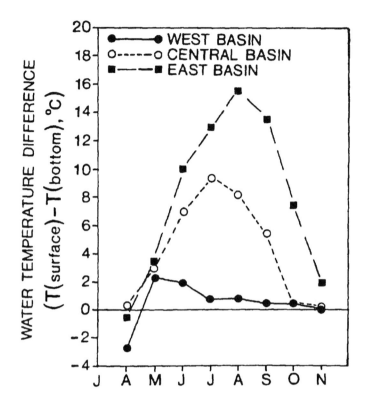

Figure 4.13. Long-term monthly means of the average difference between surface and near-bottom water temperature for selected deep water locations in Lake Erie basins (from Schertzer et al., 1987).

An outline of the annual thermal cycle in Lake Erie is given in Mortimer (1986) and can conveniently be started with conditions under winter ice cover. Because of its size and wind exposure, the whole lake cools down, in a fully mixed condition, to 34°F (1°C) or less in January before the ice cover is fully formed, with solid sheets nearshore and in bays, and with broken sheets offshore kept in intermittent motion by the wind. In mild winters, large areas of open water persist, creating a "moveable sieve with irregular openings" through which wind action keeps the water column fully mixed in contrast to the stratified situation which develops in lakes with a fully sealed ice cover. A study covering only one winter shows that apart from some weak stratification at the western end of the western basin, the remainder of the lake was isothermal (essentially, the same temperature throughout the water column) at 32°F (0.1°C) or less by late February and had become entirely isothermal from end to end at 32°F (early April) with much open water, slight warming (but with water columns everywhere isothermal) was noted, up to 34.7°F (1.5°C) in the middle of the central basin, but only up to 32.9°F (0.3°C) in the eastern basin (April 10-11). The study suggests that when the ice leaves the open water areas of the western and central basins, typically by late March, the water column is isothermal at 34°-36°F (1°-2°C). Warming then begins first in shallow nearshore water, in which stratification first appears.

During spring, significant heating of the lake occurs as a result of the increased solar radiation (Schertzer et al., 1987). Figure 4.14 illustrates basin-wide average temperature profiles for the central and eastern basins in April-October 1979. The western basin, as indicated in Figure 4.10, heats and cools at a faster rate than the rest of the lake and remains essentially a uniform temperature from top to bottom throughout the year. For the other basins, the average temperature profiles in the first survey period (April 24-26) still show essentially isothermal conditions for the central and eastern basins. In May, the eastern basin has increased in temperature but remains isothermal while the central basin has undergone significant heat gains. The thermal layers are not stable and are easily perturbed by wind events at the surface. Stratification usually begins in mid-June for the central basin; however, because of meteorological events, the third sample period (June 10-14) does not show a well-defined thermal stratification. Eastern basin heat gains are also evident in June with a relatively large temperature difference between temperatures at the surface and temperatures at the 49 ft (15

Figure 4.14. Basin-wide averaged vertical temperature profiles for the central and eastern basins of Lake Erie from lakewide temperature surveys during 1979 (from Schertzer et al., 1987.)

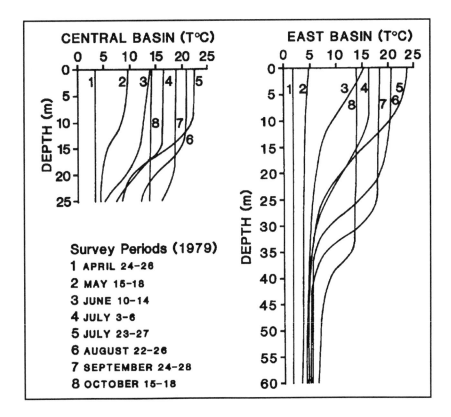

m) depth. Stratification is firmly established in the central and eastern basins by the fourth survey period in July. Maximum heat storage generally occurs in mid-August and, as indicated in the August 22-26 survey, average temperatures in the upper layers of both the central and eastern basins are decreasing in response to decreased surface heating and greater heat losses through the surface to the atmosphere. Average temperature profiles for the central basin in the September 24-28 survey indicate nearly uniform surface to bottom temperature. By the last survey, October 15-18, the central basin is isothermal and the eastern basin rapidly approaches an isothermal condition. Further heat losses result in a uniform lowering of temperature in each basin and by mid-December, Lake Erie approaches minimum temperatures thus completing the annual cycle.

Based on temperature profiles collected using accurate instruments over a variable grid of stations during the stratified season, Schertzer et al. (1987) studied the thermocline, the layer of water that separates the warmer, upper zone of water from the colder, lower zone. They determined the depth of the top and bottom of the thermocline in the central basin (Figure 4.15). The influence of the surface winds is evident in the larger depth variability of the upper boundary of the thermocline compared to the lower boundary. These data indicate that the central basin develops a thermal structure in which the depth of the thermocline can

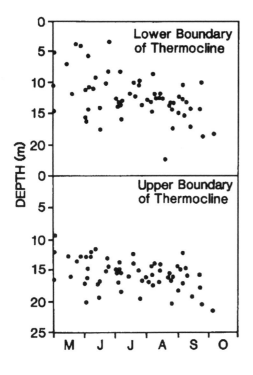

Figure 4.15. Long-term variability of depth of the upper and lower boundary of thermocline in the central basin (from Schertzer et al., 1987).

vary significantly from year to year. For any particular period during the stratified season, the range in either interface depth can be as large as 33 ft (10 m).

Lake St. Clair

Two features of Lake St. Clair greatly influence its water temperature. The first is its shallow (10 ft [3 m]) mean depth. Due to this, Lake St. Clair warms quickly in the spring and cools quickly in the fall. Also because of this, water temperatures are almost always the same from top to bottom. The second is that the water in Lake St. Clair is replaced quickly by inflow from the St. Clair River. The temperature of Lake Huron therefore has a strong influence on the temperature of Lake St. Clair. This is especially true in the western half because most of the water from the St. Clair River enters the lake from the north and middle channels. As in Lake Erie, temperatures in Lake St. Clair peak in August. On the eastern shore, temperatures average about 75°F (24°C) in July and August. On the western shore, temperatures are usually lower by 3°-7°F (2°-4°C). Temperatures are highest in the shallows near shore. A summer thermocline is rare in Lake St. Clair. In the fall, the lake is warmest near the outlet of the St. Clair River and coldest in the near-shore shallows (a reversal of the summer pattern). Water temperatures are at or just above freezing for most of the winter and begin rising in mid-March.

The average monthly surface water temperatures for Port Huron, Michigan, Belle Isle, Michigan, Marblehead Point, Ohio, and Buffalo, New York, are shown in Figure 4.16. The seasonal patterns of the four locations differ. Lake Huron water at Port Huron is the coldest of all the stations during the summer.   From Port Huron, water passes through

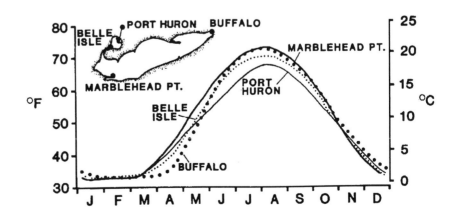

Figure 4.16. Monthly surface water temperatures at four locations. Data are from Derecki (1978) and Grumblatt (1976).

two quite shallow areas. The first is Lake St. Clair. At Belle Isle from May to October, water is warmer than at Port Huron due to Lake St. Clair's warming effect. The next shallow area is western Lake Erie. Water at Marblehead Point, in western Lake Erie, is warmer than at Belle Isle from April through October. In late fall and early winter, however, water is cooled in these shallow areas. At Buffalo, the water remains cool for most of spring because prevailing southwestern winds cause winter ice to drift to the eastern end near Buffalo. Once the ice has melted, the temperature rise at Buffalo is rapid. Buffalo has the warmest water temperatures of all four locations from October through January, because eastern Lake Erie is so deep and thus, slow to cool.

Currents

Current patterns in Lake Erie influence activities in a variety of ways. Boaters may want to take advantage of the surface currents. Shoreline property owners are interested in currents in the nearshore area. Fishermen may want information on deeper currents that could influence fish movement. Rescue groups may need to know where downed aircraft or disabled boats have drifted. Each group of users needs to know about different aspects of lake currents. The following pages supply some of that information.

The current patterns in Lakes Erie and St. Clair and the associated connecting channels are complex. Water currents are generally different at the top and bottom of the water as well as near and offshore. Surface currents are generally the same as the bottom currents in the rivers and in Lake St. Clair, but are quite different in most of Lake Erie.

Lake current patterns differ from river current patterns. Small scale current patterns differ from large scale, whole-lake current patterns. Currents also change with time, sometimes quite rapidly. These changes can seem random but are not. Currents are influenced by the thermal structure of the water, wind stress on the surface of the water, the earth's rotation, and the shape of the lake's basin. In the following review, some generalized, long-term current patterns of both the lakes and rivers will be shown along with other information which will provide an idea of what happens when the general patterns are perturbed by influences such as changing winds.

The three main causes for water movement:

1. Water that is higher in one place than in another. Gravity causes the water to flow from the high to the low place;

2. Friction between air and water associated with the surface wind causes air to drag the water with it;

3. Denser water which tends to flow to a position beneath less dense water. Density differences may be due to either differences in temperature or differences in concentration of dissolved or suspended material.

Once generated by these forces, the currents can be affected by the shore and bottom boundaries and the earth's rotation. The most obvious effect of the boundaries is that they force the water to flow parallel to themselves. The earth's rotation causes water to be deflected to the right of its motion in the Northern Hemisphere. This rightward turning effect (the Coriolis effect) has two important consequences for currents. The first is that currents will tend to flow to the right of the force moving the water. The second is that water influenced only by this force will follow a circular path.

The circular motion due to the Coriolis force is called inertial motion. However, it is only one type of periodic motion. Another major type of periodic motion, the seiche, owes its existence to the restoring force due to the water slope. The period of inertial motion depends on the latitude and the earth's rotation rate; for Lake Erie this is about 17 h. The period of seiche motion depends on gravity, water depth, and the size of the water body; for Lake Erie, seiches can have periods of 14 h or less.

General Current Patterns

Lake Erie. As stated in a report by Saylor and Miller (1984), "Efforts to measure water currents and to derive circulation patterns in Lake Erie are at best frustrating." The difficulties are due in large part to problems with the instrumentation required to accurately measure currents in the many shallow portions of the lake. Since accurate data on the currents is sparse, the general circulation pattern of Lake Erie is best shown by combining this data with mathematical models. Gedney and Lick (1972) developed a model which produced the horizontal velocities shown in Figures 4.17a-e at various water depths. A wind speed of 10.1 m/sec (23 mph) from the direction shown in the figures was used to drive the model and presumed to be uniform over the entire lake surface. It is important to note that the velocity scale varies from plot to plot.

Descriptions taken substantially from Gedney and Lick's report best tell the story. In Figures 4.17a and 4.17b, the surface water is being transported towards the eastern and southern boundaries. A subsurface

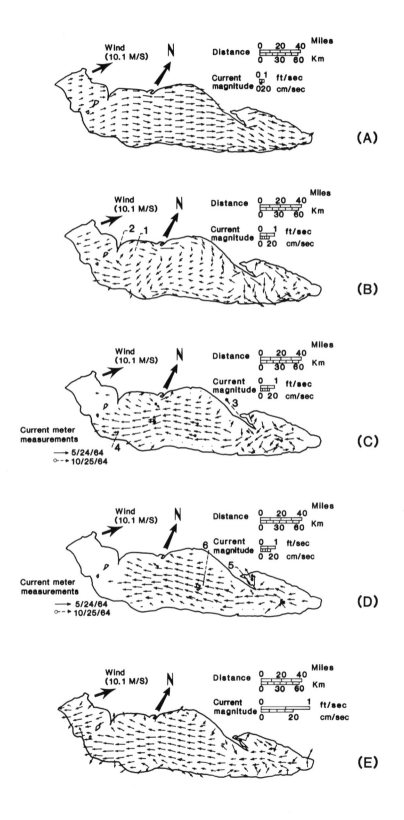

Figure 4.17. Horizontal velocities at a constant distance from surface (from Gedney and Lick, 1972): (a) 0.4 m (1.3 ft), (b) 6.7 m (22 ft), (c) 9.9 m (32.5 ft), (d) 14.9 m (48.9 ft), and (e) horizontal velocities at a constant 1.2 m (3.9 ft) from bottom).

current returns in the opposite direction (Figures 4.17c-e). In the central and eastern basins, surface currents at 0.4 m (1.3 ft) are, in general, smaller in the center of the lake than near the shore. This effect is essentially due to the relatively large subsurface return current down the center of the lake which is opposite in direction to the surface current and subtracts from it. The gyre at point 1 in Figure 4.17b is largely due to a narrow underwater ridge

In examining these figures, one should keep in mind that the current vectors are for only one wind speed and direction. The actual wind speed and direction are, of course, highly variable. Nevertheless, the wind used by the model is from the general direction expected during a large portion of the year, and the water velocity vectors are considered by many scientists to accurately depict the overall circulation pattern of Lake Erie in a reasonable manner.

According to two published reports (Federal Water Pollution Control Administration, 1968; Hamblin, 1971), in the western basin, most of the water from the Detroit River flows along the northern part of the basin and out through the Pelee Passage (the region between Point Pelee, Ontario, and Pelee Island). In several places along the shore, water is carried toward the shore by gyres. Such gyres generally exist on both sides of Lake Erie where the Detroit River water just enters the lake. The currents in the islands region south of Pelee Island are quite variable but are generally to the east. In the central and eastern basins, the current is generally to the east or southeast on the surface and opposite on the bottom.

Varying wind directions used in the model will produce current patterns different from those shown in Figure 4.17. Figure 4.18 shows the surface and bottom current patterns produced in the vicinity of the Lake Erie Islands by winds from a variety of directions. Unlike the previous set of figures, these diagrams were produced from actual current measurements collected over a 10-year period and used to create the average current maps (Herdendorf and Braidech, 1972).

The wind is usually not steady for long intervals of time. In central and eastern Lake Erie large, gyres are created by the common wind distributions and time variations (Federal Water Pollution Control Administration, 1968; Blanton and Winklhofer, 1971; 1972). There are often two gyres in the eastern basin. The southern one rotates counterclockwise, and the northern one rotates clockwise. In the central basin, there are often two large gyres. The western one rotates counterclockwise, and the eastern one rotates clockwise. These gyres strongly affect currents from near the surface to near the bottom. About a third of the

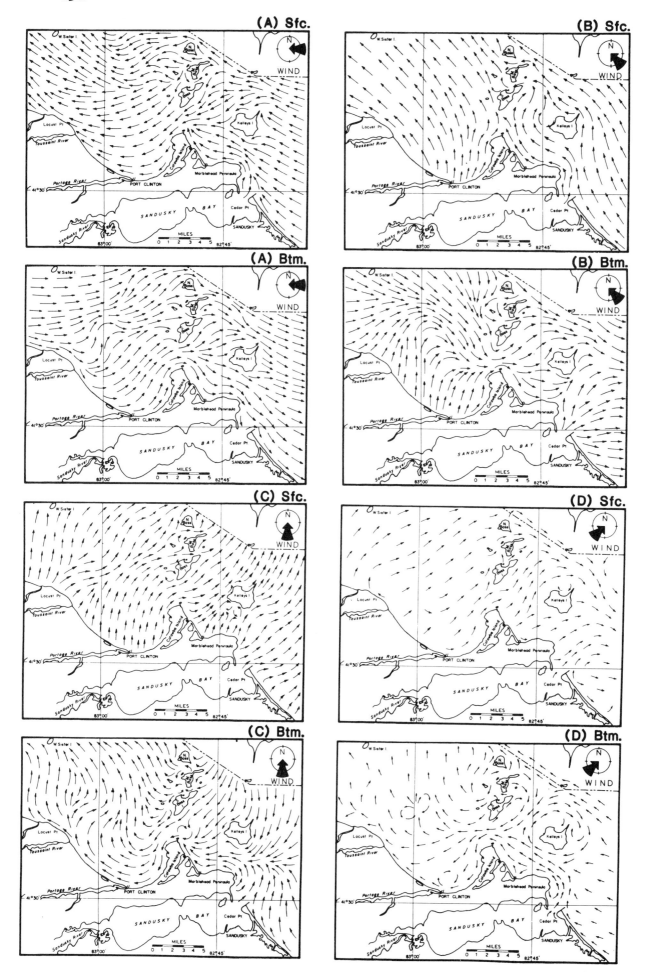

Figure 4.18. Surface and bottom currents in the eastern Lake Erie region (island region) (from Herdendorf and Braidech, 1972). (a) moderate east wind, (b) moderate southeast wind, (c) moderate south wind, and (d) moderate southeast wind.

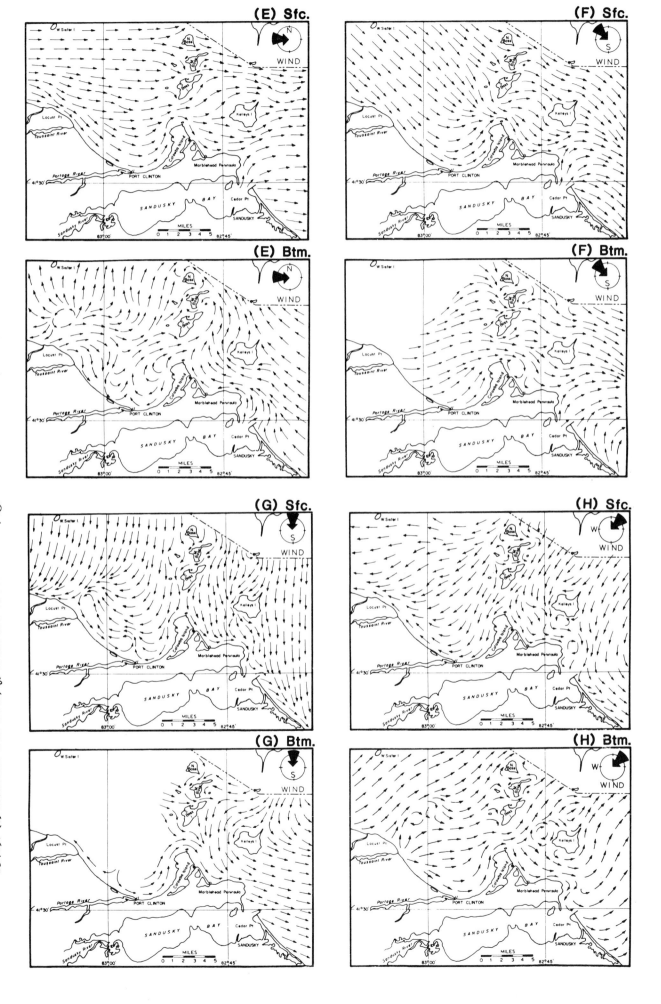

Figure 4.18 (cont). Surface and bottom currents in the eastern Lake Erie region (island region) (from Herdendorf and Braidech, 1972). (e) moderate north wind, (f) moderate northeast wind, (g) moderate northwest wind, and (h) moderate west wind.

time, one of the two gyres of the central basin predominates—usually the clockwise gyre. The central and eastern basin gyres are illustrated in Figure 4.19.

Lake St. Clair. The currents are largely dominated by the flow from the St. Clair River to the Detroit River. In most places, flow is generally toward the Detrioit River. Current speed is essentially greatest near the rivers and along a line from the north channel of the St. Clair River to the Detroit River. Figures 20a-c show circulation patterns as developed from a mathematical model. Although no data exist yet to confirm these patterns, they provide information which appears to be reasonable. The maps show the current at near-surface and near-bottom for various wind directions. There is a tendency for the upper and lower water to flow in the same direction in strong winds. Speeds are high near the Detroit River, but are usually much slower in other areas.

Figure 4.19. Common central and eastern basin gyres (from Saylor and Miller, 1983).

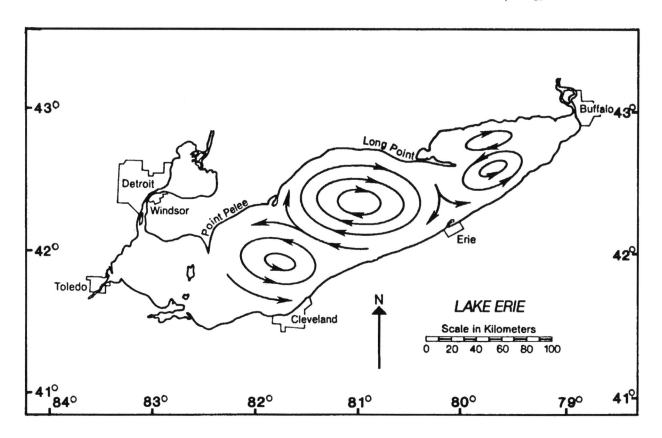

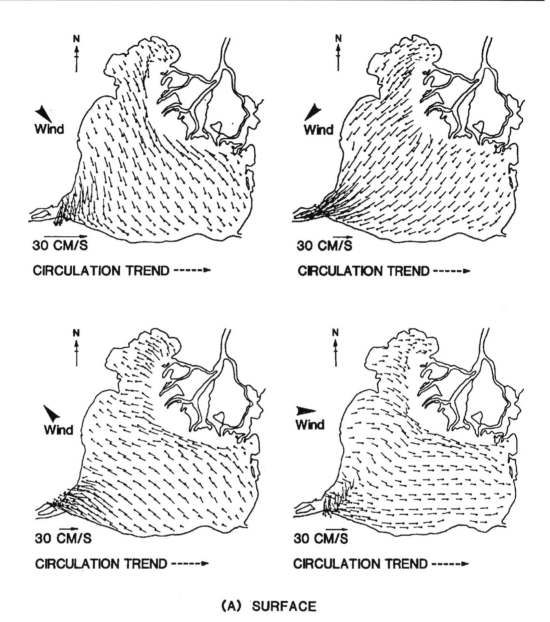

(A) SURFACE

Figure 20a. Lake St. Clair (a) surface, (b) bottom, and (c) vertically integrated circulation patterns. Winds are long term and from the northwest, northeast, southeast, and west at 8 m/sec (18 mph). Length of the current flow arrows are proportional to current velocities. A 30-cm/sec (.6 mph) current scale is shown as well as the circulation trend (dotted flow arrows). Modeled surface velocities are given in 24a (0.0 depth below the surface); near-bottom velocities are given in 24b (0.8 depth below surface—80% of the depth from the surface to the bottom); and vertically integrated velocities in 24c (current velocities at various depths are added and subtracted from each other) (from Ibrahim and McCorquodale, 1985).

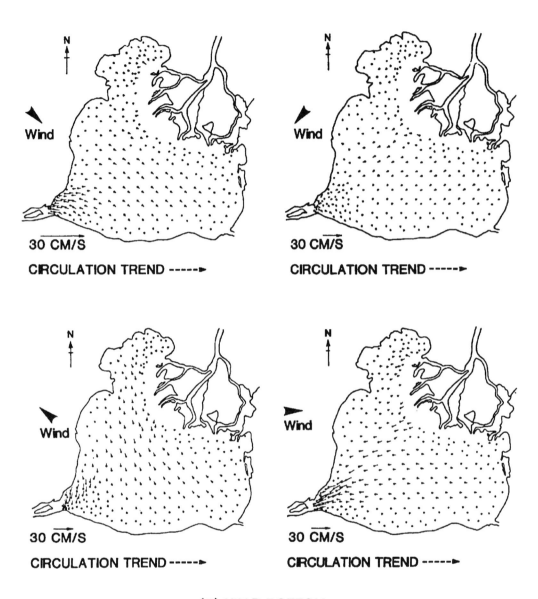

(B) NEAR BOTTOM

Figure 20b. Lake St. Clair (a) surface, (b) bottom, and (c) vertically integrated circulation patterns. Winds are long term and from the northwest, northeast, southeast, and west at 8 m/ sec (18 mph). Length of the current flow arrows are proportional to current velocities. A 30-cm/sec (.6 mph) current scale is shown as well as the circulation trend (dotted flow arrows). Modeled surface velocities are given in 24a (0.0 depth below the surface); near-bottom velocities are given in 24b (0.8 depth below surface—80% of the depth from the surface to the bottom); and vertically integrated velocities in 24c (current velocities at various depths are added and subtracted from each other) (from Ibrahim and McCorquodale, 1985).

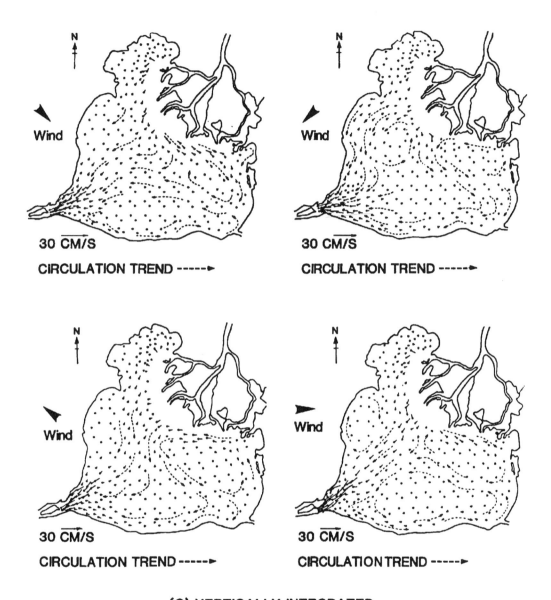

(C) VERTICALLY INTEGRATED

Figure 20c. Lake St. Clair (a) surface, (b) bottom, and (c) vertically integrated circulation patterns. Winds are long term and from the northwest, northeast, southeast, and west at 8 m/sec (18 mph). Length of the current flow arrows are proportional to current velocities. A 30-cm/sec (.6 mph) current scale is shown as well as the circulation trend (dotted flow arrows). Modeled surface velocities are given in 24a (0.0 depth below the surface); near-bottom velocities are given in 24b (0.8 depth below surface—80% of the depth from the surface to the bottom); and vertically integrated velocities in 24c (current velocities at various depths are added and subtracted from each other) (from Ibrahim and McCorquodale, 1985).

Seiche Currents

Because the sloshing action of seiches is back and forth (see Storm Surges and Seiche section in this chapter), currents they cause are also back and forth. Seiches have an effect not only on current speed, but also on direction. A longitudinal seiche on Lake Erie will cause a northeast current, followed by a southwest current, followed by a northeast current, and so on. The time for one complete cycle (for example, from NE to SW and back to NE) is the period of the seiche. The slowest cycle, the first-mode seiche, has a period of about 14 h. The second, third, and fourth modes have periods of about 9, 6, and 4 h respectively. The different sloshing modes can be mixed in any proportions. The mixing of the different seiches can make currents in a given place change in a rather complex way.

A first-mode longitudinal seiche has its largest effect in the western basin just west of Point Pelee. Here, maximum current speeds are 1 mph (0.45 m/sec) for a seiche with a wave height of 1 ft (0.3 m). Since seiche heights of 1 ft (0.3 m) are common, seiches can have a large effect on currents. Seiche currents change quickly. For example, suppose a first-mode, 1-ft (0.3-m) seiche was generating a 1 mph (0.5 m/sec) eastward current at midnight. At 3:30 a.m., 3.5 h later, the seiche current would be zero. Seven hours later at 7 a.m., the current speed would be about 1 mph (0.5 m/sec) westward. At 2 p.m., 14 h later, it would be east again with a speed of somewhat less than 1 mph (0.5 m/sec). When a first-mode seiche current reverses, it reverses everywhere. The current direction is the same throughout the lake for a first-mode seiche. That is, if current is west in one place, it is west everywhere. For a second-mode seiche, current directions are opposite in the eastern and western halves of the lake. Maximum current speeds are again in the western basin, where they exceed 1 mph/ft (5.2 km/h/m) of seiche height. In the eastern part of the central basin, they reach a maximum of about 0.5 mph/ft (0.22 m/sec/ft) of seiche height. Current speeds of first- and second-mode seiches will add. This means that if they simultaneously reach a speed of 1 mph (0.45 m/sec) east, the net flow will be 2 mph (0.9 m/sec) east. However, if one seiche current is 1 mph (0.45 m/sec) east and the other is 1 mph (0.45 m/sec) west, the two will cancel and the net flow will be zero.

The third-mode (6-h) seiche has its greatest effects on currents in the western basin and in strips across the lake near Fairport, Ohio and Erie, Pennsylvania. The fourth-mode seiche has its greatest effect in the western part of the western basin. The effects of these two modes are more local than the effects of the first two modes. Currents in the western basin are much affected by seiches of all longitudinal modes largely due to the shallow depth there. Currents in the western basin are also highly variable during periods of seiche activity.

Lake seiches can be very important to river flow. For example, if a Lake Erie seiche brings water in the western basin up a few feet, the Detroit River flow can be slowed greatly. Surface flow can even be reversed. When the seiche lowers the western basin water, the Detroit River flow will increase. Likewise, the flow of the Niagara River is affected by seiches, although somewhat less so. Seiches have little effect on the St. Clair River since seiches at its mouth and source are usually quite weak.

Inertial Currents (Oscillations)

Inertial currents, like seiche currents, have a regular, periodic character. They are more important in Lake Erie than in Lake St. Clair or the rivers. Unlike seiches, however, all inertial currents have the same period (near 17 h), and currents near the bottom move in the direction opposite surface currents when the water is stratified. Inertial currents are due to the Coriolis force. These currents are discussed in Verber, (1965, 1966) and Hamblin (1971).

The Coriolis force is due to the rotation of the earth. Because inertial currents are usually mixed with other types of currents, water does not usually follow a complete circle even if inertial currents are strong. Figure 4.21 shows the path of a particle as estimated from a 10-day

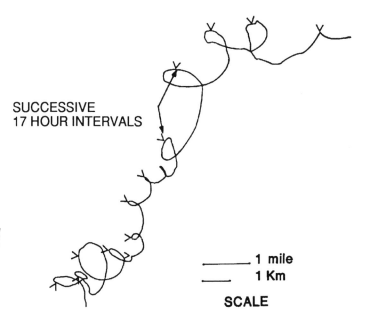

SUCCESSIVE
17 HOUR INTERVALS

1 mile
1 Km
SCALE

Figure 4.21. The looping path followed by a water parcel due to inertial currents (from Hamblin, 1971).

current history at one place in Lake Erie. The particle follows a general southwest movement. Superimposed on it, however, is a looping motion. This looping has a 17-h period and is due to inertial currents. Inertial currents are most commonly seen in regions of the lake which are stratified. Therefore, the 17-h periods of inertial currents are most common during summer in the deeper parts of the central or eastern basins of Lake Erie.

Alongshore Currents

Alongshore currents are near and parallel to the shoreline. They are caused primarily by waves breaking on the coasts and can reach 3 mph (1.3 m/sec) in storms. Figure 4.22 shows the general direction of alongshore currents on Lake Erie. Point Pelee, Pointe aux Pins, and Long Point were created by sediment carried by alongshore currents. At these places, which are all on the northern shore in Ontario, alongshore currents converge, carrying and then depositing beach material.

Current Pattern Examples

As mentioned earlier in this section, current patterns in Lake Erie are influenced by a number of factors. The generalized current patterns shown earlier serve to illustrate what the large scale currents might be

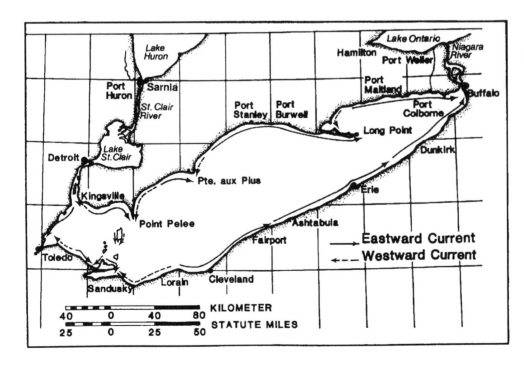

Figure 4.22. Lake Erie alongshore currents (after Herdendorf, 1975).

under certain specific conditions. Other types of currents such as inertial and seiche currents, and those caused by changing wind speed and direction, all interact to give the current observed at any instant. Each day and even each hour can bring changing conditions.

Perhaps the best way to gain additional understanding of currents and their changing nature is to look at some examples of current data collected in the lakes. Figure 4.23 shows current velocities at several locations in Lake Erie during two different 4-day periods in 1979. The first sequence shows currents at three depths around the lake. The direction and speed of the current at a point is indicated by an arrow with its foot at that location. The solid line arrows show currents in the range 15-30 ft (4.6-9 m) deep, the dotted line arrows 30-60 ft (9-18 m) deep, and the dashed line arrows greater than 60 ft (18 m) deep. Arrows show the mean daily current velocity. Currents at the very surface are not shown but would follow winds somewhat more closely. Currents on September 8 did not fit a strong overall pattern, although speeds near shore tended to be higher than those offshore. On September 9, when winds were light, speeds were generally lower but again stronger near shore. The stronger winds on September 10 raised the current speed and gave the central basin a general clockwise circulation. That pattern remained the next day, even though the wind turned to the opposite direction. This circulation pattern persisted for another 11 days.

Another sequence is shown starting on October 1 (Figure 4.23). On that day, winds were light and the central basin had a two-cell circulation pattern. Current speeds were generally low except in some places in the eastern and western basins. The stronger winds of October 2 generated faster currents but no clear overall circulation pattern emerged. However, on October 3, stronger winds turning to the southwest gave the central basin a strong counterclockwise circulation pattern which lasted for 11 days. The general circulation in the central basin on October 4 was the reverse of that for September 11.

These are fairly typical examples that illustrate several features of Lake Erie circulation: 1) the circulation pattern can change greatly within a few days; 2) speeds can change quickly; 3) the current can change at one location even if the general circulation pattern has not changed; and 4) currents only a few feet below the surface can have direction quite different from the wind direction.

To illustrate the degree of variability and periodicity in the currents, Figures 4.24a-d show hourly current speed and direction at four loca-

DAILY RESULTANT CURRENTS AT ALL DEPTHS

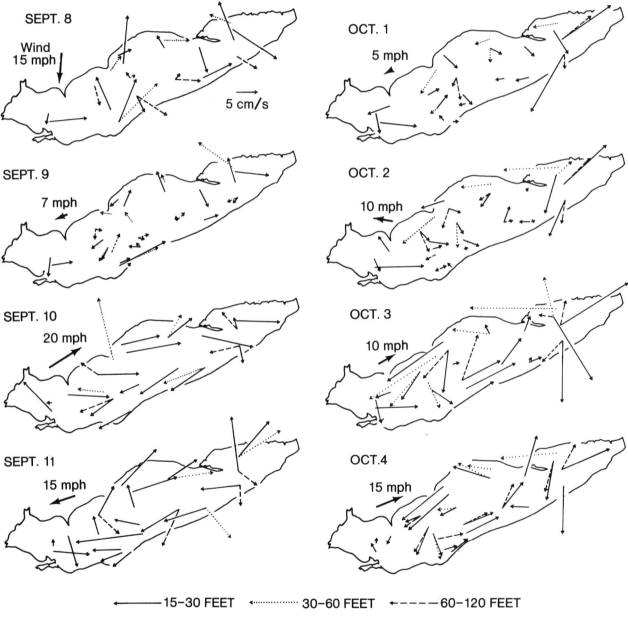

Figure 4.23. Examples of average daily currents in Lake Erie (data from J.H. Saylor).

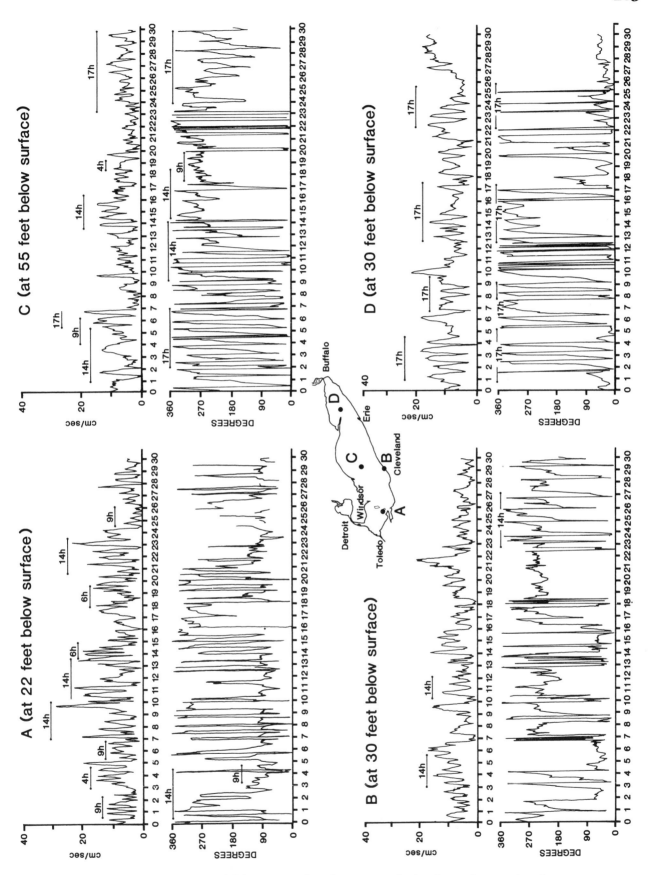

Figure 4.24. Average hourly currents during September 1979 with the four stations marked on the inset (data from G.S. Miller).

tions in Lake Erie for the month of September 1979. These examples are for locations (see inset) in the western basin (a), near shore (b), in the central basin (c), and in the eastern basin (d). The graphs show that there is a considerable variation in both speed and direction. However, much of the variation has regularities.

At location A, 22 ft (6.7 m) below the surface, there were numerous examples of currents changing with periods of 14, 9, and 6 h, the three most important seiche periods. Seiche currents were particularly strong in the channels between the Lake Erie Islands and in the western basin, because it is so shallow. At location B, 30 ft (9 m) below the surface, seiche action was much less noticeable largely because location B is near the shore which has a large influence on the currents. Nearshore current directions predominate along the shore. Currents between September 4 and September 7, and at other times of the month, followed the shoreline to the northeast (65°). Currents at 245° followed the shoreline to the southwest between September 18 and September 22 and at many other times. In fact, the current at location B persisted in one direction for long periods of time. Current speeds were, for the most part, slower than at the other locations.

Location C is in the central part of the lake. Here, seiche action was quite noticeable. Examples of current changes with 17-, 14-, 9-, and 4-h periods are shown. Inertial currents were more important here than at locations A or B because this spot is deeper and farther from shore. Between September 2 and September 7 there was an example of a continuously rotating current. Every 17 h the current returned to the same direction. At location D in the deep, eastern basin, only a periodicity of 17 h was common. These inertial currents were important here because the water is deep, stratified, and not too close to shore. Current speeds were fairly high here, but less variable than at the other locations. Figure 4.25 shows current speed distribution for one location in central Lake Erie during one year. The graph shows the frequency of speeds greater than a certain value. For example, speeds exceed 0.6 mph (0.27 m/sec) about 0.01% of the time, and they exceed 0.2 mph (.09 m/sec) about 10% of the time.

River Currents

The speed of river flows is far from uniform. Factors such as bottom slope, depth, width, shorelines, and time of year play a major role in speeding up or slowing down river currents. Figure 4.26 demonstrates some of these factors. A constriction in the river will speed up the flow, as will a steep bottom. Further, the center of the river—where it is usually deepest—will exhibit greater flow speeds than shallower shore-

Figure 4.25. Cumulative frequency of current speed at a 30 ft (9.1 m) depth at the station shown in central lake Erie for May 1979-April 1989 (data from G.S. Miller).

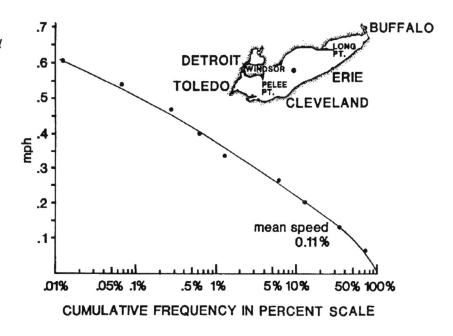

Figure 4.26. Current cross-sections of the St. Clair River (from U.S. Army Corps of Engineers data).

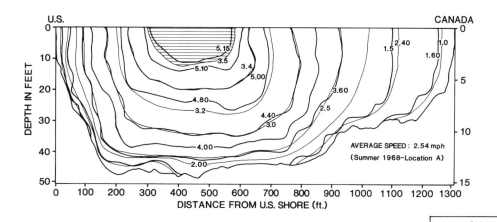

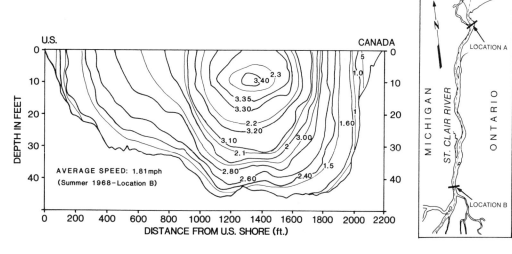

line waters. The general path of a river affects currents; for example, currents are usually the fastest, and water the deepest, on the outside of a bend. Because friction is greatest on the bottom and near the shore-lines, speeds at these areas are slower. Still, the surface is very often not the place where the greatest speeds occur; in fact, quite often the most rapid currents are under the surface. There are seasonal variations and weather affects currents on the river as well. Usually, speeds are highest after the spring thaw and slowest during the coolest part of winter. Ice jamming on the St. Clair River affects lake levels and flows in other portions of the system. Figure 4.27 shows average monthly flows in the connecting channels for 1950-79.

St. Clair River. Current speed is greatest near the Blue Water Bridge at Port Huron and least near the delta (Figure 4.26). Where speeds are great, the river is narrow and the slope is steep. Generally, hourly flow is less variable than in either the Detroit or Niagara Rivers. Monthly variation is greater, however, due to winter ice jams. Over a period of a few days, flow may increase by 20%, and occasionally by as much as 50% due to storms.

Detroit River. Speeds are highest near the Ambassador Bridge where the river is rather narrow, and in some areas of the lower river where the slope is high. Flow is quite variable on an hourly and daily basis, primarily due to setup on Lake Erie caused by strong winds that

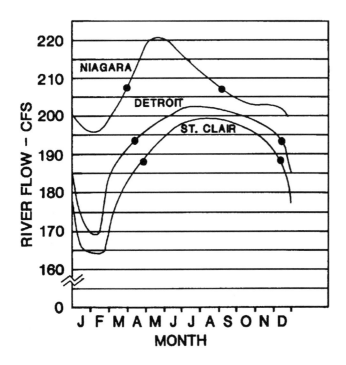

Figure 4.27. Average monthly flows in the connecting channels (from Quinn and Kelley, 1983.)

> ## GETTING USED TO CURRENT SPEEDS
>
> **Water current speeds are measured in a number of different common units. Speeds less than 1 mph can be hard to visualize. It is helpful to know that a speed of 1 mph is about 1.5 ft/sec. Here are some other conversions:**
>
> **1 mph = 1.61 km/h**
> **1 mph = 44.7 cm/sec**
> **1 mph = .87 knots**
> **1 mph = 1.47 ft/sec**
> **1 mph = .447 m/sec**

can raise or lower the lake level in western Lake Erie. The effect is great because the total drop along the Detroit River is only 3 ft, and storm surges exceeding 3 ft occur several times a year. Although the mean Detroit River flow is about 180,000 cubic ft per second (CFS) (5,094 m³/sec), its flow ranges from 50,000 CFS (1,415 m³/sec) to nearly 300,000 CFS (8,490 m³/sec). When the level of western Lake Erie exceeds the level in Lake St. Clair (due to setup or seiche action), surface currents can reverse. This reversal of normal current direction is, among all the connecting channels on the Great Lakes, a unique feature of the Detroit River.

Niagara River. Speeds are very high near the Peace Bridge, and below Grand Island speeds are high and even dangerous. This area is restricted and unsafe for boats. Flow is almost as variable as it is on the Detroit River. Seiche action and setup can significantly affect water currents. Average flows in all of the Lake Erie - St. Clair connecting channels are shown in Figure 4.27.

Waves

Surface Waves

Any casual observer of Lake Erie knows that its water is constantly in motion. That portion of water motion known as wind waves can often be either a pleasure for recreation, as in swimming in a mild surf, or a destructive force, as with storms which cause damage to shoreline property or boats. Wind waves appear on the lake surface as constantly changing crests and troughs with irregular and variable shapes. They are generally described in three categories: wave height is the vertical distance between a crest and its adjacent trough; wavelength is the horizontal distance between two successive crests; wave period is the time required for two successive crests to pass a fixed point. Thus, a wave period is the time it takes a wave to travel the distance of one wavelength. As these terms are derived from simple sinusoidal waves, wind waves have been further described by a significant wave height defined as the average height of the highest one-third of all waves and a dominant wave period defined as the period that corresponds to the peak of wave energy distribution. The "wave height" and "wave period" used here will mean "significant wave height" and "dominant wave period," respectively.

Wind waves in the Great Lakes are studied to describe the wave climate and to relate the wave characteristics with the causative force— the applied surface wind stress. Such studies aid in the design of harbors and structures placed in or on the lake, in increasing the safety of navigation and recreational activities, and in understanding the physical properties affecting shore erosion. Long-term objectives of these studies include improvement in forecasting wind waves in the Great Lakes.

The following wave statistics were derived from measurements made during the period 1981-84 by a National Oceanic and Atmospheric Administration (NOAA) NOMAD buoy located in the western Lake Erie area as shown in Figure 4.28. NOMAD buoys have been placed throughout the Great Lakes to aid in describing over-lake weather and wave conditions. The buoys first consisted of aluminum, boat-shaped hulls 20 ft (6 m) long with a 10 ft (3 m) beam and were later replaced by discus-shaped buoys, 9.8 ft (3 m) in diameter. A combination chain/synthetic line serves as a mooring. The automatic weather monitoring system is battery powered. The buoy reports wind speed and direction,

Figure 4.28. Location of NOMAD buoy.

barometric pressure, dry bulb air temperature, surface water temperature, maximum wind gusts, and one dimensional wave spectra (from which significant wave height and period can be obtained). The buoys transmit data to a satellite that retransmits the data to processing centers in Maryland. It is then disseminated over the National Weather Service communications circuits.

Observed monthly wave statistics are summarized in Figures 4.29-4.38 which show the distribution of significant wave height and wave period for the open-water season. Data are not available for other than the open-water period since the buoys are usually removed from service before the lake freezes. The figures give the percentage of time a given wave height or wave period is exceeded versus the height or period of the wave (in meters and seconds, respectively) on a logarithmic scale. For instance, the case for which wave height exceeds 2 m (6.6 ft) happens less than 2% of the time during March but more than 6% of the time during November. These results clearly indicate that waves in the autumn are much higher than those during the summer. This is due to the fact that in autumn, the atmospheric boundary layer becomes unstable, and wind speeds and wind stress across the air-water interface are enhanced.

When the water is cooler than the air just above its surface, a stable atmospheric boundary layer exists. A stable boundary layer acts like a blanket that shields the water from the winds: the wind can't get a good "bite" on the water, and waves are lower than they would be if the air and water had the same temperature. A stable boundary layer is most common over Lakes St. Clair and Erie during March-May. During these months, waves are often somewhat lower than at other times when the overland wind has the same speed.

The opposite effect occurs in the fall when the water temperature is higher than the air temperature. The water is frequently warmer than the air, and an unstable atmospheric boundary layer exists especially during October to December. During unstable boundary layer conditions, stronger surface winds frequently occur and higher waves are generated.

Internal Waves

Waves of another kind, called internal waves, are invisible to the observer on the surface and occur inside the lake along the thermocline of a thermally stratified lake. Internal waves have periods longer than surface waves, and variations of the depth of the thermocline can exceed 30 ft (9 m). Internal waves that have periods close to 17 h are some-

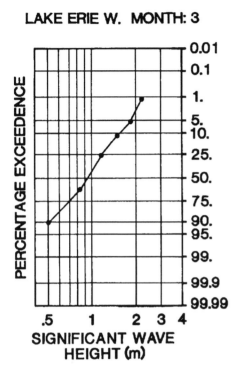

LAKE ERIE W. MONTH: 3   1982 – 1983: 674 Data

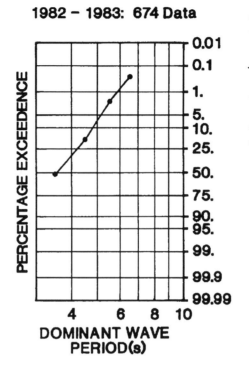

Figure 4.29. Percent average exceedance of wave height and period for the month of March at the NOMAD buoy location. Note period of record and number of data points (data courtesy of P.C. Liu).

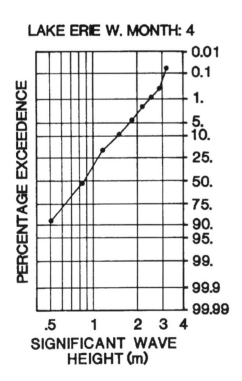

LAKE ERIE W. MONTH: 4   1981 – 1984: 166 Data

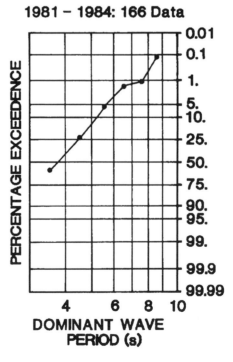

Figure 4.30. Percent average exceedance of wave height and period for the month of April at the NOMAD buoy location. Note period of record and number of data points (data courtesy of P.C. Liu).

Figure 4.31. Percent average exceedance of wave height and period for the month of May at the NOMAD buoy location. Note period of record and number of data points (data courtesy of P.C. Liu).

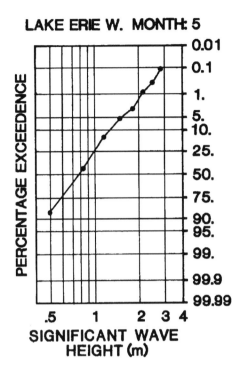

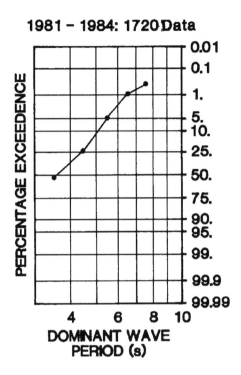

Figure 4.32. Percent average exceedance of wave height and period for the month of June at the NOMAD buoy location. Note period of record and number of data points (data courtesy of P.C. Liu).

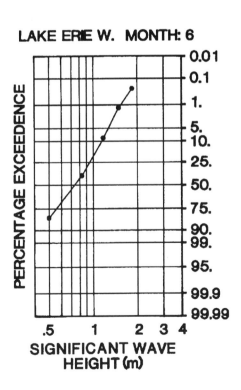

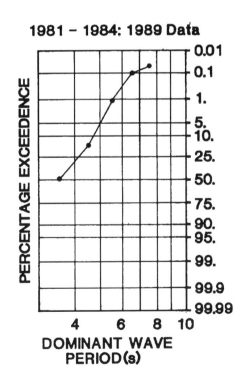

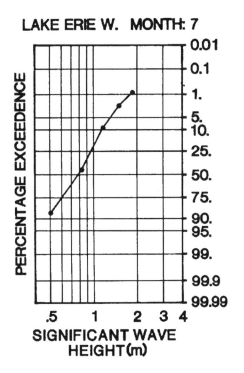

LAKE ERIE W. MONTH: 7

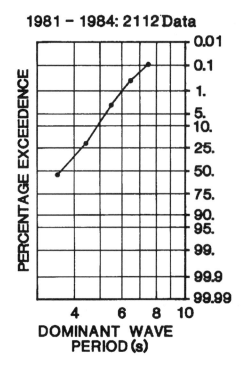

1981 – 1984: 2112 Data

Figure 4.33. Percent average exceedance of wave height and period for the month of July at the NOMAD buoy location. Note period of record and number of data points (data courtesy of P.C. Liu).

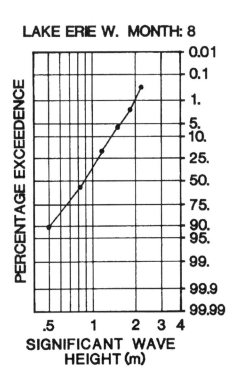

LAKE ERIE W. MONTH: 8

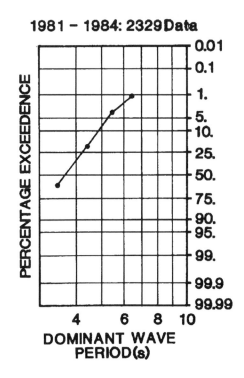

1981 – 1984: 2329 Data

Figure 4.34. Percent average exceedance of wave height and period for the month of August at the NOMAD buoy location. Note period of record and number of data points (data courtesy of P.C. Liu).

Figure 4.35. Percent average exceedance of wave height and period for the month of September at the NOMAD buoy location. Note period of record and number of data points (data courtesy of P.C. Liu).

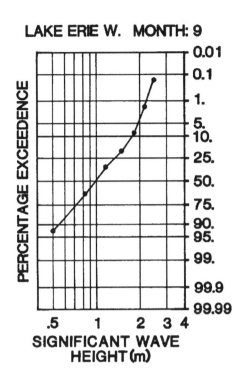

LAKE ERIE W. MONTH: 9

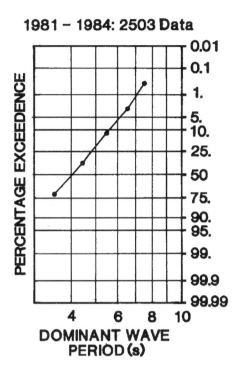

1981 – 1984: 2503 Data

Figure 4.36. Percent average exceedance of wave height and period for the month of August at the NOMAD buoy location. Note period of record and number of data points (data courtesy of P.C. Liu).

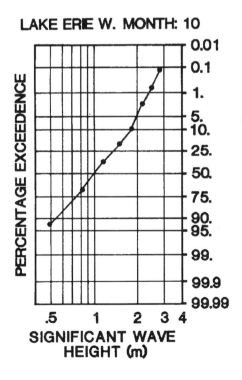

LAKE ERIE W. MONTH: 10

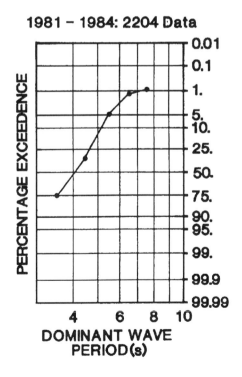

1981 – 1984: 2204 Data

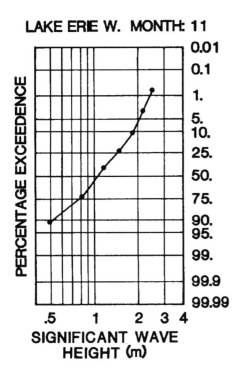

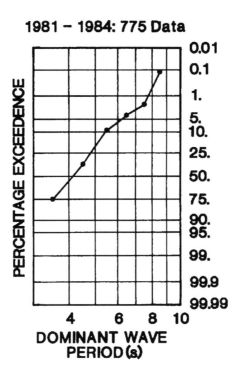

Figure 4.37. Percent average exceedance of wave height and period for the month of November at the NOMAD buoy location. Note period of record and number of data points (data courtesy of P.C. Liu).

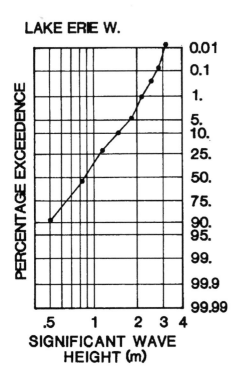

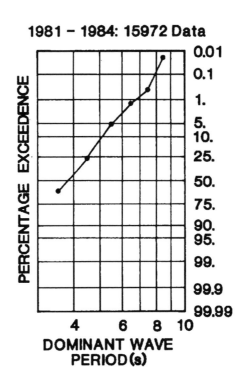

Figure 4.38. Percent average exceedance of wave height and period for the open water season (March-November) at the NOMAD buoy location. Note period of record and number of data points (data courtesy of P.C. Liu).

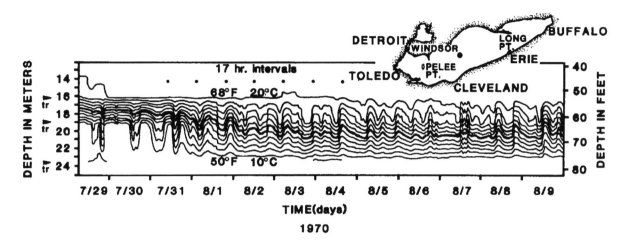

Figure 4.39. A 12-day sub-surface temperature record at one location in Lake Erie (from Blanton and Winklhofer, 1971 and 1972).

times called inertial waves. The 17-h period is discussed in the section on currents and has to do with effects of the earth's rotation.

Figure 4.39 shows the temperature record for 12 days in the summer of 1970 at one location in Lake Erie. The temperature between 40 and 80 ft (12 and 24 m) below the surface is shown in 1.8°F (1°C) intervals. The graph shows that the thermocline has a tendency to oscillate up and down about every 17 h due to internal waves; here the height was about 6 ft (2 m). The waves are always present when Lake Erie is density stratified.

Using Marine Wave and Weather Forecasting Services

Both Canadian and U.S. Government agencies provide weather reporting and forecasting services which can be received by radio. There are two types of broadcasts.

Continuous Broadcasts. Marine reports and forecasts are broadcast continuously by the Canadian Marine Coast Guard and by NOAA. NOAA broadcasts are on 162.40 MHz and 162.55 MHz. The Canadian broadcasts are on 161.65 MHz. The reports and forecasts are updated every 3 to 6 h or as necessary. Figure 4.40 shows station locations and approximate reception ranges.

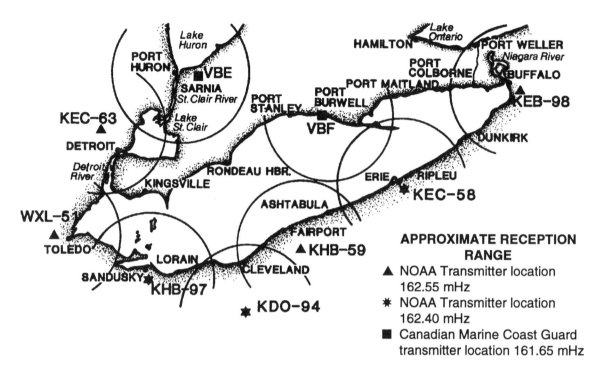

Figure 4.40. Station locations and approximate ranges of continuous broadcast marine information.

To receive these broadcasts you need a VHF-FM narrow-band receiver capable of receiving the above frequencies. Sensitivity should be at least 1 microvolt and quieting factor 20 dB. Such receivers are readily available and rather inexpensive. The NOAA stations broadcast a warning signal 13 seconds before a special announcement of severe weather. Some receivers are equipped with a warning device which can respond to this signal and alert you to these special announcements.

Channel 16 Announcements. Channel 16 (156.8 MHz) is a special radiotelephone channel. Announcements of upcoming broadcasts of marine forecasts made on this channel will tell you which other channel to turn to. Following are some of the broadcasts announced on Channel 16. Note that all times are Eastern Standard Time (EST).

LAWEB. LAWEB (Great Lakes Weather Broadcast) broadcasts give weather reports (not forecasts) and wave conditions from shore stations and ships underway. In the Lake Erie area, broadcasts are only in the navigation season. Broadcasts are at 2:30 and 8:30 (EST) both a.m. and p.m. Marine radiotelephone stations in the Lake Erie-Lake St. Clair area:

CITY	STATION	FREQUENCY	CHANNEL
Ripley, NY	KIL-929	156.850 MHz	17
Cleveland, OH	KQU-440	156.850	17
Lorain, OH	WMI	161.900	26
Toledo, OH	KIL-928	156.850	17
Algonac, MI	KIL-927	156.850	17

MAFOR. MAFOR stands for marine forecast and is a coded broadcast from the radiotelephone stations listed above. Broadcasts are every 6 h at 12:02 and 6:02 (EST) both a.m. and p.m. These forecasts complement the reports provided by LAWEB.

The coding is quite useful because it allows the forecast to be copied down on paper entirely as it is being broadcast. The forecast has several parts:

1) "MAFOR" (opening keyword)

2) day of the month

3) time forecast begins in GMT (Greenwich Mean Time). The equivalent GMT and EST are:

    0000 GMT = 7 p.m. EST

    0600 GMT = 1 a.m. EST

    1200 GMT = 7 a.m. EST

    1800 GMT = 1 p.m. EST

4) lake name (e.g. "Erie")

5) "1" (signifies North America)

6) forecast period (digit 0 - 9)

7) wind direction (digit 0 - 9)

8) wind speed   (digit 0 - 9)

9) forecast   (digit 0 - 9)

10) significant wave height in feet at downwind side of the lake

Parts (6)-(9) will be repeated as many times as necessary to specify weather changes. The codes for parts (6)-(9) are shown in Table 3.

WARNING BROADCASTS FROM RADIOTELEPHONE STATIONS.
The radiotelephone stations listed above also broadcast gale and storm warning messages. These messages are broadcast as needed and every 30 minutes for 2 h.

Table 4.3. MAFOR codes.

Part 6   G - Forecast Period

0 - Conditions at beginning of forecast period
1 - Valid for 3 hr
2 - Valid for 6 hr
3 - Valid for 9 hr
4 - Valid for 12 hr
5 - Valid for 18 hr
6 - Valid for 24 hr
7 - Valid for 48 hr
8 - Valid for 72 hr
9 - Occasionally

Part 7   D - Wind Direction

0 - Calm
1 - Northeast
2 - East
3 - Southeast
4 - South
5 - Southwest
6 - West
7 - Northwest
8 - North

Part 8 F_U Wind Speed

0 - 0 to 10 knots
1 - 11 to 16 knots
2 - 17 to 21 knots
3 - 22 to 27 knots
4 - 28 to 33 knots
5 - 34 to 40 knots
6 - 41 to 47 knots
7 - 48 to 55 knots
8 - 56 to 63 knots
9 - 64 knots and above

Part 9 W_s Forecast Weather

0 - Moderate or good visibility - more than 3 nautical miles
1 - risk of accumulation of ice on superstructures (23° to 32°F)
2 - Strong risk accumulation of ice on superstructures (below 23°F)
3 - Mist (visibility 5/8 to 3 nautical miles)
4 - Fog (visibility less than 5/8 nautical miles)
5 - Drizzle
6 - Rain
7 - Snow or rain and snow
8 - Squally weather with or without showers
9 - Thunderstorms

U.S. COAST GUARD MARINE FORECASTS. The U.S. Coast Guard broadcasts forecasts on Channel 22 (157.1 MHz). The stations and broadcast times are:

CITY	STATION	TIMES (AM and PM, EST)
Buffalo, NY	NMD47	2:55, 5:55, 8:55, 11:55
Detroit, MI	NMD25	1:55, 4:55, 7:55, 10:55

CANADIAN MARINE COAST GUARD. The Canadian Marine Coast Guard broadcasts continuously on Channel 21B (161.65 MHz) and supplements these with live broadcasts of important weather information. In addition, MAFOR and LAWEB reports are given every 3 h. The broadcast stations are:

CITY	STATION	TIMES (AM and PM, EST)
Burwell, ON	VBF	1:45, 4:45, 7:45, 10:45
Sarnia, ON	VBE	2:05, 5:05, 8:05, 11:05

Storm Surges and Seiches

One of the most spectacular features of Lake Erie is its susceptibility to water level changes due to storms. These fast and sometimes large changes are important especially near the western and eastern ends of the lake. Shoreline erosion increases when levels are high. Currents that accompany the level changes can be quite strong. Large level changes have caused serious flooding and extensive property damage in the Buffalo, New York and Toledo, Ohio areas.

Storm Surges

When a strong wind blows across a lake, it drags water with it. This causes the water level to fall on the upwind side and to rise on the downwind side, a phenomenon known as setup. During setup, the surface of the water is tilted. As long as the wind continues to blow, setup will continue. In a storm, strong winds can cause a sudden and large change in water levels called a storm surge.

Large setups and storm surges are rather common on Lake Erie. On one occasion (April 6, 1979), the difference in water level between Buffalo and Toledo exceeded 14 ft (4.3 m) because of strong winds (Hamblin, 1979; Shafiqur Rahman, 1974). On Lake St. Clair, large setups and storm surges can also raise water levels by as much as 1.5 ft (0.46 m).

Three main factors influence surge and setup magnitude:

Fetch. Fetch is the length of water over which the wind is blowing. The longer the fetch, the higher the surge or setup.

Average lake depth. The shallower the lake, the greater the effect of winds on the surge or setup.

Wind speed. The stronger the wind, the higher the surge or setup.

Lake Erie's long axis is oriented along the direction of the prevailing southwest wind. The most common wind direction is, therefore, conducive to storm surges and setups. The average depth of Lake Erie is also far less than any of the other Great Lakes (except Lake St. Clair). This shallow depth means that wind will be even more effective in generating high setups and surges. The length, orientation, and depth, then, conspire to make Lake Erie the most susceptible of the Great Lakes to surges and setups.

Figure 4.41 shows the approximate water level rise at Buffalo during southwest winds. For example, suppose the wind has averaged about 30 mph (13.5 m/sec) for the last hour at Buffalo. From the graph, if the air and water are at the same temperature, the surge would bring the water level to about 2.4 ft (0.73 m) above normal. If the water is warmer by 10°F (5°C), the surge would bring the level to about 3.5 ft (1.1 m) above normal. (Temperature has a stabilizing effect; this is discussed in the section on waves.)

About one-third of all severe storms occur in November. The frequency of storms decreases into winter and increases again in March. Storm surge frequency follows that of severe storms with a major peak in November and a minor peak in March. Almost one-fifth of all storm surges with a setup of over 6 ft (1.8 m) occur in November. The average wind speed also peaks in both November and March. Large surges are rare in the summer months (Pore et al., 1975; Caskey, 1962).

Figure 4.42a shows one example of an actual storm surge. The level at Buffalo began to rise very quickly at 8 a.m.

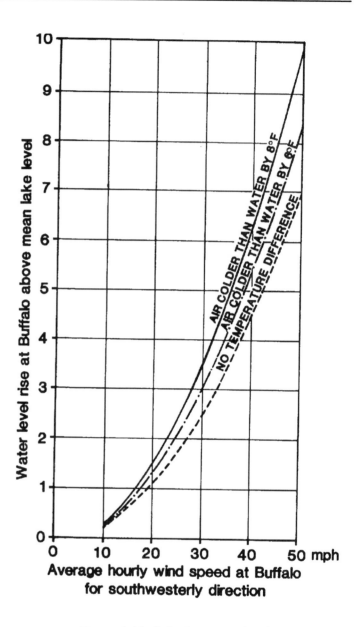

Figure 4.41. Lake Erie surge height at various wind speeds from the southwest (from Hunt, 1959).

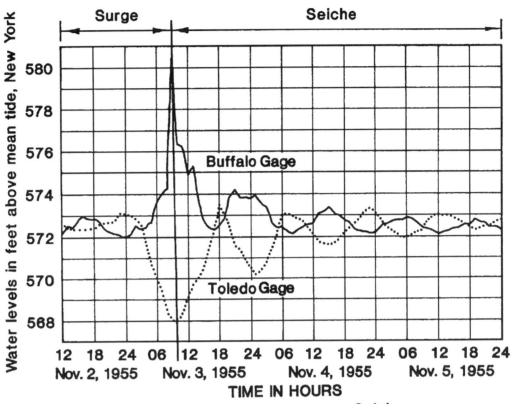

Figure 4.42a. A classical surge followed by a classical seiche in Lake Erie (from Hunt, 1959).

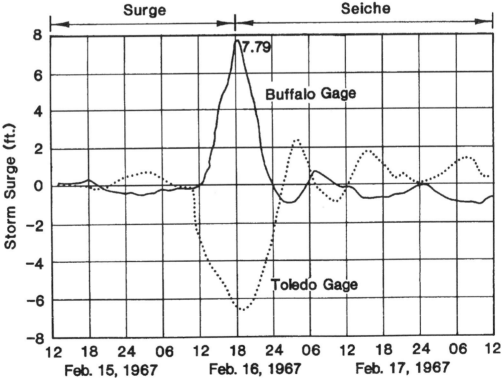

Figure 4.42b. A surge followed by a seiche in Lake Erie (from Pore et al., 1975).

Within 1 h the water level had risen more than 6 ft (1.8 m) to a height about 8 ft (2.4 m) over the mean Buffalo water level. While the water level was rising at Buffalo, it was falling at Toledo. The level changes at Toledo were, however, not as rapid as those at Buffalo because of frictional effects on the movement of water in the shallow, island-studded western basin. In this example, the rates of change were as high as 6 ft/h (1.8 m/h) at Buffalo and 1 ft/h (0.3 m/h) at Toledo.

Figure 4.42b shows another example of a storm surge. The water level at Toledo began to fall rapidly just before noon on February 15. The drop was rapid at the onset and later became less pronounced until it reached its lowest point at about 7 p.m. The total drop in water level was over 6.5 ft (2 m). While the level was falling at Toledo, it was rising at Buffalo. The level changes at Buffalo were, however, more rapid than those at Toledo. The level rise at Buffalo began slightly after the fall at Toledo. The water level rose nearly 8 ft (2.4 m) during the 6-h period from noon to 6 p.m. on February 15.

Seiches

When the wind speed diminishes, the lake levels do not quickly return to normal because of seiches or the sloshing of water in lakes. Figure 4.42a shows an example of a classical seiche which lasts for several days. Water levels at Buffalo and Toledo alternately increase and decrease because of this sloshing. For example, the peak surge level at Buffalo occurred at 9 a.m. on November 3. After that, other peaks occur, roughly every 14 h: midnight on November 3, 3 p.m. on November 4, 6 a.m. on November 5, and 7 p.m. on November 5. About half-way between these peaks are minimum water levels. The level at Toledo goes up when the level at Buffalo goes down, and vice versa. The sloshing decays and each water level peak is lower than the preceding peak by about half (not counting the initial surge peak). The amount of time between peaks in water level is called the period of the seiche. When a first-mode seiche is active on Lake Erie, water levels near Toledo and Buffalo change more than at any other place on the shore. By contrast, there is a line roughly in the center of the lake, called a nodal line, where the level does not change at all.

Figure 4.42b shows a seiche that is more typical on Lake Erie. For example, the lowest seiche level at Buffalo occurs at about 2 a.m. on February 16 and the peak level at about 7 a.m. Subsequent to that, the picture is not as clear with respect to a classic seiche period as shown in Figure 4.42a. The period of the seiche at Toledo is somewhat more regular than at Buffalo, but it is about 12 h in one case and about 16 h in another. To produce a classic surge and seiche as shown in Figure 4.42a, the wind must blow strongly and in one direction for the surge and then must stop completely, while the water sloshes back and forth. Additional examples of Lake Erie surges and seiches are provided later in this section.

The first-mode seiche has one nodal line. The second-mode seiche has two, the third has three, and so on. These higher-mode seiches have more "wiggles" or undulations in the water surface and shorter periods. While the first-mode longitudinal seiche on Lake Erie has a period of 14 h, the second-, third-, and fourth-mode seiches have periods of 9, 6, and 4 h, respectively (Platzman and Rao, 1964). The first-mode seiche has a single nodal line which runs across the lake roughly from Fairport, Ohio to Erieau, Ontario (Figure 4.43a). In this central region, the first mode's 14-h fluctuations have little effect on water levels. In both the western and eastern basins, levels are greatly affected. This is especially true west of Pelee Island, where level fluctuations can exceed fluctuations at Buffalo. The second-mode seiche has two nodes, one from Point Pelee, Ontario to Huron, Ohio, and one from near Erie, Pennsylvania to Long Point, Ontario (Figure 4.43b). Here the 9-h fluctuations in water level of the second mode are unimportant. On the other hand, the far ends of the lake and its middle are affected much more by the 9-h level fluctuations. The water levels in the central area,

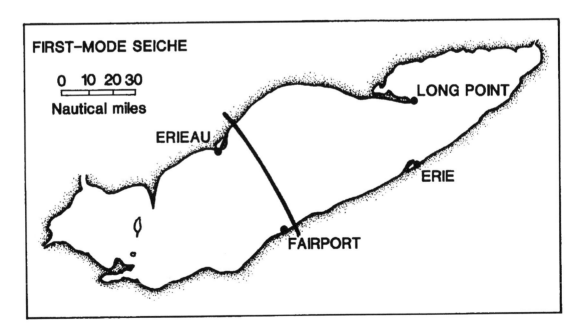

Figure 4.43a. Nodal line for first-mode seiche.

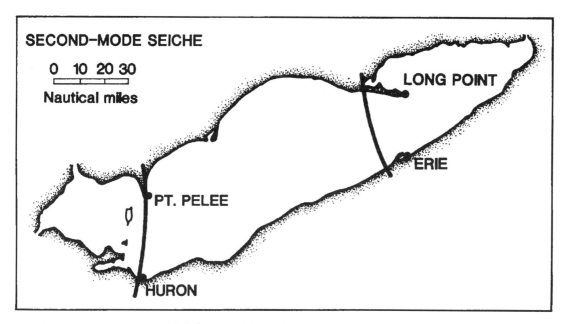

Figure 4.43b. Nodal lines for second-mode seiche.

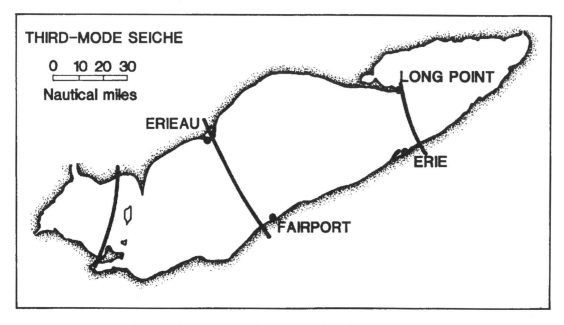

Figure 4.43c. Nodal lines for third-mode seiche.

in fact, experience much more of the second-mode seiche than the first-mode seiche. Again the level changes are most extreme in the far western region. The third-mode seiche, which has a 6-h period, has three nodes, one in the western basin, one from Fairport, Ohio to Erieau, Ontario, and one from the tip of Long Point, Ontario to near Erie, Pennsylvania (Figure 4.43c). Regions of greatest third-mode level fluctuation are in the far western end, between Huron, Ohio and Cleveland, Ohio and in the far eastern end.

The sloshing can occur not only along the length of a lake but also across its width. Sloshing across the narrow part of a lake is called a transverse seiche. Generally, transverse seiches are less important than longitudinal seiches on Lake Erie because Lake Erie is narrow and its length is oriented along the direction of prevailing winds. Only a first-mode transverse seiche on Lake Erie is ever very noticeable. The period of such seiches is slightly over 3 h (Dingman and Bedford, 1984).

Seiches change water levels more slowly than surges do. A seiche with a period of 14 h and an amplitude of 2 ft (0.6 m) (a large seiche), can change the water level by about 1 ft/h (0.3 m/hr). A 6-h seiche with an amplitude of 0.5 ft (0.15 m) can change the water level at a rate of up to 0.5 ft/h (0.15 m/hr). Unless re-excited by the weather, a seiche will decay. The amplitude decays at a rate of roughly 50% per period. For example, a 1-ft (0.3-m) seiche will be a 0.5-ft (0.15-m) seiche on its next cycle.

Surge and Seiche Climatology and Examples

Figure 4.44 shows the frequency of storm surges with magnitudes of 2 ft (0.6 m) or greater. The bar chart combines data for all months of the year over a 33-year period. Most of the surges at Buffalo are high water cases (positive storm surges), resulting from southwest winds of the winter storms passing to the north of the Great Lakes. These same storms are also responsible for most of the low water cases at Toledo.

Figure 4.45 shows wind stress and water levels at Buffalo and Toledo for October 1979. Wind stress is the force which blowing wind exerts on the water surface. The magnitude of the wind stress is shown by the length of the bars. The direction of stress, relative to the orientation of the lake, is also indicated by the bars. A bar pointing straight up represents a wind from the southwest and blowing along the axis of Lake Erie. It should be noted that the wind stress values are highly smoothed (using a low pass filter), and the water levels are not smoothed. Actual measurements would indicate that the wind stress is much more "jumpy" or erratic, as winds are in nature. The smoothing is used to simplify direct visual comparison of wind and water level fluctuations. Examples of first-mode seiches are on October 2-4, October 9-10, October 15-16, and other dates. Second-mode seiches occurred on October 8, October 13-14, and October 20-22. A third-mode seiche was evident on October 25. An example of a storm surge occurred on October 22, when winds picked up from the southwest. Other surges occurred on October 6 and 12. For most of the month, prevailing winds blew along the lake from the southwest. As a result, the Buffalo water level usually was above the Toledo water level. On a few occasions, however, the wind shifted to the northeast and caused Toledo's level to be higher than Buffalo's. This happened, for example, on October 30, when a rather small surge caused by a northeast wind raised the water level at Toledo above that of Buffalo. Seiche action also caused reversal of the levels periodically between October 9 and October 10.

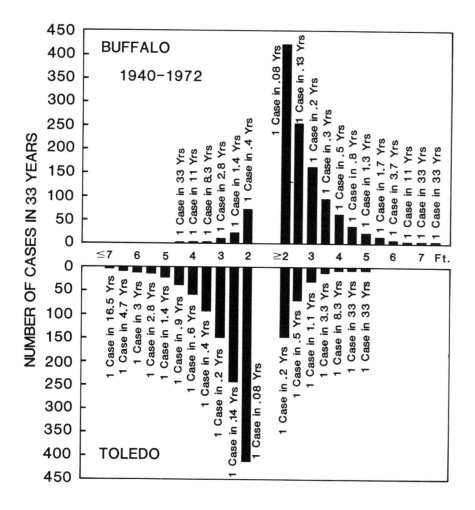

Figure 4.44. Frequencies of storm surges with magnitudes of 2 ft or more at Buffalo, New York and Toledo, Ohio during the 33-year period 1940-1972. High water cases are shown on the right side of the graph, low water cases are shown on the left (from Pore et al., 1975).

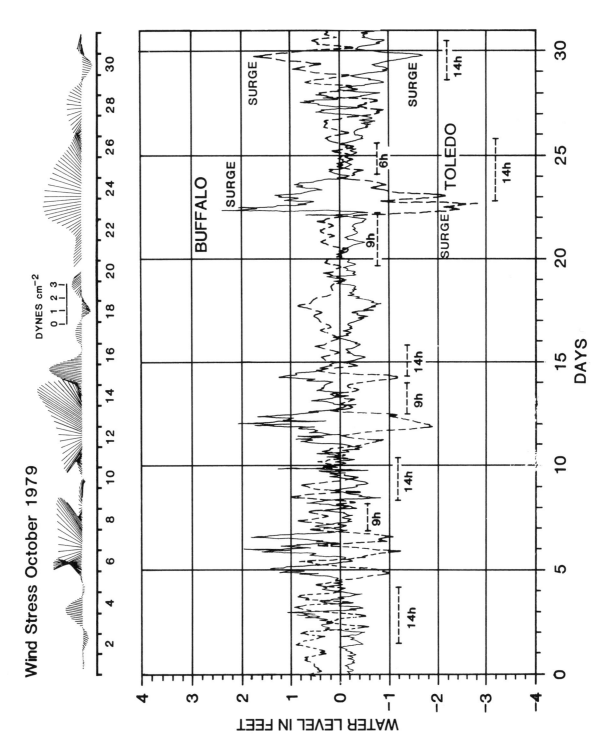

Figure 4.45. Lake levels and wind stress at Toledo, Ohio and Buffalo, New York during October 1979. Water level data are from the National Ocean Survey, Rockville, Maryland. Wind stress data are from Saylor and Miller, 1983.

Forecasts

The National Weather Service (NWS) is responsible for preparing and issuing storm surge forecasts for Lake Erie. From 1969 to 1980 the NWS used a statistically derived storm surge forecast technique to generate automated storm surge forecast guidance for Buffalo and Toledo. New methods to forecast winds over the Great Lakes were developed in 1974 paving the way for a dynamical storm surge model (Schwab, 1978) which took advantage of computer-generated winds to improve the storm surge forecasts. On the basis of comparison and verification of dynamical and statistical storm surge forecasts at Buffalo and Toledo, the dynamical forecast method has now replaced the statistical method (Richardson and Schwab, 1979). Figure 4.46 shows an example of actual water levels as compared to modeled water levels using observed winds from four weather stations around Lake Erie to drive the storm surge forecast model. It is obvious that technology transfers such as this can put science to use in warning shoreline residents of certain natural hazards.

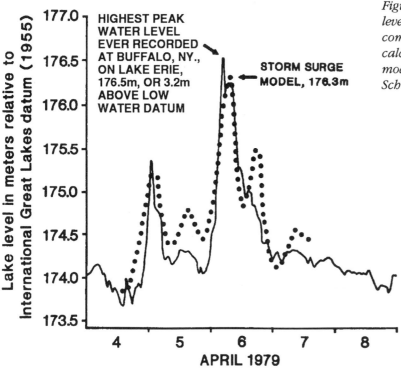

Figure 4.46. Actual water level data from Lake Erie compared with levels as calculated by the storm surge model (data courtesy of D.J. Schwab).

Ice

Ice conditions are of great interest to those who use and observe the Lake Erie region. For example, most boaters must remove their craft in the fall to protect hulls from the crushing forces of the ice. Boaters may also be interested in the time of ice dissipation in the spring. Conversely, ice fishermen and skaters are anxious for the first solid ice cover to develop and carefully watch the time of likely ice breakup.

Extent

Lake Erie. According to Assel et al. (1983),

> The small mean depth of Lake Erie and associated small thermal reserve provides this Great Lake with the most rapid response to changing atmospheric conditions. Ice cover extends over 90% of Lake Erie's surface most winters, and the ice-cover variability . . . is the largest of any of the five Great Lakes. Only during the last half of December and during April are there any persistent areas of open water. In December, these areas occupy the southern lake shore and eastern end of Lake Erie. In the last half of April, persistent open water occupies virtually the entire lake west of Long Point. . . . Ice-cover . . . has been observed to vary from open water to 90- to 100% concentration over most of [the lake's surface during the base period 1960-79.

The probability of exceeding a given percentage ice cover for half-month periods is shown in Figure 4.47. It can be seen that, for the period February 1-14, there is an over 80% chance that the lake will be over 50% ice covered, and there is only about a 20% chance the lake will still be half ice covered during the period March 16-31.

Assel et al. (1983) describe the ice extent in Lake Erie as,

> During a normal winter, ice cover usually develops in the western end of Lake Erie, west of Point Pelee, in the last half of December. During the first half of January, the west end of the lake is over 90% ice covered, and extensive ice formation takes place in the central lake basin between Point Pelee and Long Point. The eastern basin is primarily ice free. Ice forms over the entire lake surface during the second half of January, and the mid-lake basin usually becomes 70 to 90% ice covered during this period. The eastern lake basin is usually 40 to 60% ice covered at this time. During February, the entire lake normally develops a 90 to 100% ice cover. In late winter and in spring, under the influence of the prevailing winds, the ice cover usually

first recedes from the western end of the lake and northern shores, and these open water areas gradually expand eastward and southward across the lake. During March 1-15 the western lake basin and the western half of the central basin usually have 40 to 60% ice concentration, and the rest of the lake is primarily covered by 70 to 90% ice concentration. In the last half of March, the open water areas include the entire western end of the lake as well as the western half of the central basin and the northern shore of the vicinity of Long Point. These open water areas advance farther eastward during April 1-15 to include most of the lake except the area east of Erie, Pennsylvania, and primarily along, and lakeward of, the southeastern shore. Ice cover along this southeastern shore area is further reduced in extent the second half of April, and most of the remaining ice is located east of Port Colborne, Ontario. The wind can cause considerable rafting of ice cover in the eastern end of the lake, resulting in rafted ice that lasts past the end of April and well into May for some years. This rafted ice can also cause considerable navigation problems in spring.

Charts showing the extent of ice cover for selected half-month periods are given in Figure 4.48a-i.

Figure 4.47. Isopleths of percentage ice cover exceedance, Lake Erie (from Assel et al., 1983).

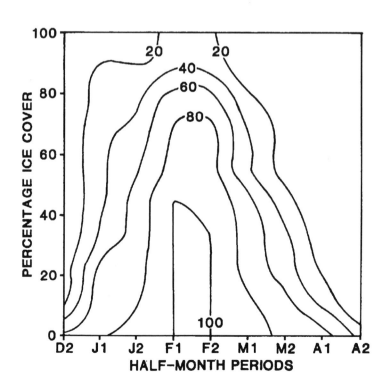

Figure 4.48a-i. Ice charts for normal ice concentration for eight half-month periods starting December 16-31 and ending April 16-30. The progression of ice concentration from open water early in the season to maximum ice cover in February and back to open water is shown. The charts were constructed from a large and long-term data base involving various sources such as aircraft and satellite observations (from Assel et al., 1983).

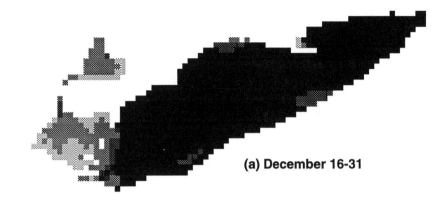

(a) December 16-31

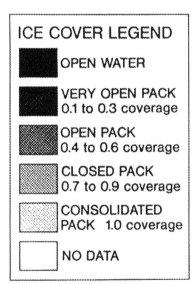

ICE COVER LEGEND

■	OPEN WATER
■	VERY OPEN PACK 0.1 to 0.3 coverage
■	OPEN PACK 0.4 to 0.6 coverage
■	CLOSED PACK 0.7 to 0.9 coverage
■	CONSOLIDATED PACK 1.0 coverage
□	NO DATA

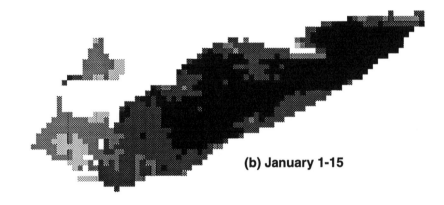

(b) January 1-15

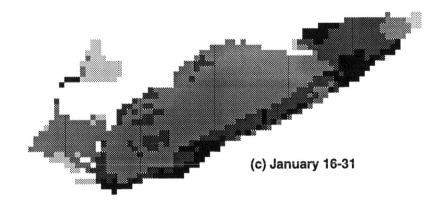

(c) January 16-31

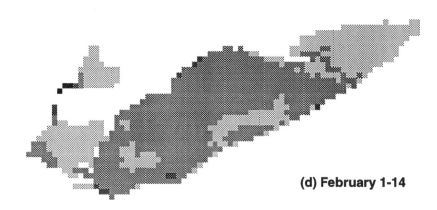

(d) February 1-14

Figure 4.48a-i. Ice charts for normal ice concentration for eight half-month periods starting December 16-31 and ending April 16-30. The progression of ice concentration from open water early in the season to maximum ice cover in February and back to open water is shown. The charts were constructed from a large and long-term data base involving various sources such as aircraft and satellite observations (from Assel et al., 1983).

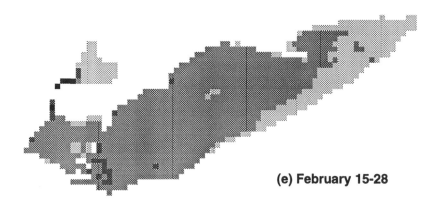

(e) February 15-28

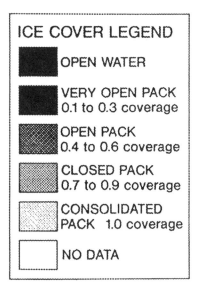

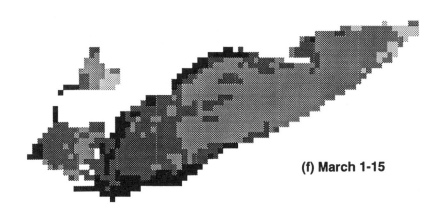

(f) March 1-15

Figure 4.48a-i. Ice charts for normal ice concentration for eight half-month periods starting December 16-31 and ending April 16-30. The progression of ice concentration from open water early in the season to maximum ice cover in February and back to open water is shown. The charts were constructed from a large and long-term data base involving various sources such as aircraft and satellite observations (from Assel et al., 1983).

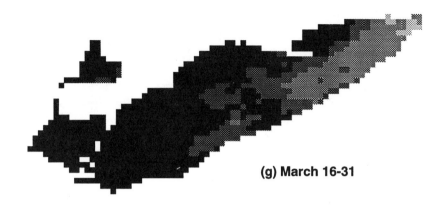

(g) March 16-31

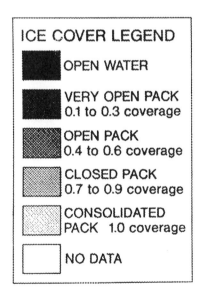

ICE COVER LEGEND

OPEN WATER

VERY OPEN PACK
0.1 to 0.3 coverage

OPEN PACK
0.4 to 0.6 coverage

CLOSED PACK
0.7 to 0.9 coverage

CONSOLIDATED
PACK 1.0 coverage

NO DATA

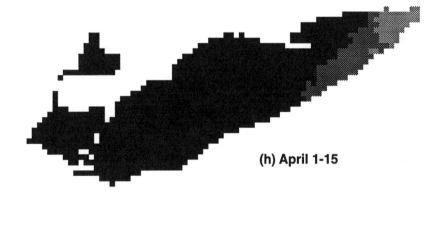

(h) April 1-15

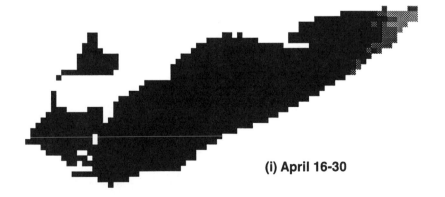

(i) April 16-30

Lake St. Clair. According to Assel et al. (1983) and Rondy (1976),

> During a normal or average winter, the ice charts (Figure 4.48a-i) show that the lake usually has near 100% ice cover in January and February. Ice covers are reduced during March 1-15 and 90 to 100% ice concentration is located in the eastern half of the lake at this time. By the second half of March, the bulk of the remaining ice cover is located along the southeastern shore. The lake is usually ice free during the first half of April. The breakup period is relatively short. As breakup progresses, winds and currents move the drifting ice to the entrance of the Detroit River where strong river currents move it out of the lake and downstream.

Thickness

Published information on the thickness and composition of ice in the nearshore zones of the Great lakes is exceedingly sparse. Many who live near Lake Erie or have visited Lake Erie often in the winter probably know the ice conditions that occur in a given area. However, such observations have not been recorded on a systematic basis, and they have usually not been published. Thus, much of this information is not available to individuals other than from friends and associates. During the 1965-66 winter season, a formal data collection network was started on all of the Great Lakes (Sleator, 1978). Observers at sites on Lake Erie and Lake St. Clair (Figure 4.49) collected information on the ice thickness on a weekly basis for over 10 years. All of the ice thickness information is for nearshore locations. Conditions at these sites can be far different from those offshore.

Bolsenga (1988) analyzed Sleator's (1978) data and found that the average freeze-up date, obtained by including the four Lake Erie/Lake St. Clair stations in the computations, occurred during the last week in December. There are no large differences between average freeze-up dates of the individual stations. The earliest average freeze-up date occurred at Brest Bay during the third week in December while that for the other stations was just one week later. The occurrence of maximum ice amounts also showed little variation. The earliest average maximum ice amount occurred during the last week in January at Brest Bay and the latest only 2 weeks later at New Baltimore-Lake St. Clair. The overall lake average occurred during the first week in February. Maximum ice amounts averaged about 13 in (33 cm) for the four stations and varied from 11 in (28 cm) at New Baltimore to 14 in (36 cm) at Brest Bay. The average breakup date for Lake Erie/Lake St. Clair occurred during the

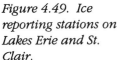

Figure 4.49. Ice reporting stations on Lakes Erie and St. Clair.

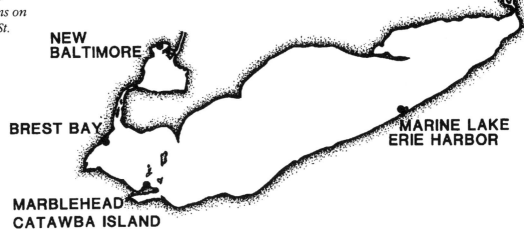

NEW BALTIMORE

BREST BAY

MARINE LAKE ERIE HARBOR

MARBLEHEAD CATAWBA ISLAND

second week in March. Average breakup dates varied little from station to station. The earliest average breakup date, the first week in March, occurred at Marblehead while the latest date, the second week in March, applied to Marine Lake, Brest Bay, and New Baltimore. The lack of variation in freeze-up, breakup, and maximum ice dates is probably attributable to the lack of water volume and the attendant heat budget factors in both Lake Erie and Lake St. Clair.

Ice growth for all stations was at an average rate of 0.30 in/day (0.76 cm/day). The lowest average growth rate was at New Baltimore (0.25 in/day [0.64 cm/day]) and the highest at Marblehead (0.35 in/day [0.89 cm/day]). The average all-station ice dissipation rate was 0.43 in/day (1.1 cm/day), which is the lowest rate for all of the Great Lakes. Lake St. Clair-New Baltimore showed the lowest (0.35 in/day [0.89 cm/day]) and Marine Lake the highest (0.50 in/day [1.3 cm/day]) average ice dissipation rates for Lakes Erie and St. Clair. Ice cover duration for the area averaged 74 days which was considerably lower than any of the other Great Lakes. Marblehead had the shortest average duration (64 days) and Brest Bay the longest average duration (83 days).

"White ice" thickness accounted for only 7% of the average total ice thickness for all stations, the lowest percentage for all of the Great Lakes. The lowest average amount of "white ice" as a percentage of total ice thickness occurred at Brest Bay (2%) and the highest at Marblehead (14%).

Ice Jams

Ice conveyed in rivers can cause particularly severe problems because of its tendency to collect in large amounts at river sections where the ice-transport capacity of that particular section is exceeded by the ice discharge from the river. In these cases, the ice comes to rest, and if the river velocity is sufficiently great, ice floes (slabs) that subsequently arrive are forced above and below each other. An ice jam can partially or almost completely block water flow in the channel. One result of an ice jam is lower water levels downstream and higher water levels upstream from the ice jam. Ice jams are not uncommon on the St. Clair River. Before installation of the ice boom on the Niagara River, ice jams caused considerable damage. Ice jams are relatively unimportant to recreation except when upstream high water levels break-up existing ice covers, and low water levels downstream create air pockets under existing ice surfaces. However, ice jams do cause flooding and impact shoreline property owners. In addition, the sudden release of an ice jam can cause physical damage to structures downstream.

Niagara River. The Niagara River is one of the most extensively studied rivers in North America with respect to ice jams. It has always carried ice in the winter and spring, and in the past, the power entities (New York Power Authority and Ontario Hydro) used ice breakers and various river structures to control the ice (Foulds, 1967). In the past, particularly destructive ice jams occurred causing severe flooding and costly power generation disruptions and demonstrated the need for additional ice control. In the winter of 1964-65, the power companies began operating the Lake Erie-Niagara River Ice Boom on a seasonal basis at the head of the Niagara River.

The Niagara River ice boom is intended to mitigate downstream ice jams by facilitating the formation of an ice arch across Lake Erie and thereby reduce the flow of lake ice into the river. The boom consists of a line of flotation buoys and large timbers attached by chains to a steel cable spanning the outlet and anchored to the bed of Lake Erie. The ice boom has been effective in lessening (but not totally eliminating) ice runs.

Detroit/St. Clair Rivers . In addition to the normal ice cover on the Detroit and St. Clair Rivers, ice jams frequently occur and at times hold back large quantities of water. Jams usually form in the Detroit River in late December or early January followed in February and March by ice jams in the St. Clair River (Bolsenga, 1968). The latter continue in April and occasionally into May. After the breaking of the jam in the St.

Clair River, each year there is frequently a jam of short duration in the Detroit River. Flow reduction due to ice jams in the St. Clair and Detroit Rivers has been shown to amount to up to 80,000 ft³/sec (2,264 m³/sec) under extreme conditions.

Ice Retardation of Water Flows

Ice retardation in the connecting channels of the Great Lakes system is one of the important mechanisms in the natural regulation of water levels and flows of the Great Lakes system. By definition, ice retardation is the reduction, or retardation, of water flows in the connecting channels due primarily to ice jams and the surface stress of a solid ice cover on moving water. (This usually occurs during the winter and early spring months when ice floes break off from the lake ice sheets and are carried into the channels.) The retardation acts as a natural water level regulating device for the Great Lakes. It performs this regulation by causing water to be stored in the upper lakes during the winter and early spring for release later during the year to the lower lakes. A hydrologic response mathematical model was used to determine the effects of ice retardation on Great Lakes water levels with the following results (Quinn, 1973).

Niagara River. The ice retardation of water flow in the Niagara River was virtually eliminated by the construction of the ice boom across the head of the river and by ice-breaking activities of the power companies along the river. Prior to this period, the ice retardation was relatively small and occurred during the months of March and April following the breakup of the Lake Erie ice sheet.

Detroit River. Ice retardation of water flow on the Detroit River is quite variable. The retardation rates are very small and it is unlikely that they would be reduced significantly by any type of regimen changes. The primary effect would be on Lake St. Clair which responds quickly to any changes in Detroit River flows.

St. Clair River. Ice retardation of water flows in the St. Clair River is primarily caused by ice drifting down from Lake Huron and jamming along the shore. Unlike the other rivers, the St. Clair River has a large amount of ice retardation. Thus, any changes in the retardation rates would be reflected in the water surface elevations of the system. The effect on the seasonal cycle of the lakes of a complete reduction (100%) in St. Clair River ice retardation is shown in Figure 4.50. It is seen that while there is a constant lowering in the seasonal profile of Lake

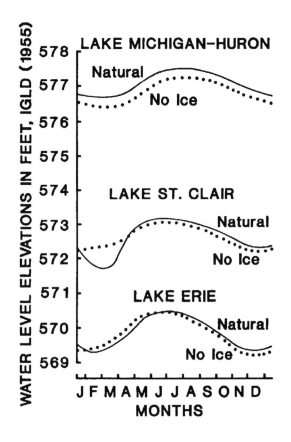

Figure 4.50. *Averge seasonal cycles (based on 1957-1966 data) of water level elevations for cases with no ice retardation in the St. Clair River (dashed line) and with natural conditions (solid line) (from Quinn, 1973).*

Michigan-Lake Huron, the net seasonal cycle remains essentially the same. For Lake St. Clair, there is a drastic change in the seasonal cycle with the water surface elevations being higher in the late winter and early spring and lower the remainder of the year than under natural conditions. It should be noted, however, that the yearly average elevation of the lake remains the same as under natural conditions. The same effect holds true for Lake Erie, though to a lesser degree.

As a result of a mammoth ice jam that occurred at the lower end of the St. Clair River in 1984, the water levels in Lakes Erie, St. Clair, Huron, and Michigan were drastically affected. The water level in Lake St. Clair dropped about 2 ft (0.6 m) during the jam. The water flowing down the St. Clair River was cut by about two-thirds because of the jam. Using the same hydrologic response model mentioned previously, it was determined that a 3-yr period would be required for the excess water in Lakes Huron and Michigan (as a result of the jam) to drain out and for levels in those lakes to return to pre-ice jam conditions.

Chapter 5

Biosphere – The Life

The biosphere encompasses all of the living organisms of the earth, its atmosphere, and its waters. Thus, the biosphere is that portion of the physical sphere capable of supporting life. Of interest in this book are the plants and animals that are dependent on the Lake Erie region for their existence.

Lake Ecology

The scientific study of lakes and other inland waters is called limnology. The aspect of this science that deals with the interrelationships between lake organisms and their environment is known as aquatic ecology. Some limnologists describe their science as the study of biological productivity in lakes as it is effected by other environmental factors. Other limnologists stress that the entire sequence of geological, physical, chemical, and biological events that operate together in a lake basin are dependent on one another (Figure 5.1). With today's wide-

Figure 5.1. Interactions within Lake Erie which determine the composition, distribution, and quantity of aquatic organisms in the lake (after Rawson, 1939).

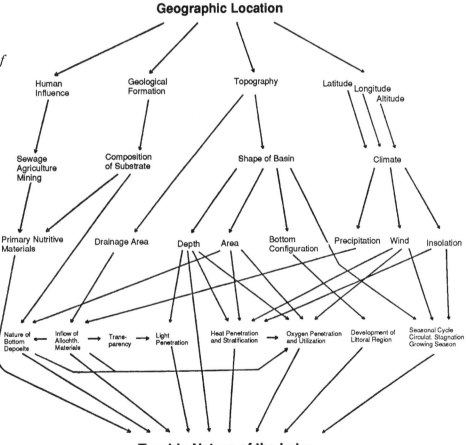

spread concern over the impact of human activity on natural environments, limnology is becoming an increasingly important practical science
(Figure 5.2). Decisions must be based on the best available limnological
information if we hope to protect, manage, or restore the quality of
lakes and streams.

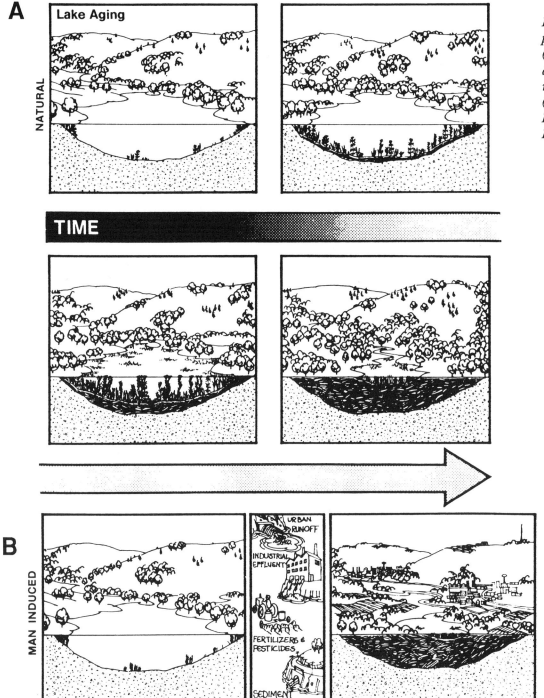

Figure 5.2. Aging processes in lakes: (A) natural aging and (B) man-induced aging (courtesy of the U.S. Environmental Protection Agency).

Physical Structure of Lake Erie

The first step in understanding a lake is to realize that it has a structure and organization that can be identified. The geological, physical, biological, and chemical characteristics of a lake are different in different parts of the lake, and they vary during the year. Certain physical phenomena in lakes occur quite independently of normal biological and chemical influences. Because water varies in density as its temperature changes, lakes in temperate climates tend to stratify, or form layers, especially during the summer.

As summer progresses, the temperature difference, and thus the density difference, between surface and bottom water masses becomes more distinct, and lakes of sufficient depth, such as the central basin of Lake Erie, generally become physically stratified into three identifiable layers (Figure 5.3). The warm, surface water layer is termed the epilimnion. Below the epilimnion there is a layer of water in which the

Figure 5.3. Thermal profiles for central and eastern Lake Erie.

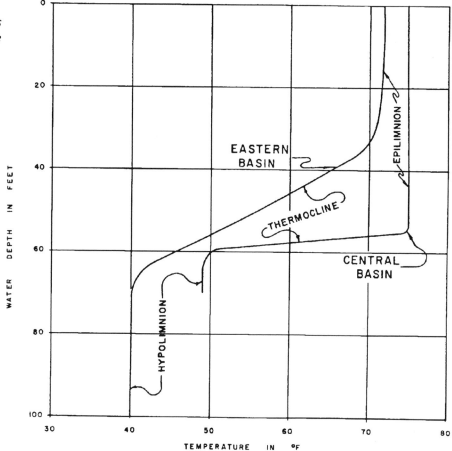

temperature declines rapidly, called the metalimnion or thermocline. Below the thermocline lies water much colder than the epilimnion, called the hypolimnion.

The density change across the thermocline provides a real physical barrier. It effectively eliminates the mixing of upper and lower waters for several months of the summer. This fact is significant for the understanding of many other aspects of limnology.

As the weather cools during autumn, the epilimnion cools too, reducing the density difference between it and the hypolimnion. As time passes, winds are able to mix the lake to greater depths, and the thermocline gradually descends. When surface and bottom waters are uniform in density, autumn winds can mix the entire lake; the lake is said to "turn over." The surface water continues to cool and eventually freezes in winter. In spring, the ice melts and the surface warming begins, starting the cycle over again.

The foregoing sequence of events are typical for the central and eastern basins of Lake Erie (Figure 5.4). Because the western basin of Lake Erie is so shallow, it is usually uniform in temperature, top to bottom (isothermal), but because of its shallowness, it responds more quickly to atmospheric temperature changes than the other basins. Only occasionally in summer does this basin stratify thermally, and then for short periods. This deprives the lower water layer of a good supply of oxygen from the atmosphere leading to rapid oxygen depletion near the bottom, drastically affecting the benthic organisms.

Biological Structure of Lake Erie

Besides being dynamic physical systems, lakes are also very complicated biological and chemical systems. There are many different kinds of plants, animals, and microorganisms that live, reproduce, and die in lakes. In the open water of a lake are found plankton—free-floating microscopic plants and animals. Nekton are larger animals, like fish, that are relatively independent of water motion because they can swim much faster than the velocity of normal currents. On the lake bottom grow many kinds of benthos, these organisms include rooted aquatic plants, snails, worms, insect larvae, and bacteria. The rates at which various organisms perform their functions contribute a great deal to the overall character of lakes. Organisms create differences in water chemistry between the top (epilimnion) and bottom (hypolimnion) of lakes, and they strongly influence the quality of the water. There are two basic life-sustaining processes in lakes just as there are on land—photosynthesis and respiration. Simplified chemical formulas for these important

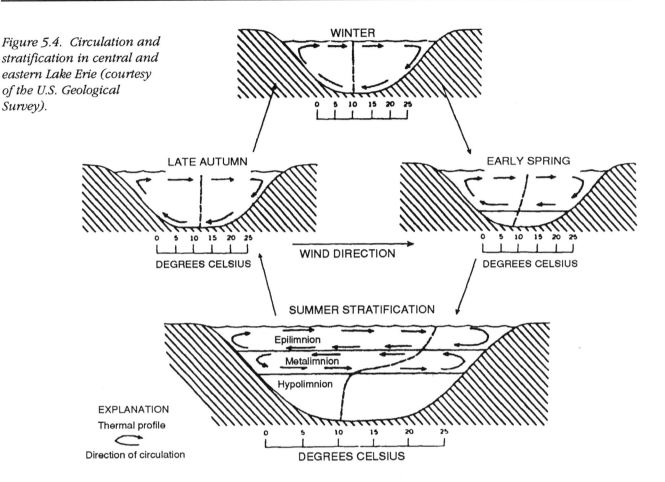

Figure 5.4. Circulation and stratification in central and eastern Lake Erie (courtesy of the U.S. Geological Survey).

process are given in Figure 5.5. Green plants are able to capture energy from sunlight in order to convert non-living, inorganic chemicals like carbon dioxide, water, and mineral compounds into living, organic plant tissue. In lakes, photosynthesis is carried on by algae and higher green plants closely related to common land plants. These plants are called primary producers because they create the organic material that is required by most other organisms for nutrients and energy. The waste product of photosynthesis, oxygen, is also used by other organisms.

Plant tissue is eaten by small animals called zooplankters. These primary consumers are then eaten by other animals, including small fish, called secondary consumers. Still larger consumers such as large fish, ospreys, and people eat them and are called tertiary consumers. All of these animals utilize food for building their own tissue by also extracting energy from the food through the process of respiration. Respiration, the oxidation of organic material, which occurs in both plants and animals, releases the energy that was originally captured from sunlight by photosynthesis. This energy is used by the animals to sustain their lives.

Photosynthesis

$$\text{Energy} + 6\,CO_2 + 6\,H_2O \xrightarrow{\text{chlorophyll}} C_6H_{12}O_6 + 6\,O_2$$
(light)   (carbon dioxide) (water)   (sugar)   (oxygen)

Respiration

$$C_6H_{12}O_6 + 6\,O_2 \longrightarrow 6\,CO_2 + 6\,H_2O + \text{Energy}$$
(sugar)   (oxygen)   (carbon dioxide) (water)

Figure 5.5. Photosynthesis and respiration processes in aquatic plants.

Meanwhile, there is excretion of wastes and death of organisms. The remains are attacked by microorganisms that decompose the material and make some of it reusable as nutrients for green-plant photosynthesis.

This whole interaction of photosynthesis and respiration by plants, animals, and microorganisms is called a food web by ecologists (Figure 5.6). Food webs are usually very complex; in any one lake ecosystem hundreds of different species could be involved.

Producers

Living green plants are confined in those regions of lakes that receive sunlight, thus photosynthesis occurs primarily in the epilimnion with maximum rates found slightly below the water surface. Large attached or rooted plants, called macrophytes, are found in shallow water. In the coastal marshes, macrophytes may represent most of the green plant material present and may account for most of the photosynthesis. Furthermore, "weed beds" are important habitats for many fish and other aquatic animals. Other parts of Lake Erie have few macrophytes. The bottom may be too rough, wave action too severe, or the water too deep. Some polluted embayments with high populations of algae or high silt concentrations have few macrophytes because little sunlight reaches the lake bottom, even in shallow water.

Algae constitute the other main group of producers. They come in countless forms and live in nearly all kinds of environments. Many are microscopic in size, growing as single cells or small colonies and are collectively called phytoplankton. Phytoplankton grow suspended in open water by taking up nutrients from solution and photosynthesizing. If their populations are dense, the water will become noticeably green

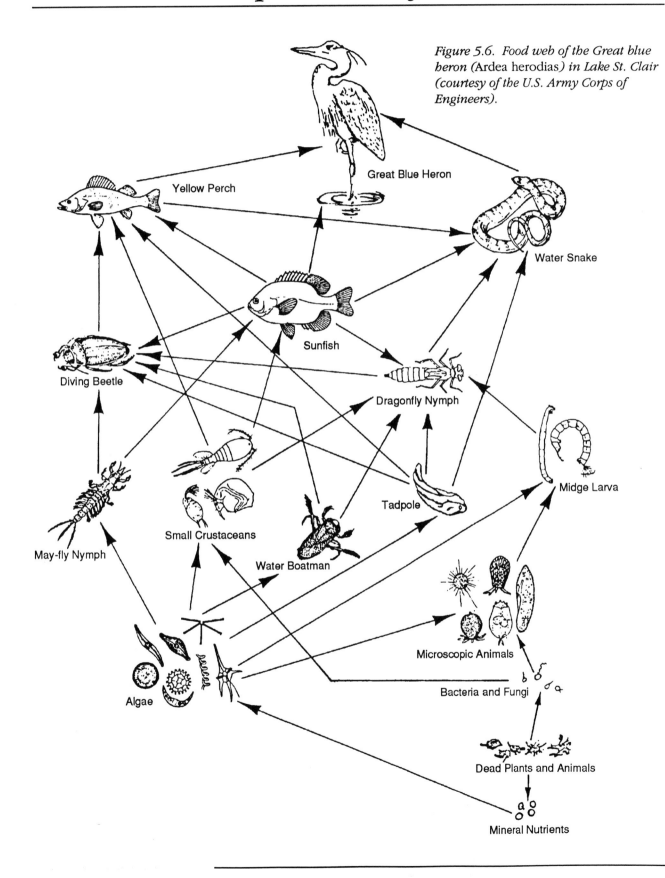

Figure 5.6. Food web of the Great blue heron (Ardea herodias) *in Lake St. Clair (courtesy of the U.S. Army Corps of Engineers).*

Great Blue Heron

Yellow Perch

Water Snake

Sunfish

Diving Beetle

Dragonfly Nymph

Midge Larva

May-fly Nymph

Small Crustaceans

Tadpole

Water Boatman

Microscopic Animals

Bacteria and Fungi

Algae

Dead Plants and Animals

Mineral Nutrients

or brown and will have low transparency. There are several groups of phytoplankton, including diatoms, green algae, and blue-green algae.

Diatoms are notable for their cell walls, which are made of silica and have remarkable geometric shapes. Both diatoms and green algae are slightly heavier than water and, therefore, rely on water turbulence to stay in the sunny epilimnion. They are generally thought to be good food for zooplankton. Blue-green algae, on the other hand, are a group less suitable as food for primary consumers. Blue greens have the ability to adjust their buoyancy; thus they can float or sink depending on circumstances of light and nutrient supply. Also, a few species are known to be able to fix nitrogen. Most plants, including diatoms and green algae, can use the essential nutrient nitrogen only if it is present in certain forms such as nitrate or ammonia. Blue-green algae, however, can also capture atmospheric molecular nitrogen (N_2) and convert it to a useful form through a process called nitrogen fixation. Blue-green algae are frequently responsible for algal blooms, which are dense growths of algae that can cover large portions of the lake's surface.

In addition to free-floating phytoplankton there are filamentous algae, which grow in long, visible, hair-like strands, and there are "rooted" algae that resemble macrophytes but have no roots, leaves, or flowers. Both of these types are usually found attached to bottom materials, debris, or larger aquatic plants.

Consumers

While photosynthesis by green plants is limited to the sunlit portions of a lake, consumers can live and grow throughout the lakes. Small animals that swim about in open water are called zooplankton. Some species can be seen with the naked eye, although they are more easily observed with a hand lens or low-power microscope. Zooplankton eat algae and are, therefore, primary consumers.

There are also many consumer animals that live at the bottom of lakes. Their feeding strategies vary widely. Some, like clams, filter small bits of organic material from water as it flows by. Others eat partially decayed organic material that has sunk to the bottom.

The best known group of aquatic consumers is fish, but individually (at the species level) their requirements for food and habitat vary a great deal. Most small fish feed primarily on zooplankton, while larger fish prey on the smaller ones. Northern pike (*Esox lucius*) are often found over beds of aquatic macrophytes suitable for spawning, whereas walleye (*Stizostedion v. vitreum*) spawn on gravel and rocky bottoms. Lake trout (*Salvelinus namaycush*) live only in very clear regions of the lake with cold, well-oxygenated deep water, but carp (*Cyprinus carpio*) are adapted to turbid parts of the lake with silt bottoms.

Decomposers

This group, which includes bacteria and other microorganisms, is the other major component in the food web. These microbes feed on the remains of aquatic organisms and, in so doing, break down organic matter, returning it to an inorganic state. Decomposers use dissolved oxygen for the decay process. Most of the decayed material is subsequently reusable-cycled as nutrition for green plants.

Energy flow through the food web

The ultimate source of energy for Lake Erie ecosystems is the sun. Only a small fraction of the total available energy from the sun enters the food chain. Even when light falls where vegetation is abundant, such as a coastal marsh, only 1 or 2% of that light is used for photosynthesis. Yet, this fraction results in the production of organic matter (from carbon, oxygen, water, and minerals) at a rate of up to 1.2 lbs/ft² per year (6 kg/m²) in Lake Erie marshes.

The passage of this energy from one organism to another takes place along a particular food chain which is made up of several trophic levels. In most communities, food chains form complex food webs involving many different types of organisms, especially on the lower trophic levels. The first step in the food chain is always a primary producer, which in freshwater aquatic ecosystems may be one of three basic types: (1) macrophytes (e.g. cattails), (2) benthic macroalgae, and (3) phytoplankton. Several studies indicate that the macrophytes are the most important primary producers in marshes. These photosynthetic organisms use light energy to make carbohydrates and other compounds which then become sources of chemical energy. Producers (autotrophs) far outweigh consumers: 99% of all organic matter in the biosphere is made up of plants, including algae. All other organisms (heterotrophs) combined account for only 1%. Food chain production is measured by the amount of energy (in calories) stored in chemical compounds or by the increase in biomass in a particular length of time. Net productivity represents the amount of light energy converted to organic matter less the amount of glucose and other compounds used in respiration.

Energy enters the animal world largely through the activities of the herbivores, the animals that eat plants and algae. Of the organic material consumed by herbivores, much is excreted undigested. Some of the chemical energy is transformed to other types of energy—heat or motion —or used in the digestive process itself. A fraction of the material is converted to animal biomass. The next level in the food chain, the secondary consumer level, involves carnivores. Only a small part of the organic substance present in the body of the herbivore becomes incorporated into the body of the carnivore. Some chains have third and fourth consumer levels, but five links are usually the limit, largely because of the waste involved in the transfer of energy from one trophic level to another.

The decomposers, which are primarily bacteria and fungi, break down dead and discarded organic matter, completing the oxidation of the energy-rich compounds formed by photosynthesis. As a result of the metabolic work of the decomposers, waste products—detritus, feces, dead plants, and animals—are broken down to inorganic substances that are returned to the soil or water to enter once more into the tissues of plants and begin the cycle again.

The flow of energy through a food chain is often represented by a graph of quantitative relationships among the various trophic levels. Because large amounts of energy and biomass are dissipated at every trophic level, these diagrams nearly always take the form of pyramids (Figure 5.7). The studies which first introduced the concepts of trophic levels were first worked out in freshwater wetlands. Juday (1943) determined the various components of the aquatic population in Weber Lake, Wisconsin as they existed in midsummer. He found that the dissolved organic matter composed about 60% of the total pyramid; the fish, only 0.5%; and the other animals, slightly less than 5% of the total pyramid.

Although much research remains to be done on food chain production and ecosystem energy relationships, particularly of freshwater wetlands, there are biological conclusions which seem to have a certain validity. For example, (1) food cycles rarely have more than five trophic levels; (2) the greater the separation of an organism from the basic source of energy (solar radiation), the less the chance that it will depend solely upon the preceding trophic level for energy; (3) at successively higher levels in the food cycle, consumers seem to be progressively more efficient in the utilization of food supply; and (4) in lake succession, productivity and photosynthetic efficiency increase from oligotrophy through to eutrophy, and then decline in lake senescence (Welch, 1952).

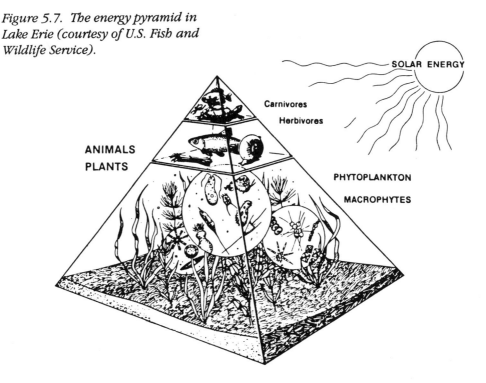

Figure 5.7. The energy pyramid in Lake Erie (courtesy of U.S. Fish and Wildlife Service).

Chemical Structure of Lakes Erie and St. Clair

Aquatic organisms modify their environment through life activities and thereby influence the subsequent chemical and biological characteristics of that environment. For example, phytoplankton extract inorganic minerals from sunlit water to create living organic material. In doing so, they release wastes including oxygen. Therefore, in photosynthetic zones of lakes, nutrients are removed, and oxygen is added to the water. Because algae gradually sink to lower depths and decompose, nutrients are redistributed from the upper water to the lake bottom.

Meanwhile, respiring organisms like zooplankton, fish, and decomposer microorganisms use oxygen and release wastes such as carbon dioxide; these organisms gradually sink to the bottom as well, further concentrating nutrients in lower waters and sediments (Figure 5.8).

Much of this biological activity occurs during the summer when maximum photosynthetic activity is driven by maximum solar radiation. But also during the summer, most of Lake Erie is stratified as explained earlier. Because biological activities are different in the epilimnion and hypolimnion, chemical characteristics are also quite different (Figure 5.8). The following sections explore key aspects of Lake Erie water quality.

A

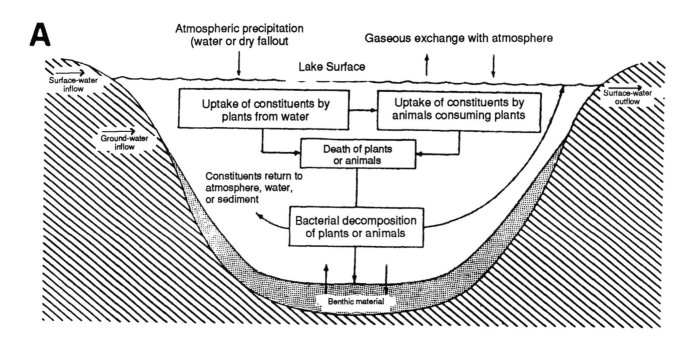

B

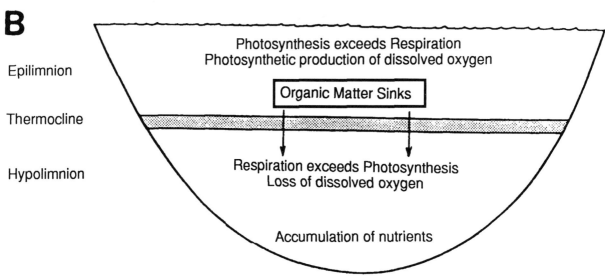

Figure 5.8. Chemical material in Lake Erie: (A) sources and cycling, and (B) biological redistribution during summer stratification (Lundquist, 1975).

The most abundant chemical constituents of Lakes Erie and St. Clair water are listed in Table 5.1. Lake Erie waters are alkaline, having a total alkalinity of 95 ppm as $CaCO_3$ and an average pH of 8.3. Total dissolved solids in the water average 173 ppm, with the highest concentrations along the south shore. In general, the concentrations of the major cations and anions increase from west to east.

Water Clarity

A simple method of measuring water clarity, employed since 1865, involves the use of the Secchi disc (Figure 5.9). This white and black disk is lowered until the observer can no longer distinguish the outline of the disc. It is then raised until it reaches a level where it again becomes visible. The length of rope is measured to determine the transparency.

Table 5.1. Mean chemical composition of Lake Erie and connecting waterways (1967-1982).

Parameter	Units	St. Clair River	Lake St. Clair	Detroit River	Western Lake Erie	Central Lake Erie	Eastern Lake Erie	Niagara River
Water temperature	°C	11.88	18.85	14.58	17.27	14.85	14.71	15.38
Secchi depth	m	0.4	1.5	1.0	0.8	3.0	4.3	------
Dissolved oxygen (D.O.)	ppm	10.4	9.5	9.3	9.8	9.4	9.9	9.7
D.O. percent saturation	%	97.4	102.0	91.9	98.1	90.6	96.6	98.4
Conductivity @ 25°C	umhos/cm	329	224	256	282	298	304	330
Dissolved solids	ppm	142.7	134.6	140.3	193.7	211.2	197.6	169.4
Suspended solids	mg/l	21.62	12.14	15.42	19.86	6.63	5.32	17.92
Alkalinity, total	mg/l	91.6	81.6	83.4	82.3	89.8	103.9	95.9
Alkalinity, phenolphthalein	mg/l	------	------	------	4.2	3.7	------	7.3
pH	SU	8.09	8.27	8.03	8.42	8.23	8.26	7.83
Calcium, total	mg/l	51.2	29.1	29.8	34.4	39.7	31.3	43.6
Magnesium, total	mg/l	18.2	7.6	7.5	7.6	9.5	8.8	9.9
Potassium, total	mg/l	3.2	1.0	1.0	1.2	1.4	1.3	1.7
Sodium, total	mg/l	47.4	4.9	6.1	8.9	10.1	9.2	13.3
Chlorides, total	mg/l	20.1	8.1	17.2	------	24.4	21.6	27.7
Sulfates, total	mg/l	16.6	16.7	16.1	32.7	25.7	25.5	30.1
Fluoride, total	mg/l	0.12	0.12	0.11	0.24	0.16	0.20	0.25
Silica, dissolved	ug/l	1.11	0.72	0.83	------	------	0.32	0.19
Ammonia, dissolved	ug/l	0.018	------	0.047	0.061	0.023	0.017	------
Nitrate + nitrite, diss.	ug/l	0.290	------	0.300	0.325	0.165	0.263	------
Phosphorus, total	ug/l	------	44.5	------	------	29.1	20.7	------
Phosphorus, dissolved	ug/l	11.9	8.1	33.8	29.3	11.8	8.1	------
Phosphorus, ortho	ug/l	12.2	------	12.1	9.2	5.8	3.4	------
Chlorophyll a	ug/l	11.9	4.7	3.4	13.5	5.6	3.1	------

Many variables affect the transparency of the water, such as algae, suspended sediments, or humic substances. Water clarity is not as great in nearshore areas due to wave agitation of sediments, and because of the addition of pollutants—such as sewage effluents and industrial effluents—from human activity. The western basin is very turbid with resulting low water clarity. Although there are differences here between

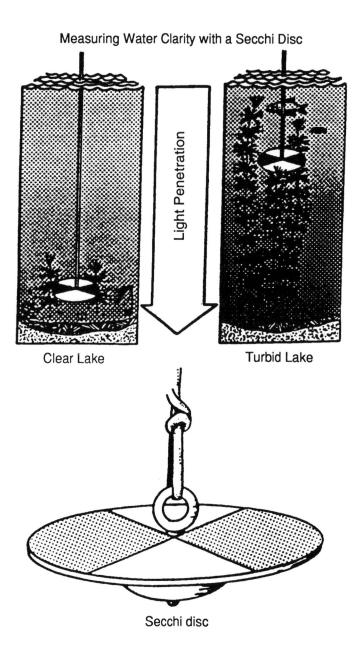

Measuring Water Clarity with a Secchi Disc

Figure 5.9. Secchi disk, simple device used to measure water transparency (Lundquist, 1975).

Light Penetration

Clear Lake   Turbid Lake

Secchi disc

inshore and offshore clarity, the difference is not as evident as that present in the central and eastern basins. Near Lorain, Ohio, along the central basin, for example, a Secchi disc would be visible 6 ft (2 m) below the water's surface. Several kilometers out from the Lorain shore, the disc is visible 10 ft (3 m) below the surface.

The western basin has, by a wide margin, the most turbid water in the Lake Erie system. This is especially true after spring and fall storm activity. After heavy rainfall, turbidity is further increased by agricultural and urban runoff.

Water clarity is better in the central and eastern basins. This is due to fewer large tributaries and deeper water. The area surrounding the deep hole of the eastern basin (210 ft or 35 m) has the greatest water clarity in the lake. Such clear areas, however, are rarely seen by visitors.

The best water clarity in the lake occurs during the winter months yet is rarely noticed because of the extensive ice coverage. However, without this ice covering to protect the water surface, intense winter storms would agitate the water column and mix bottom sediments so that the water would be more turbid than during the spring and fall. Those persons out ice fishing, or near the shoreline in the spring after the ice has moved (but before the first ice free storm), will view water that displays excellent clarity. Figures 5.10-5.13 illustrate the mean spring, summer, fall, and annual transparency patterns in Lake Erie.

Low water clarity—meaning poor visibility—in itself is not harmful to human activity or the environment. However, turbidity resulting from human activities in an environment not accustomed to turbid water can be destructive. As evidence of this, some prime fish spawning areas in the western basin have been silted over.

Eutrophication

Nutrient enrichment is a natural process usually associated with the aging of a body of water. This aging process of a lake has three stages comparable to infancy, adolescence, and adulthood. A lake in its infancy is said to be oligotrophic, or nutrient-poor. The mesotrophic stage compares to adolescence. Maximum lake age is then reached during the eutrophic stage. The eutrophication process relates to increasing productivity in the lake basin, therefore as a lake ages it moves toward a more productive status (Table 5.2).

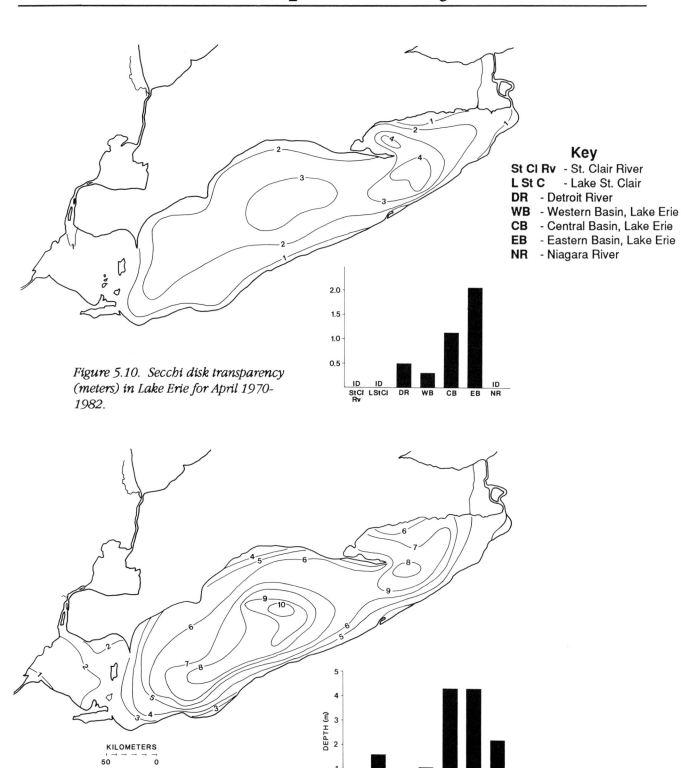

Key
St Cl Rv - St. Clair River
L St C - Lake St. Clair
DR - Detroit River
WB - Western Basin, Lake Erie
CB - Central Basin, Lake Erie
EB - Eastern Basin, Lake Erie
NR - Niagara River

Figure 5.10. Secchi disk transparency (meters) in Lake Erie for April 1970-1982.

Figure 5.11. Secchi disk transparency (meters) in Lakes Erie and St. Clair for July 1970-1982.

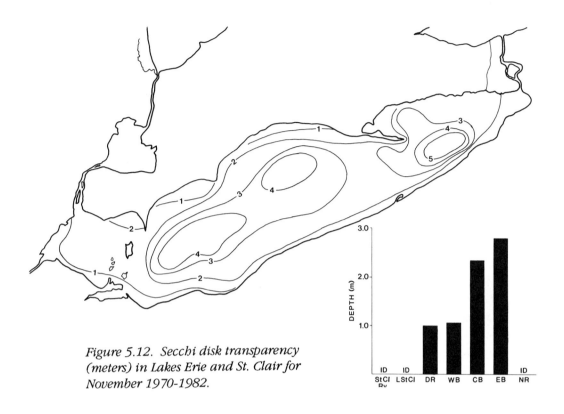

*Figure 5.12. Secchi disk transparency
(meters) in Lakes Erie and St. Clair for
November 1970-1982.*

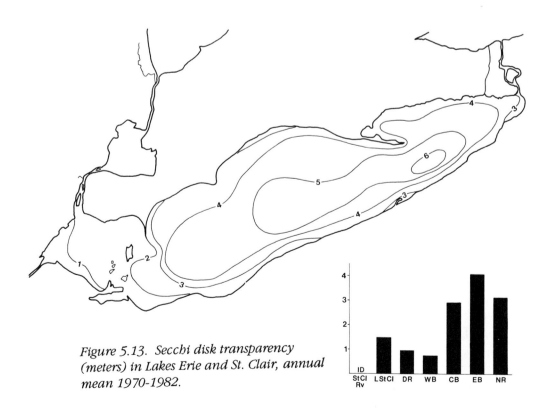

*Figure 5.13. Secchi disk transparency
(meters) in Lakes Erie and St. Clair, annual
mean 1970-1982.*

Table 5.2. Comparison of characteristics for oligotrophic and eutrophic lakes.

Oligotrophy (Lake Superior)	Eutrophy (Lake Erie)
1. Deep and steep-banked.	1. Shallow, broad littoral zone.
2. Epilimnion volume relatively small compared with hypolimnion.	2. Epilimnion/hypolimnion ratio greater.
3. Blue or green water, marked transparency.	3. Green to yellow or brownish green; limited transparency.
4. Water poor in plant nutrients & Ca++.	4. Plant nutrients and Ca++ abundant.
5. Sediments low in organic matter.	5. Profundal sediments of organic copropel.
6. Oxygen abundant at all levels at all times.	6. Oxygen depleted in summer hypolimnion.
7. Littoral plants limited, often rosette type.	7. Littoral plants abundant.
8. Phytoplankton quantitatively poor.	8. Abundant phytoplankton, mass great.
9. Water blooms of bluegreens lacking.	9. Water blooms common.
10. Profundal bottom fauna diverse intolerant of low oxygen tensions.	10. Profundal benthos poor in species; survive low oxygen.
11. Profundal benthos quantitatively poor.	11. Profundal benthic biomass great.
12. *Tanytarsus*-type midge larvae in profundal benthos.	12. *Chironomus*, the profundal midge larba; *Chaoborus* present.
13. Deep-water salmonid and coregonid fishes.	13. No stenothermal fish in hypolimnion.
14. Attached alga *Cladophora* lacking.	14. Attached alga *Cladophora* present.
15. No taste and odor problem.	15. Significant taste and odor problem.

During the natural aging process of lakes, increasing enrichment leads to increased quantities of phytoplankton which eventually die and fall to the bottom. Accumulation of organic matter in quantities too numerous to be decomposed by bacteria leads to the shallowing of the lake. The natural end to the eutrophication process is the filling in of the lake with decaying plant life. The natural aging process of a lake is very slow, and it is not probable that during a lifetime one could observe all three stages. Pollution by man, however, accelerates the aging process. In the past, references were made to Lake Erie being "dead." In actuality, there was more living material in the lake than during any previous time. Lake Erie eutrophication is being speeded by human influences. Or, it can be said, the lake is undergoing "cultural" eutrophication.

A lake's production is subject to the fertility of its watershed and groundwaters. Lakes with infertile watersheds have small nutrient loadings and are nutrient poor, or oligotrophic. Lakes with fertile watersheds, conversely, are subject to increased nutrient loading. Examining the pollution of Lake Erie first requires a look at its watershed.

In a little more than 200 years, the drainage basin was transformed from wilderness into a workhorse watershed used intensively for agriculture and industry by a population of nearly 13.5 million persons in 1980. In an extensive review of Great Lakes eutrophication, Beeton (1969) noted that changes in the biota can be related, either directly or indirectly, to human activity. Lakes showing the greatest deterioration have been in areas subjected to the greatest population growth. Increases of 100% or greater occurred between 1930 and 1960 in the Cleveland, Detroit, and Toledo metropolitan areas. Lake Erie may have aged 15,000 years since the turn of the century.

Phosphorus is necessary for unlimited algal growth in aquatic systems, and this is the nutrient most often associated with the accelerated enrichment of Lake Erie. Contributions from fertilizers, urban run-off, domestic sewage, and industrial wastewater make up the major portion of the phosphorus loaded to Lake Erie (Sly, 1976). The rich farmland in the Maumee River watershed (Figure 5.14) has received increased amounts of artificial fertilizers since the inception of the Federal Price Support Program, which restricted the number of acres a farmer could plant, but placed no restriction on yield per acre (Verduin, 1964). Detergents are also a major source of phosphorus. Phosphates are used in

TOTAL PHOSPHORUS (µg/l)

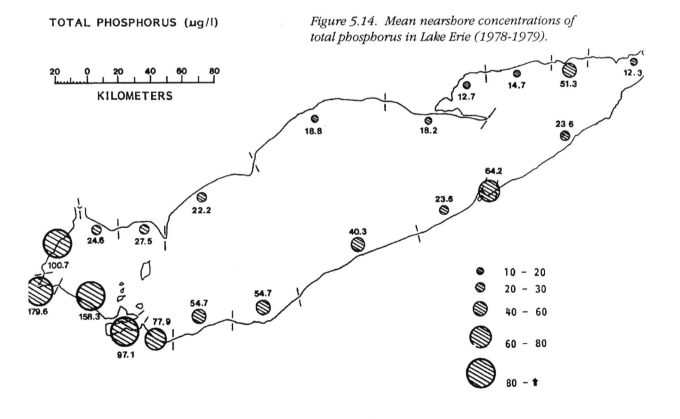

Figure 5.14. Mean nearshore concentrations of total phosphorus in Lake Erie (1978-1979).

detergents as water-softening agents to promote more efficient use of the cleaning agents. Detergents came into use in washing products after World War II. Consumption increased considerably with the advent of dishwashing machines in the late 1950s.

A five-fold increase was observed in the concentration of total phosphorus in Lake Erie between 1948 and 1968 (Verduin, 1969). This increase is one of the major causes of the cultural eutrophication of Lake Erie and of the oxygen depletion in the central basin. Much of the research conducted on Lake Erie since 1970 has focused on phosphorus. Since that time there has also been a major effort to enlarge and/or improve many of the sewage treatment plants in the Lake Erie basin. As a result of such efforts, in the 10-year period between 1971 and 1980, phosphorus contributed to Lake Erie from the Detroit River has fallen by 50% (Figure 5.15).

Excessive nutritional enrichment is the single greatest water quality problem in Lake Erie. Over-enrichment has caused undesirable interference with water supplies, recreation, and fishery. Excess nutrients can result in tremendous overproduction of aquatic plants, especially the

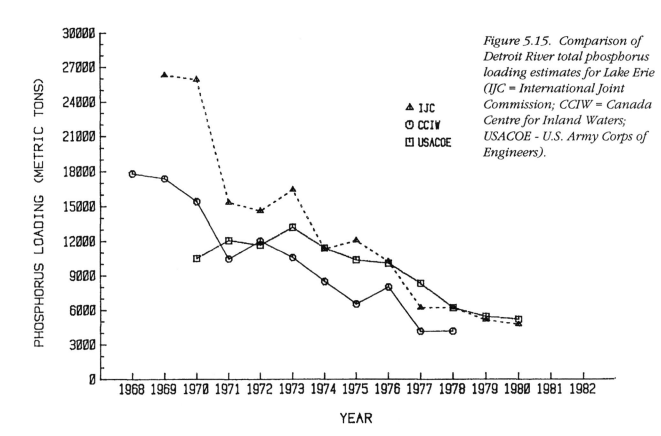

Figure 5.15. Comparison of Detroit River total phosphorus loading estimates for Lake Erie (IJC = International Joint Commission; CCIW = Canada Centre for Inland Waters; USACOE - U.S. Army Corps of Engineers).

planktonic forms. This problem has caused western Lake Erie to be classified as eutrophic (Table 5.2). Also the filamentous algae of the island region, such as *Cladophora glomerata*, flourish with high nutrient concentrations. Current and wave actions often dislodge and deposit large quantities of this attached algae onto the shoreline resulting in nuisance accumulations and obnoxious odors from the decaying bio-mass. To the public, this is very tangible evidence of excessive algal growth, frequently interpreted as environmental degradation.

The distribution of total phosphorus is dependent on many things—the productivity of the drainage basin, lake bathymetry, weather, soil erosion, status of sewage treatment plants, and agricultural practices within the watershed. The distribution of total phosphorus within the Lake Erie region varies both spatially and temporally. A representative month from each season is presented to demonstrate this variability (Figures 5.16-5.19). Highest concentrations are during springtime after the snow has melted when rains purge the surrounding drainage basin and spring storms churn lake sediment. As with all the seasons, highest concentrations occur in the southern half of the western basin and along the United States shoreline. The mid-lake sections of the central and eastern basins usually have lower levels due to a lack of point sources (effluents) and non-point sources (erosion and agricultural runoff) of total phosphorus. The July contour displays the east to west gradation of nutrients that occurs in the Sandusky sub-basin. The high value of total phosphorus adjacent to Sandusky Bay demonstrates the importance of this area to Lake Erie loading. The November contour is erratic-looking, most likely due to the effect of combining different weather years. The annual distribution shows that the Maumee River has a noticeable effect on the total phosphorus concentration of Lake Erie. The northern half of the western basin maintains low levels of total phosphorus because of the low total phosphorus concentrations in Detroit River water. The eastern and central basins are lower in concentrations and more consistent throughout the year.

Stimulated by abundant phosphorus, algae grows rapidly resulting in large concentrations of chlorophyll in the lake. Therefore, like total phosphorus, chlorophyll varies seasonally and spatially within Lake Erie. This variability of chlorophyll is explained by the availability of nutrients, water temperature, algal productivity, weather, and water clarity. To display this, spring, summer, and fall contours are presented in Figures 5.20-5.23. Maximum conditions for chlorophyll production occur during the summer. The eastern basin remains around 2.5 µg/l. In the summer, although sunlight and warm temperatures are conducive to algal growth, less nutrients are available in the eastern and central basins to

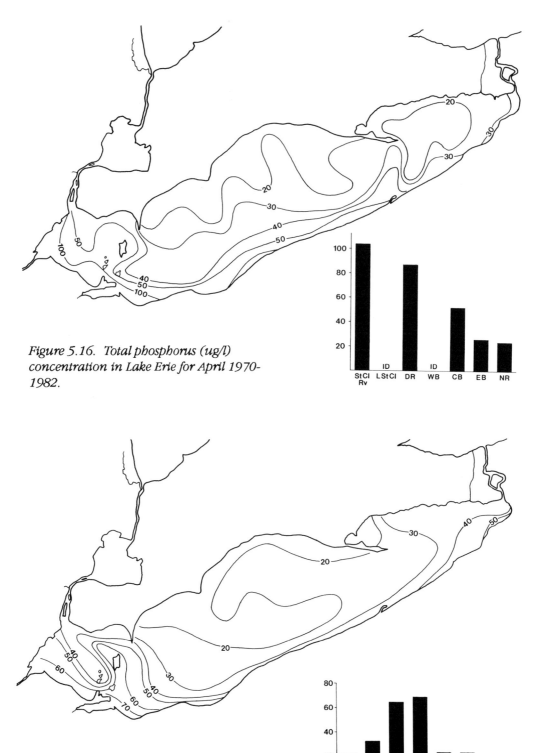

Figure 5.16. *Total phosphorus (ug/l) concentration in Lake Erie for April 1970-1982.*

Figure 5.17. *Total phosphorus (ug/l) concentration in Lakes Erie and St. Clair for July 1970-1982.*

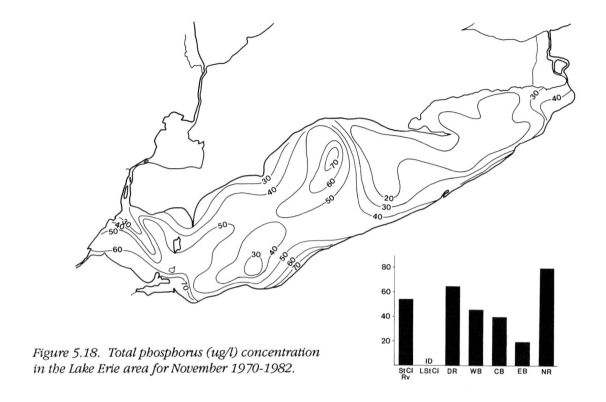

Figure 5.18. Total phosphorus (ug/l) concentration in the Lake Erie area for November 1970-1982.

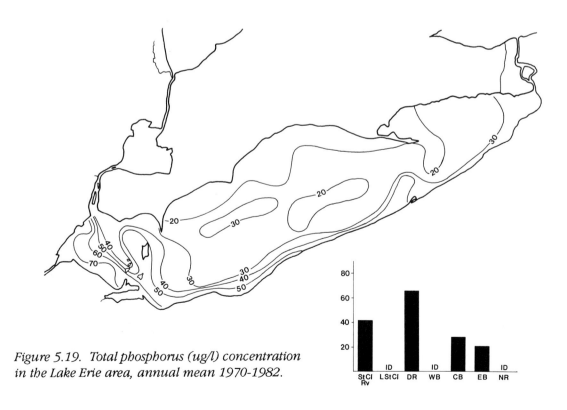

Figure 5.19. Total phosphorus (ug/l) concentration in the Lake Erie area, annual mean 1970-1982.

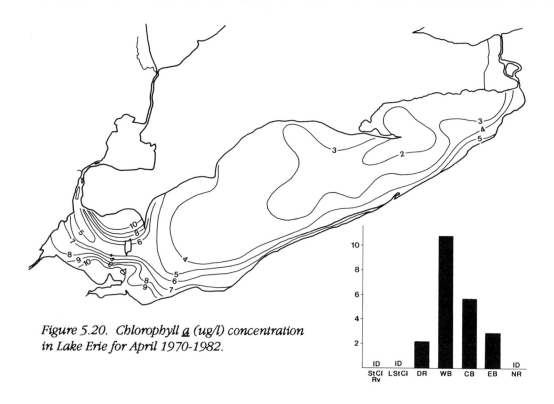

Figure 5.20. Chlorophyll a (ug/l) concentration in Lake Erie for April 1970-1982.

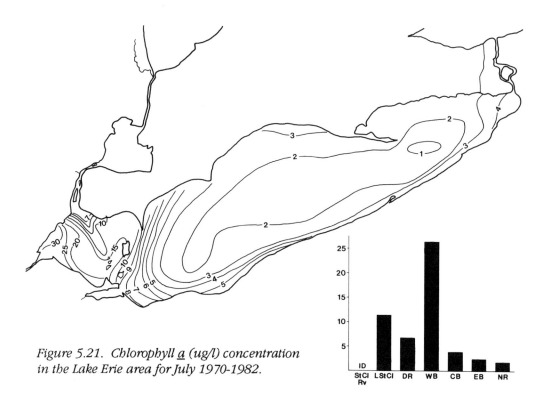

Figure 5.21. Chlorophyll a (ug/l) concentration in the Lake Erie area for July 1970-1982.

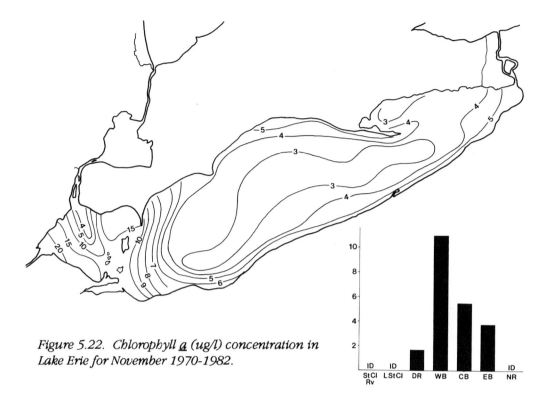

Figure 5.22. Chlorophyll *a* (ug/l) concentration in Lake Erie for November 1970-1982.

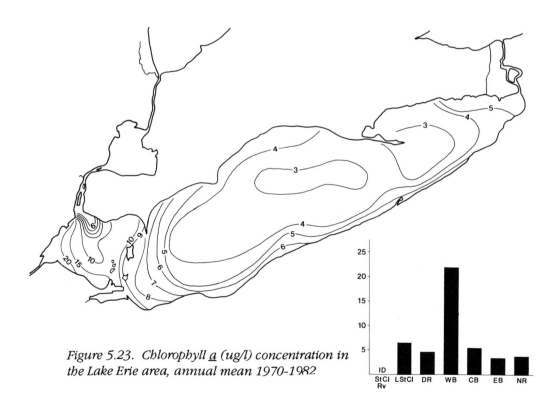

Figure 5.23. Chlorophyll *a* (ug/l) concentration in the Lake Erie area, annual mean 1970-1982.

support such growth. Springtime nutrients have settled to the bottom by this period or have been absorbed by previous algal populations. Also, once on the lake bottom, stratification in these two basins prevents the nutrients from being recycled until the fall turnover.

Trophic Status

Determining a lake's general condition, or trophy, is important because it summarizes many aspects of the lake's character. To determine which condition is present (oligotrophy, mesotrophy, or eutrophy) one must consider the lake's bathymetry, chemical nature, and biological status. To assimilate these levels of information an equation has been derived, the results of which are presented in Figure 5.24. From these results, Lake Erie is shown to have four trophic levels: eutrophic, eutrophic/mesotrophic, mesotrophic, and oligotrophic.

The western basin is predominantly eutrophic except for a narrow band of eutrophic/mesotrophic and mesotrophic waters along the Ontario shoreline. This area is affected by the higher quality Lake Huron water that is forced against the shoreline. The Sandusky sub-basin is eutrophic/mesotrophic since this area has combined features of the western and central basins. As more turbid western water approaches this deeper and wider region, the water mass moves more slowly and allows some of its sediment to settle. This part of the lake exhibits the fastest sedimentation rate. Remaining portions of the central and eastern basins are mesotrophic while deeper areas are oligotrophic.

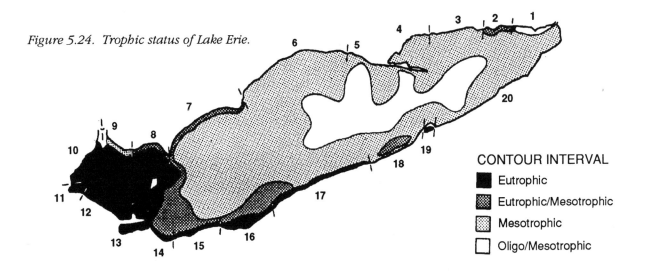

Figure 5.24. Trophic status of Lake Erie.

CONTOUR INTERVAL
- Eutrophic
- Eutrophic/Mesotrophic
- Mesotrophic
- Oligo/Mesotrophic

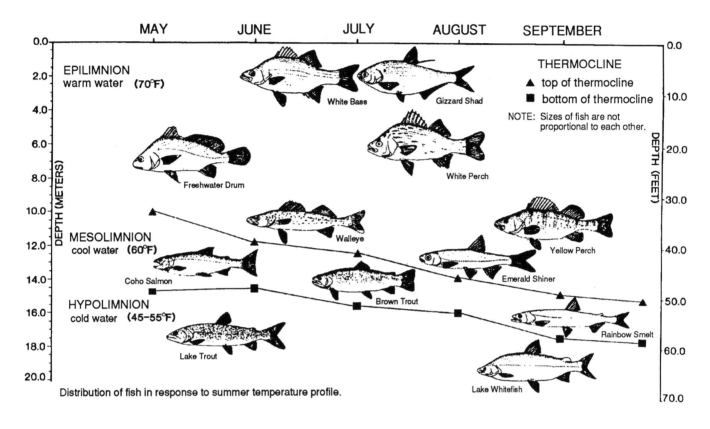

Distribution of fish in response to summer temperature profile.

Figure 5.25. Lake Erie thermal structure showing the mean annual trend in hypolimnion thickness for the central basin (1970-1982).

Oxygen Depletion

In the central basin during late summer, this is one of the least obvious but one of the most serious pollution problems. To comprehend how this depletion occurs, it is necessary to understand the physical condition—stratification—that must exist before oxygen depletion occurs. In early May, surface waters (the epilimnion) of the central basin warm more quickly than the bottom waters (the hypolimnion). Surface water temperatures may be over 68°F (20°C) while bottom temperatures rarely exceed 50°F (10°C). This results in a middle depth—the mesolimnion—that evidences rapid temperature change—the thermocline. The epilimnion is still relatively high in the water column in early June. But as surface waters continue to warm, the epilimnion volume increases with a simultaneous decreasing hypolimnion volume (Figure 5.25). Mixing of the hypolimnion water with the oxygen-rich epilimnion water is impeded by the temperature density gradient of the mesolimnion.

During the period of stratification (late May to mid-September), dissolved oxygen content of the hypolimnion depletes steadily (Figure 5.26) due to the oxidation of reduced metallic species and organic matter (Burns and Ross, 1972).

Interest in the dissolved oxygen concentration of the central basin was initiated in 1930 (Fish, 1960). Results of 15 surveys between 1930 and 1982 are presented in Figure 5.27.

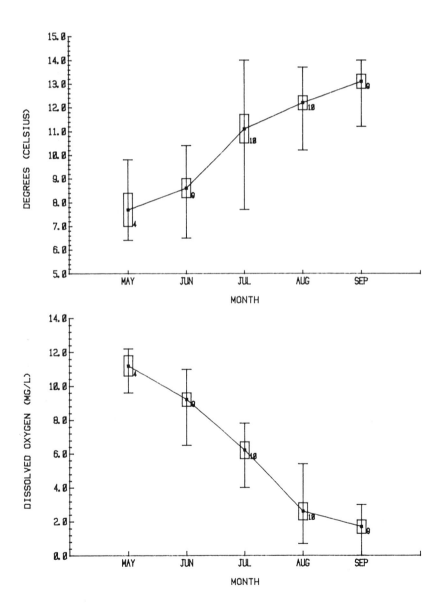

Figure 5.26. Mean annual trends in hypolimnion temperature and dissolved oxygen for the central basin of Lake Erie (1970-1982).

*Figure 5.27.
Distribution of
phyolimnion
anoxia in
central Lake Erie
(1930-1982).*

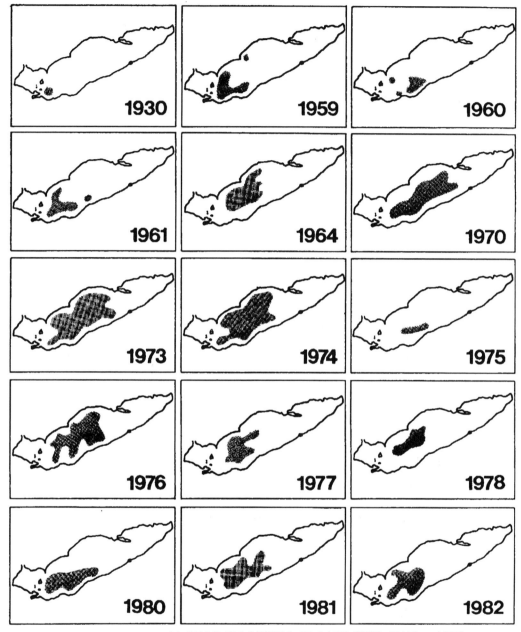

DISTRIBUTION OF ANOXIA IN LAKE ERIE (1930 - 1982).

Depletion of oxygen in the hypolimnion, produced three major effects—one of chemical importance and two of biological importance. When oxygen is still present in the hypolimnion, phosphorus is precipitated as insoluble ferric phosphate. Under anoxic (oxygen-depleted) conditions, the reduction to iron causes precipitation of ferric sulfide

(FeS), freeing phosphate (PO_4) to dissolve in the hypolimnion waters. This phosphorus "regeneration" in the central basin of Lake Erie has been an internal source of nutrients. Even if phosphorus loading to Lake Erie is reduced, improvements in the central basin will be slow over the next 15 years. This is due to the phosphorus regeneration mechanism (Burns, 1985).

Many bottom-dwelling organisms are adversely affected by low oxygen levels. There are numerous reports of changes in species composition in Lake Erie. Most noticeable has been the change from the oxygen-dependent mayfly larvae to oxygen-independent tubificid worms. Mayfly larvae (Figure 5.28) comprised a major portion of the fishery food supply before their disappearance in 1954.

The species composition of fish in Lake Erie has also changed as a result of low dissolved oxygen. A minimum of 5 ppm (or mg/l) dissolved oxygen has been reported as a requirement to support fish life. This being the case, the fish cannot remain in the hypolimnion in the late summer months since dissolved oxygen levels are normally less than 5 mg/l from August 1 until the end of the stratified season (normally mid-September).

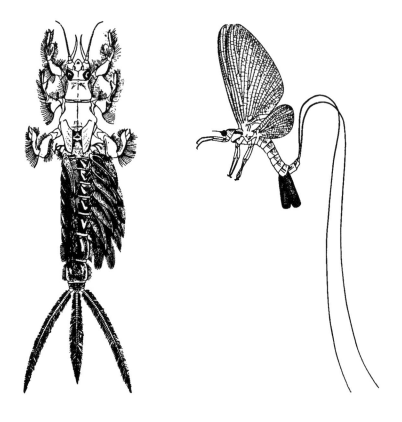

Figure 5.28. Nymph (A) and emergent form (B) of the mayfly Hexagenia (after Pennak, 1978). This mud-burrowing insect was extirpated from Lake Erie in the 1950s due to low oxygen concentration.

Lake Flora and Fauna

The classification of lake organisms is given in the Biological Structure section based on the role (niche) of the organism within the community. Another approach to organism classification in aquatic ecology is by their habitat. The habitat of an organism is the place where it lives, or the location where one would expect to find it. The ecological niche, on the other hand, is the position or status of an organism within its community and ecosystem resulting from the organism's structural adaptations, physiological responses, and specific behavior (inherited and/or learned). The ecological niche of an organism depends not only on where it lives but also on what it does. By analogy, it may be said that the habitat is the organism's "address," and the niche is its "profession."

Based on the habitat approach, Lake Erie organisms are classified as (Figure 5.29):

Neuston. Organisms resting or swimming on the water surface.

Plankton. Floating organisms, both plants (phytoplankton) and animal (zooplankton), whose movements are more or less dependent on currents.

While some of the zooplankton exhibit active swimming movements that aid in maintaining vertical position, plankton as a whole is unable to move against appreciable currents. In practice, net plankton is that which is caught in a fine-meshed net which is towed slowly through the water; nanoplankton is too small to be caught in a net and must be extracted from water collected in a bottle or by means of a pump.

Periphyton. Organisms (both plant and animal) attached or clinging to stems and leaves of rooted plants or other surfaces projecting above the bottom (some scientists use the German term *aufwuchs* for this group).

Benthon. Organisms attached or resting on the bottom or living in the bottom sediments.

Nekton. Swimming organisms able to navigate at will (and hence capable of avoiding plankton nets, water bottles, etc.).

Avifauna. Organisms with the ability to fly, especially the birds of a given region.

Biosphere - The Life

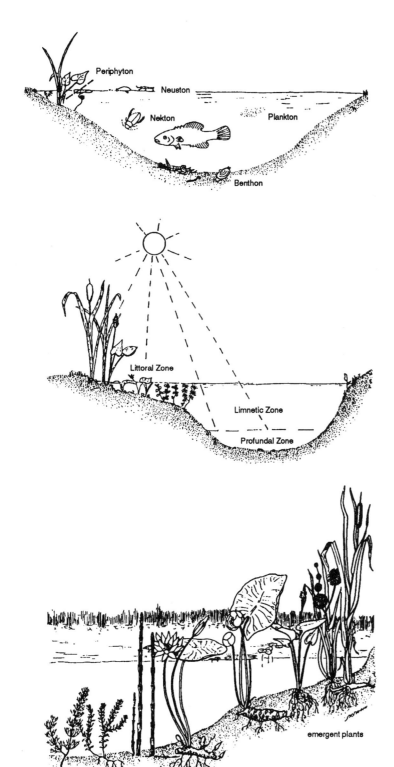

Figure 5.29. Lake Erie area environments: (A) types of littoral organisms, (B) areas of population in lentic (lake) water, and (C) zonation at the margin of a lake (from Klotts, 1966).

Neuston

This is the community of flora and fauna associated with surface tension.

The difference in density between the water and the air above is on the order of 1,000 times. This great density difference produces a film with which small organisms are associated.

Resting on this film is often a thick layer of organic substances such as lipoproteins. This layer and the material collecting in it support the animals known as the epineuston. Two common, but often unobserved, animal taxa in this assemblage are small arachnids (water mites) and tiny insects known as springtails. These insects have a markedly hydrophobic cuticle fitting them for such a habitat. The water striders, consisting of two hemipteran (bug) families, are among the most conspicuous of the epineuston (Figure 5.30).

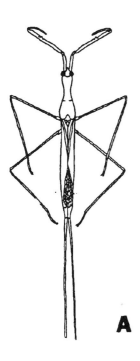
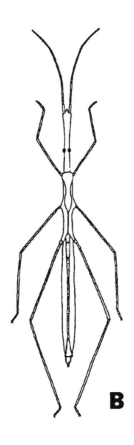
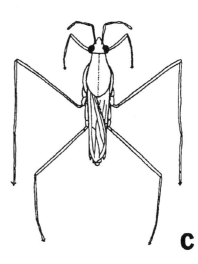

Figure 5.30. Neustonic insects: (A) water scorpion, (B) marsh treader, and (C) water strider (after Pennak, 1978).

The conspicuous green covering on some ponds is made up of the duckweeds (*Lemna* spp.), another component of the neuston. These tiny angiosperms float with rootlets hanging in the water below the surface. The dusty or oily appearance of some pond surfaces is due to an epineustic microflora. Floating algal groups such as the chrysophyceans, euglenophytes, and chlorophyceans contribute to this appearance.

The hyponeuston is the community living at and under the surface film. A host of algae and protozoans can be found here. They provide food for other organisms, such as mosquitoes, which in turn are preyed upon by top-minnows, such as *Gambusia*.

Plankton

Phytoplankton. These are the algae of open lakes and streams whose movements are dependent on currents for the most part, and they consist of a diverse assemblage of nearly all major taxonomic groups. Phytoplankters can be single floating cells or floating colonies in the forms of spheres, globes, or filaments. The cell walls can be composed of cellulose (green algae) or silica (diatoms). The western basin of Lake Erie, with its high nutrient concentrations, is an excellent media for phytoplankton. The most common algal groups found in the lake are the Bacillarophycea (diatoms), Chlorophyceae (green algae), Cyanophyceae (blue-greens), and Crytophyceae (cryptomonad algae) (Figure 5.31).

There are several environmental factors which interact to regulate spatial and temporal growth of phytoplankton populations. These include basic physiological requirements of temperature and light and the means of remaining within the photic zone long enough to complete growth and reproduction. Densities of phytoplankton populations are largely affected by the availability of inorganic and organic nutrients and by herbivorous predation and parasitism.

The following size classification and terminology is in current use:

NAME	SIZE RANGE
Macroplankton	>500 μm
Microplankton (net plankton)	50-500 μm
Nanoplankton	10-50 μm
Ultraplankton	0.5-10 μm

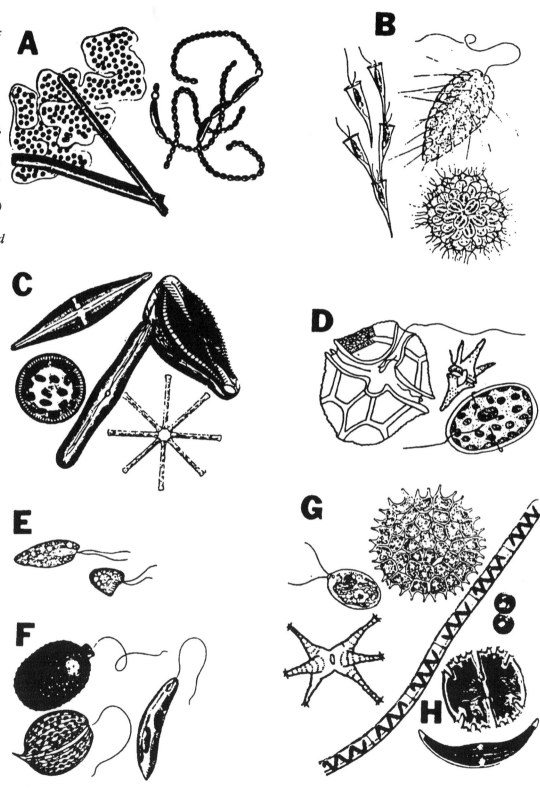

Figure 5.31. Phytoplankton: (A) blue-green algae, (B) golden-brown algae, (C) diatoms, (D) dinoflagellates, (E) cryptomonads, (F) euglenoids, (G) green algae, and (H) desmids (after Cole, 1983 and APHA, 1985).

Plankton is collected in the field with a tow net either vertically or horizontally. The plankton net is both a qualitative and quantitative sampling device. The sample may be quantified by using a flow meter calculating flow rates to determine the volume of water filtered through the net.

The alga population of Lake Erie is composed mainly of diatoms (~75%). Two periods of peak plankton abundance occur yearly. A spring pulse consists almost entirely of diatoms and the most predominant genera are *Asterionella, Fragilaria, Melosira,* and *Synedra.* These genera are indicators of eutrophic conditions. Early summer is characterized by green algae such as *Pediastrum* and *Spirogyra.* In August and September, blooms of blue-green algae are common with *Anabaena, Nostoc,* and *Anacystis* the most dominant. A bloom of *Oscillatoria* and *Aphanizomenon* often occurs during the hot days of August, too. This annual cycle of algal forms is illustrated in Figure 5.32.

Zooplankton. These are the animals of the plankton community. They are herbivores (phytoplankton eating), carnivores (zooplankton eating), and omnivores (phytoplankton and zooplankton eating). These animals are capable of some degree of locomotion and are divided into three major groups: the rotifers, and two small crustacean forms, the cladocerans and copepods (Figure 5.33).

Figure 5.32. Seasonal cycle of phytoplankton populations in Lake Erie (from Lundquist, 1975).

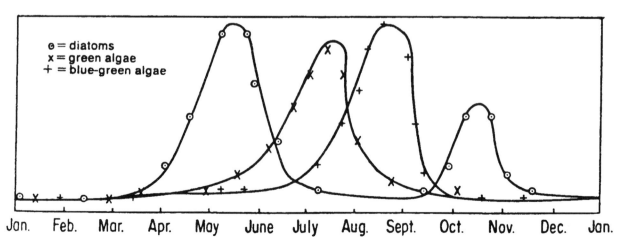

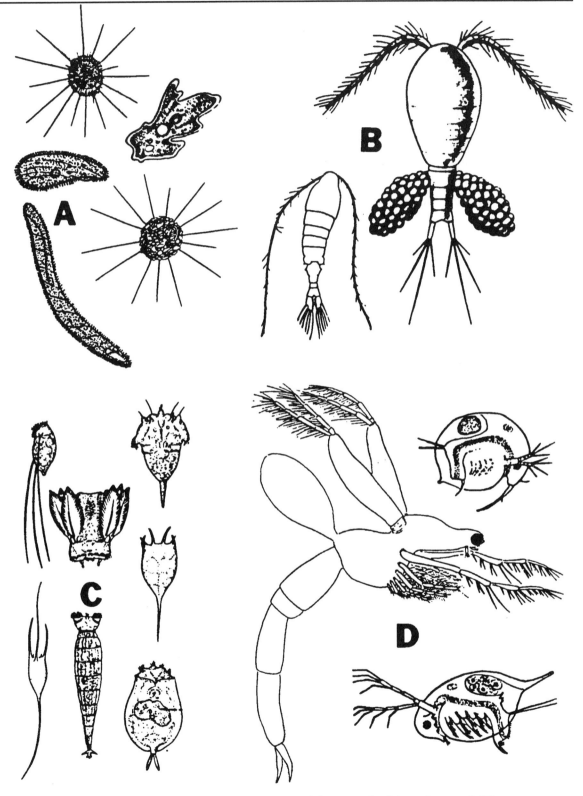

Figure 5.33. Zooplankton: (A) protozoans, (B) copepods, (C) rotifers, and (D) cladocerans (after Cole, 1983 and APHA, 1985).

Rotifers compose a large class of the pseudocoelomate (fake body cavity) Phylum Aschelminthes which are essentially microscopic, their length ranging between 100 and 500 micrometers (μm). Most rotifers, both sessile and planktonic, are nonpredatory. Omnivorous feeding occurs by means of ciliary direction of living and detrital particulate organic matter into the mouth cavity.

Rotifers occur in a variety of aquatic habitats, but most are largely sessile and associated with substrate in the littoral region of lakes. The vast majority of rotifers encountered under natural conditions are females. Males are known for relatively few species and are much smaller than females, degenerate and seldom live for more than a few days. Common examples in Lake Erie include *Synchaeta*, *Keratella*, and *Brachionus*.

Copepods form an order within the Class Crustacea. They are categorized into three distinct groups: the suborder Cyclopoida, Calanoida, and Harpacticoida. The body length ranges from 0.3 to 3.2 mm, but the great majority are less than 2.0 mm long. Identification of the suborders is based mainly on morphological details of appendages and feeding habits (Figure 5.34).

Calanoid copepods feed largely by filtration of plankton. Their antennae are used as screws to produce a current from which particles are filtered by mouth parts modified for seizing and biting. The food consists mainly of unicellular plant and animal organisms and organic

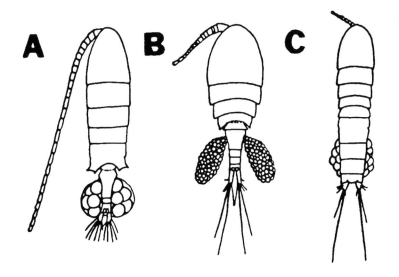

Figure 5.34. Freshwater copepods: (A) calanoid, (B) cyclopoid, and (C) harpacticoid (after Edmondson, 1963). Note that only the left antennae are shown.

debris. Harpacticoid copepods are almost exclusively littoral, inhabiting macrophytes, mosses, littoral sediments, and particulate organic matter. Cyclopoid copepods are primarily littoral benthic species and the calanoid copepods are exclusively planktonic in the pelagic zone.

Littoral and plankton copepods are easily collected with a plankton net or dipnet. Many species may be obtained by drawing nets through rooted aquatic vegetation and by skimming the bottom. To collect harpacticoids, the top centimeter or two of mud and debris should be scooped up, brought into a laboratory, and allowed to settle. The harpacticoids can be found moving about at the mud-water interface and can be removed with a pipette or eye dropper.

Cladocerans, the water fleas, vary in size with individuals ranging from 0.2 to 3.0 mm. They are very common, good swimmers, and are a preferred fish food. The common *Daphnia* have been favorite objects of observation by students and professional biologists. All have a distinct head, and the body is covered by a bivalve carapace. Light sensitive organs usually consist of a large compound eye and a smaller ocellus. The second antennae are large swimming appendages and constitute the primary organs of locomotion.

Complex movements of the thoracic legs produce a constant current of water between the valves. These movements further serve to filter food particles from the water and collect them in a groove at the base of the legs. This stream of food is fed forward to the mouth parts where the particles are ground between the surfaces of the mandibles then transported into the mouth. Algae, protozoans, organic detritus, and bacteria are the chief foods for cladocerans. A few genera, such as *Polyphemus* and *Leptodora*, are predaceous and have legs modified for seizing.

Seasonal succession is variable among cladoceran species and within species for different lake conditions. Some are perennial species that over-winter in low population densities as adults rather than as resting eggs. They exhibit maximum numbers in surface layers during colder periods in the spring and in the cooler hypolimnetic and metalimnetic layers during summer stratification. Common open water and limnetic forms in Lake Erie include *Daphnia longispira*, *D. pulex*, *Bosmina*, and *Eubosmina*. The greatest abundance of species may be collected in the vegetation at margins of lakes and rivers.

The zooplankton in Lake Erie has doubled in the past 50 years. The dominant genera include: *Cyclops* and *Diaptomus* (Copepoda); *Daphnia*,

Bosmina, and *Leptodora* (Cladocera); *Keratella, Asplanchna,* and
Synchaeta (Rotifera). Zooplankton populations are low during the
winter months. Adult crustaceans are rare in the spring and fall, but
nauplic (immature copepods) are most abundant in late spring and form
an important part of the diet of larval fish. The adult crustaceans
achieve the greatest abundance during the summer (Figure 5.35) and
also serve as a significant link in the food chain of Lake Erie fishes.

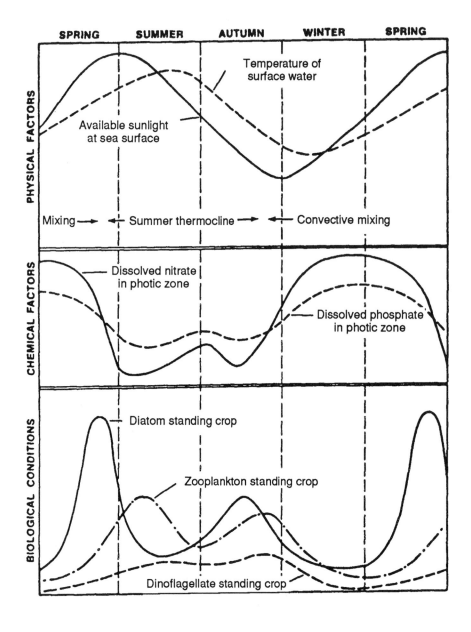

*Figure 5.35. Seasonal
fluctuation in physical and
chemical factors which in
turn influence phytoplankton
and zooplankton populations
in Lake Erie (after Sumich,
1984 [redrawn from Riley
1946 and 1947]).*

Periphyton

These are microfloral growths upon a substrate (Figure 5.36). Among the algal communities, the following subdivisions are used: (1) epipelic algae and the flora growing on sediments (fine, organic); (2) epilithic algae growing on rock or stone surfaces; (3) epiphytic algae growing on macrophytic surfaces; (4) epizoic algae growing on surfaces of animals; and (5) epipsammic algae as the rather specific organisms growing on or moving through sand. The general word psammon refers to all organisms growing on or moving through sand.

A sixth group of algae found aggregated in the littoral zone is the metaphyton which is neither strictly attached to substrate nor truly planktonic. The metaphyton commonly originates from true phytoplankton populations that aggregate among macrophytes and debris of the littoral zone as a result of wind-induced water movements. In other situations, the metaphytonic algae derive from fragmentation of dense epipelic and epiphytic algal populations (Wetzel, 1975).

Benthon

These are the organisms that are attached or sessile on the lake bottom or are found living in the substrate (Figures 5.37-5.40). This definition includes not only zoo-benthos but also phyto-benthos, the attached algae, and higher aquatic plants found growing on the substrate. A typical benthic habitat within an aquatic ecosystem consists of many different kinds of organisms and many species of each type. This component of the aquatic community may include the molluscs (i.e. snails and clams), the immature and mature stages of aquatic insects (i.e.

Figure 5.36. Periphyton communitues in Lake Erie.

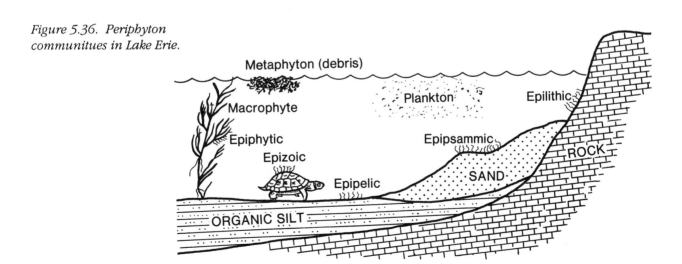

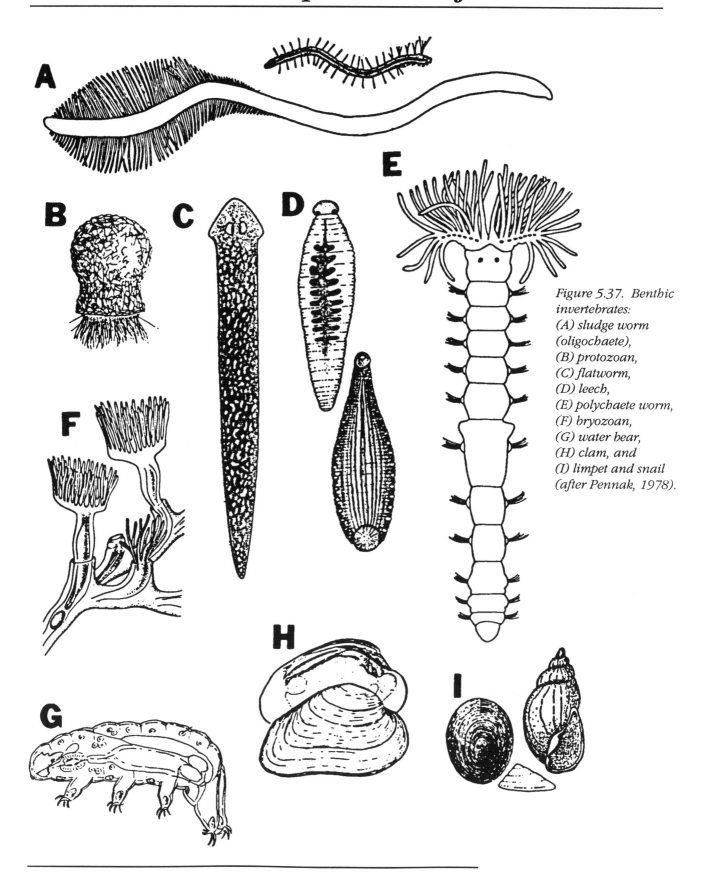

Figure 5.37. Benthic invertebrates: (A) sludge worm (oligochaete), (B) protozoan, (C) flatworm, (D) leech, (E) polychaete worm, (F) bryozoan, (G) water bear, (H) clam, and (I) limpet and snail (after Pennak, 1978).

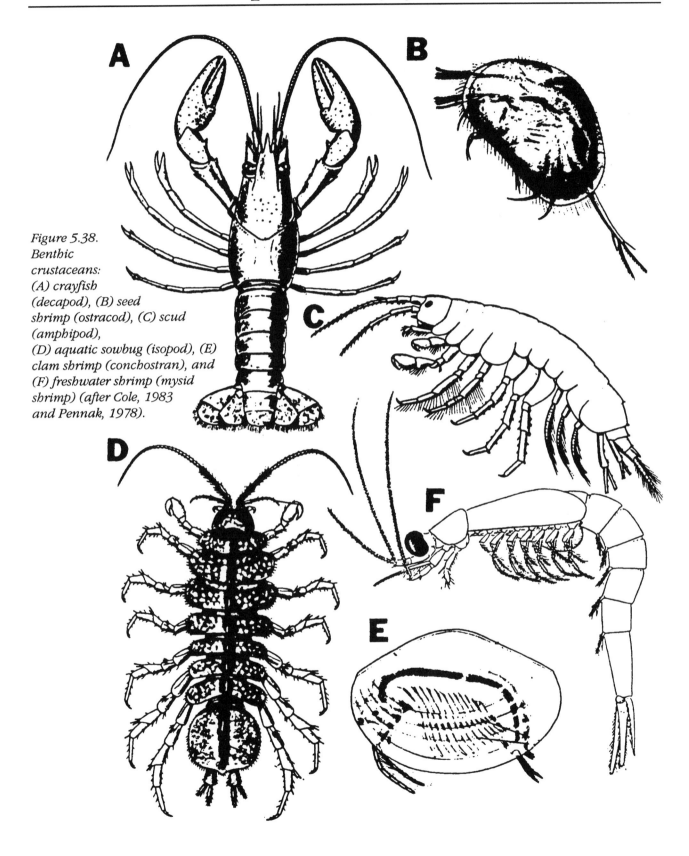

Figure 5.38. Benthic crustaceans: (A) crayfish (decapod), (B) seed shrimp (ostracod), (C) scud (amphipod), (D) aquatic sowbug (isopod), (E) clam shrimp (conchostran), and (F) freshwater shrimp (mysid shrimp) (after Cole, 1983 and Pennak, 1978).

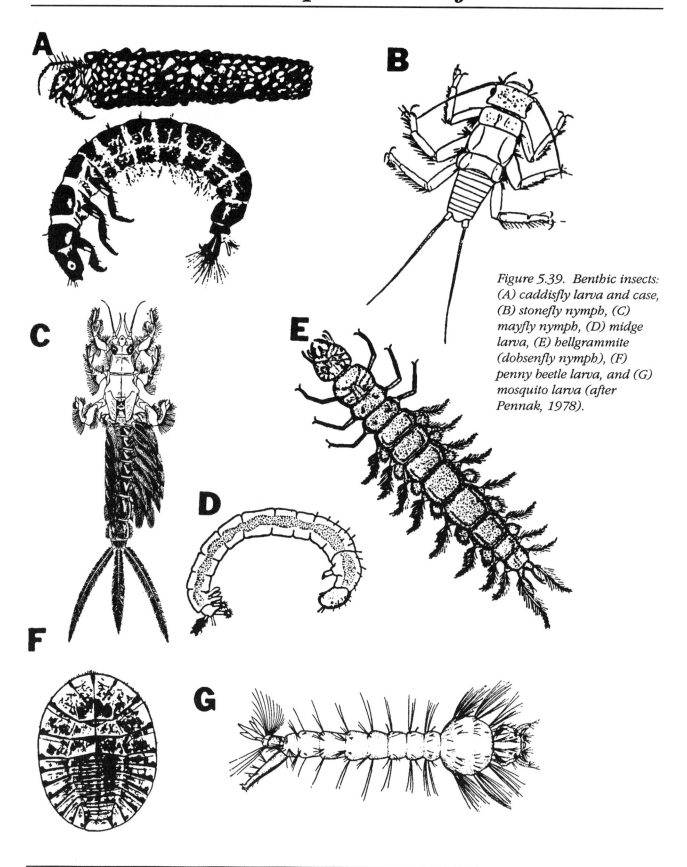

Figure 5.39. Benthic insects: (A) caddisfly larva and case, (B) stonefly nymph, (C) mayfly nymph, (D) midge larva, (E) hellgrammite (dobsenfly nymph), (F) penny beetle larva, and (G) mosquito larva (after Pennak, 1978).

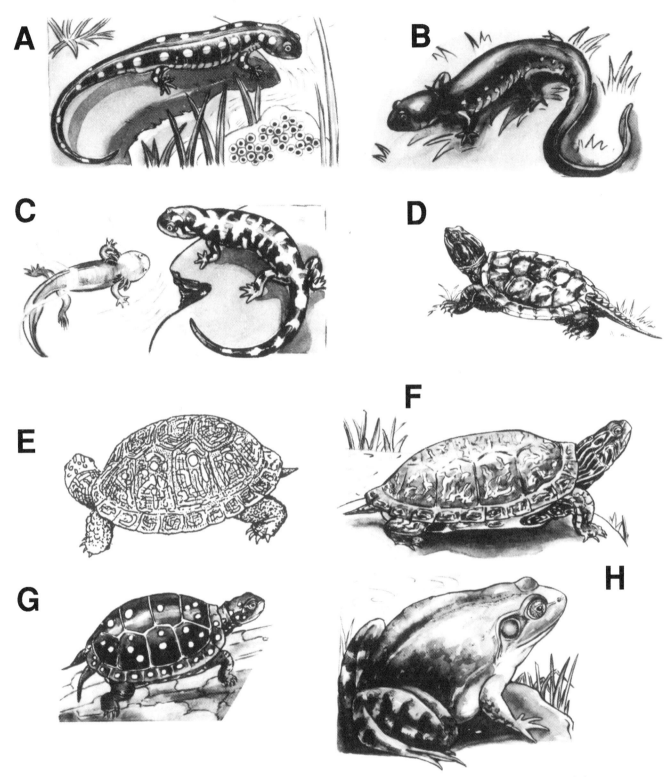

Figure 5.40. Benthic invertebrates: (A) spotted salamander, (B) Jefferson's salamander, (C) tiger salamander, (D) snapping turtle, (E) Blanding's turtle, (F) map turtle, (G) spotted turtle, and (H) bullfrog (after Buck, 1955).

mosquitoes, midges, mayflies, stonefly nymphs, and caddisfly larvae), and many other groups including some amphibians and reptiles (Figure 5.40). Benthic plants include the attached algae *Cladophora*, *Ulothrix*, and *Bangia* with *Valisneria* and *Potamogeton* representatives of aquatic vascular plants.

The distribution and density of benthic organisms is quite dependent upon the type of substrate. Burrowing forms like chironomids and oligochaetes are most common in soft mud bottoms, whereas dragon-flies would be most common in shallow water with emergent vegetation, and some of the mayflies and caddisflies would be most abundant in a pebble-cobble substrate.

The benthos are an important link in the food chain and provide an indicator of the current state of health of the lake. Sampling the sediments and the benthos is done with dredges such as an Eckman, Ponar, or Petersen. These are quantitative sampling devices, as is the Surber Sampler which is used for streams.

The bottom fauna of Lake Erie is composed principally of the aquatic earthworms, midge larvae, fingernail clams, and snails. Most of these forms are pollution tolerant and occur in greatest concentrations near the mouths of the Detroit, Maumee, and Raisin Rivers. Pollution sensitive organisms such as amphipods, mayfly nymphs, larger clams and caddisfly larvae are scarce near the river mouths and more abundant in the islands area. The benthic community of bottom animals in the lake and nearby ponds is an accumulation of diverse and abundant organisms occurring in several different substrates; mud, sand, clay, gravel, and rock. The oligochaetes comprise over 60% of the total bottom fauna, particularly in the soft mud which is the most common sediment. Chironomid larvae make up less than 20% and sphaerid clams 10% of the benthos. The remaining percentage of the benthic fauna includes isopods, leeches, and crustaceans. A new invader to the lake is the zebra mussel. The benthic population of western Lake Erie is representative of eutrophic but not grossly polluted waters.

A myriad of factors affect the species composition and the numbers of individuals that live in a particular lake at any moment. Primary factors that determine Lake Erie's ecology are such things as climate and total abundance of inorganic nutrients. Some species have been eliminated from a lake because they cannot tolerate one or more of the lake's characteristics. Other species have been out-competed by organisms that are better suited to the environment. Some species flourish for a period of time and then give way to other species that are more compatible with changed conditions. Planktonic organisms are particularly noteworthy in this respect. Plankton communities are characterized by seasonal successions as species become more and then less dominant during the year. Other organisms—like fish—that must maintain stable populations continuously in order to reproduce have to be tolerant of aquatic conditions year round.

Nekton

Some insects (Figure 5.41) and water snakes (Figure 5.42) are good swimmers, although fish are the largest and most visible nektonic organisms in our aquatic ecosystems. Fish are cold-blooded animals with backbones, gills, and fins and are dependent on water as a medium in

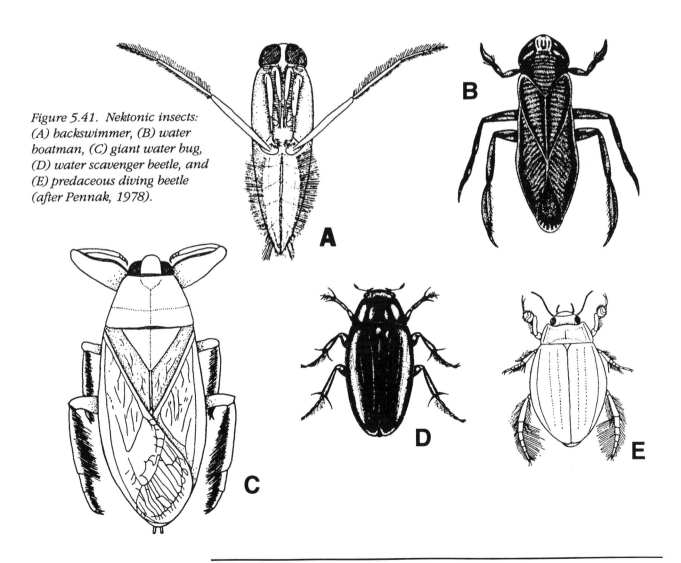

Figure 5.41. Nektonic insects: (A) backswimmer, (B) water boatman, (C) giant water bug, (D) water scavenger beetle, and (E) predaceous diving beetle (after Pennak, 1978).

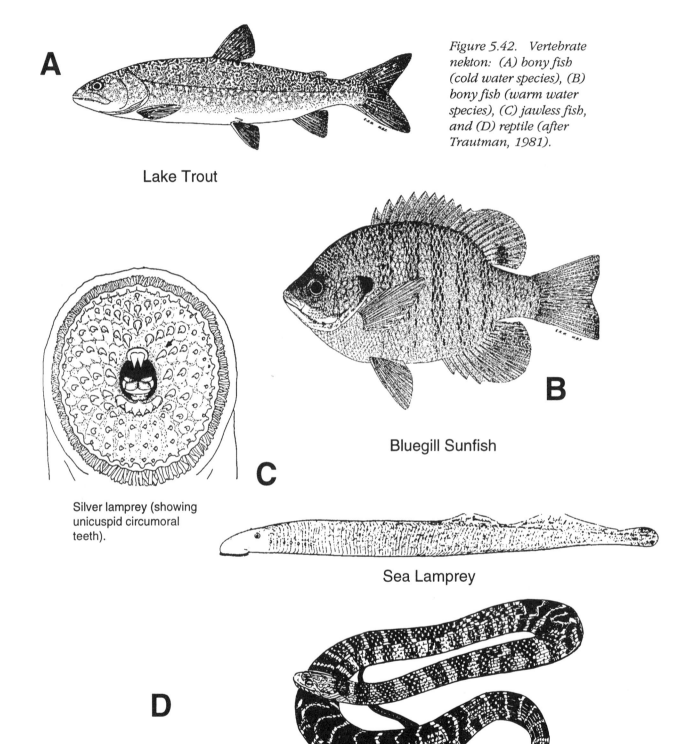

A

Lake Trout

Figure 5.42. Vertebrate nekton: (A) bony fish (cold water species), (B) bony fish (warm water species), (C) jawless fish, and (D) reptile (after Trautman, 1981).

B

Bluegill Sunfish

C

Silver lamprey (showing unicuspid circumoral teeth).

Sea Lamprey

D

Water Snake

which to live. At an estimated 40,000 species, fishes are the most numerous of the vertebrates. It is really no wonder that there are so many different kinds of fishes when their antiquity and the extent and variety of their habitat are considered.

Lake Erie, in its nearly 200-year history of commercial fishing, has produced greater numbers and varieties of commercial species of fish than any other Great Lake, accounting for nearly half of the total fish production from the Great Lakes. Annual production for the past 50 years has averaged approximately 25,000 tons with at least 17 species significant in the landings at one time or another.

The western basin has long been considered to have the most valuable fish spawning and nursery grounds in the lake, and is the location of intense sport fishing. Ninety-five species of fish have been reported from the water surrounding the islands. These species have differed in abundance and dominance throughout recorded time. No other large lake has experienced such extensive changes in the drainage basin, the lake environment, and the fish populations over the last 150 years (Hartman, 1973). Deforestation and prairie burning led to the watershed erosion and eventual siltation of spawning grounds. Many marsh areas were drained and lake-to-river spawning migration of sturgeon, walleye, and other fishes was blocked by mill dams. The accelerated use of detergents and fertilizers increased the nutrients in the lake. The present phosphate loading to Lake Erie is about 12,000 tons each year. As a result of this nutrient loading, phytoplankton biomass increased 20-fold between 1919 and 1963, and the oxygen demand from decomposition of these algae degraded the oxygen regimes in the western and central basins by the 1950s. The once extremely abundant mayfly nymphs (Figure 5.28) were destroyed as the hypolimnion became anoxic. The sequence of disappearance or severe depletion of fish species was as follows: lake trout (*Salvelinus namaycush*), sturgeon (*Acipenser fulvescens*), lake herring (*Coregonus artedii*), lake whitefish (*Coregonus clupeaformis*), sauger (*Stizostedion canadense*), and blue pike (*Stizostedion vitreum glaucum*).

The argument as to what really caused the decline of Lake Erie fishes has been ongoing for many years. The following are the most commonly accepted reasons for the decline: (1) changes in the watershed such as erosion and siltation of stream beds and inshore lake areas, and construction of dams in tributaries; (2) an extensive, ineffectively controlled commercial fishery; (3) nutrient loading, destruction of flora and fauna, and reduction of dissolved oxygen; and (4) the competitive and predatory activities of invading species.

Dominant species today are perch, bass, channel catfish (*Ictalurus punctatus*), alewife (*Alosa pseudoharengus*), gizzard shad (*Dorosoma cepedianum*), carp (*Cyprinus carpio*), goldfish (*Carassius auratus*), drum (*Aplodinotus grunniens*), and emerald shiner (*Notropis atherinoides*). The gizzard shad is one of the most abundant **rough fish** species in the lake. Important commercial and sport fish in the lake include walleye (*Stizostedion v. vitreum*), yellow perch (*Perca flavescens*), white perch (*Morone americana*), smallmouth bass (*Micropterus dolomieui*), white bass (*Morone chrysops*), channel catfish (*Ictalurus punctatus*), and smelt (*Osmerus mordax*).

The abundance of walleye in western Lake Erie increased throughout the 1970s. During the 1960s, the "fishable" population of walleye (age two and older) was below 2 million fish. The Ohio Division of Wildlife estimates that the fishable population present in 1982 was 25 million walleye. This represents a more than 10-fold recovery of walleye within a decade. The increased population has been attributed to good young-of-the-year recruitment into the fish stock, favorable climate conditions, and the international management programs to control sport and commercial harvests which are coordinated by the Great Lakes Fishery Commission.

The Lake Erie and Lake St. Clair region has been called the "walleye and sports fishing capital of the world." Because these lakes are the shallowest, warmest, and most nutrient enriched of the Great Lakes, they are also the most biologically productive. Futhermore, because the fisheries productivity of these bodies of water is not dependent upon one species, there is no time of the year when one cannot find excellent fishing for a popular sport species. In the 300 mi (480 km) between the head of the St. Clair River at Lake Huron and the mouth of the Niagara River at Lake Ontario, fishermen can catch over 20 different sport species. The following section describes these species plus a few other bait, forage, endangered, and parasitic fish of interest (Figure 5.43).

Walleye (*Stizostedion v. vitreum*). This fish, for many anglers, is "king" of Lake Erie. In addition to being a favorite gamefish, walleye is also renowned for its flavor. Lake Erie's western basin has been the most popular fishing location. This area, however, is rivaled by a tremendous walleye fishery in Lake St. Clair and a rapidly growing fishery in the central and eastern basins of Lake Erie.

Walleyes are the largest members of the perch family (*Percidae*). In Lake Erie and Lake St. Clair, fish in the 9-10 lbs (4 to 5 kg) range are not uncommon, and occasionally, fish in excess of 15 lbs (7 kg) are taken.

The walleye, which is also called yellow pike, wall-eyed pike, and pickerel by sportsmen, is frequently confused with the sauger (*Stizostedion canadense*) which is taken occasionally throughout the region but is most common in western Lake Erie and Lake St. Clair. Both species have large fang-like teeth, but saugers have fully-scaled cheeks, whereas walleye have few scales, if any, on their cheeks. (The carved out cheek meat of walleye is considered by many to be a delicacy). Sauger also have dark spots between the spines of the spinous dorsal fin, whereas walleye lack the spots but have one large dark blotch at the base of the dorsal fin. Yellow perch (*Perca flavescens*) in addition to being smaller than walleye, lack the large canine teeth and have dark vertical bands on their sides. Blue pike (*Stizostedion v. glaucum*), now considered extinct, was silvery in color and had much larger eyes.

Walleye are a native species of the region and were an important source of food for the early pioneers and the natives before them. Records from the late 1700s indicate that they were probably common in the lakes and all the tributaries in the region. Walleye spawn over clean rock or gravel reefs or riffles beginning in the spring when the water temperature reaches about 40°F (4°C). A single female can lay well over a quarter of a million eggs. Dams on many of the region's tributaries have prevented the fish from reaching their spawning riffles and eliminated the population from those streams. The major spawning areas are now the reefs in the western basin of Lake Erie, Lake St. Clair, the Maumee River, the Sandusky River, and the Thames River. These three tributaries attract throngs of anglers when the walleye run in the spring.

Figure 5.43. Fishes of Lake Erie (after Trautman, 1981).

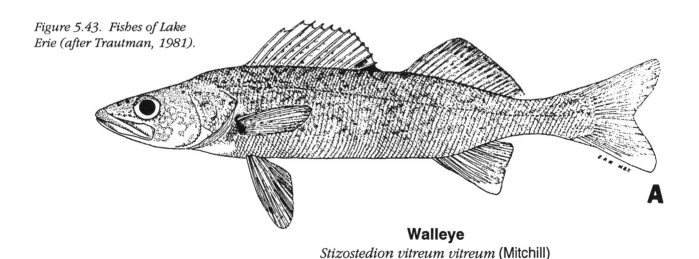

Walleye
Stizostedion vitreum vitreum (Mitchill)

Traditionally, saugers are thought to tolerate more turbid or muddy water than walleye, and both species are considered to be light-sensitive sight feeders which are most active at twilight. Possibly due to the high turbidity of Lake Erie and Lake St. Clair, the "twilight active" rule appears to fail as limit catches are frequently taken at mid-day. Walleye have been known to feed extensively on yellow perch but in this region, emerald shiner, gizzard shad, and smelt are the dominant food items. Very young walleye are plankton and insect feeders, but they become fish eaters before they are 3 months old and 3 in (8 cm) long. They are difficult to raise in hatcheries because they require live food and may become cannibalistic.

A fallacy about walleye is that they occur only at the bottom over hard-rock reefs or riffles. The advent of sophisticated depth finders or fish finders has shown that walleye are frequently suspended in schools or clusters midway between the bottom and the surface in open water. In this situation, the wise fisherman uses the count-down technique to estimate the depth of his lure as it sinks below the surface and attempts to draw the lure through the school.

Walleyes were a major portion of the commercial and sport catches until the late 1950s when the population severely diminished. In 1970 a commercial ban was placed on walleye by the State of Ohio. Since that time the species has rebounded dramatically.

Walleye can be taken throughout the year by anglers in the region. Open lake boat fishermen generally drift or cast weight-forward spinners tipped with nightcrawlers or troll with crank baits. All three methods are very effective. River fishermen frequently use spoons, spinners, and Rapalas.

River fishing is best during April and May. June and July are best for the western basin of Lake Erie and Lake St. Clair, although August and September may provide trophy fishing in these areas. Central and eastern basin fishing starts a little later but is often excellent well into September or October. Because walleye feed all winter, many ice fishermen have taken large fish using emerald shiners and other live bait.

White Bass (*Morone chrysops*). This species is a member of the bass family, Serranidae, as are some of the more common marine and commercial fishes such as the groupers and jew fishes. The white bass is easily distinguished from the black basses (largemouth and smallmouth), which are members of the sunfish family. The characteristics which sets the white bass apart are its silver coloration, two completely separate dorsal fins, a spiny dorsal fin, and a soft dorsal fin of nearly equal height.

The distinction between the white bass and its close relative, the white perch, is more difficult. The distinguishing characteristics of the white perch are its second and third anal spines which are almost equal in size. The white perch lacks the dark horizontal lines which are often prominent on white bass. Anal spines of the white bass get progressively larger from front to back. The most exact distinction between the two species is the number of soft rays in the anal fins. The white bass has 13, and the white perch has 10.

White bass occur throughout the Lake Erie region but are probably most important as sport and commercial species only in Lake Erie. The white bass is a schooling species which is often classified as a mid-water (less than 20 ft or 6 m deep) or a surface swimmer. This species is rare near the bottom or at depths greater than 20 ft (6 m).

The white bass is primarily an open water species, but moves onto shallow reefs or up tributaries to riffles for spawning in May and June. It spawns by broadcasting its eggs and sperm over the bottom, where they lie unattended until they hatch about 2 days later. In addition to the many reefs and shoals in the area, the primary spawning tributaries are

Figure 5.43 (continued). Fishes of Lake Erie (after Trautman, 1981).

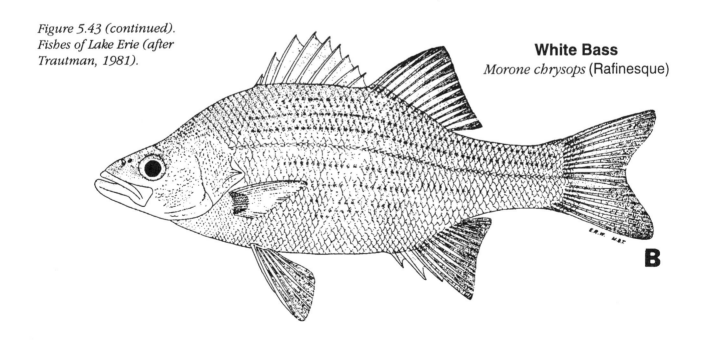

White Bass
Morone chrysops (Rafinesque)

B

the Maumee, Sandusky, and Thames Rivers. Excellent fishing is provided during these runs when thousands of fish crowd into these tributaries.

After hatching, white bass first feed on zooplankton and aquatic insects. White bass rapidly become piscivorous (fish eaters) and truly deserve their nickname, "freshwater sharks." White bass 3 in (8 cm) long are frequently found with a stomach full of 1 in (3 cm) shiners and gizzard shad. They swim in large schools and are crepuscular, feeding most actively at dawn and dusk.

Experienced anglers know that flocks of gulls will often lead to actively feeding schools of white bass because of the bass's hunting and feeding tactics. Schools of bass swim up underneath large schools of forage fish, trapping the school against the surface. As the small fish leap out of the water in an attempt to avoid being eaten, they attract another predator, the gull.

When bass are feeding in this fashion, they are in a frenzy similar to that observed in sharks, hence their nickname. At these times, bass will hit almost anything an angler casts in the water, although small spoons, spinners, and jigs are the preferred lures. Because they have an oil content which is higher than that of walleye and perch but lower than that of trout and salmon, they should be iced immediately after capture to slow decomposition and avoid a strong fishy taste.

Their voracious feeding habits and an abundance of available food in the region allow white bass to grow rapidly. They can reach lengths in excess of 9 in (23 cm) by the time they are a year old. Sexual maturity is reached by the age of 3 years. These fish rarely live longer than 8 years and usually do not exceed 15 in (38 cm) in length.

With one exception, white bass are not active in the winter and consequently are seldom taken by anglers. That one exception occurs near thermal discharges. There are over 25 hot-water discharges from electric power plants or industries in the region. Because white bass can be found in large numbers at these discharges during all seasons, fishing thermal discharges can greatly increase one's catch.

Yellow Perch (*Perca flavescens*). This species, like the walleye and the sauger, is a member of the perch family, Percidae. This family is characterized by a dorsal fin which is completely divided into a spiny and soft-rayed portion. Yellow perch has the reputation of being the best-tasting fish in the region.

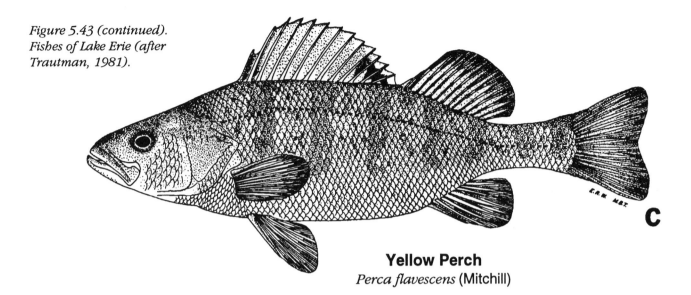

*Figure 5.43 (continued).
Fishes of Lake Erie (after
Trautman, 1981).*

C

Yellow Perch
Perca flavescens (Mitchill)

The perch is a schooling species and is an angler's delight throughout the region. It lacks the fang-like teeth of the walleye and sauger, but nevertheless strikes hard for its size, which is normally around 8 in (20 cm) in Lake St. Clair and often 10 in (25 cm) or more in the central and eastern basins of Lake Erie.

Perch which feed on aquatic insects and small fish, are almost always found near the bottom in less than 60 ft (18 m) of water. Preferred bait is a small shiner or minnow, fished about 1 ft (0.3 m) above the bottom. Because of its schooling nature, spreaders are often used, allowing the skillful angler to catch two perch (a doubleheader) at once.

Yellow perch seem to prefer temperatures of 65°-75°F (18°-24°C) but are active throughout the year. In fact, they are the most abundant catch for ice fishermen.

Perch generally reach maturity and spawn when 3 years old during late April or May when the temperature reaches 50°F (10°C). The eggs are laid in gelatinous ribbons draped over aquatic plants, twigs, or branches in shallow water (less than 20 ft or 6 m deep). They seldom enter streams in significant numbers.

Native to the region, yellow perch have been a mainstay for both sport and commercial fisheries for years. Because of their torpedo shape, schooling behavior, and active and migratory swimming patterns, yellow perch have been very susceptible to harvest by commercial gill netters. On the Canadian side of Lake Erie, commercial fishermen harvest over 4000 tons of perch annually. Regulations reducing the commercial harvest in Lake St. Clair and the Ohio portion of Lake Erie have been successful in rehabilitating the yellow perch stocks and restoring this sport fish, which is considered a major asset to the region's economy.

White Perch (*Morone americana*). Surprisingly, the white perch is not a member of the perch family, Percidae, but rather a member of the bass family, Serranidae, and is a close relative of the white bass. (See the section on white bass for distinguishing characteristics of white bass and white perch.)

The white perch is not a native of the Lake Erie region. They arrived through the St. Lawrence Seaway, and the first specimen was observed in 1954. Only since the 1980s have white perch become abundant in Lake Erie. In the Hudson River and Atlantic coastal estuaries, white perch frequently attain lengths of 12 in (30 cm). However, in the Lake Erie region, lengths of 8 in (20 cm) are more common.

Fisheries scientists are working to gain an understanding of the role of white perch in the Lake Erie area fish community. Spawning and feeding habits and locations, and interactions with native species are all

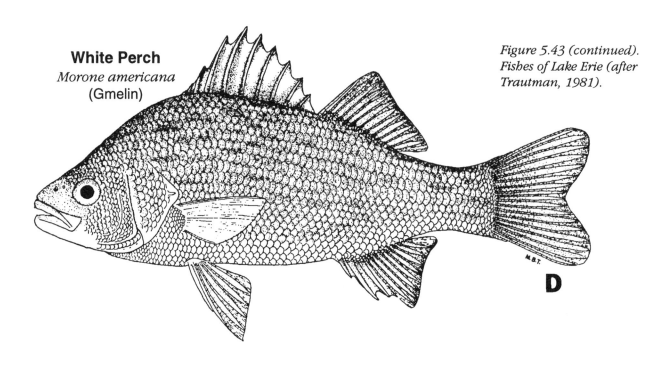

White Perch
Morone americana
(Gmelin)

Figure 5.43 (continued). Fishes of Lake Erie (after Trautman, 1981).

D

aspects of the white perch which interest scientists. Although the fish most closely resembles the white bass in appearance and taste, its food, behavior, and growth are more similar to the yellow perch. The increasing white perch population will most likely cause anglers to find a large number of these fish in their creel in the future.

White perch are occasionally taken on small spoons and spinners from the surface or mid-water in a fashion similar to that for white bass. However, white perch are most frequently caught near the bottom using nightcrawlers, crayfish, small spoons or spinners, jigs, and jigs tipped with minnows or nightcrawlers. They are hard strikers and put up an excellent fight. Because of their moderate oil content, they should be iced immediately to minimize decomposition and protect the flavor.

Freshwater Drum (*Aplodinotus grunniens*). This species is the only freshwater member of the drum family, Scienidae, and probably the most misunderstood fish in the region (in addition to being one of the most abundant). The drum is found throughout the Midwest, as far north as southern Manitoba, and as far south as northern South America. The drum has been given almost 30 names throughout this range including grunter, bubbler, gray bass, white bass, reef bass, silver bass, gray perch, white perch, Catawba dolphin, and buffalo fish. In the Lake Erie/Lake St. Clair region, drum are most frequently called sheepshead.

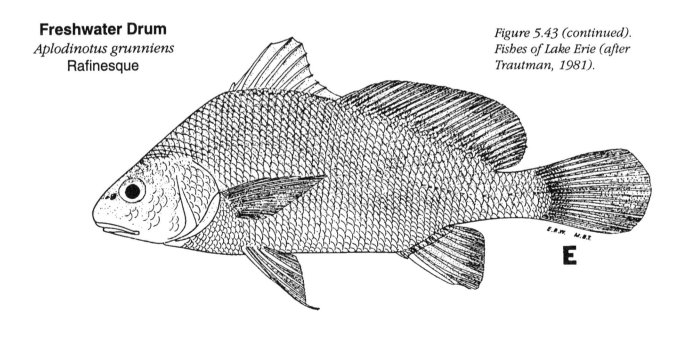

Freshwater Drum
Aplodinotus grunniens
Rafinesque

Figure 5.43 (continued). Fishes of Lake Erie (after Trautman, 1981).

Like their marine relatives, drum make a drumming sound with their swim bladder. This can be felt and heard when holding the fish after capture. This sound is heard most frequently at spawning time.

Drum have a yellow or whitish belly and silver sides with an olive or bronze cast. They have a subterminal mouth and a rounded tail. They can be distinguished from white bass and white perch by the rounded tail and from carp and suckers by the 8-9 spines in the dorsal fin. These spines are lacking in carp and suckers. Drum lack the canine teeth of the walleye and sauger and are the only species in the region with a lateral line that extends onto the tail.

Many people feel drum are a "trash" fish and are scavengers similar to carp and suckers. Conversely, with the exception of eating more molluscs, the diet of the drum is actually quite similar to that of the walleye. They begin life as a zooplankton feeder, switch to benthic insects and molluscs, and then add fish to their diet. Another part of the misunderstanding is that the flesh is poor quality. This has been dis-proved in numerous taste tests. However, because drum have a moder-ately high oil content similar to that of the white bass, they should be iced immediately after capture to insure the highest quality meat and prevent a strong fishy taste.

The drum is a late-spring or early-summer spawner (approximately 66-70°F or 19-21°C). It is a broadcast spawner with males and females swimming together in shallow water (less than 20 ft or 6 m) and releas-ing the eggs and milt together. A large oil globule in the egg makes it semi-buoyant and allows it to drift with the current. This prevents the egg from being buried in silt. Females lay between 100,000 and 500,000 eggs which hatch in 2-3 days. Growth during the first year of life is rapid but slows down quickly thereafter. Drum in excess of 25 lbs (11.3 kgs) have been taken in Lake Erie but 1-5 lb (0.5-2.3 kgs) specimens are more common.

Drum prefer water between 5 and 60 ft (1.5 and 18.3 m) in depth. At twilight they have been observed in shallow nearshore areas moving rocks with their snouts and eating crayfish and molluscs which have been disturbed.

Drum are native to the region and most common in Lake Erie. They are excellent fighters and will hit almost anything. Frequently, a walleye fisherman will hook a fish which puts up a good fight and will invari-ably say "It's either a big walleye or a small drum." The best method for drum is a worm fished still or bounced along the bottom.

Largemouth Bass (*Micropterus salmoides*). This species is a member of the sunfish family, Centrarchidae. It is prized by anglers for its fighting nature on the line and its tasty flesh in the pan. It is distinguished from the smallmouth by its dark lateral band and a jaw which extends back beyond the eye. Further differences are presented in the section on smallmouth bass.

Because of habitat requirements, largemouth bass are much less abundant than smallmouth bass in this region. Largemouth prefer water temperatures as high as 80-82°F (26.7-27.8°C), non-flowing waters containing aquatic vegetation, and low turbidity. Preferred bottom types include soft muck and organic debris, gravel, sand, and hard, nonflocculent clays. They are seldom found at depths greater than 20 ft (6 m). Because of these habitat requirements, Lake St. Clair and the marshes around Lakes Erie and St. Clair are the best places to fish for largemouth bass.

The largemouth is a nest builder which spawns in late spring or early summer. The male usually constructs a nest on rocky or gravelly near-shore areas in shallow water, although occasionally, eggs are deposited in leaves and roots of aquatic vegetation. The eggs are slightly smaller than smallmouth eggs and hatch in 3-4 days. As with smallmouth, the fry rest in the gravel for 5-8 days before rising above the nest forming a tightly packed school. They remain over or in the vicinity of the nest and under the protection of their father for almost a month before they disperse, at which time they are about 1 in (2.5 cm) long.

Figure 5.43 (continued). Fishes of Lake Erie (after Trautman, 1981).

Northern Largemouth Blackbass
Micropterus salmoides salmoides
(Lacepede)

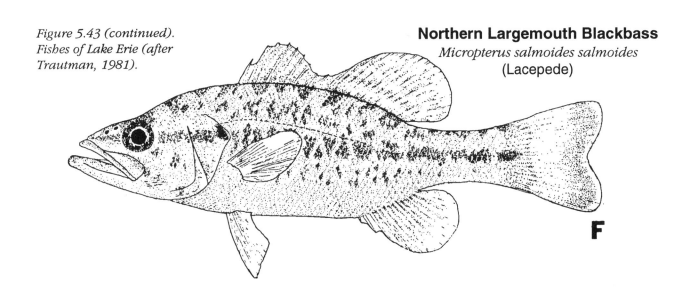

F

Smallmouth Bass (*Micropterus dolomieui*). This is Ohio's state fish, a fisherman's delight. It may pack more fight—pound for pound—than any fish alive. The smallmouth and the largemouth are members of the sunfish family, Centrarchidae.

Smallmouth bass look much like largemouth bass, but as the name indicates, they have a smaller mouth. The rear end of the smallmouth's jaw does not extend beyond the eye, whereas the rear end of the largemouth's jaw does. Other distinctions can be equally as subtle including the facts that the spiny portion of the dorsal fin of the small-mouth is gently curved, whereas the largemouth has a larger hump in the spiny dorsal, and the notch between the spiny and soft-rayed por-tion of the dorsal fin of the smallmouth bass is shallow, whereas that of the largemouth is much deeper. The most frequently used distinguish-ing characteristic by most sportsmen is the presence of a dark lateral band on largemouth bass which is lacking on smallmouth bass.

Smallmouth bass are available throughout the region. Ideal small-mouth bass territory contains protective cover such as large rocks and boulders or fallen trees and submerged logs. Smallmouth enthusiasts point out that these bass are frequently taken on the deepwater side of a submerged ledge or dropoff. They prefer clear water with temperatures ranging from 67 to 73°F (19 to 23°C). They are most abundant around the islands of western Lake Erie but are also taken in huge numbers in Lake St. Clair and around the rocky breakwalls of the ports on both lakes. Whereas the yellow perch is primarily a lake fish, the smallmouth bass is equally at home in streams and lakes. In the tributaries around

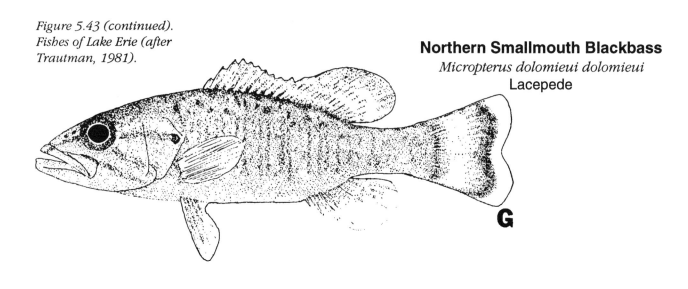

Figure 5.43 (continued). Fishes of Lake Erie (after Trautman, 1981).

Northern Smallmouth Blackbass
Micropterus dolomieui dolomieui
Lacepede

G

Lakes St. Clair and Erie, smallmouth are most frequently taken in pools below riffles.

Spawning activity normally begins in the spring when water temperatures reach 55-65°F (13-18°C) (May-July). The male builds a nest in gravel in quiet water near shore or down stream from an obstruction where the water is also quiet. These nests, 2-4 ft (0.6-1.2 m) in diameter, are easily observed when walking along the shoreline. Females will lay 2,000-10,000 eggs which are fertilized and guarded by the male. Nests are normally near deeper water or other protection for the male. The eggs hatch in 2-3 days, but the newly hatched larvae drop down into the gravel and remain in the nest for 6 more days. When the larvae or fry rise out of the gravel they, will stay over the nest swimming in a dense, dark cloud under the protection of their father before dispersing. Zooplankton is their first food, but soon aquatic insects, crayfish, and fish are added to their diets. They are also not above cannibalizing their brothers and sisters. At this stage, the fingerlings are 2-3 in (5-7.5 cm) long and are easy to recognize because of their tri-colored tail. The basal third is orange-yellow, the middle third is dusky in the form of a vertical bar, and the distal third is whitish.

It is evident that from the time of the arrival of Europeans until about 1900, the smallmouth was extremely abundant in the region. It was a valuable food source for both Europeans and Indians during times of food shortages. They were captured with spears, gigs, bows and arrows, jacklights in canoes and boats, hook and line, seines, nets, weirs, and guns. Their initial vulnerability to spears has been reduced by turbidity resulting from increased erosion. Commercial fishing for the black basses is now prohibited, but they have failed to regain their former abundance. Records indicate that in the late 1800s several tons were taken daily during the season with hook and line around the Erie islands.

Anglers no longer measure their catches in tons, but limit catches are common during the spring and fall. Once on the line, the fun begins. To say smallmouth are acrobatic is an understatement; this fish even may try to jump in the boat or walk on its tail. It is most common to catch fish from 1 to 4 lbs (0.5 to 1.8 kgs), but trophies in the 6 lb (2.7 kgs) range are not uncommon.

During the spring, successful fishermen often use jigs, jig/minnow combinations, spinners, and spinner/nightcrawler combinations that are bounced along the bottom or drawn just above the bottom in the shallows where spawning is likely to be occurring. It is also quite effective to use crank baits, rappalas, or flies at this time of year. Because they are catching fish off their nests, sportsmen often use catch-and-release techniques during the spring. This simply means handling the fish and removing the hook gently before carefully returning the fish to the water. Because it has been shown that the home range of smallmouth bass is within a 0.5 mi (0.8 km) diameter, you may catch the same fish near that spot later in the year or next year.

During the fall, the bass move offshore into deeper water with catch results indicating the fish can be densely packed in small areas. Jigs, jig/minnow, or jig/nightcrawler combinations are used, as are deep diving crank baits and live bait. Some anglers have even been fortunate enough to catch a doubleheader (two fish at once) using spreaders and minnows.

Northern Pike (*Esox lucius*). This fish is a relative of the muskie and a member of the pike family, Esocidae. It is very similar in appearance to the muskie: its body is long and cylindrical with a single spineless dorsal fin set well back on the body. Its flattened snout is lined with long sharp canine teeth. The cheek is fully scaled, and the upper half of the gill cover is scaled. The body is frequently covered with light spots on a dark background.

The feeding behavior and diet of pike are very similar to those of muskies. They are primarily fish eaters, but have been known to take birds, rodents, and small mammals. The pike also is a sight feeder, preferring to lurk in the cover of vegetation while waiting for its prey to pass. Pike have been known to eat items half their own size.

Figure 5.43 (continued).
Fishes of Lake Erie (after
Trautman, 1981).

Northern Pike
Esox lucius Linnaeus

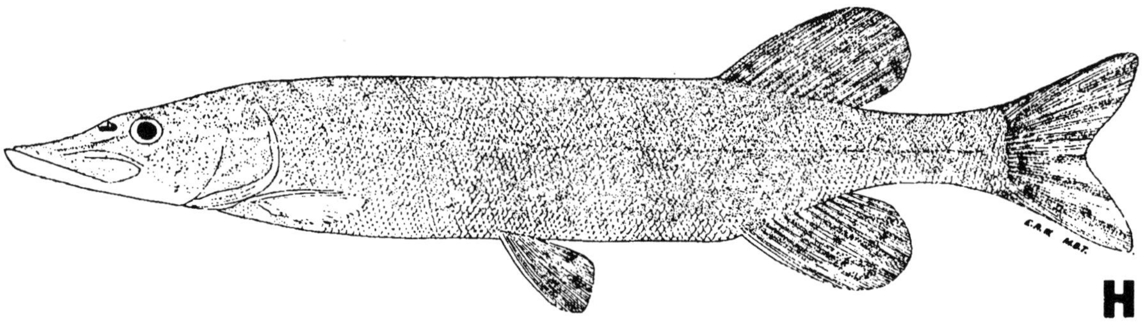

Northerns prefer bays, marshes, and pools in low-gradient streams with clear water and plenty of vegetation. They migrate in winter and early spring to shoreline marshes and ascend tributaries to headwater marshes to spawn on aquatic vegetation. This normally occurs before, during, and immediately after ice-out and just before the muskies spawn. After hatching, pike fry remain attached to the vegetation for their first few days of life.

Pike grow rapidly. Males are mature at age 2-3 while females reach maturity between the ages of 3 and 4. In the Great Lakes, few pike live beyond 12 years or grow larger than 40 lbs (18 kg), and 4 ft (1 m) in length.

Northern pike are native to the Lake Erie/Lake St. Clair region and were one of the earliest commercial species. The exact number of northerns and muskies harvested is difficult to determine because early records give only combined totals of the two. In 1885, the Lake Erie harvest of the two fish was 263,840 lbs (119,678 kg). These fish were taken with seines and speared through holes in the ice. They were then stacked in wagons and transported to Cleveland, Toledo, and Detroit for sale. By 1945, largely due to destruction of spawning habitat, the harvest had fallen to 3,764 lbs (1707 kg).

Today northerns are not taken commercially, but sportsmen are still quite successful during the spring in Lake St. Clair, Sandusky Bay, and the Niagara River. As with the muskie, northerns will put up a good fight, and their flesh is quite tasty. Anglers are most successful trolling or casting spoons or crank baits near shallow vegetation.

Muskellunge (*Esox masquinongy*). The muskie is a member of the pike family, Esocidea. Muskie and northern pike are characterized by a long cylindrical body, a long flattened snout (duck bill), huge canine teeth, smooth scales, and a single dorsal fin which lacks spines and is placed far back on the body. Muskies can be distinguished from northern pike by the scales on the cheeks and the pattern of spotting. Muskies have scales on the upper half of the cheeks and gill cover. Northern pike have scales on the upper half of the gill cover, but the entire cheek is scaled. Muskies have dark spots on a lighter background on their body, and on their dorsal, caudal (tail), and anal fins. Northern pike have light spots on a dark background.

The muskie is the largest and most ferocious predator in the Great Lakes. Muskies are sight feeders which frequently will rest in vegetation or other cover and then rush out to seize their prey. These attacks can literally be a charge, covering distances of 50 ft (15 m) or more. After grasping their prey in powerful jaws, muskies often return to their place of cover to eat. Although they frequently grab their food items broadside, muskies, as do most predators, will normally rotate their prey and swallow them head first. This is probably a good example of natural selection at work. If food items such as catfish or bullheads are eaten tail first, they will invariably get caught in the predator's throat. Thus, fish that eat other fish tail first have been selected against by dying with prey lodged in their throat.

Muskies remain active during the summer and are occasionally seen at the surface rolling in the sun. They are predominantly fish eaters, eating suckers, perch, sunfish, black bass, minnows, catfish, and probably any other fish they desire. Large muskies have also been known to eat muskrats, mallards, and small dogs and have been seen leaping from the water to snatch a redwing blackbird perched on a cattail.

Muskies spawn in early spring shortly after ice-out in shallow water (less than 2 ft or 61 cm) among dense vegetation. They frequently run up tributaries to find these shallow, marshy areas. Muskies grow very rapidly, and females grow faster than males. Consequently, trophy fish are often females. In the Great Lakes region, muskies are second only to sturgeon in size, with individuals as long as 6 ft (2 m) weighing in at over 100 lbs (45 kg). Fish most frequently taken by sportsmen are 25 to 50 in (65 to 127 cm) long and weigh 5-40 lbs (2-18 kg). Muskies reach maturity at 3-5 years of age. Most fish taken by anglers are 5-15 years old, but specimens greater than 20 years of age have been taken. Many fish will prey upon muskie fry and fingerlings, but once a muskie is an adult, man is his only enemy.

Great Lakes Muskellunge
Esox masquinongy masquinongy Mitchill

Figure 5.43 (continued). Fishes of Lake Erie (after Trautman, 1981).

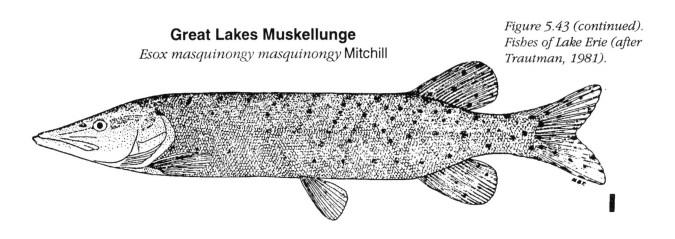

Muskellunge are native to the Lake Erie/Lake St. Clair region and due to their extreme abundance, quality flesh, and ease of harvest, they were one of the first species to become commercially important. Prior to 1850, muskies were harvested in huge numbers by spearing the fish through holes in the ice over riffles and by dragging seines in these areas and in the marshes where they spawn. Large fisheries existed in Maumee Bay, the Maumee River, Sandusky Bay, and the Sandusky River. Indeed, in the early 1900s, a harvest of 100 muskies per day from Maumee Bay was not unusual.

This fishing pressure coupled with the draining and diking of wetlands, channelizing streams, and siltation from agricultural run-off have greatly reduced the muskie population. By 1950, the population in Lake Erie was so low that it was in danger of being extirpated. However, healthy populations do exist in Lake St. Clair and the Niagara River and are providing anglers with a great deal of fishing pleasure.

Many a muskie fisherman will say that it takes an average of 90 hours of fishing per muskie. Obviously, this depends on the location and skill of the angler, but suffice it to say that they are not easily caught. However, the same angler will tell you that the fight was worth the wait.

Muskies can be taken on almost anything. Occasionally one even hears of the small boy who caught a muskie from the dock with a bobber and a worm. However, the most frequently used method is to troll a very large spoon or pike minnow at a high speed near vegetation. When it hits, you know it. Breaking water on the strike is not unusual. Nor is it unheard of for muskies to charge or even ram a boat. The battle is not over when the fish is in the landing net. Many muskie and pike fishermen carry a "muskie club" to quiet the fish once it's in the boat. Other anglers bear scars from trying to remove hooks from muskies. Obviously the muskie is a challenge to any sportsman.

Bluegill (*Lepomis macrochirus*). This fish is a member of the sunfish family, Centrarchidae, as are the large and smallmouth bass, pumpkinseed, green sunfish, orange-spotted sunfish, long-ear sunfish, and rock bass. The members of this family have rough ctenoid scales as in the perch family but with the exception of the largemouth bass, all Centrarchidae have spiny and soft-rayed dorsal fins which are connected and confluent. In addition, the perch family is generally torpedo-shaped while the sunfish are deep-bodied and laterally flattened having a leaf shape that ichthyologists call a "gibbose" body form.

The bluegill is distinguished from other sunfish by the following combination of characteristics: pointed pectoral fins, a small mouth, and a dark blotch at the distal, basal portion of the dorsal fin. Bluegills often have an emerald-bluish or a blue luster with silver reflections on their sides. The belly can be whitish, yellow, orange, or a rusty-red. Fish from clear water often have 5-9 vertical bars on their sides. These bars are often absent on fish from turbid or muddy water.

Bluegills generally prefer non-flowing, quiet waters with low turbidity which have bottoms consisting of sand, gravel, or organic debris. The presence of beds of aquatic vegetation, tree stumps, fallen trees, or other cover is almost essential. However, with these ideal habitat characteristics and the absence of predators, bluegill frequently over-populate and become dwarfed or stunted in their growth.

Bluegill spawn in shallow (normally less than 4 ft or 1 m) water in early summer when water temperatures reach 65°F (18°C). Males build

Northern Bluegill Sunfish
Lepomis macrochirus macrochirus Rafinesque

Figure 5.43 (continued). Fishes of Lake Erie (after Trautman, 1981).

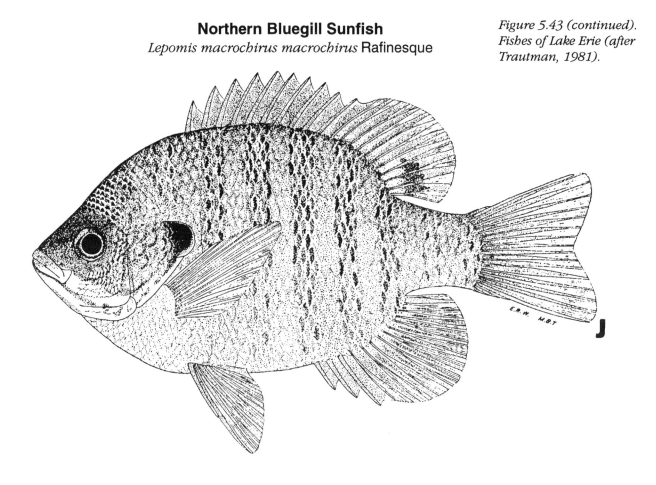

nests in sand, gravel, or occasionally mud and guard the nest and fry until they reach the swimming stage. In farm ponds and marshes which are crowded, competition for spawning grounds can be fierce. It is not uncommon to see a cluster of nests less than 5 ft (2 m) apart with a male bluegill hovering over each nest. Fry feed mainly on zooplankton but soon add aquatic insects and small fish to their diet. Males reach sexual maturity at 2-3 years of age and females at 3-4 years of age.

Bluegill feed from surface to bottom, are easy to catch, taste great, and put up a good fight. In fact, it's been said that there is no point in trying to raise a 5 lb (2 kg) bluegill, because nobody would be able to land it.

In the Lake Erie/Lake St. Clair region, bluegill and other sunfish are most frequently captured in coastal marshes, bays, and marinas. In fact, young children frequently catch goodly numbers of fish with small hooks and worms while the boat is tied to the dock. However, bluegill are probably most fun to catch with spinners or poppers and ultra-light tackle or by fly fishing. They are also active during the winter and considered a real delicacy by ice fishermen.

Channel Catfish (*Ictalurus punctatus*). This species and the brown bullhead are members of the catfish family, Ictaluridae. Catfish are characterized by a fleshy adipose fin on the back between the caudal fin and the dorsal fin, forked tail, scaleless body, flattened head, mouth surrounded by barbels, and sharp heavy spines at the origin of the pectoral and dorsal fins.

Many misinformed anglers believe that they can be "stung" by the barbels. This is totally untrue. The belief that barbels can inflict an injury probably arose when someone was accidentally poked with a pectoral or dorsal spine. When dragged along the lake bottom, the barbels of catfish and bullheads are used for taste and help the fish locate food.

Catfish are native to the Lake St. Clair/Lake Erie region. They have long been prized sport and commercial fish because of their high quality flesh and fine fighting characteristics. They should be skinned prior to eating. Because they are primarily nocturnal (active at night), they can often be taken as easily at night as during the day.

Contrary to popular belief, catfish prefer clean water with clean sand, gravel, or boulder bottoms, but may also be found over silt bottoms

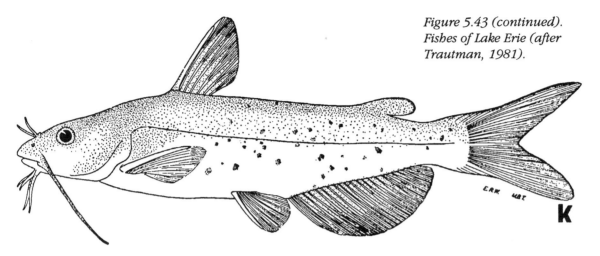

Figure 5.43 (continued).
Fishes of Lake Erie (after
Trautman, 1981).

Channel Catfish
Ictalurus punctatus (Rafinesque)

when the rate of deposition is slow. They are seldom found over muck or beds of aquatic vegetation.

Channel catfish migrate in and out of small streams to spawn in late spring or early summer. Males build nests in holes, logs, gravel, or rocks. The number of eggs laid by an adult female varies from 4000 to 100,000. The eggs hatch in 5-10 days. After hatching, the young can often be seen almost rolling along the bottom in a very dense cloud. Initially the young eat mostly insects, however, they soon begin to eat snails, fingernail clams, crayfish, tree seeds, and fish. They grow rapidly, reaching sexual maturity in 5-8 years and some have been known to live as long as 25 years.

They are commonly taken by anglers fishing live bait, especially worms and crayfish, at the bottom. However, they also feed occasionally on a variety of spinners, crank baits, and spoons. Once on the line, catfish are known for their twisting, turning moves and great fight.

Brown Bullhead (*Ictalurus nebulosus*). This bullhead is a member of the catfish family, Ictaluridae. Brown bullheads are characterized by a fleshy adipose fin on the back between the dorsal and caudal fin, scaleless body, flattened head, mouth surrounded by barbels, and sharp heavy spines at the origin of the dorsal and pectoral fins. The brown bullhead has a caudal fin which is almost totally straight, distinguishing it from the channel catfish with its forked tail. Two other species of bullheads, the yellow and the black bullhead, are found in the Lake Erie/Lake St. Clair region but are far less abundant than the brown bullhead. Yellow bullheads can be distinguished from browns and blacks by their pure white chin barbels. Browns can be distinguished from blacks by the size of the serrations on the back side of each of the pectoral and dorsal fins. The serrations on black bullheads are little more than small bumps while those on brown bullheads are much larger and will catch your finger if you drag it against them.

Bullheads are native to the Lake Erie/Lake St. Clair region and are of some commercial and sport significance. They spawn in early summer in nests prepared in mud, sand, or vegetation. Each female lays 2,500 to 15,000 eggs. One or both parents care for the eggs by fanning them to keep them aerated. The eggs hatch in about 1 week, but the fry remain under the protection of the parents until they are 1 in (3 cm) long. They are primarily bottom feeders eating mollusks, insects, fish, crayfish, snails, and fingernail clams. They reach sexual maturity at age 3 and seldom live longer than 6-8 years.

Bullheads are almost always caught at the bottom and most frequently with live bait. They are very popular with children because they are easy to catch and fight well. They are often caught off docks at marinas. As with catfish, bullheads should be skinned before cooking.

Figure 5.43 (continued). Fishes of Lake Erie (after Trautman, 1981).

Brown Bullhead
Ictalurus nebulosus (Lesueur)

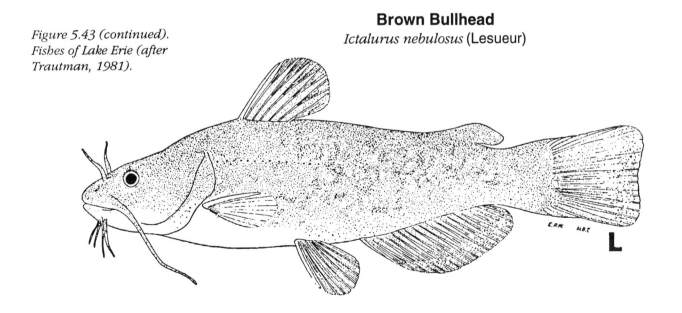

Carp (*Cyprinus carpio*). To the surprise of most people, carp is a member of the minnow family, Cyprinidae. They are characterized by a single, long dorsal fin, the first ray of which is a spinous ray with a double row of serrations on the posterior side. Carp also have very large scales and four fleshy barbels around the mouth. Some carp are scaleless or partly scaled. These individuals are commonly called "mirror" or "leather" carp. Carp are most frequently confused with goldfish, but goldfish lack barbels. However, carp frequently hybridize with goldfish, and the resulting offspring often bears some of the characteristics of both parents. Frequently these hybrids have only two barbels which are shorter than those of the pure carp.

Carp are not native to the Lake Erie/Lake St. Clair region. They were stocked in our waters from Europe and Asia by the U.S. Fish Commission to serve as a food resource. The first individuals in the region were stocked in Fremont, Ohio in the fall of 1879. Stocking continued until 1896. Owners of land where carp were planted frequently destroyed their waterfowl to protect the "delicate" carp. The obvious proliferation of this species is one of the reasons fishery managers are so cautious when considering stocking exotic species.

Common Carp
Cyprinus carpio Linnaeus

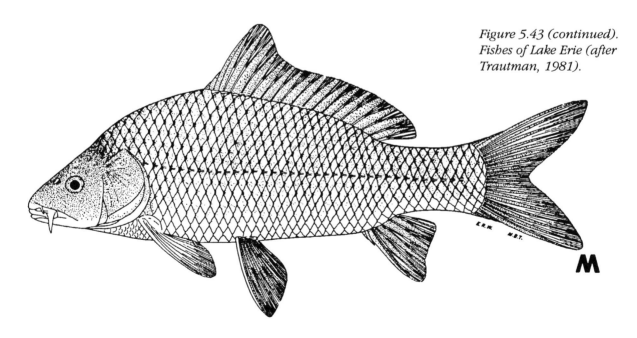

Figure 5.43 (continued). Fishes of Lake Erie (after Trautman, 1981).

Carp are most abundant in ponds, lakes, and low-gradient, warm streams with an abundant supply of organic matter. In this region, they are also common in diked and undiked marshes where they frequently cause problems by increasing turbidity and uprooting aquatic plants as they feed. They are tolerant of all types of bottoms and clear or turbid water.

In this region, carp spawn from late spring through summer at temperatures ranging from 65° to 80°F (18° to 27°C). However, most activity occurs in May and June in shallow, quiet, nearshore water where they create quite a display. A group of carp will splash about together spewing forth milt and eggs. The fry grow rapidly and although they are preyed upon by a variety of fish when young, from the time they reach 1-2 lbs (0.5-0.9 kg) until they die some 20 years later, they go unmolested by other fish. Males generally become sexually mature at 3-4 years of age, and females reach maturity about a year later. Each female will lay up to 350,000 eggs in a single season.

Carp are sought by commercial fishermen to be sold live to Jewish markets in cities such as Detroit, Cleveland, Buffalo, Rochester, and New York. Because of their feeding habits, anglers seldom catch carp. However, those that have will tell of a real battle with one of the region's strongest fish.

Smoked carp is truly a delicacy—making the difficult cleaning process well worth the trouble.

Rainbow Smelt (*Osmerus mordax*). The smelt belongs to the family Osmeridae. It is a slender fish seldom exceeding 8 in (20 cm) in length. Although small in size, it has many canine teeth and is easily distinguished from other fish by teeth on its tongue and the presence of an adipose fin. Smelt are predominantly silver buty the dorsal surface may take on a bluish hue and the ventral surface is often white with a silver cast.

Smelt prefer the deeper, cooler waters of the region during all seasons. The preferred temperature range is 45°-52°F (7°-11°C). Consequently, they are frequently found in the mid-water zone near the thermocline.

Smelt are not native to the region. In fact, the entire present population can be traced back to a single introduction into Crystal Lake in Benzie County, Michigan in 1912. The first records from Lake St. Clair date back to 1932, while Lake Erie's first record is from 1936.

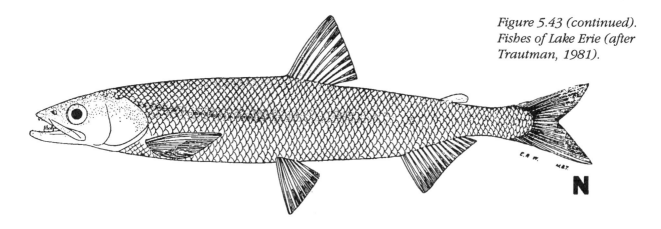

Figure 5.43 (continued).
Fishes of Lake Erie (after
Trautman, 1981).

Rainbow Smelt
Osmerus mordax (Mitchill)

Smelt run into tributaries to spawn over gravel beds, but also spawn on shallow reefs and shoals in the open lake and nearshore areas during early spring. At this time they can be easily dip-netted in large numbers. This is, for all practical purposes, the only harvest time or technique used by sportsmen.

After spawning, smelt grow rapidly and reach maturity in 2-3 years. They are preyed upon by most of the region's predators, but they too are a predator, feeding on plankton, aquatic insects, small fish, and other smelt.

On the Canadian side of Lake Erie they are fished heavily by commercial fishermen using trawls and gill nets, and are shipped as far as Japan.

Lake Trout (*Salvelinus namaycush*). This species is a member of the salmon and trout family, Salmonidae, and is the largest trout inhabiting the waters of this region. As with the other species of this family, lake trout have very fine cycloid scales and an adipose fin. They also have a forked tail, large mouth, and dark vermiculations (worm-like markings) on their back. They usually have light spots on their sides.

Lake trout are native to the region, but due to their extremely cold temperature requirements, Lake Erie is the southernmost boundary of their range. Here, they are located in the deep, cold water below the thermocline. During the spring and fall, they occasionally venture into shallower water.

Lake trout are primarily fish eaters and cover many miles in search of food. They are fall spawners on deep gravel beds where the eggs are deposited at night. The average adult weighs 9-10 lbs (4-5 kg) but specimens have been taken weighing over 50 lbs (23 kg). Adults are not sexually mature until they are 6-7 years old. This late maturity is one reason this species is very susceptible to over-fishing.

Because of their temperature preference, lake trout in this region relocated to the central and eastern basins of Lake Erie. Due to over-fishing and habitat degradation, the population of this species has been drastically reduced since 1850. The main forms of habitat degradation have been siltation of spawning grounds and eutrophication causing oxygen deficiencies below the thermocline. New York has stocked some in Lake Erie in recent years which has probably prevented the complete extirpation of the species. It is doubtful whether any natural reproduction occurs in the region.

In recent years a hybrid produced by fertilizing lake trout eggs with brook trout (*Salvelinus fontinalis*) sperm has become popular. This hybrid, called splake, appears to grow faster than either of the parents yet retains their fighting characteristics.

Lake Trout
Salvelinus namaycush (Walbaum)

Figure 5.43 (continued). Fishes of Lake Erie (after Trautman, 1981).

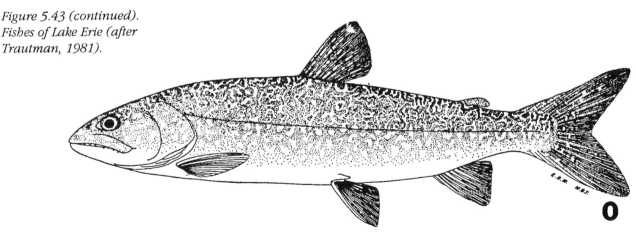

Gizzard Shad (*Dorosoma cepedianum*). This fish is a member of the herring family, Clupeidae. Gizzard shad are silver in color, deep bodied, and slab-sided (laterally compressed). The gizzard shad has two very distinct characteristics: a dark spot above the pectoral fin and behind the gill cover, and a greatly elongated final ray of the dorsal fin.

Shad are plankton feeders and as a result are almost never captured by sportsmen. As fry, they feed on zooplankton, but as their digestive system develops they switch to phytoplankton. The abundance of algae in the lakes assures the shad of a plentiful food supply. Shad may be the single most abundant fish in the region and are eaten by almost all predators. The angler who accidentally cuts open the stomach of his catch while filleting will almost certainly find gizzard shad.

There is some disagreement as to whether gizzard shad are native to the region. The first record of their presence was in 1948 at the mouth of the Cuyahoga River. However, some ichthyologists feel that they were probably here long before that but in relatively low numbers. There is little doubt that their current population is significantly larger than in the past.

Shad prefer quiet waters and are found in both clear and turbid environments. They do, however, require an abundant supply of phytoplankton. They spawn in shallow water on vegetation. It appears

Eastern Gizzard Shad
Dorosoma cepedianum (Leseuer)

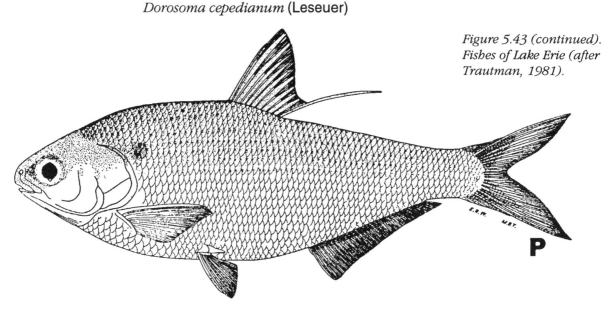

Figure 5.43 (continued). Fishes of Lake Erie (after Trautman, 1981).

that Lake Erie may be the northernmost boundary of their range. Consequently they are very sensitive to temperature and often have large winter kills during harsh weather.

After hatching, shad grow extremely rapidly reaching 4-6 in (10-15 cm) in length by the end of their first growing season. As a result, they receive little predator pressure after their first year because they are too large.

The shad is a schooling species and because of its preferences for warmer temperatures, is often found around thermal outfalls, where it creates serious problems at water intakes by clogging screening devices.

Because gizzard shad are quite oily, they spoil rapidly and are not very tasty. They currently have no market value for human consumption but are sold for animal feeds and bait.

Emerald Shiner (*Notropis atherinoides*). This shiner is a member of the minnow family, Cyprinidae. The sides of emerald shiners are silvery and show an emerald green band when viewed from certain angles. The back is usually olive green, and the stomach is silver-white.

When sportsmen in this region request shiners for bait, they are referring to the emerald. When emeralds are in short supply, bait

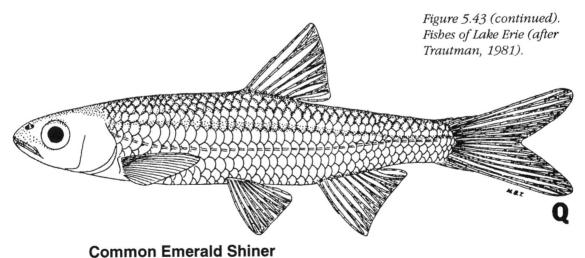

Figure 5.43 (continued). Fishes of Lake Erie (after Trautman, 1981).

Common Emerald Shiner
Notropis atherinoides atherinoides **Rafinesque**

dealers frequently switch to fathead minnows, *Pimephales promelas*, which they refer to as chubs.

The emerald shiner is a surface or mid-water species and is rarely found at the bottom. It prefers large lakes or rivers with little if any detectable flow. It is a favorite prey item of many of the region's predators. It prefers clear water when it feeds on zooplankton and on aquatic insects near the surface during the evening.

Since 1980, this population has undergone some extreme fluctuations and appears to be decreasing. Many fishery biologists feel that decline is caused by growing predator populations.

Chinook Salmon (*Oncorhynchus tshawztscha*). The chinook or king salmon is a member of the trout and salmon family, Salmonidae. All members of this family have very delicate, cycloid scales and an adipose fin. The chinook, in appearance, is most like the coho salmon or steelhead trout, although it is much larger than both of the others. Chinook have black spots on their back, dorsal fin and on the entire caudal fin. They also have black gums on the lower jaw. Coho salmon lack spots on the lower lobe of the dorsal fin and have grayish gums on the lower jaw. Steelhead have a forked tail and a white mouth. The chinook has 14-19 anal rays, the coho has 12-15 anal rays, and the steelhead has 9-12 anal rays.

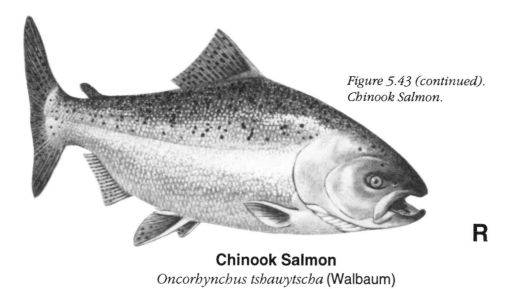

Figure 5.43 (continued).
Chinook Salmon.

R

Chinook Salmon
Oncorhynchus tshawytscha (Walbaum)

Chinook are not native to the Great Lakes but were first introduced into this region between 1873 and 1878. They are native to the Pacific coast of North America from Monterey, California to Alaska. They run up many of the coastal streams to spawn.

In the Great Lakes, chinook spend their adult lives in the open lake but return to the stream where they were born when they are mature and ready to spawn. Chinook are fish eaters and prefer cold, clear water. Consequently, they are found near the bottom but usually at depths less than 100 ft (30 m).

During the fall when the temperature reaches about 65°F (18°C), chinook move shoreward and usually remain within a quarter mile of shore until they move upstream to spawn. This normally occurs from September to November. While in nearshore areas, they normally exhibit three types of behavior related to their pre-spawning migrations: stream searching, stream testing, and false runs. Stream searching involves moving back and forth along the shoreline very close to shore looking for streams. Stream testing involves running up streams other than the one in which they will eventually spawn. False runs occur when a fish runs in and out of the stream in which it will spawn. Near-shore trolling with flatfish, spoons, wobblers, spinners, and diving crank baits is quite effective at this time.

When the chinook finally run upstream to spawn, they will build nests in large gravel beds near riffles. After spawning they return to the lake and die within 2 weeks. The eggs over-winter in the nests and hatch in the spring. However, primarily because temperatures do not remain cold long enough, the eggs seldom hatch. Consequently, all chinook salmon in the region must be started in hatcheries and planted in streams as fingerlings. These fingerlings remain in the stream from several months to a year before moving out into the lake. When they are 4-7 years old they will return to spawn. At this time, fish in excess of 30 lbs (14 kg) are not uncommon. Most fish return when they are 4-5 years old. However, some precocious males return when they are 2-3 years old. Ohio has stopped stocking chinook because of poor returns. However, Michigan, New York, and Pennsylvania still stock the valiant fighter.

Many of the same lures used in the lake are also used in the streams. Another very successful technique is to bury a hook in the back or pouch of spawn. In some places fish managers place fences or wires across streams to stop the fish and give anglers more time to harvest them. In these locations, snagging is frequently permitted since the fish will die after spawning anyway.

Eight to ten pound (4 to 5 kg) test line is normally a minimum for chinook. Also, the reel must have plenty of line to play the fish and a good drag. Chinook are tremendous fighters cannot be easily landed.

In this region, chinook are normally taken during the summer with downriggers in the central and eastern basins of Lake Erie. During the fall, they are taken in the Niagara River and the nearshore area and tributaries along the south shore of Lake Erie.

Coho Salmon (*Oncorhynchus kisutch*). The salmon is a member of the salmon and trout family, Salmonidae. All of these fish have very delicate, cycloid scales and adipose fins. For a discussion of identifying characteristics and fishing techniques, see the section on chinook salmon.

The coho is often considered the smaller brother of the chinook. Its behavior and spawning characteristics are quite similar; however 8 lbs (4 kg) would be an average size for coho compared to 20-30 lbs (9-14 kg) for chinook. One reason for this is that prior to moving into its spawning stream, the chinook stays in the lake until it is 4-7 years old. Coho return to spawn when they are only 3 years old.

Coho Salmon
Oncorhynchus kisutch (Walbaum)

*Figure 5.43 (continued).
Fishes of Lake Erie (after
Trautman, 1981).*

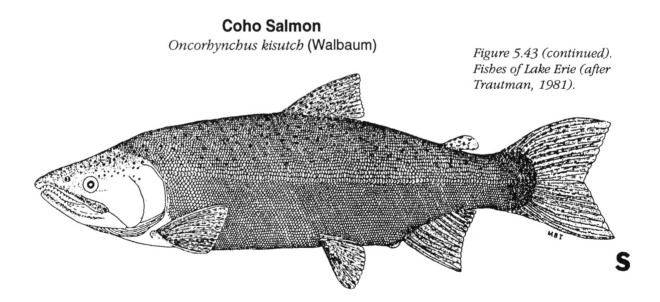

S

Coho, like chinook, are not native to this region, but were introduced along with the chinook in 1873. Michigan, Ohio, Pennsylvania, and New York all have stocking programs. Consequently, coho are much more plentiful than chinook, and although smaller, they pack a real wallop and hours of fishing enjoyment.

The best methods of capture are downriggers in the deep waters of Lake Erie's central and eastern basins during the summer followed by nearshore and river fishing when the runs begin.

Steelhead (*Salmo gairdneri*). The steelhead or lake-run rainbow trout is a member of the salmon and trout family, Salmonidae. The steelhead, like all members of this family, has very delicate, cycloid scales and an adipose fin. Rainbow trout spend their entire life in clear, clean, fast-flowing streams. The steelhead is a lake-run rainbow, meaning that after it hatches from a nest in gravel near a riffle in a stream, it moves to one of the Great Lakes to live.

Behaviorally, steelhead differ in several important ways from their relatives the chinook and the coho. Steelhead frequently do not die after spawning and have been known to spawn for 5 consecutive years. Whereas chinook and coho spawn in fall, the steelhead spawn in fall or spring with the majority selecting spring immediately after ice-out. Steelhead often follow chinook and coho into streams in the fall and

Figure 5.43 (continued). Fishes of Lake Erie (after Trautman, 1981).

Rainbow Trout
Salmo gairdneri Richardson

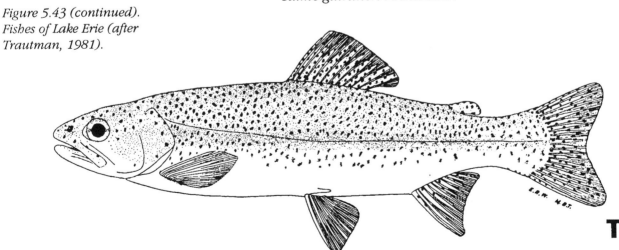

have been known to eat their eggs. Because their eggs only require 4-7 weeks to hatch, there is some successful steelhead reproduction in the region.

Steelhead are not native to the region, but were introduced from the Pacific coast as were the chinook and coho in 1885 and 1886. Because they require cold, clear water, the best streams are those which are spring-fed.

After hatching, young steelhead are zooplankton feeders, but quickly switch to insects and fish. In Lake Erie, they are primarily a mid-water species. When they are in the open lake they are most frequently observed in the hypolimnion of the central and eastern basins. In these locations they feed primarily on smelt, gizzard shad, and emerald shiners, although they have been known to delight fly-fishermen by striking flies at the surface.

Males generally reach maturity at age 3, whereas females take a year longer. They continue to grow all of their lives and although the average weight is 6-10 lbs (3-5 kg), fish over 20 lbs (9 kg) are not unheard of in the lake.

They are a sportsman's delight in that they fight hard, almost always break water, and taste great no matter how they are prepared.

Brown Trout (*Salmo truttta*). This species is a member of the salmon and trout family, Salmonidae. As such, it bears a certain resemblance to the chinook, coho, steelhead, and lake trout in that is has small, delicate, cycloid scales and an adipose fin. Brown trout have 9-10 rays in the anal fin. They also have black spots on the back and sides as do the chinook, coho, and steelhead but are easily distinguished from these species because the spots (often reddish or brown in appearance) are surrounded by small white or bluish halos. Like the steelhead, brown trout also lack spots on the head and tail.

Brown trout are not native to this region but were introduced from Europe and western Asian into Michigan and New York waters in 1883. The first Ohio planting in the Lake Erie drainage basin was in Cold Creek (Sandusky Bay) in 1930.

Brown trout generally prefer cold, clear streams with an abundance of insects (which they feed on), and a temperature regime which seldom exceeds 65°F (18°C), and never exceeds 75°F (24°C).

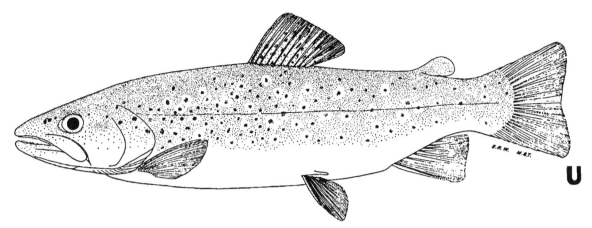

*Figure 5.43 (continued).
Fishes of Lake Erie (after
Trautman, 1981).*

Brown Trout
Salmo trutta Linnaeus

It requires great skill to catch brown trout because they are wary. They are most frequently found in shallow water where they can hide around boulders, weed beds, etc. In this region, they are normally captured in tributaries or near the mouths of tributaries as they begin their spawning runs. Browns are fall spawners and do not die after spawning. They ascend tributaries to gravel bars where females scoop out nests called "redds" (name given to most nests of salmonid species) where the eggs are deposited. After spawning, she covers the eggs with gravel and leaves the nest. Some natural reproduction occurs in the region, but most fish captured by anglers are the result of annual stocking programs conducted by Michigan, Ohio, Pennsylvania, and New York.

Brown trout are primarily insect and fish eaters that seldom weigh over 10 lbs (5 kg). They are difficult to catch, and once hooked put up a real battle. Fishermen should watch for their sharp teeth including a set on their tongue.

Sea Lamprey (*Petromyzon marinus*). This unusual fish, also called the "vampire of the deep," is a member of the lamprey family, Petromyzontidae, and is parasitic on fish. It is eel-like in appearance, has no paired fins, and lacks true bones. It has a circular, suction cup-like mouth which it uses to attach itself to the side of a fish. It then rasps a hole and sucks out blood and body fluids.

The sea lamprey has been in the lower St. Lawrence drainage since early post-glacial times. It could not migrate beyond Niagara Falls until

1829 when the Welland Canal was completed. However, for some unknown reason the sea lamprey did not take advantage of the route; the first specimen in Lake Erie was not recorded until 1921, and the first spawning run was not observed until 1932.

Sea lampreys are sight feeders. Consequently, they are most effective in clear water where they can see their future host at a great distance. Because they rasp a hole in the side of their host, they are most effective on large fish (more blood) with small delicate scales. Salmon and trout meet these requirements and therefore have been the hardest hit by the invasion of the lamprey.

Lamprey run up streams to spawn in gravel beds during the spring. They are not tolerant of silt or pollutants and die after spawning. The young lamprey, called "ammocoetes," live as filter feeders buried in the gravel for 6 years before they mature. As adults, they are free-swimming parasites for only 1 year before they return to spawn and die. Adults reach lengths of up to 3 ft (91 cm).

The sea lamprey never was a serious problem in the Lake Erie/Lake St. Clair region because the water was turbid, there were few suitable spawning streams, and there were few salmonids—the lamprey's preferred food. However, the upper lakes (Lakes Huron, Michigan, and Superior) were hit hard by the sea lamprey. Eventually, control measures were required. A chemical, TFM, was dripped into the spawning streams where it killed the ammocoetes. This procedure is still in use today.

Occasionally, fish are caught with a lamprey attached to the side or which have round scars from earlier lamprey attacks. It should also be noted that not all species of lampreys are parasitic, and these non-parasitic forms are common in tributaries in the region.

Figure 5.43 (continued). Fishes of Lake Erie (after Trautman, 1981).

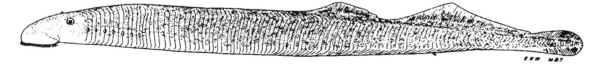

Sea Lamprey
Petromyzon marinus Linnaeus

V

Blue Pike (*Stizostedion vitreum glaucum*). The blue pike fishery collapsed in 1959 and is now considered extinct by most ichthyologists. The blue pike is a subspecies of the walleye and a member of the perch family, Percidae. The blue pike looked much like a walleye but had larger eyes and was gray to silver in color with a bluish-silver back. It was somewhat smaller than a walleye and had softer flesh. It avoided the turbid waters of the western basin and was most abundant in the eastern two-thirds of the lake. It was a very important commercial and sport species.

Lake Sturgeon (*Acipenser fulvescens*). This fish is a member of the sturgeon family, Acipenseridae. They have bony plates, lack scales, and are huge fish—some are over 8 ft (2 m) long and weigh approximately 300 lbs (136 kg). Due to over-fishing and the destruction of spawning habitat, these fish are quite rare in the region.

The sturgeon is a bottom feeder primarily eating molluscs and insects. In May and June, they run up tributaries and spawn in shallow water over gravel.

A significant factor in their depletion is the fact that they do not become sexually mature until they are 20 years old and 4 ft (1 m) long. In the late 1800s they caused commercial fishermen so much trouble by breaking nets that they were often simply thrown up on the beach to rot and were occasionally piled and burned. Later as markets developed, the flesh was smoked, the eggs were converted into caviar, the oil rendered, and the bladders converted into isinglass.

Figure 5.43 (continued). Blue Pike.

Blue Pike

Stizostedion vitreum glaucum Hubbs

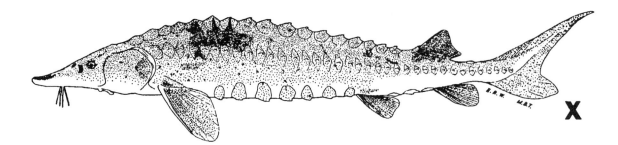

X

Lake Sturgeon
Acipenser fulvescens Rafinesque

Figure 5.43 (continued). Fishes of Lake Erie (after Trautman, 1981).

Avifauna

The Lake Erie region abounds in both land- and waterbirds and exhibits marked seasonal variety. Spring migration begins in February, with birds appearing soon after the break up of the ice. In general, migration is earliest in the southwest around Toledo and progressively later to the east and north. There may be enormous gatherings of waterfowl at the beginning of the migration season. Branches of the Atlantic and Mississippi migratory routes pass over the western end of the Lake Erie region; over one million ducks and geese use these flyways during migration (Figure 5.44). The marshes here are used by nearly two-thirds of North America's 100,000 tundra (whistling) swans.

Migratory movements of birds are greatly influenced by the weather. In the early spring, birds may arrive with warmer weather systems but will return south if wintry conditions arise. Migrants tend to congregate in specific areas—islands, points of land, shorelines, habitat edges (e.g. where woods meet open fields), marshes, and river mouths.

By June, most birds are settled into nesting and breeding grounds where they remain until the fall migration. Some species may begin this migration as early as July. By August, most shorebird migration is underway. In September, a wide variety of species may appear, and by October, landbird passage is at its peak (hunting season also begins at this time). Weather plays a role in migration patterns; in autumn, cold weather triggers migration, and warm weather halts such movement. During prolonged periods of poor weather, southward-moving landbirds will concentrate in protective habitats such as wooded areas along the lake. Hawk flights, meanwhile, occur on cool, sunny days with winds from the north or northwest. The most spectacular of these flights is

Figure 5.44a. Mississippi waterfowl migration flyways in North America (Lincoln, 1950).

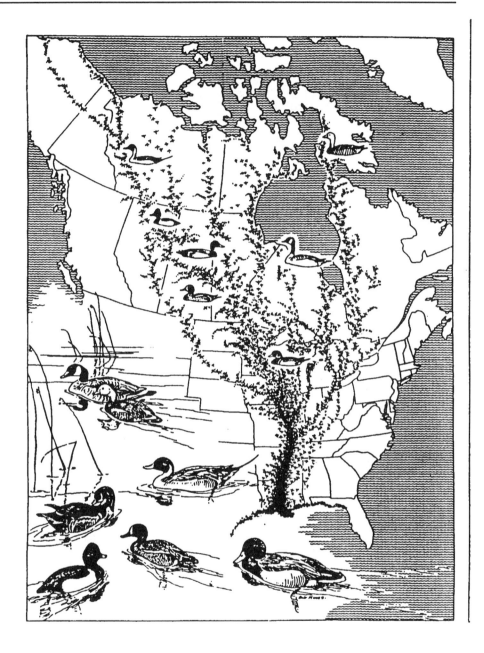

that of broad-winged hawks which travel in large flocks of up to 100 birds or more. In late September, large chickadee and blue jay movements may occur. Waterfowl assemble into large migratory flocks by November.

Winter is the time when birds are present in their smallest numbers, though some Audubon Society "Christmas counts" have exceeded 100

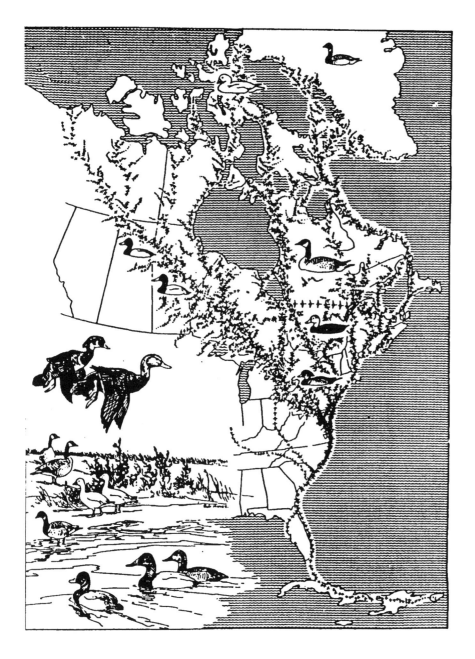

Figure 5.44b. Atlantic waterfowl migration flyways in North America (Lincoln, 1950).

species. These northern migrants and permanent residents are found where there is available food and shelter—such as in evergreen and mixed woodlands—and also where there is open water, especially at warm water outlets from power plants.

The Lake Erie region supports a wide variety of birds which are divided into several groups: waterbirds, wading birds, game birds, birds of prey (raptors), and songbirds which includes perching birds (passerines) and non-perching birds (non-passerines). The term landbirds in this section refers to the last three groups.

Waterbirds. This group embraces all members of the waterfowl family—swans, geese, and ducks—plus other birds that obtain their food mainly from the water. Gulls and terns are included in this heading. Also included are American coots and the moorhens (formerly called gallinules) because of their water-oriented behavior (Figure 5.45).

Wading Birds. This category includes the long-legged, shallow-water waders such as egrets and herons and the shorebirds like sandpipers and plovers (Figure 5.46).

Figure 5.45. Waterbirds of Lake Erie's rocky coasts (after Pettingill, 1970). In the air, left to right: Parasitic Jaeger (rare), Common Tern, Caspian Tern, Ring-billed Gull, Herring Gull. On the water, left to right: Bufflehead, Cormorant, Common Merganser, Common Loon, Mallard.

The water-margin habitat produces a great deal of plant and animal life which supports these species. The abundance of insects, mollusks, crustaceans, fish, and aquatic plants is the basis for such a broad collection of bird families near the lakes and rivers.

Birds of the marsh and shoreline are an interesting segment of life in wet marginal areas. They do not, though, have direct economic importance or gamebird value. Most feed on animal life; some of the long-legged species eat fish extensively (Figure 5.47).

Upland Game Birds. Principal birds in this group include the ring-necked pheasant, American woodcock, and mourning dove. Although the woodcock is related to the shorebirds, its habitat differs slightly by including lowland woods and upland fields. Additionally, it is a well-known game species. Most of these upland game birds primarily eat plant matter.

Raptors. The term "birds of prey" is applied to species of this group which feed on vertebrates and is used in this sense to include hawks, vultures, eagles, and owls. These predators balance populations of many species that often, if not checked, cause local or wide-ranging

Figure 5.46. Wading birds of Lake Erie's sandy shores (after Pettingill, 1970). Left to right, front row: Dowitcher, Yellowlegs, Semipalmated Sandpiper, Ruddy Turnstone. Middle row: Common Snipe, Killdeer, Semipalmater Plover, Spotted Sandpiper, Avocet (rare), Marbled Godwit (rare). In the background: Great Blue Heron, Black-crowned Night Heron, Glossy Ibis.

harm to the environment. Great horned owls, for example, feed extensively on mice and rats. Game managers note that raptors benefit prey species by eliminating sick and weak individuals. By helping to balance these populations, birds of prey, along with other predators, benefit all ecosystems.

A bird's size, build, and structure of talons and bill allows observers to infer what that bird eats. Larger species may be able to handle large prey, while smaller species generally choose prey in proportion to their size. Thus, while eagles feed on medium-sized fish, squirrels, rabbits, and ducks, smaller members of the hawk family (e.g. Cooper's hawk) hunt rats, mice, and small birds. Members of the raptor group generally have strong talons and bills for holding and tearing their prey. The red-tailed hawk—a large bird with powerful beak and talons—may pursue squirrels, rabbits, rats, and mice. The red-shouldered hawk, on the other hand, is nearly equal in size to the red-tailed hawk, but it feeds primarily on mice, reptiles, birds, and large insects due to its relatively weak beak and talons.

Songbirds. The "songbird" group of passerines and non-passerines encompasses landbirds not covered in the previous categories. It includes such unmelodious species as the American crow, European starling, and common grackle.

Most songbirds are migratory. Many that winter in the south nest in this area, while some Arctic songbirds venture to the Lake Erie region for the winter. Other songbirds are permanent residents, remaining throughout the year.

In addition to attracting the interest of human observers, songbirds are economically important in two ways: (1) many species help control insects that are harmful to crops, orchards, forests and gardens; and (2) conversely, some species damage fruit orchards, vineyards, or grainfields with their feeding activity.

Reading Suggestions. There are several good books available on the subject of bird identification and location. The following are recommended:

1. Bull, J. and J. Farrand, Jr. The Audubon Society field guide to North American birds, eastern region. A.A. Knopf, NY, 776 pp. (1977).
2. Geffen, A.M. A birdwatcher's guide to the eastern United States. Barron's, Woodbury, NY, 346 pp. (1978).

3. Goodwin, C.E. A bird finding guide to Ontario. University of
    Toronto Press, Toronto, 248 pp. (1982).

4. Peterson, R.T. A field guide to the birds east of the Rockies (4th
    edition). Houghton Mifflin, Boston, 384 pp. (1980).

5. Scott, S.L. (ed.). Field guide to the birds of North America. National
    Geographic Society, Washington, DC, 464 pp. (1983).

6. Thomson, T. Birding in Ohio. Indiana University Press,
    Bloomington, 265 pp. (1983).

7. Peterjohn, B.G. The birds of Ohio. Indiana University Press,
    Bloomington, 237 pp. (1989).

Common bird names used in this section align with the 1983 American Ornithologists' Union (AOU) checklist of North American Birds. This reference should be consulted for current scientific names of bird species and families.

Figure 5.47. Marsh birds of Lake Erie's wetlands (after Pettingill, 1970). From the left, perching or standing: Red-winged blackbird, Long-billed Marsh Wren, American Bittern, American Coot, Common Moorhen, Virginia Rail. In the water: Pied-billed Grebe. In the air: Northern Harrier.

Birding Sites

The following discussion details noteworthy birding sites around the shores of Lake Erie and Lake St. Clair, beginning at the head of the St. Clair River and progressing counter-clockwise around the region. For convenience of presentation, the region has been divided into 14 segments. Each description contains general locations for good birdwatching and notes on species which should be present at various times of the year.

Most sites are natural areas, but a particular type of site deserves special note. Ontario sewage lagoons are mentioned because they are significant birding areas in relation to their size. The fertile waters may yield marsh, mud flat, or open water, depending on management techniques, and this in turn attracts many birds. Permission is usually required before entering municipal lagoons. Birdwatchers displaying responsible behavior generally are tolerated.

St. Clair River (Michigan and Ontario). The head of the St. Clair River is perhaps the best spot in Ontario for birds such as jaegers, Sabine's gulls, and large concentrations of other waterbirds near shore in late fall. Canatara Park, to the east, has wild natural areas, lake viewing, and a small lake which attracts waterfowl and marshbirds. Many landbirds are seen here in spring. Point Edward, overlooking Lake Huron and the river, usually features many landbirds, including hawks, that move along the shore during spring and fall migrations. The St. Clair Parkway (County Road 33) follows the river south from Sarnia to Walpole Island. This route is particularly rewarding from late fall to early spring when gulls and ducks congregate on the open water. A place of particular interest is Willow Park, an active site for gulls. The Port Huron wetland, located south of the town near the north end of Stag Island, attracts canvasbacks and other waterfowl in the winter when open water is maintained by thermal discharges from nearby power plants. Near Corunna, Stag Island is a wetland that attracts waterfowl and marsh- and shorebirds. The marsh at Algonac State Park serves as a staging and wintering ground for canvasbacks.

Lake St. Clair (Michigan and Ontario). Exceptional opportunities exist for observing waterfowl and marshbirds at the St. Clair Flats wetlands (Figure 5.48). These extensive marshes along the northwest shoreline of Lake St. Clair were formed by sediment deposition in the mouth of the St. Clair River. This complex consists of wetlands on Bouvier Bay and at Dickinson, McDonald, North, Middle, Green, Harsens, and Bruchner Islands (all lie within the St. Clair Flats Wildlife Area). The islands comprise a delta of the St. Clair River and are charac-

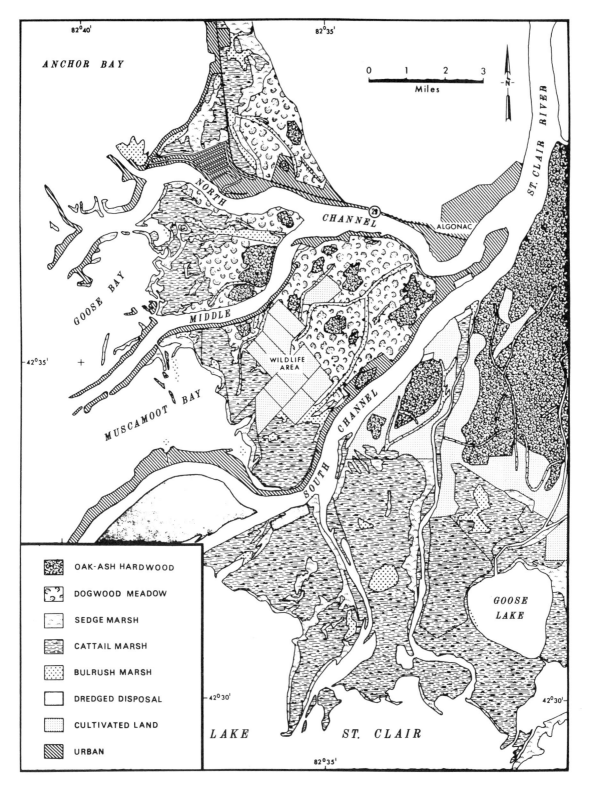

Figure 5.48. Vegetation zones of the St. Clair Delta marshes (after Raphael and Jaworski, 1982).

teristically marshy except for some wooded areas on Harsens and Dickinson Islands.

Harsens Island is most accessible, being serviced by the Champion Ferry (carrying both passengers and automobiles). Heated power plant discharges keep some water open throughout the winter. Canvasbacks and redheads gather in this open water, often numbering up to 2,000 or more. Lesser numbers of other ducks also congregate here. From the beginning of March to early April, one of the main attractions is the large number—up to 30,000—of tundra swans that rest here for 2 or 3 weeks on their way north. Some species seen in the fall include the Canada goose, mallard, black duck, pintail, green-winged, blue-winged and cinnamon teal, redhead, canvasback, common goldeneye, merganser, wood duck, bufflehead, scaup, American wigeon, and American coot. In addition to waterfowl, short-eared owls and rough-legged hawks have been reported in Bouvier Bay wetland during the winter.

Nesting species in the St. Clair Flats include the common snipe, pied-billed grebe, American bittern, king rail, sora, American coot, black and common terns, marsh wren, great egret, swamp sparrow, black-crowned night-heron, green-backed heron, and many of the waterfowl mentioned for the fall. Of special note is a great blue heron rookery near the center of Dickinson Island.

Walpole Island lies within the Lambert Indian Reservation and is also part of the St. Clair Flats wetland. This island is of critical importance to migrating waterfowl. There are two ways to reach this island: by ferry from Algonac, or across the bridge on Kent Road 32. There is a network of dirt roads, but most of the area is relatively inaccessible. The island features a rookery of black-crowned night-herons and great egrets. Extensive woodland areas offer typical species though the area is best known for its waterfowl. For extended excursions into the marshes, permission should be obtained from the Indian Reservation headquarters.

Anchor Bay, on the Michigan shore, is heavily utilized by migrant diving ducks as a feeding and resting site, particularly in the vicinity of Marsac and Swan Creeks. The Clinton River wetlands include Black Creek marsh near the creek's mouth, Belvidere Bay marsh, and Grass Island marsh in Lake St. Clair. In spring, summer, and fall, one may find dabbling ducks, American coots, terns, and shorebirds nesting, feeding, or resting in this area. In addition, shorebirds and geese use these wetlands during migration. Nearby L'anse Creuse Bay is used by such migrant ducks as redheads, canvasbacks, mallards, and blue-winged teal.

Detroit River (Michigan and Ontario). From Detroit, crossing the river on the Douglas MacArthur Bridge leads to Belle Isle Park, one of America's largest urban island parks. Here one may find nesting common terns, among the many local species. The west and south sections of the island are utilized by migrant and wintering ducks. Just south of here is Mud (Spoils) Island, where there is a large nesting area of ring-billed gulls and common terns.

Grosse Ile and nearby islands are prime locations for seeing swans and ducks in the winter. This reach of the Detroit River often has some of the largest populations of wintering ducks in the Midwest. Thousands of lesser scaup, canvasbacks, common goldeneyes, and redheads concentrate in open water when the river is partly iced over. Buffleheads are present in small numbers. In fall and spring, Bonaparte's gulls are seen. Stony Island supports nesting great blue herons, black-crowned night-herons, and great egrets. Gibraltar and Celeron Islands host typical wetland birds including blue-winged teal, mallards, lesser scaup, herons, gulls, terns, king rails, and spotted sandpipers.

Scenic views of the Detroit River are available along the Windsor waterfront and south along Highway 18 to Amherstburg. Waterfowl are seen here in migration periods and during the winter. Ojibway Park, a city park at the southeast end of Windsor, lies adjacent to Ojibway Prairie Provincial Nature Preserve. During spring and fall migrations, this area features an abundance of blue jays, warblers, thrushes, flycatchers, and, on occasion, rarities such as the Kentucky warbler, yellow-crowned night-heron, and summer tanager. Continuing south, the mouth of the Canard River is especially worthwhile for waterbirds. Ducks gather here on the extensive marshes, especially large numbers of canvasback in the fall. Shorebirds may be numerous as well, depending on the water level. South of the Canard River is the community of Edgewater Beach; there is a sewage lagoon nearby with additional birdwatching opportunities.

Western Lake Erie (Michigan). On Lake Erie near the mouth of the Detroit River, Pointe Mouillee can be found. Pointe Mouillee State Game Area is a point of departure for the large hawk migrations that cross the Detroit River into Canada. Common and black terns and waterfowl such as black ducks, mallards, gadwalls, blue-winged teal, and wood ducks nest here. Other migrating birds using this location include tundra swans, Canada geese, snow geese, and diving and dabbling ducks. Rockwood Road wetlands, north of Pointe Mouillee, may host ruddy ducks, great blue herons, green-backed herons, great egrets, black-crowned night-herons, ring-billed gulls, and common terns.

While to the south, Swan Creek wetlands occupy the estuarine mouth of the creek and offer birdwatchers opportunities to observe marsh birds.

In Monroe, Sterling State Park is important to migrating hawks, waterfowl, shorebirds, and passerines. It is also a nesting site for common terns, black terns, and waterfowl. The River Raisin wetlands lie on the north and south sides of the river mouth at Monroe. Birds recorded in this area include the mute swan, mallard, black duck, canvasback, double-crested cormorant, belted kingfisher, great blue heron, great egret, black-crowned night-heron, American coot, and red-tailed hawk. The mouth of the River Raisin and Bolles Harbor provide nesting sites for common terns, black terns, and waterfowl. This is also a migration area for waterfowl, shorebirds, passerines, and hawks. The river mouth area is the only known nesting location of yellow-crowned night-herons in the Great Lakes.

Maumee Bay (Michigan and Ohio). The Erie State Game Area, on North Maumee Bay, is a noteworthy location particularly for waterfowl. Slightly south along the beach toward the tip of North Cape there is an extensive wetland to the west. The first 0.5 mi (0.8 km) of shore is part of the game refuge; the remainder is public hunting ground. Erie Marsh provides nesting sites for waterfowl. Also seen here are Bonaparte's gulls, great blue herons, and great egrets. North Maumee Bay has many wetlands, including Woodtick Peninsula, Erie Road, Bay Creek, Flat Creek, Indian Island, Halfway Creek, the Ottawa River mouth, and Carland Beach. Woodtick Peninsula attracts spring flights of shorebirds, waterfowl, passerines, and hawks. The Atlantic and Mississippi flyways cross here at the west end of Lake Erie. This peninsula is also a nesting area for common terns, black terns, and waterfowl. Turtle Island, a remnant of a sand spit several miles offshore, supports nesting herring gulls.

Landbirds are common throughout the year in the undergrowth and trees along the Maumee Bay shore. These birds are most numerous during migrations. Principal waterbirds are the thousands of tundra swans in the spring, and great black-backed gulls, which are uncommon on the Great Lakes. In May, August, and September, when westerly winds may lower the lake level, shorebirds gather on the exposed mud flats and sand bars. In late summer, great egrets are common along the marsh and shore. Spectacular flights of waterfowl are seen in the fall at sunset when large flocks pass to the fields and marshes to feed.

Two wetlands for waterfowl and gulls are located near the Toledo waterfront. Detwiler wetland is located on the west shore of Maumee

Bay within Toledo city limits. This wetland is immediately north of the Maumee River mouth between Bay View and Cullen parks. Otter Creek wetland lies along the estuarine portion of Otter Creek, extending inland from the stream's mouth at the Maumee River. This wetland is nestled in the busy Toledo harbor area within the city limits of Oregon. Birders may see shorebirds in season such as Hudsonian and marbled godwits, willets, and American avocets. In late fall, many diving ducks visit the waters of the bay. Maumee Bay State Park, with its meadows, wet woods, and marshes, serves as a wildlife haven. Summer birdwatchers may see such unusual species as dickcissels, bobolinks, western mead-owlarks, rails, and bitterns. In the winter, northern harriers (marsh hawks) and short-eared owls may be present.

The Toledo Harbor Dike, a man-made landfill covered with upland grass, is located at the mouth of the Maumee River and is a nesting area for herring and ring-billed gulls. Although no nests have been observed recently, common terns can be seen in the area during nesting season. Upstream on the Maumee River is Grassy Island which has a wooded swamp and a cattail marsh that provide habitat for many migrant and resident birds. In the winter, the Maumee River rapids, located between the villages of Maumee and Grand Rapids, do not freeze and often provide the only open water in the vicinity. As a result, thousands of ducks may seek the rapids area. This portion of the river is also a feeding area for gulls. In August and September, when the water is low, shorebirds often congregate along the exposed river bottom. U.S. Route 24 runs close to the rapids on the north shore.

The Toledo Area Metropolitan Park District operates eight units which are open daily and are free of charge. Perhaps the best for birdwatching is Oak Openings Metropark. The main entrance is on Wilkins Road just north of Swan Creek. Varied habitats here include open oak woods, swamp forests, bogs, wet and dry prairies, and bare dunes. Habitats in the park are intermixed and closely adjoined so that they attract correspondingly varied birdlife in a relatively small area. One may observe great crested flycatchers, scarlet tanagers, Acadian flycatchers, wood thrushes, veeries, redstarts, rose-breasted grosbeaks, golden- and blue-winged warblers, yellow-breasted chats, rufous-sided towhees, yellow-throats, horned larks, and Henslow's, vesper, lark, and field sparrows.

Two other rewarding parks, especially during migrations, are Wild-wood Preserve Metropark, located on West Central Avenue (U.S. Route 20), and Pearson Metropark in Oregon on State Route 2. The first is unique in this predominantly flat county in that it has three large, ridged ravines. This park is predominantly oak forest with 10 mi (16 km) of hiking trails. Pearson Metropark offers hiking trails that lead through woods and past several ponds. In late April and May, many migrating landbirds are present here. Nesting bird species include the eastern wood pewee, red-headed woodpecker, black-capped chickadee, barn swallow, white-breasted nuthatch, gray catbird, house wren, wood thrush, brown thrasher, red-eyed vireo, cerulean warbler, common yellow throat, northern oriole, scarlet tanager, indigo bunting, and rose-breasted grosbeak.

Western Lake Erie Marshes (Ohio). The Ottawa National Wildlife Refuge, bordering western Lake Erie, includes three separate refuges that total over 12 mi² (30 km²). The complex is administered by the United States Fish and Wildlife Service (USFWS). It is renowned as one of the best overall birdwatching areas in Ohio. The western-most section is Cedar Point National Wildlife Refuge which lies between Maumee Bay State Park and Cooley Canal. About 3 mi (5 km) to the east along the lakeshore is the Ottawa National Wildlife Refuge, for which the complex is named. This refuge includes the Navarre Marsh unit, which is leased to the USFWS by Toledo Edison, and the Darby Marsh unit to the east.

The third component of the complex is West Sister Island, lying 9 mi (14 km) offshore. This island constitutes Ohio's only federally-designated wilderness area. Great blue herons, black-crowned night-herons, great egrets, and herring gulls nest here in great numbers. West Sister Island is not open to the public.

The only public access permitted in the Ottawa complex is at the Ottawa unit along a system of trails reached from the main entrance on State Route 2, midway between Toledo and Port Clinton. A pamphlet describing the 8 mi (13 km) of trails and their wildlife is available at a bulletin board in the parking lot.

The most spectacular bird concentrations are seen during spring and fall migrations. Ottawa Refuge functions as a pivotal point for waterfowl. It is here that many Mississippi and Atlantic flyways users separate on their southward migrations. They rejoin here during their northerly spring flights. Mallards, black ducks, Canada geese, and tundra swans are among the waterfowl which gather. Notable among the 143 nesting species at Ottawa are several pairs of bald eagles—a federally-endangered species and the United States' national bird. The Columbus (Ohio) Zoo has successfully placed eaglets (born in captivity) in the nests here. Over 280 species, highlighted by 4,000 resident Canada geese, have been reported throughout this complex. Among these species are the snow goose, wood duck, northern shoveler, dunlin, Wilson's phalarope, Forster's tern, barn and snowy owls, red-headed woodpecker, red-breasted nuthatch, winter wren, cedar waxwing, Philadelphia vireo, and common redpoll. A checklist of Ottawa refuge birds is available from the USFWS.

Magee Marsh State Wildlife Area, about 13 mi (21 km) west of Port Clinton on State Route 2, is administered by the Ohio Department of Natural Resources, Division of Wildlife (ODNR, DOW). Tucked along the lakeshore at Magee Marsh is Crane Creek State Park where the Crane Creek Wildlife Experiment Station is headquartered. A popular bird trail winds along the south edge of the park, providing opportunities to view a variety of habitats and birds. The warbler migration here in the spring attracts many birdwatchers.

Major species of waterfowl using these Lake Erie marshes are the mallard, black duck, American wigeon, and Canada goose. Blue-winged teal nest here, and sizeable concentrations of these ducks are found in fall migration, along with lesser numbers of pintails, gadwalls, green-winged teal, wood ducks, canvasbacks, redheads, American coots, and moorhens (gallinules). Under normal fall conditions, several thousand black ducks, mallards, and wigeons use these marshes, with peak duck populations occurring in mid-November. Spring flocks of migrating waterfowl begin to arrive in February. Tundra swans appear from late March to the end of April.

Waterbirds common to the area are double-crested cormorants, gulls, terns, and American coots, as well as a wide variety of shorebirds. The area also attracts large warbler concentrations during spring and fall migrations. Birds of prey include bald eagles, turkey vultures, and several species of hawks and owls. Over 300 species of birds are listed for this wildlife area, ranking it as one of Ohio's major birdwatching areas. Also of interest is the Sportsman's Migratory Bird Center which houses a large collection of birds found in the area. An observation platform for the marsh is located at the center.

The nearby Toussaint Wildlife Area, located north of Oak Harbor on State Route 92, is managed by ODNR for waterfowl. Also abundant are ring-necked pheasants and shorebirds.

Metzger Marsh State Wildlife Area is situated in the southeast corner of Lucas County off State Route 2 near the village of Bono. Divided between open water and cattail marsh and open to the lake, the marsh is subject to fluctuating water levels. Large varieties of waterfowl and shorebirds are present during spring and fall migrations. During warmer months, herring, ring-billed, and Bonaparte's gulls, plus several species of terns, may be observed on the sandbars.

Little Portage Wildlife Area is located on State Route 53 about 5 mi (8 km) west of Port Clinton. This area is bounded by Portage and Little Portage Rivers and is a combination of river marsh and low-lying agricultural ground. A portion of this area is diked for water level control to enhance waterfowl usage. Waterfowl and shorebirds of many varieties are found during spring and fall migrations. Wood ducks, mallards, and blue-winged teal nest here. The Port Clinton Marsh, located at the mouth of the Portage River, is another shorebird migration area where egrets and other wading birds are also present.

East, West, and Middle Harbors provide excellent waterfowl habitat along the east shore of Catawba Island peninsula. At least 20 species of transient waterfowl gather on the marsh and harbor from late March to April and from late September to October. Situated 6 mi (10 km) east of Port Clinton is East Harbor State Park on Route 240. Much of the park consists of sandy beach, marsh, and open water. Boats may be rented nearby for exploring the marsh, where in May and June, pied-billed grebes, black-crowned night-herons, American and least bitterns, mallards, black ducks, king and Virginia rails, soras, black and common terns, marsh wrens, and red-winged blackbirds are found. Bald eagles may occasionally soar overhead.

Lake Erie Islands (Ohio and Ontario). The islands district of western Lake Erie (Figure 5.49) supports a great variety of birds from early spring through late fall. Several islands are reached by boat, ferry and airplane; others are not easily accessible or off-limits.

South Bass Island, located about 4 mi (6 km) north of Catawba Point, is accessible by ferries from Port Clinton and Catawba. Although some 50 species of birds nest on South Bass Island, the outstanding ornithological events are the hawk, waterfowl and songbird migrations. Spring hawk migration peaks from April 10-May 1 as sharp-shinned, Cooper's, red-tailed, red-shouldered, and broad-winged hawks pass over. Red-breasted and hooded mergansers are among the most conspicuous diving ducks in Put-in-Bay Harbor in early spring and late fall. Songbirds are best seen between May 1 and May 20, and September 20 and October 10 during the first 3 hours of daylight and on rainy, cloudy, or windy days. At such times hundreds of vireos and warblers may be observed as they pass through. Thousands of blackbirds and hundreds

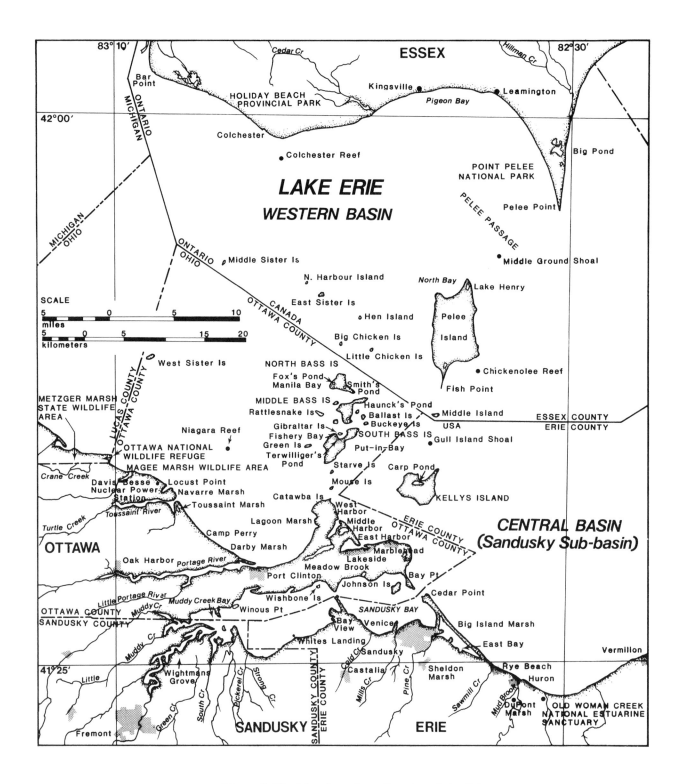

Figure 5.49. Islands region of western Lake Erie.

of blue jays are also seen in spring and fall migrations. The wooded area along the island's west shore is the best place to find concentrations of these migrants.

Terwilliger's Pond on South Bass Island opens onto Fishery Bay. In this pond mallards, belted kingfishers, great blue herons, and black-crowned night-herons feed or roost.

In spring and fall, nearly all species of North American ducks visit the bay between Gibraltar and South Bass Islands, the open water near the south shore of South Bass, and waters off of East Point. Migrating shorebirds appear on island mudflats in July. Commonly seen species include the greater and lesser yellowlegs, solitary and spotted sandpipers, semipalmated plover, ruddy turnstone, sanderling, and least sandpiper.

Uninhabited Green Island lies west of South Bass Island. It is a nesting area for herring gulls and a migration stop for passerines. Typical woodland species are found here.

Ballast Island is privately owned and lies east of Middle Bass Island. It is a nesting site for herring gulls, and late in the summer ring-billed and Bonaparte's gulls are present.

Middle Bass Island lies between North Bass and South Bass islands and is serviced by ferries from Port Clinton, Catawba, and South Bass Island and by planes from Port Clinton and South Bass Island. In addition to typical woodland species, gulls also nest here. During migration, several species of gulls and terns may be observed. Late summer brings Caspian terns and Bonaparte's gulls. Haunck's Pond on the island's northeast end serves as a feeding area for great blue herons and great egrets.

North Bass Island is 15 mi (24 km) northwest of Sandusky, Ohio and north of South and Middle Bass Islands. North Bass Island has two wetland areas: Smith's Pond, located on the southeast end of the island, and Fox's Marsh on the southwest end. These marshes serve as nesting areas for waterfowl. This island likewise is a migration stop for waterfowl, shorebirds, and some passerines (e.g. blackbirds, American robins, and blue jays). The island is also a feeding area for black-crowned night-herons and great blue herons.

Kelleys Island lies southeast of South Bass Island, 4 mi (6 km) north of Marblehead Point. It is served by a ferry from Marblehead. Kelleys is ringed by 29 km (18 mi) of rocky shoreline. Two cattail marshes are of special interest—Kelleys Pond near the village on the south shore, and Carp Pond near the north shore which host nesting waterfowl. This island is a major shorebird, waterfowl, and passerine stopover site during migration and is the site of the last eagle nest on any of the islands.

Ontario's Lake Erie islands offer a variety of waterbirds comparable to that of the nearby Ohio islands. Only Pelee Island, though, can be visited by public conveyance. Other Canadian islands are privately owned or designated as provincial nature preserves.

Pelee Island is the largest and most populated of the Canadian islands. It is located about 8 mi (13 km) southwest of the tip of Point Pelee (on Ontario's mainland) and is served by daily ferries from Sandusky, Ohio and Leamington, or Kingsville, Ontario. Passengers making this lake crossing may observe gulls, terns, and other waterbirds while in route. Air service is also available from Port Clinton and Sandusky.

Lake Henry, in Lighthouse Point Provincial Nature Reserve, hosts colonies of double-crested cormorants and herring gulls and serves as a feeding area for herons and great egrets. Later in summer, shorebirds and Caspian terns gather, especially if mud flats are exposed. In September, many raptors fly past this point. Upland areas in the Lighthouse Point area support Carolina wrens, blue-gray gnatcatchers, white-eyed vireos, and northern and orchard orioles during the summer. Brown's Point, southeast of Lighthouse Point, hosts many typical Carolinian species. The airport, near the east center of the island, may yield upland sandpiper, bobolinks, and both western and eastern meadowlarks. At the southeast end of the island is an undisturbed open savannah tract, and birders may note yellow-breasted chats, song sparrows, and other open-field species. Rafts of loons, grebes, and diving ducks sometimes congregate offshore in Lake Erie during migration.

The southernmost extremity of the island is encompassed by Fish Point Provincial Park Reserve including Fox Pond (actually a marsh area) and Mosquito Bay. Great egrets, black-crowned night-herons, king rails, common moorhens, coots, black ducks, and mallards have been recorded at Fox Pond. Great horned owls, red-bellied woodpeckers, winter and Carolina wrens, blue-gray gnatcatchers, and prothonotary warblers may also be present in the breeding season. Other birds of interest include the ring-necked pheasant, yellow-billed cuckoo, barn owl, eastern screech owl, and eastern bluebird. During migration this area provides exceptional birdwatching.

Middle and Hen Islands, two of the privately-owned Canadian islands, function as nesting sites for herring gulls. Big Chicken Island, a cobble covered uninhabited island, is a teeming nesting site for herring gulls and double-crested cormorants. Most of the space on this tiny island is used for the nesting activities of these birds.

East Sister Island is thickly wooded, but the southeast corner can be marshy during high lake levels. Colonies of great blue herons as well as black-crowned night-herons, double-crested cormorants, great egrets, herring gulls, and woodland species nest in this Provincial Nature Reserve. Middle Sister is also designated as a Provincial Nature Reserve. Great blue herons, black-crowned night-herons, egrets, and herring gulls nest here. Both East Sister and Middle Sister Islands may not be visited without permission from Ontario's Ministry of Natural Resources.

Sandusky Bay (Ohio). The several extensive wetlands of Sandusky Bay serve as excellent locations for observing waterfowl and shorebirds. In spring it is an important feeding and resting area for migrants. Just inside the bay near downtown Sandusky is a man-made island—Sandusky Turning Point—which supports a large nesting colony of herring gulls. Bay View, Willow Point, Whites Landing, and Pickerel Creek wetlands are located along the southern shore of the bay. These areas are privately owned; Bay View, Willow Point, and Whites Landing are managed for waterfowl. Within these wetlands are the Moxley/Strohm Marsh and Willow Point Marsh State Wildlife Area. A heron rookery is established at the Moxley/Strohm Marsh.

Muddy Creek Bay, located at the western end of Sandusky Bay, is the most extensive wetland on the Ohio shore. Most of this wetland is privately owned and managed for waterfowl propagation and hunting.

Winous Point Marsh and Ottawa Club Marsh support nesting areas for great blue herons and duck species that include pintail, green-winged teal, gadwall, northern shoveler, wood duck, redhead, and scaup. Gulls and terns are commonly seen overhead; ospreys are present during migration; and red-tailed hawks, Cooper's hawks, and several pairs of bald eagles nest in the vicinity.

Not far from the south shore of Sandusky Bay, Resthaven Wildlife Area, on State Route 269 in Castalia, is managed by ODNR. A great variety of waterfowl is found during migration times. Wood ducks, mallards, black ducks, blue-winged teal, and American woodcocks nest in the area.

A pond located in Castalia does not freeze in winter because of a steady flow of water from underground springs. Waterfowl are abundant here after nearby waters freeze over and may be observed and photographed at extremely close range. Species attracted to these open waters include the pied-billed grebe, horned grebe, Canada goose, mallard, black duck, gadwall, pintail, teals, American wigeon, wood duck, common goldeneye, hooded merganser, and northern shoveler.

At the east end of Sandusky Bay, along the inside of Cedar Point sand spit, are several marshy areas including Big Island, Pipe Creek, Hemming Ditch, East Bay, Plum Brook, and the Plum Brook Creek wetlands. Another wetland lies across the narrower entrance to the bay on Bay Point. These areas are important migration sites for shorebirds, passerines, and hawks. At the base of Cedar Point is Sheldon's Marsh State Nature Preserve (previously known as Sheldon's Folly). This 387 acre preserve consists of upland and swamp forests, emergent marsh, sandy beach, waterfowl refuge, natural marshes, successional farm fields, and dense undergrowth. This varied habitat furnishes nesting sites and migration cover for a great number of waterfowl and other birds including the prothonotary warbler—rare for this area. Nearly 300 species have been sighted here, the more common being rufous-sided towhees, blue-gray gnatcatchers, red-winged blackbirds, eastern kingbirds, at least 20 species warblers, mallards, and great blue herons. This nature preserve is also a resting stop for migrant bald eagles and ospreys. Also of interest: a nearby nesting pair of eagles uses this area for fledging their young. Hundreds of birdwatchers come each spring to observe the incredible numbers of birds resting at Sheldon's Marsh prior to their journey across Lake Erie.

Nearby Sawmill Creek wetland has mallards, great blue herons, eastern kingbirds, and red-winged blackbirds. Migratory birds, including ospreys and bald eagles, use these areas for feeding and resting.

About 3 mi (5 km) east of Sandusky Bay is the Huron River wetland located within the Huron city limits, near the mouth of Mud Brook at its junction with the Huron River. Part of this area is managed as a State Nature Preserve by ODNR. Marsh habitat here attracts many species of shorebirds and passerines. Great blue herons, bitterns, killdeer, spotted sandpipers, and blue-winged teal are common resident species, while ospreys and tundra swans are noteworthy visitors. A major number of Bonaparte, ring-bill, and herring gulls use this area in the winter.

Old Woman Creek State Nature Preserve and National Estuarine Research Reserve, located at the mouth of Old Woman Creek 2 mi (3 km) east of Huron, is also managed by ODNR's Division of Natural Areas and Preserves (Figure 5.49). This preserve encompasses a beach, swamp forest, freshwater estuary, woods, prairie, fields, and marsh. Nearly 300 species, representing 42 families, have been reported here. There is a visitor center and a 1 mi. hiking trail with an observation deck overlooking the estuary.

Central Lake Erie (Ohio). In Lorain Harbor, warm water discharges from an Ohio Edison power plant maintains a large area of open water in the inner harbor during cold weather. Birders may see a great number of waterbirds, even into mid-winter. Herons, mallards, scaup, redheads, canvasbacks, common goldeneyes, buffleheads, mergansers, and gulls may be present. The breakwater area may yield common loons, horned grebes, diving and dabbling ducks, and oldsquaws. Rare birds seen at these two areas include red-throated loons, red-necked grebes, greater white-fronted geese, common eiders, harlequin ducks, scoters, jaegers, black-legged kittiwakes, and glaucous, common black-headed, and little gulls.

Encircling greater Cleveland are 10 reservations of the Cleveland Metropolitan Park system, sometimes referred to as the "Emerald Necklace." Birdwatching is available at each unit and is especially rewarding at the Rocky River, Hinckley, Huntington, and North Chagrin reservations.

Rocky River Reservation is a narrow, winding, wooded parkway about 20 mi (32 km) long that stretches through several suburbs and Cleveland's western limits. This ribbon of valley land extends along the Rocky River and provides habitats which include swamp, hardwood forest, several small ponds, and a lagoon. During migration, herons, dabbling ducks, mergansers, and many species of warbler and finch pass through this area. Nesting species include the green-backed heron, red-shouldered hawk, ring-necked pheasant, killdeer, spotted sandpiper, great horned owl, barred owl, belted kingfisher, eastern wood pewee, rough-winged swallow, American crow, Carolina wren, yellow warbler, common yellowthroat, American redstart, indigo bunting, American goldfinch, rufous-sided towhee, and song sparrow.

The Big Creek Parkway portion of the Metropark system lies in Middleburg Heights and features the Lake Isaac waterfowl refuge. An observation area off the parkway provides opportunities to observe the migrant and resident Canada geese, mallards, black ducks, wood ducks, scaup, redheads, pied-billed grebes, and American coots on Lake Isaac. A trail leads around the lake through old fields and small ravine areas.

Huntington Metropark, on the lakeshore in Bay Village, attracts birds to its beach, ravine, and forest habitats. The beach and overlooking cliff provide views of the gulls, terns, and shorebirds here. During spring and fall migration a tremendous variety of birds may appear in the waters off the rock piers, ranging from Bonaparte's gulls to common loons to brant. In early spring great flocks of red-breasted mergansers—interspersed with several diving duck species—congregate offshore.

Hinckley Metropark reservation lies 20 mi (32 km) south of Cleveland on County Road 44. The east branch of the Rocky River has been dammed to create a sizeable lake which, coupled with the stream, provides many sites for observing waterfowl and shorebirds. The area is most noted, though, for the annual return of its turkey vultures. In March, these birds, amidst a great deal of human festivities, return to establish nests in the Buzzard's Roost area. In spring and fall, migrating ducks and herons are also seen. Noteworthy nesting birds at Hinckley include wood ducks, ring-neck pheasants, spotted sandpipers, mourning doves, black-billed cuckoos, pileated woodpeckers, alder flycatchers, yellow warblers, blue-winged warblers, cerulean warblers, hooded warblers, northern orioles, red-winged blackbirds, rose-breasted grosbeaks, and song sparrows.

North Chagrin Reservation is a large tract of wooded hills along the Chagrin River west of SR 92 and south of U.S. Route 6. Nature trails and an aerated pond that maintains open water during the winter are two of this park's attractions. Canada geese, mallards, American black ducks, and American wigeons usually remain for the winter. During spring migration, many birds pass through the park and a large species list may be quickly compiled. A nearby waterfowl sanctuary has observation platforms for viewing the resident and migrant birds.

Shaker Lakes Regional Nature Center lies at the boundary of Cleveland Heights and Shaker Heights on North Park Boulevard. Many types of habitat are present including lake, stream, field, marsh, and ravine. Over 160 species of birds have been sighted here. Transient grebes, herons, ducks, and shorebirds visit these lakes. During spring migration, smaller landbirds—particularly warblers—are abundant in bordering trees and shrubs.

In fall, winter, and early spring, waterbirds and waterfowl may be seen along the Lake Erie shore inside the Cleveland Harbor breakwater. Natural habitats at Perkins Beach, Edgewater Park, and Gordon Park attract a great number of these migrants because of surrounding human activity. Views are available at Gordon Park on the east shore, Edgewater Park on the west shore, and at Burke Lakefront Airport in downtown Cleveland. At the Cleveland Electric Illuminating Company plant on East 71st Street, warm water discharged into the lake maintains open water during cold weather. Close to the shore many species of waterfowl congregate during the winter. Among unusual birds listed for this site are red-throated loons, red-necked grebes, black scoters, purple sandpipers, red phalaropes, red-necked (northern) phalaropes, parasitic jaegers, glacuous gulls, kittiwakes, Forster's terns, and snowy owls. During March and April, migrating mourning doves, blue jays, common flickers, and other landbirds may fly past in great numbers. Migrating hawks are frequently seen flying eastward along the shoreline. Trees and bushes here often teem with warblers during the peak of spring migration.

Although not a conventional birdwatching site, the Cleveland Museum of Natural History bears mention. Located near downtown Cleveland, it houses a collection of nearly 27,000 bird skins and 4,200 egg sets from all over the world. A series of rooms in the museum's Exhibition Building is devoted to birds common to Ohio. On Sunday mornings from mid-April to mid-May, the museum sponsors birdwatching walks at several locations. These are conducted in conjunction with the Cleveland Metropark system.

Continuing east along the lakefront one reaches White City Park. Despite the park's limited size, a surprisingly large number of shorebirds stop here during southward migration. The variety of gulls found may include Iceland, glaucous, herring, great black-backed, common black-headed, ring-billed, and Sabine's and the black-legged kittiwake. Pomarine and parasitic jaegers have been spotted in September and October. In the summer and fall, this park is an excellent location for rare shorebirds such as the American avocet, Hudsonian godwit, willet, red phalarope, red-necked phalarope, and stilt sandpiper.

Holden Arboretum, east of Cleveland, with its trails, ponds, ravines, and over 5,000 varieties of plants, is a scenic and popular birdwatching area. Most of the warblers that occur in Ohio may be seen here. The arboretum's Corning Lake has an aeration system which keeps it free of ice in the winter. This attracts large numbers of waterfowl, including tundra swans and Canada geese.

Summer birds include pied-billed grebes, wood ducks, turkey vultures, several hawk species, cuckoos, owls, ruby-throated hummingbirds, belted kingfishers, red-headed woodpeckers, eastern kingbirds, several vireo and warbler species, northern orioles, indigo buntings, and chipping sparrows.

Little Mountain, at an elevation of 1,200 ft (370 m), lies within the Holden Arboretum on Sperry County Road north of U.S. Route 6. This scenic "mountain" is noted as the nesting site for several species that rarely nest elsewhere in Ohio. These birds include the least flycatcher, red-breasted nuthatch, solitary vireo, and Blackburnian warbler. Other nesting birds found here are the black-throated green warbler, black-and-white warbler, cerulean warbler, American redstart, broad-winged hawk, and ruffed grouse. Little Mountain is also a productive site for transient landbirds during spring and fall migrations.

Mentor Marsh is located 30 mi (50 km) east of Cleveland on the shore of Lake Erie near the Grand River. A State Nature Preserve off Corduroy Road, it is designated for wildlife habitat preservation and is well-known for its abundant bird migrants. The marsh is jointly administered by the ODNR and the Cleveland Museum of Natural History. This national, natural landmark consists of sand dunes, swamp forest, upland forest, open fields, and open marsh. The diverse habitat attracts over 100 bird species, including 20 warblers. Among birds found here are the common loon, horned and pied-billed grebe, gadwall, mallard, American black duck, pintail, American wigeon, ring-necked duck, scaup, green-winged teal, wood duck, bufflehead, ruddy duck, hooded merganser, Cooper's hawk, herons, egrets, bitterns, black-bellied plover, ruddy turnstone, sandpipers, gulls, Caspian tern, cuckoos, barred owl, belted kingfisher, pileated woodpecker, eastern kingbird, horned lark, swallows, winter wren, red-breasted nuthatch, and snow bunting.

Nearby Headlands Beach State Park, which encompasses Ohio's largest state-owned beach, is famous for many kinds of wildlife and provides nesting grounds for waterfowl, shorebirds, and warblers. Loons, grebes, and diving ducks are frequently seen here, as are such rarities as the oldsquaw and the three scoter species.

At closeby Fairport Harbor, large numbers of gulls congregate in the protected water, especially in the spring and fall. Rare species found here include the eared grebe, scoters, whimbrel, purple sandpiper, and pomarine and parasitic jaegers.

Farther to the east near Ashtabula, an excellent example of a small estuarine wetland, the Arcola Creek mouth is located at the community of Driftwood. This area is owned and maintained by the Cleveland Museum of Natural History as a nature preserve and research facility. Birdwatching opportunities are best during migration when waterfowl pass through the area. Geneva State Park on SR 534 is primarily a natural beach area with stands of mixed hardwoods and old fields. It is productive for observing shorebirds, but waterfowl are not exceptionally abundant due to the lack of cover.

Ashtabula River wetland lies on non-forested landfill deposits inside the Ashtabula harbor breakwalls. The harbor and surrounding natural area are used by wintering and migrating waterfowl and shorebirds. Species recorded here include the great blue heron, mallard, black duck, canvasback, common goldeneye, bufflehead, oldsquaw, mergansers, and Bonaparte's ring-billed, and herring gulls.

Eastern Lake Erie (Pennsylvania and New York). Jutting into Lake Erie near the outskirts of Erie, Pennsylvania is a curved peninsula over 7 mi (11 km) long known as Presque Isle. This land encloses Erie Harbor and comprises Pennsylvania's Presque Isle State Park. The entire length of the sand spit can be travelled via a paved highway (SR 832) which can be reached from SR 5 west of Erie. Nowhere in the Lake Erie region is such a varied habitat of lagoons, marshes, and sand dunes—and the associated bird life—found in such a limited area. All seasons are productive for bird observation at Presque Isle State Park. During an "open" winter, waterfowl are numerous and include scaup, common goldeneyes, common mergansers, buffleheads, mallards, black ducks, canvasbacks, redheads, and others. Some winters, evening and pine grosbeaks, redpolls, crossbills, snowy owls, and rough-legged hawks may visit. Several species of gull are present throughout the year. In mid-March flocks of tundra swans arrive to spend several days at Erie Bay. April is the best month to see duck species in the park's bay and lagoons. A great variety of migrants appears in May including warblers, shorebirds, and hawks.

Nesting species at Presque Isle include the spotted sandpiper, killdeer, song sparrow, yellow warbler, red-eyed vireo, eastern wood pewee, black-capped chickadee, house wren, wood duck, pileated and other woodpeckers, green-backed heron, black duck, common snipe, Virginia rail, sora, black tern, least bittern, and bank swallow. Common terns have recently faltered in nesting on Gull Point, due to disturbances by recreationists who are unaware of the tern's nesting habits. This designated sanctuary requires respectful use.

During July and August, migrating shorebirds are abundant at Presque Isle. Sanderlings, black-bellied and semipalmated plovers, lesser and greater yellowlegs, and least, semipalmated, Baird's, pectoral, and stilt sandpipers may be seen. Dunlins arrive with flights of October waterfowl. At certain times in the fall, thrushes, kinglets, and many sparrow species teem in the undergrowth. As fall progresses into winter, dark-eyed juncos, tree sparrows, and snow-buntings return.

Chautauqua Gorge, near the town of Westfield, New York, has nesting populations of bald eagles and herring gulls, and migratory landbirds are abundant. Canadaway Creek Nature Sanctuary, off of SR 5 (West Lake Road), is owned by the Nature Conservancy, Inc. This sanctuary, with typical stream and lakeshore habitats, is a major stopover for migratory birds. Among the 140 species recorded for this area are the black-crowned night-heron, wood duck, hooded merganser, red phalarope, willet, Caspian tern, tufted titmouse, and common redpoll. Farther to the east, nesting colonies of ring-billed gulls and common terns are found on the Buffalo breakwater. In recent years, the tern population has declined, possibly because of pressure from gulls.

Niagara River (New York and Ontario). The environs of the Niagara River are primarily known for fall and winter birdwatching, especially for ducks and gulls along the river and gorge. The river runs over 44 mi (70 km) from Fort Erie to Niagara-on-the-Lake. The Niagara Parkway follows nearly the entire length of the river. During peak periods in late fall, a day or more may be spent birdwatching in the area as large flocks of gulls and ducks assemble here. A few kilometers downstream from the falls, the Niagara River Gorge hosts a nesting colony of herring gulls. Fourteen species of gulls have been recorded in the area.

Duck numbers along the Niagara River increase in November. Species present at this time may include canvasback, scaup, common goldeneye, bufflehead, oldsquaw, common merganser, mallard, black duck, gadwall, American wigeon, Barrow's goldeneye, scoters, harlequin ducks, loons, and grebes. Shorebirds include purple sandpipers, which are often found into the winter. Other wintering species include the mockingbird, tufted titmouse, house finch, and Carolina wren, along with many waterbirds. The Niagara River is less rewarding at other times, though in early autumn, large movements of common nighthawks and purple martins may occur.

At Fort Erie, the Kift Farm is situated near the head of the Niagara River where it connects to Lake Erie. This farm and the surrounding area are noted for its waterfowl, shorebird, passerine, and hawk migrations. Black terns have been reported as nesting here.

The Grand Island wetlands include Buckhorn Island, Green Creek, Spicer Creek, Staley Road, Beaver Island State Park, Beaver Island, and

West River Road marshes. Waterfowl found in these wetlands include Black ducks, mallards, American wigeons, scaup, canvasbacks, common goldeneyes, oldsquaws, buffleheads, American coots, and mergansers. Portions of this wetland area are owned by both public and private groups. Buckhorn Island and Beaver Island State parks are included within this complex. Herring and ring-billed gulls nest on Buckhorn Island. This island is also a migration area used by waterfowl, passerines, and hawks. Southeast of Buckhorn Island, common terns and ring-billed gulls may nest. Strawberry Island is a nesting area for black terns and waterfowl and a migration area for waterfowl, passerines, hawks, and shorebirds.

The area surrounding St. Catharines, Ontario, at the lower end of the Welland Canal, fosters extensive birdwatching as it encompasses the Lake Ontario shoreline, and reservoirs and woods along the Niagara Escarpment. Port Weller, the entrance to the canal, is northeast of St. Catharines and is a likely place to observe gulls. The entire area supports productive waterbird observation. The Happy Rolphe Bird Sanctuary and Children's Farm is located nearby at the north end of Read Road on Lake Ontario. There are feeding stations for native birds, three ponds for waterfowl, and other attractions for children. The facility is open from mid-May to mid-October. West of here, at the mouth of Twelve Mile Creek and Martindale Pond, Port Dolhousie hosts many waterbirds. The areas around the escarpment feature many landbirds and are reached from Highway 406.

Eastern Lake Erie (Ontario). There are many birdwatching areas of interest near Port Colborne. In Wainfleet Bog, northwest of town, one may see northern harriers (marsh hawks), short-eared owls, Lincoln's sparrows, and whip-poor-wills. Permission from a private farm is needed to enter the bog. Nearby Morgan's Point, on the lake shore, attracts shorebirds and waterfowl, while migrants often concentrate in the undergrowth and woods.

Marshlands along Ontario's Grand River, west of Dunnville, are observable from vantage points on bridges and sideroads. Grant Point near Port Maitland yields shorebirds, gulls, and ducks. There is also a small sewage lagoon northeast of Dunnville that attracts additional birds.

Selkirk Provincial Park, near Port Dover, is one of the most productive in Ontario. As a migrant concentration point it is second only to Point Pelee, and it serves as a major staging area for waterfowl. Port Dover Harbor sometimes hosts gulls of several species. The pond along the river behind the town is generally a rewarding birdwatching area.

About 5 mi (8 km) north of town is a great blue heron rookery. Marshes along the small creek between Port Dover and Nanticoke may also warrant investigation.

Turkey Point Provincial Park has a large pond which attracts an assortment of ducks during migration. North of here, ruffed grouse and pileated woodpeckers can be seen at Backus Woods. St. Williams Forestry Station on Highway 24 also yields birdwatching opportunities. Some species with more northern ranges are found here.

The village of Port Royal provides birdwatching opportunities at its cemetery and along Big Creek. Also of note is Port Royal Waterfowl Sanctuary locally known as Lee Brown's. To the west, marshes narrow into swampland where prothonotary warblers have been recorded. Swans and other waterfowl may be seen in the fields in spring. Lee Brown's provides viewing of these areas, and snow and white-fronted geese may also be present here.

Long Point is an enormous sandspit with lengthy beaches backed by high sand dunes on its southerly lake side. On the north side is Long Point Bay and extensive marshes. Between these two areas are varying amounts of forest and grassland. The marshes are rich in bird-life including many characteristic marsh species. Terns and little gulls (probable) nest here though these nest areas are fairly inaccessible. American woodcocks occur in the wooded areas. Enormous numbers of waterfowl concentrate on the open water toward the end of March and beginning of April. Birdwatching sites are available along both shore-lines and in the deciduous woodlands. There is controlled waterfowl hunting on the point, but much of the area north of Long Point Provincial Park and Big Creek Marsh is a sanctuary where undisturbed bird-watching opportunities exist.

Central Lake Erie (Ontario). Perhaps the best viewing between Long Point and Port Stanley is from the mouths of major streams at Port Burwell and Port Bruce. The town of Port Stanley is best known for its proximity to Hawk Cliff, but the sewage lagoon, beaches, and harbor are also productive areas. Hawk Cliff lies east of town and is a prime location for hawk observation and banding in the fall. It also yields fall migrants—both landbirds and waterfowl—that move along the Lake Erie shoreline. Broad-winged hawks, sharp-shinned hawks, and American kestrels are seen in September; there are sharp-shinned hawks, red-tailed hawks, and turkey vultures in October and red-tailed hawks in November. Over 30,000 broad-winged hawks may be seen in one day. A total of 15 raptor species occur regularly. Flights are usually heaviest during northwest winds with light cumulus clouds, and are not present on rainy days or during southerly winds. The Fingal Wildlife Management Area, on CR 16, is managed for bobwhite and other species. There is also a small waterfowl feeding area and an observation tower here.

North of the lakeshore near the town of Dutton is one of the finest woodlots along the Thames River; it is on private property in South Ekfrid Township. These woods are one of the few consistent sites to see red-bellied woodpeckers as well as other woodpecker species and wood ducks. Directions to this property are available in the town of Dutton. Permission is required before entering the woods. In this area, many roads running south from Highway 3 to the lake provide lake views. John E. Pierce Provincial Park, near the community of Tyrconnell, supports a large assortment of landbirds.

The sewage lagoons northwest of Blenheim and Rondeau Provincial Park west of town are productive bird areas. Marshes at the north end of Rondeau Bay may host marsh-and shorebirds under proper conditions. On the inner bay side of the park are extensive marshes and a 5 mi (8 km) walking trail. Little gulls are present in summer and several rare waterbirds may visit. In March, tundra swans gather in the bay and a pair of bald eagles nests along the edge of the marsh. The main area of the park is covered by Carolinian hardwoods rich in fauna and flora. Cerulean and prothonotary warblers and Acadian flycatchers nest here. This is one of the few southern Ontario locations for prothonotary warblers. Three hundred and twenty-three species of birds have been recorded in Rondeau, and 126 of these presently nest or have nested here. The park teems with migrants, though the concentration is less than that of Point Pelee to the west. The park's configuration also makes it more difficult to explore. An entrance fee is required, and the park has interpretive programs and many trails. Bird lists are available, and naturalists will assist in locating present species.

Erieau Harbour offers a lake and bay view where herons, ducks, gulls, shorebirds, and, infrequently, bald eagles may be present. Just outside the village is a pond and marsh area (McGeachy Pond) which is used by ducks, gulls, and shorebirds. Nearby fields often yield migrant shorebirds, and Brewer's blackbirds nest there.

Western Lake Erie (Ontario). The area south of Highway 3 between Leamington and Wheatley—including the shoreline, Wheatley Harbor, and marshes along Hillman Creek—is productive for birdwatching. In Wheatley Provincial Park, lagoons and a creek attract waterbirds, while ducks and gulls may be seen on the lake. There is also a sewage lagoon in the campground that attracts many birds.

Point Pelee National Park lies southeast of Leamington. This massive sandspit which juts into Lake Erie offers outstanding opportunities for birdwatching throughout the year. Within the park are diverse habitats of sandy beach, cattail marsh, and one of the few remaining Carolinian deciduous forests in Canada.

The park is open all year with the best birdwatching during migration periods. A feature of migration in fall is the sight of birds leaving the point: birds congregate at the point's extreme south tip before striking out across the lake. In winter, stragglers are often present. Late April to early May is a peak period to see southern rarities, and late May yields shorebirds if suitable habitat is available. In July, large swallow flights begin; migrations continue with fall shorebird flights in August. In September, accipiter migration is heavy along with other hawks and landbirds. October and November yield waterfowl, including tundra swans.

Although not as productive for nesting birds as Rondeau, Point Pelee is a principal location to observe nesting Carolina wrens, yellow-breasted chats, blue-gray gnatcathcers, white-eyed vireos, and orchard orioles. Rarities are less predictable in fall but migrant numbers are higher than in the spring. Over 100 species may be seen in 1 day during peak periods in mid-May and mid-September. A map and checklist are available at the gate. The interpretive center staff will assist in locating unusual birds. Noteworthy areas within the park include waters off the point, where large flocks of red-breasted mergansers are seen in the spring and fall, the point's beaches for gulls and shorebirds, and the woods and undergrowth for songbirds. Visitors are warned not to walk past the line of bushes at the end of the point because migrant birds resting here do not generally return once they have been alarmed.

The road between the visitor centre and the point, the nature trail starting at the centre, and the trail through Tilden's Woods all offer views of migrant landbirds, while the marsh boardwalk provides the chance to observe marsh birds. Field areas may yield such sparrows as LeConte's, grasshopper, sharp-tailed, and Henslow's. All of Point Pelee is considered excellent birdwatching territory.

Holiday Beach Provincial Park is 9 mi (15 km) southeast of Amherstburg on CR 50. It is best known as a hawk observation point, but waterbirds may be present as well since it borders the Big Creek marshes and Lake Erie. Canada and snow geese, often numbering in the thousands, may be viewed from close range. Great egrets and herons are common in the summer. A baited waterfowl feeding sanctuary located east of the park has a viewing facility.

Fall hawk migration at Holiday Beach is the heaviest in Ontario. From September to November one may see broad-winged, sharp-shinned, and red-tailed hawks, and turkey vultures flying in "kettles"—spiralling, cylindrical formations. Over 30,000 broad-winged hawks may be observed in 1 day. In all, 15 raptor species occur in migration. When soaring hawks are very high, viewing may be better at Hawk Cliff near Port Stanley, Ontario.

Wild Game

Coastal and nearshore areas of Lake Erie and Lake St. Clair offer a variety of hunting opportunities. Both public and private marsh areas are managed for waterfowl and wetland mammals, while rural upland areas along the coast provide habitat for ring-necked pheasants, American woodcocks, eastern cottontails, squirrels, and white-tailed deer (Figure 5.50). Seasons and regulations vary throughout the Lake Erie Region. Hunters should contact the following state and provincial natural resources agencies for current information:

Michigan -

Department of Natural Resources
Wildlife Division
District 14
2455 N. Williams Lake Rd.
Pontiac, MI 48054
Phone: (313) 666-1500

Public Access Stamp Program
Wildlife Division
Box 30028
Lansing, MI 48909
Phone: (517) 373-1263

Ohio -

Department of Natural Resources
Division of Wildlife
Fountain Square
Columbus, OH 43224
Phone: (614) 265-6330

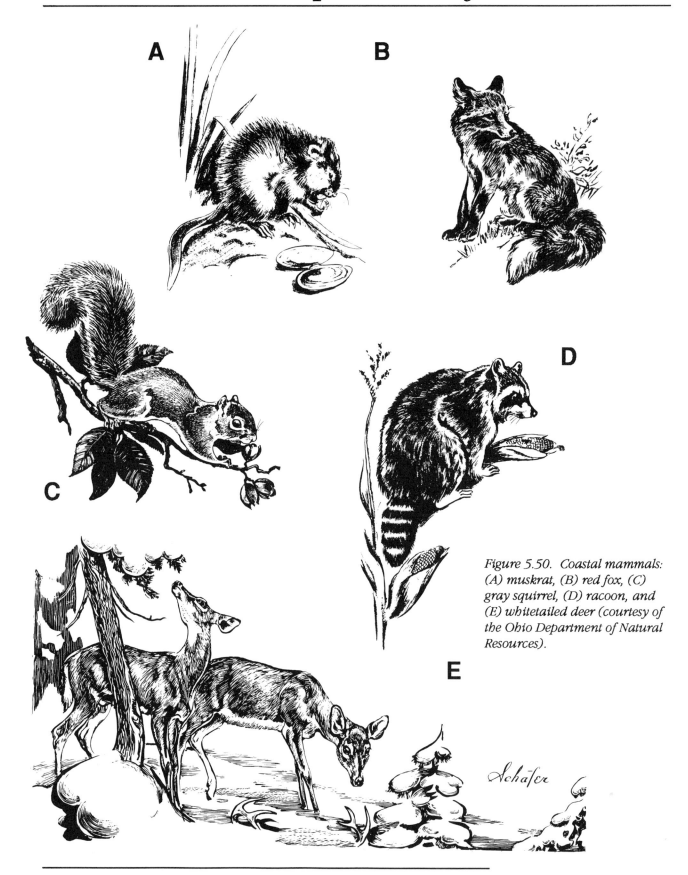

Figure 5.50. Coastal mammals:
(A) muskrat, (B) red fox, (C)
gray squirrel, (D) racoon, and
(E) whitetailed deer (courtesy of
the Ohio Department of Natural
Resources).

Wildlife District Two
952 Lima Avenue
Findlay, OH 45840
Phone: (419) 422-6757

Pennsylvania -

Game Commission
P.O. Box 1567
Harrisburg, PA 17105-1567
Phone: (717) 787-5529

Northwest Division Headquarters
P.O. Box 31
1509 Pittsburgh Road
Franklin, PA 16323
Phone: (814) 432-3187

New York -

Department of Environmental Conservation
50 Wolf Road
Albany, NY 12233
Phone: (518) 457-3522

DEC Regional Office
128 South Street
Olean, NY 14760
Phone: (716) 372-0645

Ontario -

Ministry of Natural Resources
Wildlife Branch
2nd Floor, Whitney Block
Queen's Park
Toronto, Ontario M7A 1W3
Phone: (416) 965-4251

Long Point Waterfowl Management Unit
Ministry of Natural Resources
Port Rowan, Ontario N0E 1M0
Phone: (519) 586-2133

Waterfowl

Ducks are generally divided into two groups—"divers" and "dabblers." Diving ducks include the canvasback, redhead, ring-necked duck, scaup, bufflehead, goldeneye, old-squaw, scoters, and also the hooded, red-breasted, and common mergansers. These birds are found on open water in lakes, bays, and wide rivers; they seldom come ashore. Their tails lie nearly even with the water and their legs are set toward the rear of the body. Diving ducks must run across the water against the wind to become airborne.

Dabbling ducks are also called marsh or puddle ducks. They frequent shallow marshes, ponds, rivers, and creeks and often feed in grain fields. Included in this group are the mallard, black duck, northern shoveler, pintail, blue-winged teal, green-winged teal, gadwall, American wigeon, and wood duck. Their rumps are high as they sit in the water and the legs are near the center of the body. When taking off, they jump almost vertically from the water.

Although the American coot is not a member of the duck family, it is generally classed with ducks in hunting regulations. Coots are good swimmers and are often found with groups of diving ducks. They feed on aquatic plants and often serve as indicators of this food to ducks.

Canada geese are successful waterfowl judging from their wide distribution and abundance. They are seen during migration periods resting at wildlife management areas, marshes, larger lakes, and feeding in corn and grain fields. They also feed on aquatic plants and small animals found in mud.

Another goose that provides hunting opportunities, although to a lesser degree, is the snow goose. It has two color phases which used to be considered two separate species—the white "snow" goose and the gray "blue" goose. They may be present in grasslands, grainfields, and wetlands.

Upland Birds

The ring-necked pheasant is a beautiful and delicious gamebird which was imported from the Orient in the late 1800s. It is a bird of the flatlands and thrives in areas of intense farming when there is adequate cover and sufficient food. During the winter, pheasants concentrate in corn fields, brushy woodlots, and dense field edges. When flushed, they rise almost vertically with a loud whirring of wings.

Ruffed grouse hunting is a challenging sport due to the rough terrain the bird inhabits. The ruffed grouse is also a fast and elusive flyer. It has excellent protective coloration and often will not flush until almost stepped upon. Grouse habitat includes three general areas: young forests of mixed hardwoods; mixed stands of hardwood shrubs, saplings, and brush-vine tangles; and moist areas with dense shrubbery. In good habitat, fall populations average one bird per 12 to 20 acres (5 to 8 hectares). Population fluctuations may arise due to reproductive success and survival. The birds tend to feed in the late afternoon in openings or along swamp edges. It may be possible to find them here away from protective covering. In fall and winter, ruffed grouse feed on acorns, beechnuts, and buds.

The American woodcock is a tricky aerialist and can add spice to a hunt and a meal to the table. These birds are well-suited for bird dogs due to their scent and their tendency to remain still. Woodcock are found in similar habitat as the ruffed grouse (i.e. low-ground tag alder, apsen, upland woods, and stream and marsh edges in lowland thickets). They usually avoid thick grass. Their diet is mainly comprised of earthworms, and thus may be found in areas of moist soil in dense thickets. Most woodcock migrate south by November, but small numbers spend the winter near springs and seeps.

The wild turkey is North America's largest game bird, weighing up to 24 lbs (11 kg). These birds were extirpated in many areas due to habitat destruction and over-hunting. They have responded, though, to re-establishment efforts. Turkeys usually feed in flocks, mostly on the ground where they scratch for insects, acorns, and fruit. Occasionally they feed in trees or vines. Hardwood-pine forests interspersed with openings are prime turkey habitat in spring. Areas with highest turkey populations also have streams and lakes. When escaping danger, wild turkeys prefer running to flying. They take flight only when surrounded. Their excellent eyesight and hearing make it difficult for them to be surprised. Turkeys tend to roost in tree tops, away from ground predators. Many hunters are successful early in the morning as the turkeys leave their roosts to feed.

Wetland Mammals

The muskrat—a stocky aquatic rodent—is found in marshes, swamps, lakes, ponds, and ditches that provide still or slowly running water and vegetation in the water and along the banks. Cattail, bulrush and bur-reed marshes are ideal. In spring it moves to den sites among marsh vegetation and in autumn it builds conical homes about 7 ft (2 m) wide and 3 ft (1 m) tall from available vegetation. (When abandoned, these homes may provide nesting sites for ducks or geese.) In areas where it is not possible for these huts to be built (because of fluctuating water levels or swift currents), the muskrat will burrow into the bank at the edge of the water. Muskrats feed on cattail shoots, arrowhead, celery grass, and certain invertebrates. The muskrat in turn is preyed upon by the mink, hawk, owl, weasel, raccoon, and fox. It is trapped in great numbers for its pelt.

Classed as furbearers, raccoons are trapped and hunted. They are found in many types of habitat but are especially abundant in woodlots with nearby wetlands. They frequent water and are found along most streambanks and lakes. Most of their foraging is done in water as they seek shellfish, frogs, snails, and clams. They also eat eggs, mice, berries, nuts, and corn. Large hollow trees are common den sites, but nests may also be in burrows or crevices. Raccoons do not hibernate but sleep for long periods during winter months.

The red fox has several color variations but all feature a white-tipped tail. The tree-climbing gray fox, generally grayish with black and rust, has a black-tipped tail. Both species prefer a general mixture of forest and open country. Agricultural lands with woodlots and brushy areas near wetlands are ideal for red fox; denser woodlots may attract gray fox more readily. The red fox is also found in many other habitat types, possibly even infringing on suburban areas. This fox often uses previously dug burrows; woodchuck holes frequently become fox dens. Both species are fairly omnivorous, eating freshly killed or rotting animals and a variety of plant material. They do not hibernate but forage their territory in all seasons. Keen senses of sight, smell, and hearing make them a challenging quarry, although the red fox is thought to be more sporting because is leads its pursuers on a long, devious chase rather than climbing trees like the gray fox.

The opossum is the oldest and most primitive species, and the only marsupial in North America. Preferred habitat is farmland, especially wooded pastures near water. They may also become established in suburbs and urban areas. When in danger the opossum hisses and bares its 50 teeth. More often it will "play possum"—an automatic reaction to stress. The opossum does not hibernate but may remain in its den for days in extremely cold weather. Dens are typically found in wooded areas near water. The opossum continues to maintain its numbers and expand its range in spite of human encroachment.

The mink is the elusive and prized catch of fur trappers. It was the first wild animal to be domesticated for fur in the United States. The mink is active at night when it engages in most of its hunting. Mink are also observed traveling or hunting in daylight hours. Mink are classed as carnivores—their food includes muskrats, rabbits, birds, crayfish, frogs, and fish. They are generally difficult to catch. Mink travel a regular route and complete circuits of such routes in about 1 week. They function well in water or on land. In the wild, mink dens are usually near water and may be in hollow logs, under tree roots or stumps, or in riverbanks. Most mink hunting is done with dogs specially trained to track mink.

Related to the mink, the long-tailed weasel inhabits a variety of habitats including brushlands, prairies, and forests. Their dens may be located in nearly any sheltered, undisturbed spot: old foundations, logs, rock piles, stumps, or even underground. Weasels spend most of their time hunting for food—mainly mice, rats, and birds. The pelt of the weasel is considered to be of high quality.

Upland Mammals

The eastern cottontail rabbit is a common and popular small game animal. They live in a wide variety of habitats but are most abundant in open lands bordered by thickets and brushy areas with burrows which provide quick escape and protective cover. "Travel lanes" are important, too, since rabbits prefer feeding near cover.

Cottontails will nest wherever there is adequate food and cover including shrubby pastures, hay fields, open fields, unkept orchards, and mowed lawns. They feed on twigs, fruit, bark, buds, stems, and grain.

A productive time to start a rabbit hunt is in the morning because nighttime tracks—especially after a new-fallen snow—are still fresh. Working along heavy cover edges should yield a single track to follow.

Three species of squirrel provide hunting opportunities, including the fox squirrel, the gray squirrel and its black color variant, and the red squirrel. Their food supply consists of nuts, acorns, berries, and buds from elms and maples. They are found wherever there are middle-aged and mature stands of trees; the three species, though, differ slightly in preferred habitats. Nests and tree-trunk dens are used for sleeping and raising young. Unlike other members of the squirrel family (the wood-chuck, ground squirrel, and chipmunk), the game squirrels do not hibernate but instead remain in their holes for long periods during very cold weather.

The woodchuck, or groundhog, provides small game for the hunter who cannot travel far from home; "chucks" may live right up to the edges of suburbs and cities. Burrows are located in fields near towns, forest edge, heavy brush, creeks, and undisturbed cover in agricultural areas. The woodchuck lives close to its food supply of fruit, forage crops, small grains, and vegetative matter. Because woodchucks may eat some crop plants, most farmers grant permission to hunt if requested. Although hunted extensively, woodchucks are seldom eaten. However, woodchuck meat is excellent if properly prepared.

The woodchuck hibernates in winter by rolling its body into a ball. It may emerge during occasional warm spells in winter and early spring. It has been estimated that woodchucks spend 75% of their lives asleep.

The white-tailed deer is considered a forest mammal and thrives in habitats with diverse food and cover, including varying timber stands. Deer are often found along forest edges browsing brushy openings. They feed on grass, twigs, buds of dogwood, yellow birch, and maple trees, cedar and pine needles, aspen leaves, and some farm crops.

Many persons imagine a deer to be larger than its true size. Average males or "bucks", however, are only 36-42 in (91-107 cm) tall at the withers (the highest point on a deer's back) and weigh around 180 lbs (82 kg). Females or "does," are somewhat smaller and weigh an average of 120 lbs (54 kg). A deer's age can only be determined by looking at its teeth; antler size is controlled primarily by available food (although antlers tend to be larger on older bucks). Approximately 90% of all bucks taken by hunters are younger than 2 1/2 years old.

Deer have an acute sense of hearing but may not be able to tell from which direction a sound emanates. They may even investigate unfamiliar noises. Deer lack an instinctive fear of humans but generally acquire this through contact.

There are two general rules for a successful deer hunt. The first, perseverance, though simple is sometimes not heeded. Stay in the woods and keep hunting; it pays off. The second involves choosing a hunting area. Some locations have a great many deer while others not so many. Aerial photographs are available for most areas from agencies such as the U.S. Conservation Service or Geological Survey. These may be helpful in determining the location of deer habitats, particularly forest edges, hill, and hollows. The landforms of most areas have also been mapped, and these maps can lead to a successful hunt. Topographic maps are available from state and provincial natural resource agencies.

Black bear populations in any area are small in comparison to most other animals. Added to this is the fact that bears generally remain out of sight. Signs that a bear is in the woods include overturned logs and stones, trampled bushes, torn-apart tree stumps, and low branches torn from trees.

Bears are omnivorous—they will eat a wide variety of food. Insects are an important part of their diet along with grasses, fruits, nuts, birds, eggs, carrion, fish, and honey. A bear needs forage space, climbing trees, adequate food, and secluded areas. Prime bear country provides these elements. A bear's coat is shiny black often with a patch of white on the chest, and the muzzle is brown. The young are usually born in January while the female is in her winter den. From one to five cubs may be in the litter, each weighing about 8 oz. (225 gm). In a year they will gain 60-100 lbs (27-45 kg). A 200 lb (180 kg) bear is considered to be of medium size.

In the Lake Erie region bear hunting is uncommon and confined to the upland areas surrounding the eastern end of the lake such as Cattaraugus County, New York.

Coastal Wetlands

Lake Erie and its connecting waterways lie in the highly industrialized region of the north-central United States and southeastern Canada. However, within this region of intense human activity are located many areas of natural beauty. The coastal wetlands are one of the most fascinating natural features available for visitors to enjoy. What are wetlands? Quite simply they are areas of wet soil which promote the growth of a wide variety of aquatic vegetation. Names such as marshes, swamps, flats, bogs and fens have been applied to wetlands in the Great Lakes region (Figure 5.51).

Coastal wetlands differ in several ways from inland wetlands. The coast is subject to temporary (short term) water level changes. Seiches and storm surges affect the wetlands adjacent to the shorelines of Lake Erie and Lake St. Clair by raising and lowering the lake level as much as 6 ft (2 m) in a single day! Long-term cyclic water level changes, related to precipitation and the water budget of the Great Lakes basin, also affect the coastal wetlands. Such fluctuations, occurring over a number of years, may cause wetland plants to die off, erode, or be displaced. Not all coastal wetlands exhibit senescence, the aging process associated with inland wetlands. This process leads from open ponds to densely vegetated marshes and eventually, to dry fields. Because of the fluctuating water levels, constant rejuvenation of wetland plant communities

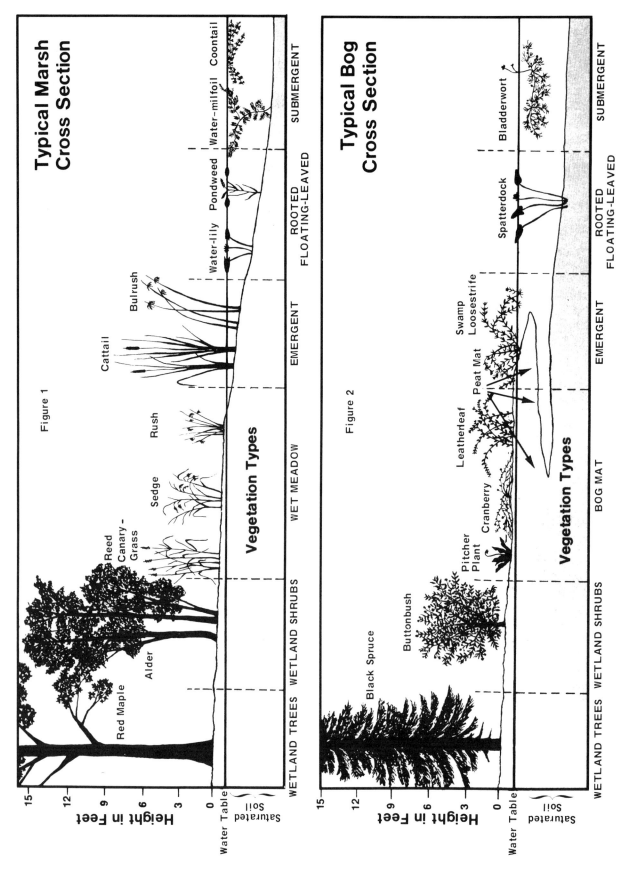

Figure 5.51. Vegetation zones of a Lake Erie coastal marsh and a coastal plain bog (courtesy of the New York Sea Grant Program).

occurs along the shorelines. Coastal wetlands also show a diversity of land forms not normally encountered in other wetlands environments. Largely the result of major elevation changes of the Great Lakes associated with the retreat of the glacial ice sheets, landforms such as deltas, barrier bars, beaches, spits, lagoons, and natural levees have been deposited along the shores. Many of these geomorphic features promote the formation of wetlands, each with distinctive features resulting in the great variety and diversity of coastal wetlands found in the region.

Origin of Coastal Wetlands

The basins occupied by Lake Erie and Lake St. Clair were shaped by glacial ice scour, and their physical features and hydrology differ greatly from regions not exposed to the Pleistocene ice sheets. In terms of earth history, the construction of the basins has recently been completed. The lakes, with their present outlets and water levels, date back less than 5,000 years. The processes of stream and coastal erosion/accretion have made only modest changes in the original topography, but these changes are significant in the origin and development of coastal wetlands.

Prior to the Pleistocene Ice Age, the Great Lakes were non-existent, but the area was dissected by well-developed valleys of several major streams. When the continental ice cap developed to a thickness of 10,000 ft (3,000 m) in northeastern Canada, it spread southward into the present Great Lakes region. Tremendous amounts of bedrock were eroded and the debris was entrained in the ice mass. As the ice sheets slowly melted and retreated progressively northward, this entrained debris was released, and vast irregular deposits of till were laid down on the scoured bedrock surface. Occasionally blocks of ice were also entrained in the till and eventually formed kettle lakes.

Once Lake Erie became established, shoreline processes provided favorable sites for coastal wetlands. The most significant processes included: (1) delta construction, (2) estuary development, and (3) sand bar/dune formation, creating coastal lagoons. Although the gross configuration of Lake Erie has been little altered since the last glacier retreated to the north, these processes have fostered the creation of many wetlands. Except where bedrock is exposed or protective works constructed, the glacial or lacustrine (lake sediment) overburden comprising the shores is still vulnerable to changes which can work to the benefit or destruction of coastal wetlands.

Kettle Lake Wetlands

These small lakes are one of the most characteristic features of the coastal uplands adjacent to the Great Lakes. As mentioned earlier, they are formed by the incorporation of ice blocks in the material that washed out from a melting ice front. The glacial outwash, consisting of sand, gravel, and silt was derived from the drift or moraine underlying or bordering the ice. As the mass of ice melted, a basin was left in the drift, and if the basin penetrated below the water table, a body of water known as a kettle lake came to occupy the site of the original ice block. The kettles are extremely variable in shape and size; some are less than 100 ft (30 m) across, such as Fern Lake near the Lake County-Geauga County border in Ohio, while others, such as Trout Lake, Wisconsin, have a diameter of nearly 3 mi (5 km). In general, the depth of kettle lakes does not exceed 165 ft (50 m). Bogs are the most common wetlands in kettle lakes.

Kettle lakes which are protected from wind and are poorly drained often become bog lakes. They first become fringed by floating mats of sedge vegetation growing inward to encroach upon the open water; this change is accompanied by a drop in pH as the waters become more acidic. The succession then continues as the mat covers the lake surface and sphagnum moss (*Sphagnum* sp.) and ericaceous shrubs, such as leatherleaf (*Chamedaphne calyculata*) and Labrador tea (*Ledum groenlandicum*), become established. When growth exceeds decomposition, the lake basin begins to fill and peat deposits are formed. Ultimately a sequence of tree species, commonly tamarack (*Larix laricina*) followed by black spruce (*Picea mariana*) leads to a climax forest association.

Delta Wetlands

A stream reaching a body of standing water, such as the St. Clair River flowing into Lake St. Clair, at times builds a deposit or delta composed of the stream's sediment load. These deposits are commonly the site of extensive wetland development. Not all rivers build deltas; deltas may be lacking at the mouths of streams which enter the Great Lakes because their mouths are so exposed to wave and current action that sediments are removed as rapidly as they are deposited. Some streams also lack deltas because they carry so little load.

Although each delta has its own individual form, four basic outlines are recognized: (1) arcuate, triangular outline, (2) digitate, bird-foot type, (3) cuspate, tooth-shaped form, and (4) estuarine, drowned valley (Strahler, 1971).

The typical arcuate delta originates at an upstream apex and radiates lakeward by means of branched distributary channels to form a triangular shape. Sediments reaching the lakes from the distributary mouths are swept along the coast by wave-induced currents to form curved bars enclosing shallow wetland lagoons; the delta shoreline is thus arcuate in plan, bowed convexly outward. The digitate or bird-foot delta contains long extensions of its branching distributaries into open water. This type of delta requires a gently sloping lake bottom in front of the river mouth, such as Lake St. Clair (Figure 5.48), on which natural levees can be built up quickly. The cuspate or tooth-shaped delta is normally formed when the stream has a single, dominant mouth. Sediment from this mouth builds the delta forward into deeper water while wave action sweeps the sediment away from the discharge to form a curving beach on both sides of the mouth, concave toward the lake. An estuarine delta commonly fills a long narrow estuary that resulted from drowning of the lower part of the river valley because of a rise in lake level. Estuarine deltas are characterized by depositional islands containing wetlands.

Delta growth occurs when a stream enters a standing body of water as a jet or plume. The jet velocity is rapidly checked and sediment is deposited in lateral embankments (natural levees) in zones of less turbulence on either side of the jet, thus extending the stream channel into the lake. The stream repeatedly breaks through the embankments to occupy different radii (distributary channels) and in time produces a deposit in semi-circular form, closely analogous to the alluvial fans found at the base of mountain ranges. The natural levees serve to isolate shallow interdistributary ponds and marshes containing fine muds and organic detritus or peat. The sediment structure of most deltas on the Great Lakes is produced by three sets of beds: (1) bottomset, (2) foreset, and (3) topset. Bottomset beds consist of fine-grained materials (silt and clay) carried farthest offshore and laid down on the bottom of the lake embayment into which the delta is being built. Foreset beds are somewhat coarser (fine sand), and they represent the advancing front of the delta and the greater part of its bulk; they usually have a distinctly steeper slope (dip) than the bottomset beds over which they are slowly advancing. Topset beds lie above the foreset beds and are in reality a continuation of the alluvial plain of which the delta is the terminal portion. It is on the foreset beds that delta wetlands normally develop. Unlike deltas formed along the ocean, freshwater deltas do not contain aggregates of fine particles induced by electrolyte flocculation (due to the dissolved salts in the sea). Therefore, fine particles are carried offshore in lakes and are not incorporated into the delta sediments.

Delta wetlands are not numerous in the Lake Erie Region, but where they do occur, such as the St. Clair Delta, they account for some of the highest quality marshland in the Region. Delta marshes are often gradational to estuary, river, and floodplain wetlands as one moves inland from the lake.

Freshwater Estuary Wetlands

The lower courses of several tributaries to the Great Lakes, particularly the more southerly lakes, are characterized by estuarine-type or drowned stream mouths. The flooded flat areas adjacent to these estuaries afford ideal sites for wetland development. The lower 15 mi (25 km) of the Maumee River, which flows into Lake Erie at Toledo, Ohio and possesses the largest drainage of any Great Lakes tributary, is an excellent example of a freshwater estuary. The formation of this estuary on Lake Erie is the result of a series of geologic events related to Pleistocene glaciation. The flow of the Maumee River was reversed from its southwestern direction when the glacial lakes drained from the Erie Basin, as the ice sheet melted, exposing a lower Niagara River outlet. At that time, river velocities were accelerated by the base-level lowering, and the Maumee Valley was cut deeply into lacustrine deposits, glacial tills, and bedrock. With the weight of the ice removed, the outlet eventually rebounded and produced a rise in lake level. The lake encroached up the valley and formed the present drowned stream mouth which is analogous in many ways to a marine estuary. Virtually all of the tributaries entering Lake Erie on the Ohio shore have estuarine-type lower reaches and attendant wetlands, where lake water masses affect water level and quality for several miles upstream from traditional mouths.

The Maumee River estuary begins near Perrysburg, Ohio at the most downstream bedrock riffle. As the water enters the estuary from the river, its velocity abruptly diminishes except during major runoff events, causing sedimentation of suspended particles. The deposits have formed a series of elliptical islands which foster wetland formation. Similar deposits are found in the Sandusky River estuary and in the mouth of the Detroit River.

Coastal Lagoon Wetlands

In large bodies of water such as the Great Lakes, the shifting of sediments by nearshore currents can form basins where wetlands eventually develop. If sediments are deposited across the mouth of an embayment, a tributary outlet or a freshwater estuary, the blockage may result in the formation of a new pond or lagoon. Wave activity, too, has formed bars of sand and gravel, which likewise have closed off the mouths of embayments.

The usual way in which a lagoon capable of supporting a wetland is formed is by accretion of a bar across some irregularity or indentation of the coastline. The term bar is used here in a generic sense to include the various types of submerged or emergent embankments of sand and gravel built on the lake bottom by waves and currents. One of the most common types of bars associated with wetlands in the Great Lakes is a spit. This feature is a sand ridge attached to the mainland at one end and terminating in open water at the distal end. Spits that have extended themselves across, or partially across, embayments are termed baymouth or barrier bars. Commonly, the axis of a spit will extend in a straight line parallel to the coast, but where currents are deflected landward or unusually strong waves exist, growth of a spit may be deflected landward, resulting in the creation of a recurved spit or hook. Several stages of hook development may produce a compound recurved spit with a series of ponds separated by beach ridges. These ponds have provided excellent sites for wetland development along the Great Lakes.

Kormondy (1969) described wetland succession in beach ponds on the 4 mi (7 km) long sand spit, Presque Isle, near Erie, Pennsylvania. Owing to a combination of its sandy shore and exposure to violent lake storms, this spit developed as a series of hooks with the establishment of numerous, fingerlike beach ponds over the past several thousand years. The ponds are created when an elevated bar of sand develops, thereby isolating a small portion of the lake; the ponds are seldom more than 330-660 ft (100-200 m) long, 33-66 ft (10-20 m) wide, and 3 ft (1 m) deep. Some of the ponds are destroyed in a few days, months, or years by subsequent storms which either breach the sand bar or blow enough sand to fill in the depression. The better protected ponds survive these geological processes only to be subject to a biological fate—wetland succession (Figure 5.52). A 4-year-old pond is characterized by sparse pioneer vegetation, such as stonewort algae (*Chara* spp.), bulrushes (*Scirpus* spp.), cattail (*Typha* spp.), and cottonwood (*Populus deltoides*) seedlings. At 50 years, filling has occurred in the basin and encroaching vegetation has reduced the open water portion to about half of its former area. The major vegetation then consists of water milfoil (*Myriophyllum exalbescens*), cattail, bulrushes, bluejoint grass (*Calamagrostis canadensis*), willow (*Salix* spp.), bayberry (*Myrica pensylvanica*), and cottonwood. After 100 years the open water portion is almost obliterated and the vegetation has increased in complexity. The dominant forms then include water milfoil, pondweed (*Potamogeton* spp.), yellow water-lily (*Nuphar advena*), bulrushes, bluejoint grass,

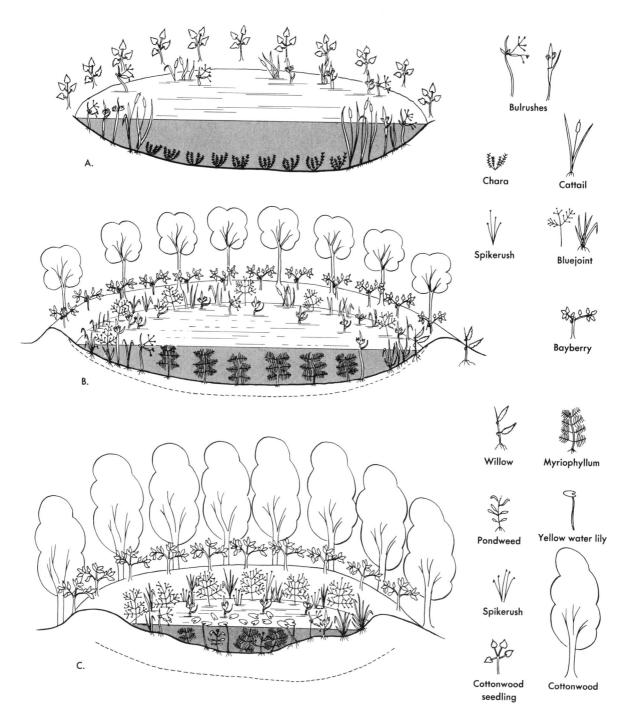

Figure 5.52. *Wetland succession in a Lake Erie beach pond at Presque Isle, Pennsylvania:
(A) 4 years old, (B) 50 years old, and (C) 100 years of age (from Kormandy, 1969, 1984).*

spikerush (*Eleocharis* spp.), bayberry, and cottonwood. Sparseness of distribution and limitation of plant species mark the early ponds; increased density and heterogeneity characterize the older ponds, a striking contrast. From this analysis of succession, Kormondy concluded that the ponds or lagoons at the northeast end of Presque Isle are the youngest, and that the spit has grown from the southwest because the ponds are increasingly older in that direction.

Value of Coastal Wetlands

The value of coastal wetlands is immense but often unrecognized. In recent years there has been an increasing awareness of the valuable resources our Great Lakes coastal wetlands and the urgent need to protect and conserve these ecosystems. Traditionally, wetlands conservation efforts have been aimed at protecting waterfowl breeding sites, and to a lesser degree, fish spawning and nursery habitat. More recent efforts toward preservation are based on the knowledge that wetlands provide additional benefits, including flood control, shore erosion protection, nutrient cycling, accumulation of sediments, and the supply of fundamental material for aquatic food webs. Some of the more important functions and values of coastal wetlands are outlined below:

1. Natural biological functions
   a. net primary productivity
   b. food chain (web) support

2. Habitat for aquatic and wetland species

3. Aquatic study areas, sanctuaries and refuges

4. Hydrologic support functions
   a. shoreline protection from wave attack
   b. storage of storm and flood waters
   c. water purification through natural filtration, sediment trapping and nutrient cycling uptake
   d. groundwater recharge

5. Cultural or auxiliary values including consumptive and nonconsumptive recreation as well as aesthetic value.

Wetland Flora and Fauna

The Lake Erie and Lake St. Clair wetlands are actually composed of a variety of habitats including open ponds, cattail/reed marshes, earthen dikes, barrier beaches, delta flats, and wooded swamps. Collectively, these habitats are known as the coastal marsh complex. Each habitat attracts its own species of plants, birds, mammals, reptiles, amphibians, and in some cases, fish. The result is more variety in plant and animal life than in any other area of equal size in the interior of the bordering states and province. Some of the coastal marshes, particularly those in the St. Clair Delta, are still very primitive. Such marshes have been visited by no more than a handful of people in the last several decades, while others are intensely managed for the benefit of specific purposes, such as waterfowl propagation. The prominent plants and animal groups found in Lake Erie region wetlands are presented in the following paragraphs.

Vegetation

An estimated 800 species of vascular plants (sometimes referred to as the higher plants) are found in the marsh communities of the Lake Erie region (Stuckey, 1978). Of these, less than 100 species are trees and shrubs. The majority are the emergent, submergent, and floating leaved aquatic plants of the wetlands (Figure 5.53). Although often unnoticed, aquatic plants are widespread and can either promote or hinder recreational activities. As providers of food and cover for animals ranging from plankton to geese, aquatic plants are a key element in the life and productivity of the lakes and their wetlands. Conversely, this vitality often reaches levels where it hinders human activities. Some aquatic plants, for instance, may clog marinas or swimming and fishing areas with abundant or excessive growth. In view of such diverse attributes and effects, understanding the Lake Erie region's aquatic plants will require additional investigation.

The wetland communities are of several types. New York's major wetland concentration is located along the Niagara River. These wetlands are largely non-wooded and associated with depressional areas. Further west, throughout the eastern and central basins at Lake Erie, most wetlands are associated with stream mouths and isolated sand spits (such as Presque Isle, Long Point, and Point Pelee); the perched (elevated) wetland of Mentor marsh is a notable exception. Stream mouth and beach pond wetlands generally have both wooded and non-wooded components. Except for the few sand spits mentioned above, most of these marsh areas are relatively small in size.

Wetlands of the western basin are, in general, large expanses of low-lying shoreline. Many have been preserved by diking to combat the adverse effects of recent high water episodes. Throughout the Lake Erie coastal zone, dominant wetland species include cattail (*Typha* spp.), bur

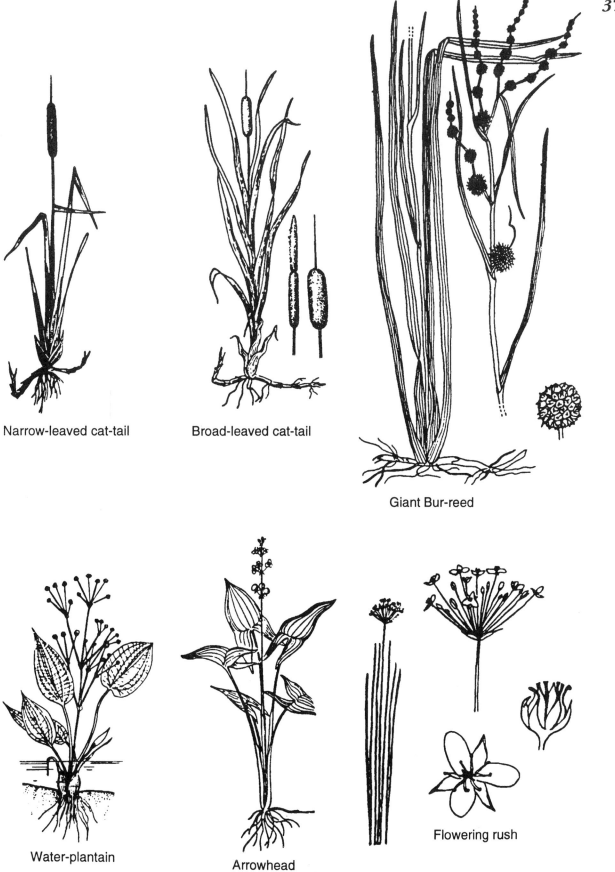

Narrow-leaved cat-tail

Broad-leaved cat-tail

Giant Bur-reed

Water-plantain

Arrowhead

Flowering rush

Figure 5.53. Aquatic plants of Lake Erie coastal marshes (after Fassett, 1940 and New York Sea Grant Program, Rawinski et al., 1979).

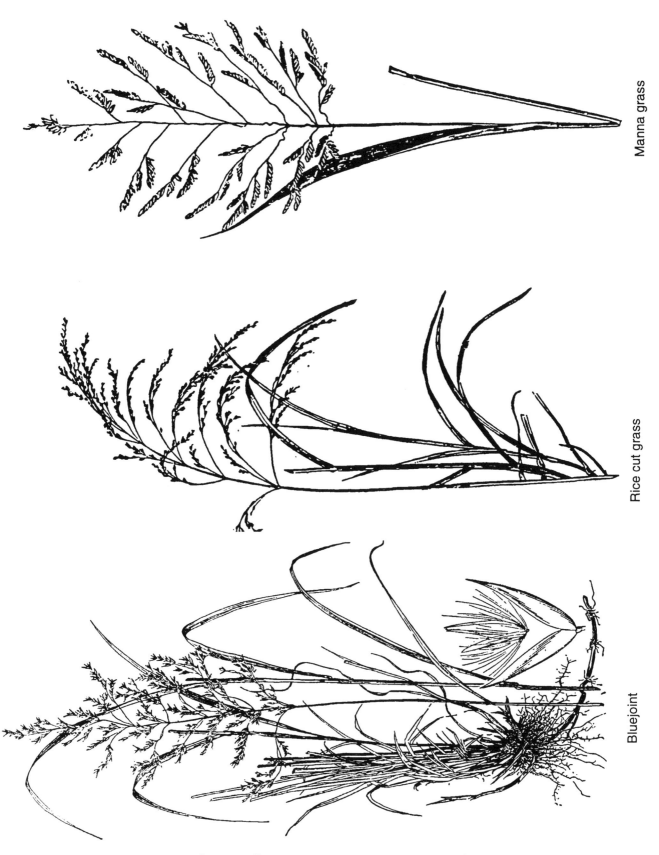

Manna grass

Rice cut grass

Bluejoint

Figure 5.53 (continued). Aquatic plants of Lake Erie coastal marshes (after Fassett, 1940 and New York Sea Grant Program, Rawinski et al., 1979).

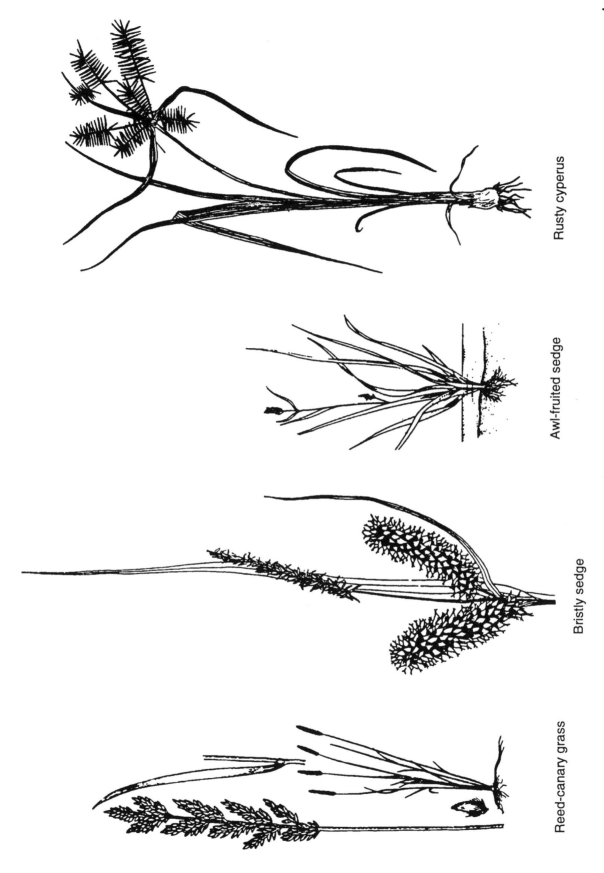

Rusty cyperus

Awl-fruited sedge

Bristly sedge

Reed-canary grass

Figure 5.53 (continued). Aquatic plants of Lake Erie coastal marshes (after Fassett, 1940 and New York Sea Grant Program, Rawinski et al., 1979).

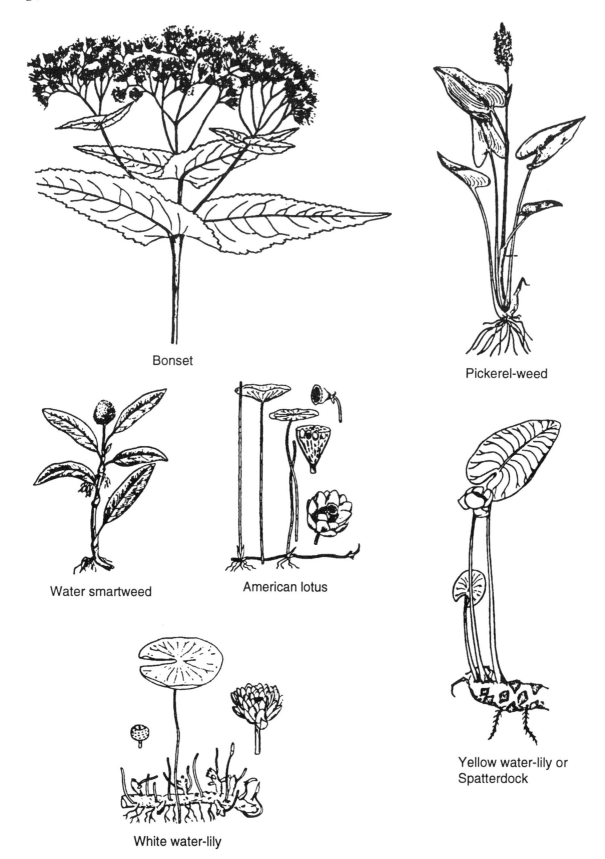

Bonset

Pickerel-weed

Water smartweed

American lotus

Yellow water-lily or Spatterdock

White water-lily

Figure 5.53 (continued). Aquatic plants of Lake Erie coastal marshes (after Fassett, 1940 and New York Sea Grant Program, Rawinski et al., 1979).

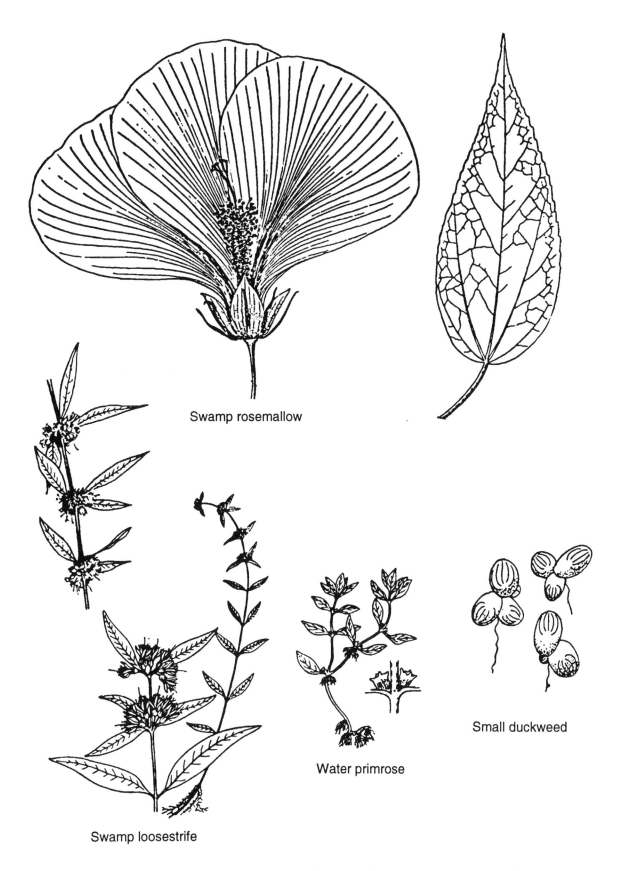

Swamp rosemallow

Swamp loosestrife

Water primrose

Small duckweed

Figure 5.53 (continued). Aquatic plants of Lake Erie coastal marshes (after Fassett, 1940 and New York Sea Grant Program, Rawinski et al., 1979).

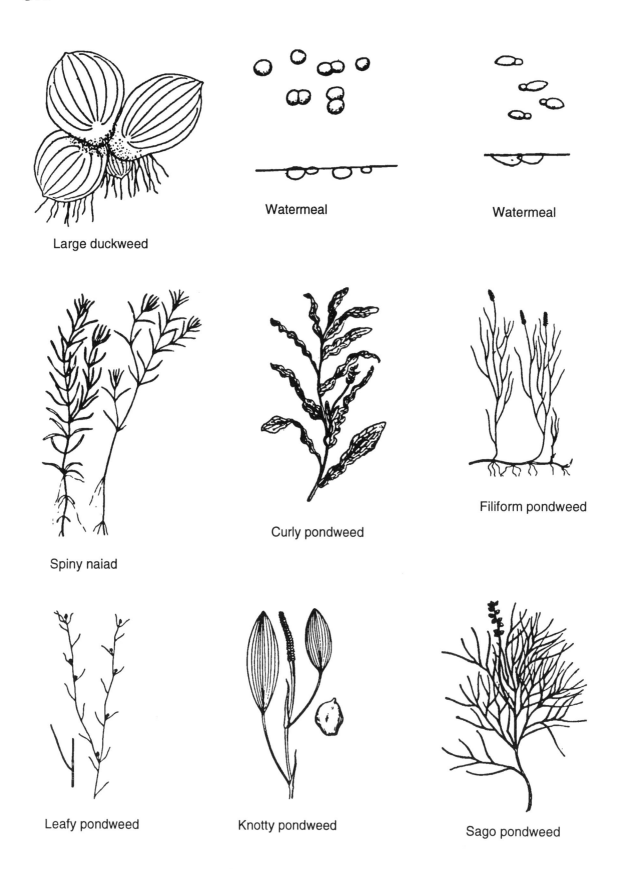

Large duckweed

Watermeal

Watermeal

Spiny naiad

Curly pondweed

Filiform pondweed

Leafy pondweed

Knotty pondweed

Sago pondweed

Figure 5.53 (continued). Aquatic plants of Lake Erie coastal marshes (after Fassett, 1940 and New York Sea Grant Program, Rawinski et al., 1979).

379

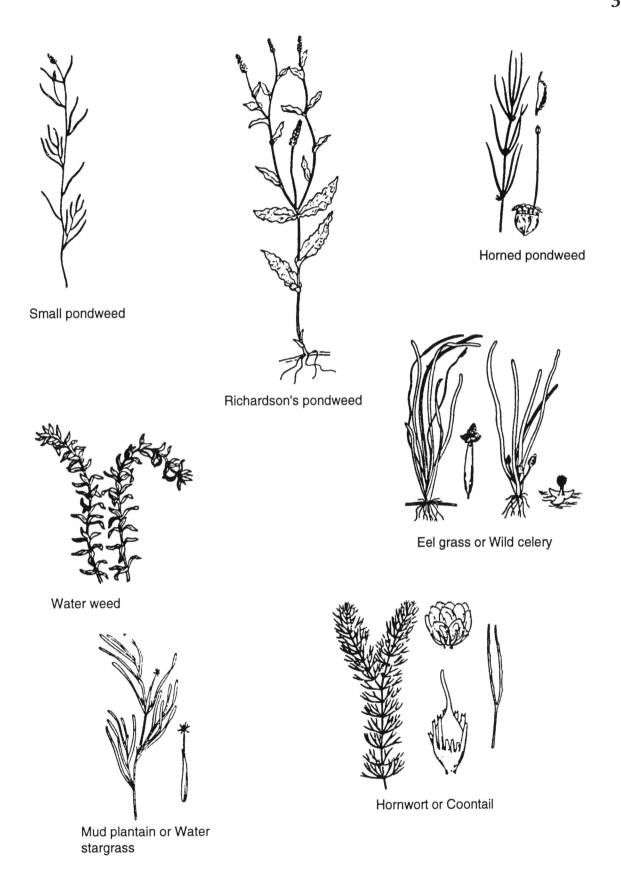

Small pondweed

Richardson's pondweed

Horned pondweed

Water weed

Eel grass or Wild celery

Mud plantain or Water
stargrass

Hornwort or Coontail

Figure 5.53 (continued). Aquatic plants of Lake Erie coastal marshes (after Fassett, 1940 and New York Sea Grant Program, Rawinski et al., 1979).

reed (*Sparganium* spp.), grasses (*Echinochloa* spp., *Leersia oryzoides*, *Calamagrostis canadensis*), spatterdock (*Nuphar advena*), water lily (*Nymphaea* spp.), and water smartweed (*Polygonum coccineum*). Vegetational composition varies greatly among wetlands, with greatest species diversity occurring in the wetlands of the western basin. If lake levels were to be lowered, the size and quality of vegetated coastal wetlands on Lake Erie would increase, particularly in stream mouths and embayments.

The west shore of Lake Erie includes 40,000 acres (160 km²) of marsh, most of which is owned by private clubs. Several marshes, such as the state-owned Magee Marsh and the privately owned Winous Point Club, are under intensive management for increasing waterfowl breeding population. Most of these marshes are natural lowlands separated from Lake Erie by a stable beach ridge. The sandy beach is strewn with clam shells, small rocks, and pebbles washed ashore during storms. Several species of grasses, sandbar willow (*Salix interior*), staghorn sumac (*Rhus typhina*), and many other low plants characterize the beach ridge plant community. Behind the beach ridge is a hardwood swamp zone. Cottonwood (*Populus deltoides*) and black willow (*Salix nigra*) are in abundance and hackberry (*Celtis occidentalis*), sycamore (*Platanus occidentalis*), staghorn sumac, and river-bank grape (*Vitis riparia*) are common. The beach ridge and hardwood swamp are probably the most stable communities. Severe storms can result in changes in the biota, but these changes are usually temporary.

The managed marshes are often surrounded and transected by earthen dikes. Cottonwood, black willow, rough-leaved dogwood (*Cornus drummondii*), staghorn sumac, river-bank grape, and several grasses are common on the dikes. Wherever there is standing water throughout most of the year, cattail (*Typha* spp.), softstem bulrush (*Scirpus validus*), white water lily (*Nymphaea tuberosa*), water milfoil (*Myriophyllum exalbescens*), sago pondweed (*Potamogeton pectinatus*), and curly pondweed (*Potamogeton crispus*) are abundant.

Waterfowl management is essentially control of plant succession based on seasonal needs of ducks and geese. Intensive and economical management is best achieved by control of water levels, since fluctuation of water levels has a marked influence on the succession of aquatic plants. Marsh managers obtain the best results from drawdown (lowering of water level by use of dikes and/or pumps) in May to create a nesting habitat for the summer, and reflooding in the fall to attract large numbers of fall migrants. Partial reduction of water levels, rather than complete drying of the soil, exposes knolls used for nesting and leads to an interspersion of suitable submerged, emergent, and shoreline vegetation. Experimental water drawdown tests conducted at Locust Point have shown that with partial drawdown, dense growths of smartweed (*Polygonum* spp.)—a good waterfowl food—developed in exposed areas. Partially flooded areas developed dense stands of emergent plants such as bulrush (*Scirpus* spp.), water milfoil, and spikerush (*Eleocharis* spp.). In marshes where the water was not drawn down, less desirable growths of water lilies and arrowhead (*Sagittaria* spp.) formed most of the plant cover.

The most extensive growth of wetland plants occurs in the massive St. Clair Delta marshes. The marshes on the Michigan side of the delta have been greatly altered since settlement of the region, but the Ontario side still contains mainly primitive wetlands.

Fish

Lake Erie and Lake St. Clair support a greater diversity of fish stocks and a higher biomass of fish per unit area than the other Great Lakes. Commercial fish production has been high throughout the history of the fishery which has operated regularly since 1815, averaging approximately 20,000 tons per year since 1915. Production from these lakes often surpasses the combined commercial catches of the other four Great Lakes combined. An extensive and economically valuable recreational fishery has developed largely since 1950 and continues to expand, particularly with the resurgence of walleye (*Stizostedion v. vitreum*) populations in western Lake Erie.

Wetlands are important to fish production because they provide spawning and nursery habitat for wetland-dependent species, cover for juvenile and forage fish, and feeding areas for predator fish (Figure 5.54). Approximately 43 species of fishes are, or once were, associated with the coastal marshes of Lake Erie. Twenty-six of these species are currently of significant recreational, commercial, or prey value. Fishes associated with coastal marshes can be divided into two categories: (1) species directly dependent on coastal marshes as adult habitats or spawning and nursery areas, and (2) species not dependent on marshes for such uses but which are usually common in coastal marshes, apparently making opportunistic use of them as spawning, nursery, and feeding areas. The first category includes species such as northern pike (*Esox lucius*), longnose gar (*Lepisosteus osseus*), bowfin (*Amia calva*), bullheads (*Ictalurus* spp.), and crappies (*Pomoxis* spp.), whose dependence on aquatic vegetation has been well established. The second category includes common nearshore and bay species such as gizzard

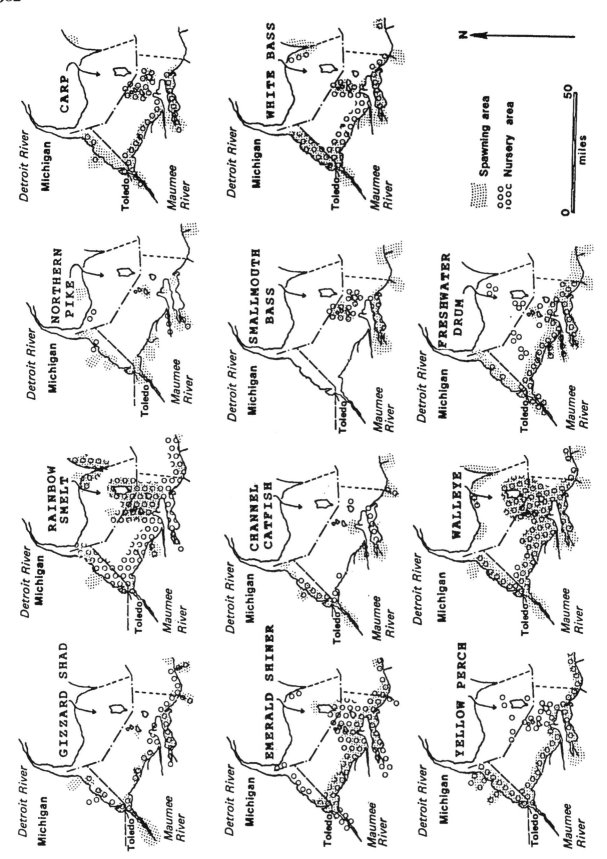

Figure 5.54. Spawning and nursery grounds for important western Lake Erie fish species (after Goodyear et al., 1982).

shad (*Dorosoma cepedianum*), quillback (*Carpoides cyprinus*), white sucker (*Catostomus commersoni*), white bass (*Morone chrysops*), white perch (*Morone americana*), channel catfish (*Ictalurus punctatus*), and yellow perch (*Perca flavescens*), which are often seen in coastal marshes during some part of their life history but do not appear to have a strict dependence on aquatic vegetation.

Most of the fish fauna inhabiting wetlands appears to consist of non-salmonid, warm water or cool water species such as carp (*Cyprinus carpio*), northern pike (*Esox lucius*), bullheads (*Ictalurus* spp.), and buffalos (*Ictiobus cyprinellus*). Because of the predominance of clayey and organic-rich substrates in wetlands, there is a prevalence of bottom feeders (e.g., bullheads, channel catfish, carp, and buffalo). Often as much as 90% of the standing fish crop of coastal marshes consists of forage species such as carp and freshwater drum (*Aplodinotus grunniens*). The standing crop of fish in productive wetlands can run as high as 500 lbs/acre (90 kg/hectare). Large predator fish, such as northern pike, rely on visual contact for locating their prey and require clear water as do some minnows, such as emerald shiners (*Notropis atherinoides*). Siltation due to agricultural development of northwestern Ohio has eliminated much of this type of environment. As the waters have become more silt-ladened, the clear water fish have been replaced by other species including carp, bullheads, and buffalo which are tolerant of turbidity and siltation.

Northern pike usually broadcast their eggs in shallow sedge marshes or in flooded fields. Carp also broadcast their eggs over vegetation and debris in warm, shallow embayments and marshes. Because many fish species spawn only on specific substrate types, modification of wetlands through direct habitat loss, addition of suspended solids, and alteration of flow regime has resulted in the elimination or degradation of wetland spawning environments.

The introduction of externally-derived detritus, including particulate organic matter, along with algae, duckweeds, and other aquatic plants provide food for herbivorous fish and other forage species. In turn, the abundance of these forage fish, as well as large numbers of juvenile fish, attract predator fish to wetlands for feeding. Predator fish, such as northern pike may feed at dusk and at dawn in shallow waters but usually return to somewhat cooler or deeper waters for resting during the day. Thus, links between open waters and the shallow wetlands are essential. Spring floods, seiches, and other high-water periods provide access to the wetlands for feeding and spawning fish. In contrast, during periods of low or obstructed flow, links to adjacent wetlands are broken, and the isolated wetland populations may suffer from higher water temperatures, reduced dissolved oxygen, and a concentration of chemical effluents. Carp Pond on Kelleys Island—typically barred across in late summer—suffers these problems.

Researchers have studied the movements of fishes into and out of Lake Erie coastal wetlands. In Rondeau Bay, Ontario, two groups of yellow perch reside in the bay: (1) two- and three-year-old migratory perch which concentrate near the mouth of the bay and migrate daily into the lake, and (2) two- and three-year-old non-migratory perch which remain in the bay. Movement occurs primarily at sunrise and sunset. Based on plankton counts and examination of stomach contents, the migratory group appears to enter the lake during the day to feed on the water flea *Daphnia*. Other studies of fish movement into and out of a coastal wetland of Sandusky Bay, Ohio reveal that the exchange of all fish species between the wetland and bay is substantial. Movements in each direction are almost equal, with direction of movement apparently determined by positive rheotaxis (tendency to be attracted to flowing water). Direction of flow varies with the fluctuating water levels in Sandusky Bay. The principal species moving through the culvert are, in order of abundance, gizzard shad, brown bullhead (*Ictalurus nebulosus*), carp, freshwater drum, white crappie (*Pomoxis annularis*), pumpkinseed (*Lepomis gibbosus*), goldfish (*Carassius auratus*), and black crappie (*Pomoxis nigromaculatus*). Peak adult movement appears to be related to spawning activity in the spring, with juveniles moving out of the wetland in summer.

Studies of the effect of carp on vegetation in the Erie Shooting Club marsh on the Michigan shore of Lake Erie were made by comparing enclosed, carp-free areas with similar areas open to carp. This research demonstrates that carp significantly decrease the abundance of aquatic vegetation in the marsh. Carp have a selective effect on certain submersed plants, particularly in the spring growing season, when plants are young and delicate. Carp retard the growth of plants by feeding on them, uprooting them, and increasing turbidity of the water. This species can be extremely deleterious in waterfowl marshes because they selectively destroy those submersed plants most attractive as waterfowl food.

Reptiles and Amphibians

Snakes, turtles, frogs, and salamanders are common in the Lake Erie and Lake St. Clair wetlands. At least 28 species of amphibians and 27 species of reptiles inhabit the Lake Erie region. Since all amphibians are dependent on water (or heavy moisture) for breeding, most of those species found in the Lake Erie drainage basin may exist at least seasonally in coastal wetlands. Many of the reptiles are primarily terrestrial, although they may be found crossing wetlands or inhabiting meadows, brush, or forest areas bordering coastal wetlands. The presence of water, food, and cover, as well as relative isolation from cultural development, are among the factors which contribute to the importance of wetlands in maintaining a diverse and abundant herpetofauna. The snapping turtle, eastern spiny soft-shell, bullfrog, and green frog are edible species harvested in some coastal wetlands. Of the turtles, the snapping turtle is the largest, attaining a weight of up to 50 lbs (110 kg). Many reptiles and amphibians also serve as food sources for fish, birds, and mammals utilizing the wetlands.

The mudpuppy (*Necturus maculosus*) and the red-spotted newt (*Notophthalmus viridescens*) are generally associated with submersed aquatic vegetation, and the four-toed salamander (*Hemidactylium scutatum*) is often associated with sphagnum in bog habitats. These three species will usually be associated with wetlands. Most other perennially aquatic frogs and salamanders in the Lake Erie coastal region live in a variety of aquatic habitats, including wetlands, where the abundance of cover is conducive to large populations. These species include the bullfrog (*Rana catesbeiana*), green frog (*Rana clamitans*), northern leopard frog (*Rana pipiens*), and pickerel frog (*Rana palustris*). Semi-aquatic species such as the small-mouthed salamander (*Ambystoma texanum*), Tremblay's salamander (*Ambystoma tremblayi*), blue-spotted salamander (*Ambystoma laterale*), silvery salamander (*Ambystoma platineum*), spotted salamander (*Ambystoma maculatum*), and tiger salamander (*Ambystoma tigrinum*), as well as semiaquatic climbing frog (*Pleudacris triseriata*), cricket frog (*Acris crepitans*), and spring peeper (*Hyla crucifer*), may be found in Lake Erie coastal wetlands or their margins. Primarily terrestrial amphibians such as the wood frog (*Rana sylvatica*), Fowler's toad (*Bufo woodhousei fowleri*), American toad (*Bufo americanus*), red-backed salamander (*Plethodon cinereus*), marbled salamander (*Ambystoma opacum*), and slimy salamander (*Plethodon glutinosus*) may occur in coastal wetlands during their respective breeding seasons.

The aquatic and semiaquatic reptiles of the Lake Erie coastal wetlands include the map turtle (*Graptemys geographica*), midland painted turtle (*Chrysemys picta marginata*), snapping turtle (*Chelydra serpentina*), spotted turtle (*Clemmys guttata*), stinkpot (*Sternotherus odoratus*), Blanding's turtle (*Emydoidea blandingi*), spiny soft-shell (*Trionyx spiniferus*), garter snake (*Thamnophis sirtalis*), brown snake

(*Stereria dekayi*), ribbon snake (*Thamnophis sauritus*), queen snake (*Natrix septemvittata*), northern and Lake Erie water snakes (*Natrix s. sipedon* and *N. S. insularum*), Kirtland's water snake (*Natrix kirtlandi*), eastern milk snake (*Lampropeltis doliata triangulum*), and Butler's garter snake (*Thamnophis butleri*). The massasauga (*Sistrurus catenatus*) is largely a swamp and bog inhabitant which appears uncommonly in coastal wetlands, while the colorful fox snake (*Elaphe vulpina*) is almost wholly restricted to and common in the coastal marshes of western Lake Erie.

Birds

In general, wetland habitat along Lake Erie supports a diversity of bird life. Resident and migratory species of waterfowl, waterbirds, wading birds, shore birds, raptors and perching birds use the region for nesting, feeding and resting. Noteworthy migratory species which utilize the shoreline environment include the bald eagle (*Haliaeetus leucocephalus*), osprey (*Pandion haliaetus*), and Kirtland's warbler (*Dendroica kirtlandii*). Waterfowl commonly observed in the wetlands of southwestern Lake Erie are mallard (*Anas platyrhynchos*), wood duck (*Aix sponsa*), black duck (*A. rubripes*), pintail (*A. acuta*), blue-winged teal (*A. discors*), American wigeon (*A. americana*), and Canada goose (*Branta canadensis*), as well as great blue heron (*Ardea herodias*) and great egret (*Casmerodius albus*).

Several species of endangered birds have been recorded in the coastal wetlands of Lake Erie. Bald eagles nest successfully in the Locust Point wetland complex in Ottawa County, Ohio. King rails (*Rallus elegans*) have been recorded from several wetlands and are known to breed in the vicinity of Catawba Island. The common tern (*Sterna hirundo*) has been observed in the Toledo area. Other birds endangered or threatened in states bordering Lake Erie and which have been recorded in the coastal zone of the lake include the Caspian tern (*Sterna caspia*), piping plover (*Charadrius melodus*), Cooper's hawk (*Accipiter cooperii*), red-shouldered hawk (*Buteo lineatus*), marsh hawk or northern harrier (*Circus cyaneus*), and sharp-shinned hawk (*Accipiter striatus*). Some other birds such as the black-crowned night heron (*Nycticorax nycticorax*), barred owl (*Strix varia*), and American bittern (*Botaurus lentiginosus*) are uncommon.

The Great Lakes lie along the path of three bird migration corridors which comprise the Central, Mississippi, and Atlantic flyways. Each corridor, in turn, is a web of routes as opposed to a single, narrow band rigidly followed by waterfowl. In general, fall movements of dabbling ducks, e.g., mallard and blue-winged teal, are from the northwest, across the Great Plains, to the Gulf Coast of Texas and Louisiana. Diving ducks and redheads exhibit a more east-west migration pattern but may winter along either the Gulf or Atlantic coasts.

As waterfowl migrate between breeding grounds and wintering areas, they stop to rest and feed in wetlands with an abundance of food, low wave energy, and little human disturbance. Canvasbacks (*Aythya valisineria*), redheads (*Aythya americana*), American wigeon, ring-necked ducks (*Aythya collaris*), and coots (*Fulica* spp.) feed extensively on submersed plants, whereas shovelers (*Anas clypeata*), oldsquaw (*Clangula hyemalis*), goldeneye (*Bucephala clangula*), and mergansers (*Mergus* spp. and *Lophodytes cucullatus*) appear to prefer crayfish, small fish, and other animal foods. Black ducks, mallard, pintail, teal (*Anas* spp.), scaup (*Aythya* spp.), and bufflehead (*Bucephala albeola*), select from both plant and animal foods. Canada geese, and common mallard also feed heavily on waste grains in agricultural fields. Food availability may be more important than food preference, especially during the spring migration when food supplies are less abundant.

Mammals

Cattail marshes provide excellent food and building material for furbearers such as muskrat (*Ondatra zibethicus*). Many other species such as raccoons (*Procyon lotor*) and white-tailed deer (*Odocoileus virginianus*) occupy multiple habitats, of which wetlands are only one. All told, about 20 kinds of mammals can be found in the marsh complex. Muskrat is the most important furbearer. Its harvest in southeastern Lake Erie wetlands ranks Ohio among the top fur-producing states and accounts for 70% of Ohio furs. The high productivity of muskrat in this region is a direct result of management practices which maintain stable water levels in the wetlands. Red and gray foxes (*Vulpes fulva* and *Urocyon cinereoargenteus*) are also frequent visitors to the wetland margins, feeding on rabbits, rodents, and marsh birds.

The coastal wetlands of Lake Erie are important for many mammalian species. The Eastern cottontail (*Sylvilagus floridanus*), woodchuck (*Marmota monax*), and striped skunk (*Mephitis mephitis*) chiefly utilize the dikes of managed wetlands. Fox squirrels (*Sciurus niger*) are found most commonly in the wooded perimeter of wetlands. White-tailed deer are only transient members of wetland communities. Long-tailed weasels (*Mustela frenata*), mink (*M. vison*), and red fox are uncommon to most Lake Erie wetlands. Generally there is a smaller variety of mammalian fauna in the Lake Erie island wetlands than in mainland wetlands.

One of the most significant environmental changes in Lake Erie was the draining and filling of the massive coastal marsh system at the western end of the lake. Prior to 1850, an extensive coastal marsh and swamp system, consisting largely of an area known as the Black Swamp (Figure 5.55), covered an area of approximately 1,500 mi² (4,000 km²) between Vermilion, Ohio, and the mouth of the Detroit River and extended up the Maumee Valley into Indiana. This area was largely cleared, drained, and filled to provide agricultural land, lumber, and transportation routes, so that at present only about 40 mi² (100 km²) of coastal marshland remains. Most of this remaining marshland is encompassed by dikes. Between 1850 and 1900, as coastal marshes were drained and filled for conversion to agriculture, dikes were constructed to protect farmlands from seasonal flooding and to separate them from adjacent open water and unfilled marsh. During this time, the marshes of western Lake Erie gained considerable fame as waterfowl hunting areas. After 1900, the rate of loss of the remaining marshlands accelerated due to increasing development pressure, changing lake levels,

Environmental Changes in Coastal Wetlands

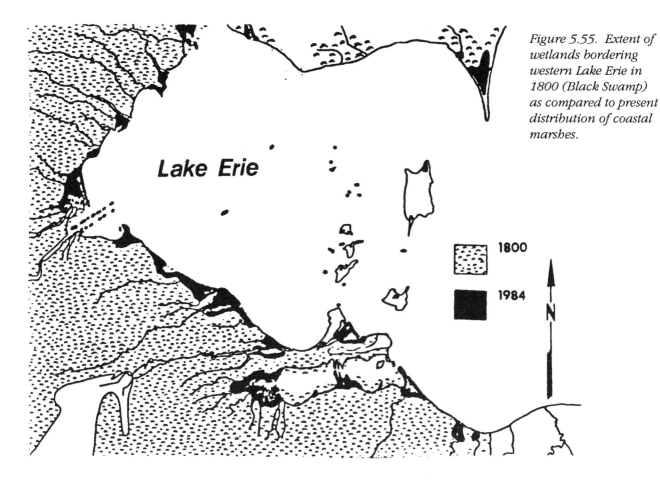

Figure 5.55. Extent of wetlands bordering western Lake Erie in 1800 (Black Swamp) as compared to present distribution of coastal marshes.

increasing agricultural siltation, and wave erosion. Groups of wealthy sportsmen interested in preserving quality waterfowl hunting in the area purchased most of the remaining marshland around western Lake Erie. Marshes were then enclosed by a second generation of dikes equipped with gates and pumps to protect them from flooding, siltation, and wave erosion and to permit water level regulation for the production of aquatic plants used by waterfowl. Since 1950, many of these privately owned marshes were acquired by the natural resource agencies to be used as wildlife refuges, public hunting and recreation areas, natural areas and preserves, and state/provincial parks.

The management of these marshes for fisheries presents two special problems. First, water levels in these marshes must be maintained at levels optimal for production of aquatic plants used by waterfowl and for control of dike erosion. During high lake water levels or high watershed runoff periods, particularly in spring, gates must be opened or pumps run to remove excess water and minimize dike erosion and silt deposition. During low lake water levels, particularly during late summer and fall, lake water must be introduced to the marshes in order to maintain minimum water levels for aquatic plant production. This may be done with either pumps or by opening gates. The gate method takes advantage of storm-induced high lake levels to admit water to the marshes, thus saving pump operating costs. The timing of these operations is generally dictated by climate and weather conditions, and marsh managers are often unable to provide access or egress to fish which might otherwise use the marshes as spawning and nursery areas. Low water levels maintained during the summer are also conducive to dissolved oxygen depletion and summerkill of fish. Second, marsh managers are compelled to exclude carp from controlled marshes, since this species readily overpopulates marshes, consumes desirable aquatic vegetation, and roils the water thereby increasing turbidity and decreasing production of aquatic plants. Marsh managers are very reluctant to open gates unnecessarily during late spring and summer, when carp spawning runs occur, even if desirable species are thereby excluded. Certain "marshes" are kept dewatered during spring and summer for the production of cash crops (such as soybeans) then flooded for waterfowl attraction during the fall.

Observing Coastal Wetlands

Inventories of Great Lakes wetlands have revealed that at least 150 individual wetlands or wetland complexes are found along the coast between the head of the St. Clair River and the mouth of the Niagara River (Herdendorf et al., 1981). Taken together, the United States and Canadian coastal wetlands of Lake Erie, Lake St. Clair, and the St. Clair,

Detroit and Niagara rivers cover an estimated 130,000 acres (530 km²). Many of the finest marshes and swamps are owned and managed by federal, state, and provincial agencies as wildlife preserves. Most of these agencies have established visitors' centers, nature trails, or observation towers to accommodate the interested traveler. Fifteen of the best locations to observe coastal wetlands in the region are described below.

St. Clair Flats

The St. Clair Flats wetlands complex is located on the delta formed at the mouth of the St. Clair River as it flows into Lake St. Clair. Approximately 8,500 acres (35 km²) of wetlands lie on the Michigan side of the border and 20,000 acres (80 km²) lie in Ontario. Major islands in the delta include Walpole Island, Dickinson Island, McDonald Island, North Island, Middle Island, Green Island, Harsens Island, Bruchner Island, Squirrel Island, and St. Anne Island. Most of the United States portion of the delta marshes lie within the Lake St. Clair National Wildlife Refuge and the St. Clair Flats State Wildlife Area. The Canadian portion of the wetlands is largely within the Walpole Island Indian Reservation.

On the various islands of the delta, five major and three minor plant zones can be seen. These include from driest to wettest habitat: (1) oak-ash hardwood forest, (2) dogwood-grass zone, (3) sedge marsh, (4) cattail marsh, and (5) bulrush marsh. The other easily identifiable plant zones which are small and limited in distribution include: (1) canal-pond-abandoned channel aquatic plant zones, (2) lake and bay bottom communities, and (3) reed grass zones (Jaworski and Raphael, 1978).

Oak-ash hardwood forest occurs in the upper portion of Dickinson, Harsens, Squirrel, Walpole, and St. Anne Islands. Major species of this forest include red ash (*Fraxinus pennsylvanica*) and swamp white oak (*Quercus bicolor*). Associated species occurring in this forest include pin oak (*Quercus palustrus*), bur oak (*Quercus macrocarpa*), shagbark hickory (*Carya ovata*) and cottonwood (*Populus deltoides*).

The dogwood-grass zone occurs as a transition zone between the forest and the wetter sedge marsh. Infrequent flooding and human disturbance (burning and mowing) may prevent this zone from reverting to hardwood forest. Major species composing this zone include blue-joint grass (*Calamagrostis canadensis*), soft rush (*Juncus effusus*), quaking aspen (*Populus tremuloides*), gray dogwood (*Cornus racemosa*), and red osier (*Cornus stolonifera*). Associated species include: foul meadow grass (*Poa palustris*), marsh fern (*Dryopteris thelypteris*), spike rush (*Eleocharis erythropoda*), swamp milkweed (*Asclepia incarnata*), silverweed (*Pontentilla anserina*), vetch (*Vicia angustifolia*), cottonwood, silky willow (*Salix sericea*), swamp rose (*Rosa palustris*), wild grape (*Vitis palmata*), and hawthorn (*Crateagus* sp.).

The sedge marsh comprises a narrow zone located between the dogwood-grass zone and the cattail marsh, as well as along eroding lake and bay shorelines, particularly on the American side of the delta. This plant zone may also occur along lower distributary channels and on old shorelines now stranded in the cattail marsh. The sedge marsh occurs in wet sites which are occasionally flooded; however, permanent water depth does not exceed 10 in (25 cm). Major species of the sedge marsh include blue-joint grass and sedges (*Carex stricta, C. lasipcarpa, C. sartwellii, C. lanuginosa, C. lacustris*). On eroding shorelines nightshade (*Solanus* sp.) and common comfrey (*Symphytun officinale*) may also occur.

The cattail marsh is a broad zone located on lower portions of the delta where permanent water depths exceed 6 in (15 cm). Zones of cattail also occur on inundated shoulders of river channels, on lower ends of distributary channels, and on crevasses. Pure stands of cattail are associated with peaty or clayey sediments in the St. Clair Delta. The major species present is narrow-leaved cattail (*Typha angustifolia*). In small, shallow open water areas, duckweed (*Lemna minor*), water milfoil (*Myriophyllum alterniflorum*), and bladderwort (*Utricularia vulgaris*) are abundant.

The bulrush marsh is prevalent inside abandoned river channels and in cattail marshes where open water and sandy sediments occur. Water depths in these wetlands average 3 ft (1 m). The major species of the bulrush marsh is hard-stem bulrush (*Scirpus acutus*). Buttonbush (*Cephalanthus occidentalis*) occurs as an associate in the bulrush marshes.

The canal-pond-abandoned channel aquatic plant zones occur in artificial canals, openings in the marshes, and abandoned river channels where water depths range from 1 to 3 ft (0.3 to 1 m). While communities vary in composition, the most frequently occurring species are duckweed, pickerel weed (*Pontederia cordata*), elodea (*Elodea canadensis*), smartweed (*Polygonum amphibium*), and water milfoil. Associated species include yellow pond lily (*Nuphar rubrodiscum*), white water lily (*Nymphaea tuberosa*), and pondweed (*Potamogeton* spp.), as well as green algae (*Cladophora glomerata*).

The lake and bay bottom communities occur along low wave energy lake bottoms and nearshore environments of bays such as Little Muscamoot Bay. Water depths range from 1 to 5 ft (0.3 to 1.5 m). Major species occurring in this zone include wild celery (*Vallisneria americana*), pickerel weed (*Pontederia cordata*), yellow pond lily (*Nuphar rubrodiscum*), smartweed, water milfoil, narrow-leaved cattail, hard-stem bulrush, and American bulrush (*Scirpus americanus*).

The reed grass (*Phragmites communis*) zone consists of small, scattered clumps of reed grass throughout the delta at or just below the water level. Reed grass zones are especially prevalent in Middle, South, and Bassett channels.

Major game fish (Figure 5.56) in the delta region include: northern pike (*Esox lucius*), largemouth bass (*Micropterus salmoides*), yellow perch (*Perca flavescens*), bullheads (*Ictalurus* spp.) and sunfishes (*Lepomis* spp.). Common waterfowl, marsh birds, and raptors observed in the wetlands include: Canada goose (*Branta canadensis*), mallard (*Anas platyrhynchos*), black duck (*Anas rubripes*), blue-winged teal (*Anas discors*), wood duck (*Aix sponsa*), hooded merganser (*Lophodytes cucullatus*), common merganser (*Mergus merganser*), great blue heron (*Ardea herodias*), black-crowned night-heron (*Nyticorax nycticorax*), American bittern (*Botaurus lentiginosus*), American coot (*Fulica americana*), herring gull (*Larus argentatus*), common tern (*Sterna hirundo*), red-tailed hawk (*Buteo jamaicensis*), and northern harrier (*Circus cyaneus*).

Marsh mammals are abundant in the St. Clair Flats wetlands. Annually over 5,000 muskrats (*Ondatra zibethicus*) are trapped in the Michigan marshes. Red fox (*Vulpes vulpes*), raccoon (*Procyon lotor*), mink (*Mustela vison*), striped skunk (*Mephitis mephitis*), and white-tailed deer (*Odocoileus virginianus*) also forage in the delta wetlands.

Detroit River

The mouth of the Detroit River contains several small islands and one major island, Grosse Ile. Most of these islands are fringed by coastal wetlands where development has not destroyed them. These wetlands are generally non-wooded marshes dominated by cattails (*Typha* spp.). The most noteworthy marshes can be found on Gibraltar Island, Cherry Isle, Celeron Island, Horse Island, Round Island, Elba Island, Calf Island, Stony Island, Grassy Island, and Grosse Ile.

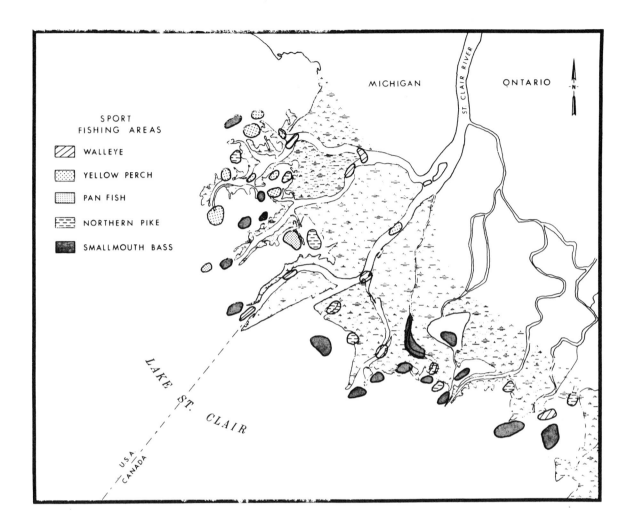

Figure 5.56. Sport fishng areas in the vicinity of the St. Clair Delta (Jaworski and Raphael, 1978).

    The following fish are known to spawn in coastal wetlands of the lower Detroit River: lake sturgeon (*Acipenser fulvescens*), northern pike, carp (*Cyprinus carpio*), channel catfish (*Ictalurus punctatus*), largemouth bass (*Micropterus salmoides*), smallmouth bass (*Micropterus dolomieui*), bluegill (*Lepomis macrochirus*), yellow perch (*Perca flavescens*), and walleye (*Stizostedion v. vitreum*). Commercial fishing in the Detroit River has been discontinued for several decades. Non-salmonid sport fishing for carp, channel catfish (*Ictalurus punctatus*), bullheads (*Ictalurus* spp.), yellow perch, walleye, and white bass (*Morone chrysops*) is common along the Detroit River wetlands where several launching facilities provide anglers with access to the river. Test netting in the vicinity of Grosse Ile has yielded 45 species of fishes, the most abundant of which are northern pike (*Esox lucius*), carp, goldfish (*Carassius auratus*), carp x goldfish hybrids, goldenshiner (*Notemigonus crysoleucas*), blacknose shiner (*Notropis heterolepis*), white sucker (*Catostomus commersoni*), brook silverside (*Labidesthes sicculus*), rock bass (*Ambloplites rupestris*), pumpkinseed (*Lepomis gibbosus*), black crappie (*Pomoxis nigromaculatus*), and yellow perch.

The dominant water birds utilizing the wetlands of Cherry Isle include: mallard (*Anas platyrhynchos*), blue-winged teal (*Anas discors*), wood duck (*Aix sponsa*), ruddy duck (*Oxyura jamaicensis*), belted kingfisher (*Ceryle alcyon*), great blue heron (*Ardea herodias*), green-backed heron (*Butorides striatus*), black-crowned night-heron (*Nyticorax nycticorax*), great egret (*Casmerodius albus*), common moorhen (*Gallinula chloropus*), herring gull (*Larus argentatus*), ring-billed gull (*Larus delawarensis*), Caspian tern (*Sterna caspia*), and lesser yellowlegs (*Tringa flavipes*).

Mouillee Marsh

Located along the shore of western Lake Erie about 5 mi (8 km) south of the Detroit River mouth, this marsh is the most extensive wetland on the Michigan shore of Lake Erie (1,400 acres or 5.7 km²). Most of the wetlands are within the Pointe Mouillee State Game Area. The estuarine mouths of the Huron River and Mouillee Creek are located near the center of the marsh. Portions of the marsh are protected by onshore and offshore dikes. A sandy barrier beach, known as Pointe Mouillee, also separates the marsh from Lake Erie.

Cattails (*Typha* spp.) are the natural dominant species in Mouillee Marsh. However, portions of the marsh are managed for waterfowl and such food plants as smartweed (*Polygonum* spp.), pigweed (*Amaranthus* spp.), and bur reed (*Sparganium* spp.) are propagated in diked management areas, to the exclusion of cattails. Approximately 20 species of fish are found in Mouillee Marsh. Carp (*Cyprinus carpio*) is the most abundant. Forage species such as gizzard shad (*Dorosoma cepedianum*), alewife (*Alosa pseudoharengus*), emerald shiner (*Notropis atherinoides*), and spottail shiner (*Notropis hudsonius*) also utilize the marsh. Common amphibians and reptiles include bullfrog (*Rana catesbeiana*), green frog (*Rana clamitans*), leopard frog (*Rana pipiens*), cricket frog (*Acris crepitans*), western chorus frog (*Pseudacris t. triseriata*), American toad (*Bufo americanus*), fox snake (*Elaphe vulpina*), brown snake (*Storeria dekayi*), snapping turtle (*Chelydra* serpentina), and midland painted turtle (*Chrysemys picta marginata*). Canada goose (*Branta canadensis*), black duck (*Anas rubripes*), mallard (*Anas platyrhynchos*, gadwall (*Anas strepera*), blue-winged teal (*Anas discors*), and wood duck (*Aix sponsa*) are common nesting species in Mouillee Marsh. Muskrat (*Ondatra zibethicus*) are dependent on the marsh for food, shelter, and breeding areas, whereas opossum (*Didelphis virginiana*), red fox (*Vulpes vulpes*), raccoon (*Procyon lotor*), mink (*Mustela vison*), and striped skunk (*Mephitis mephitis*) utilize the marsh as a foraging area.

Maumee Bay

This bay lies at the mouth of the Maumee River and is formed by Cedar Point (locally known as little Cedar Point to avoid confusion with the point of the same name on the east side of Sandusky Bay) on the east and Woodtick Peninsula on the west. These two sand spits provide the shelter necessary for wetland development. The former lies within the Cedar Point National Wildlife Refuge (administered as a part of the Ottawa National Wildlife Refuge), and the latter lies partially within the Erie State Game Area (administered by the Michigan Department of Natural Resources). The Cedar Point marshes extend westward along the south shore of the bay to Maumee Bay State Park. Estuarine wetlands also occur along the Maumee River valley between Rosford and the first bedrock riffles at Perrysburg.

The major plant species thriving in the Maumee Bay marshes include narrow-leaved cattail (*Typha angustifolia*), broad-leaved cattail (*Typha latifolia*), jewelweeds (*Impatiens* sp.), marsh-mallow (*Hibiscus palustris*), blue-joint grass (*Calamagrostis canadensis*), and swamp milkweed (*Asclepia incarnata*). In the transition zone between open water and the cattail stands, soft-stem bulrush (*Scirpus validus*) and American bulrush (*Scirpus americanus*) are the dominant species.

Fish found in the Maumee Bay wetlands include bowfin (*Amia calva*), carp (*Cyprinus carpio*), yellow perch (*Perca flavescens*), largemouth bass (*Micropterus salmoides*), white bass (*Morone chrysops*), green sunfish, (*Lepomis cyanellus*), yellow bullhead (*Ictalurus natalis*), gizzard shad (*Dorosoma cepedianum*), and walleye (*Stizostedion v. vitreum*).

The historical occurrence (1936) of Forster's tern (*Sterna forsteri*) has been reported for these wetlands. A bald eagle (*Haliaeetus leucocephalus*) nest is active on Cedar Point. The most common waterfowl are mallard (*Anas platyrhynchos*), black duck (*Anas rubripes*), green-winged teal (*Anas crecca*), blue-winged teal (*Anas discors*), northern shoveler (*Anas clypeata*), and American coot (*Fulica americana*).

Tundra swans (*Cyngus columbianus*) and snow geese (*Chen caerulescens*) also utilize the area for resting during spring migration. The area sustains resident populations of 200 to 300 each for mallards (*Anas platyrhynchos*) and Canada geese (*Branta canadensis*) and smaller numbers of blue-winged teal (*Anas discors*).

Locust Point

This point is a low, gently curved headlands on the south shore of western Lake Erie between Toledo and Sandusky, Ohio. Flanking this point, to the east and west, are 8,600 acres (35 km²) of prime coastal marshes, mostly in federal or state ownership. This wetland complex includes 4 units of the Ottawa National Wildlife Refuge (Cedar Point Marsh, Ottawa Marsh, Navarre Marsh, and Darby Marsh) and three areas administered by the Ohio Department of Natural Resources (Metzger Marsh, Magee Marsh, and Crane Creek State Park). All of these wetlands are protected from Lake Erie flooding by extensive earthen and rip-rap dikes. The federal areas, some of which are former hunting club preserves are now managed as waterfowl refuges by the U.S. Fish and Wildlife Service. Controlled waterfowl hunting is permitted in some parts of the state wildlife areas. Several nature trails are open to visitors in both the federal and state refuges and a fine swimming beach is located at Crane Creek State Park.

Because the marshes are managed for waterfowl, most of the aquatic plants present are excellent duck food. Walter's millet (*Echinochloa walteri*) is the dominant grass. Marsh plants associated with this species include soft-stem bulrush (*Scirpus validus*), hard-stem bulrush (*Scirpus acutus*), catchfly grass (*Leersia lentiuclaris*), mild water-pepper (*Polygonum hydropiperoides*), smartweed (*Polygonum pennsylvanicum*), and cattail (*Typha* spp.). A recent invader, purple loosestrife (*Lythrum salicaria*) produces a beautiful violet flower but offers little food value for wildlife. This plant propagates readily and is a threat to many Lake Erie wetlands.

A fishing survey in connection with an environmental evaluation of the Davis-Besse Nuclear Power Station located on Locust Point, revealed 48 species of fish in Lake Erie and the coastal wetlands. Of these, only seven species were found in Navarre Marsh which borders the station:

bowfin (*Amia calva*), gizzard shad (*Dorosoma cepedianum*), goldfish (*Carassius auratus*), carp (*Cyprinus carpio*), largemouth bass (*Micropterus salmoides*), black crappie (*Pomoxis nigromaculatus*), and white crappie (*Pomoxis annularis*).

Major waterfowl species found in the vicinity of Locust Point are mallard (*Anas platyrhynchos*), black duck (*Anas rubripes*), American wigeon (*Anas americana*), wood duck (*Aix sponsa*), pintail (*Anas acuta*), blue-winged teal (*Anas discors*), and Canada goose (*Branta canadensis*).

The wetlands in this complex also provide important nesting and feeding habitat for bald eagles (*Haliaeetus leucocephalus*). Three pairs of bald eagles have been observed nesting here in recent years. Ospreys (*Pandion haliaetus*) use the area for feeding and resting during migration.

As with most of the Lake Erie marshes, the muskrat (*Ondatra zibethicus*) is the most important furbearer. Other mammals common in the marshes and earthen dikes are woodchuck (*Marmota monax*), eastern cottontial (*Sylvilagus floridanus*), striped skunk (*Mephitis mephitis*), and white-tailed deer (*Odocoileus virginianus*).

Lake Erie Islands

Small wetlands can be found on most of the larger islands in western Lake Erie. Several of the more prominent ones are listed below:

Island	Wetland
Pelee Island	Fish Point Swamp
Pelee Island	Lighthouse Point Marsh
Kelleys Island	Carp Pond
South Bass Island	Terwilliger's Pond
North Bass Island	Manila Bay/Smith's Pond
North Bass Island	Fox's Marsh
Middle Bass Island	Haunk's Pond
East Sister Island	East Sister Swamp

Typically, these wetlands occupy depressions behind sand spits or barrier bars that have been built by alongshore currents. These low, protected areas eventually became the sites of lush growths of vascular aquatic plants. Lagoons with openings to the lake, such as Carp Pond, Terwilliger's Pond and Manila Bay, serve as spawning and nursery grounds for several warm-water fish species such as carp (*Cyprinus carpio*), white crappie (*Pomoxis annularis*), bluegill (*Lepomis macrochirus*), and yellow perch (*Perca flavescens*).

The protected marsh in Haunck's Pond provides an excellent example of aquatic plant zonation in response to water depths. Eight zones have been identified extending from open water to a shrub shoreline:

Zone	**Zone**
1 - open water	5 - cutgrass
2 - water lily	6 - jewelweed
3 - dock	7 - tall grass
4 - cattail	8 - shrub shoreline

Each of these zones is transitional in nature, and in no zone does one species dominate to the exclusion of all other species.

Major species occurring in the open water zone are unattached floating plants such as duckweeds (*Lemna minor, L. trisulca*), water-flaxseed (*Spriodela polyrhiza*), and water-meal (*Wolffia columbiana*), and submersed aquatic plants such as sago pondweed (*Potamogeton pectinatus*), water milfoil (*Myriophyllum exalbescens*), elodea (*Elodea canadensis*), and coontail (*Ceratophyllum demersum*). July water depth in this zone ranges up to 3 ft (1 m).

Major species composing the water lily zone are spatterdock (*Nuphar advena*) and white water lily (*Nymphaea tuberosa*). Species associated with this zone include water-plantain (*Alisma subcordatum*), arrowhead (*Sagittaria latifolia*), and pickerel weed (*Pontederia cordata*). The water lily zone is actually several distinct zones, together occupying a major portion of the wetland. July water depth in this zone ranges up to 3 ft (1 m).

Two species of dock (*Rumex crispus, R. verticillatus*) comprise the major cover of the dock zone. Plants thriving under the dock cover include spatterdock white water lily, sedges, and in some areas rice cutgrass (*Leersia oryzoides*). Occasional hummocks support swamp-loosestrife (*Decodon verticillatus*) and buttonbush (*Cephalanthus occidentalis*). July water depth in this zone ranges up to 1.5 ft (0.5 m).

Narrow-leaved cattail (*Typha angustifolia*) and broad-leaved cattail (*Typha latifolia*) are co-dominant species of the cattail zone. Thriving as associates in this zone are sedges (*Carex cristatella, Scirpus atrovirens, S. validus*), soft rush (*Juncus effusus*), bur reed (*Sparganium eurycarpum*), cutgrass and river bulrush (*Scirpus fluviatilis*). Early summer water depth in this zone ranges up to 6 in (15 cm). However, this zone is predominantly a mudflat.

In early summer, 2-6 in (5-15 cm) of water covers the cutgrass zone. At this time water-plantain (*Alisma subcordatum*) and spatterdock are common associates of cutgrass. As water levels fall, associated species are limited to sedges (*Carex cristatella, C. comosa, Cyperus strigosus, Scirpus atrovirens, S. validus*), spike-rushes (*Eleocharis intermedia, E. obtusa*), and ditch stonecrop (*Penthorum sedoides*). The jewelweeds, *Impatiens capensis* and *I. pallida*, occur in the jewelweed zone nearly to the exclusion of other species. However, in wetter areas, cutgrass, spatterdock, and dock occur. Additional associates of this zone include cattail (*Typha* spp.), sedges (*Cyperaceae*), rushes (*Juncus* spp.), monkey-flower (*Mimulus ringens*), skullcap (*Scutellaria epilobiifolia*), and *Iris* sp.

The tallgrass zone is primarily composed of reed-canary grass (*Phalaris arundinacea*), and blue-joint grass (*Calamagrostis canadensis*), which in some areas attains a height of 6 ft (2 m). Jewel-weed (*Impatiens* spp.) and cattail are the only herbaceous associates. Small hummocks in this zone support white ash (*Fraxinus americana*), hackberry (*Celtis occidentalis*), and choke cherry (*Prunus virginiana*).

The shrub zone is composed primarily of saplings of species found in the nearby swamp forest such as bur-oak (*Quercus macrocarpa*), hackberry (*Celtis occidentalis*), slippery elm (*Ulmus rubra*), and white ash (*Fraxinus americana*). Low growing plants occurring in this site include choke cherry, prairie rose (*Rosa setigera*), and common elder-berry (*Sambucus canadensis*).

Most of the island wetlands are privately owned, but several can be viewed from nearby roadways, including Haunk's Pond. Carp Pond lies within Kelleys Island State Park and is open to visitors.

Sandusky Bay

This bay contains several distinctive wetlands extending from the mouths of the Sandusky River and Muddy Creek at the far western end of the bay, along the south shore to the vicinity of the Sandusky Bay bridges, to the sand spits of Cedar Point and Bay Point at the eastern extremity of the bay. The wetlands at the western end of the bay are the most extensive in private ownership on the Ohio shore of Lake Erie (4,300 acres or 17 km²). These wetlands are largely non-wooded and protected by earthen and rip-rap dikes. They are mostly managed for waterfowl hunting and propagation and to a lesser extent, trapping and propagation of furbearers. Much of this marshland and the wetlands in the vicinity of the bay bridges are divided by a network of dikes into a number of marsh units, which are managed individually for waterfowl habitat. If dikes were not utilized, it is likely that the erosive action of the waves would eliminate much of the wetland vegetation. In the open water of the marshes, the dominant plant species vary from year to year, but the most common ones are coontail (*Ceratophyllum demersum*), duckweeds (*Lemna* spp.), water-milfoil (*Myriophyllum exalbescens*), water-smartweed (*Polygonum coccineum*), American lotus (*Nelumbo lutea*), white water lily (*Nymphaea tuberosa*), spatterdock (*Nuphar advena*), pondweeds (*Potamogeton* spp.), and water-stargrass (*Heteranthera dubia*). The ability to regulate water levels in managed marsh units has proven to be a useful tool in altering species composition and thereby increasing waterfowl food and nesting cover.

The dominant nesting waterfowl of these marshes are mallard (*Anas platyrhynchos*) (72%), black duck (*Anas rubripes*) (16%), and blue-winged teal (*Anas discors*) (9%). The adult great blue heron (*Ardea herodias*) population of these wetlands is estimated at over 3,000 birds; one rookery alone at Winous Point has 1,200 breeding pairs. Nesting bald eagles (*Haliaeetus leucocephalus*) have also been reported in this area.

The muskrat (*Ondatra zibethicus*) is the most important furbearer and receives the greatest trapping pressure in these wetlands. During the November-March trapping season, over 5,000 muskrats are taken each year from the Winous Point Marsh (northwest shore of Sandusky Bay). Other marsh mammals trapped for their pelts include raccoon (*Procyon lotor*), opossum (*Didelphis virginiana*), mink (*Mustela vison*), and red fox (*Vulpes vulpes*).

The marshes at the eastern end of Sandusky Bay are considerably different. They are not protected by dikes but rather, they benefit from the natural protection provided by the sand spits at the entrance of Sandusky Bay. The mouth of the bay is an area of converging along-shore currents. One set of currents has built Bay Point spit in a south-easterly direction and another set has constructed Cedar Point spit in a northwesterly direction. These two spits are now separated by the 40 ft (13 m) deep Moseley Channel. The tip of Bay Point is accreting at a rate of 10 ft (2 m) per year, but further growth of Cedar Point has been halted by the construction of a 1.6 mi (2.6 km) long jetty at the tip to keep the channel open for navigation.

Wetlands and open ponds occupy depressions between sand ridges on both of these spits. Bay Point wetlands are relatively undisturbed. Although privately owned, the fine beaches are open to the public for swimming and camping. Cedar Point wetlands were probably similar to those of Presque Isle, but they have since been modified to accommodate a major amusement park. The Cedar Point sand spit also provides natural protection for marshes which have developed between Big Island (near the mouth of Pipe Creek within the city of Sandusky) and Sawmill Creek at the base of the spit. These marshes are typically dominated by cattails (*Typha* spp.) and spatterdock (*Nuphar advena*).

Similar wetlands can be found at East Harbor State Park. In the shallow depression between Marblehead Peninsula and Catawba Island (also a peninsula), sand spits have formed lagoons known as West Harbor, Middle Harbor, and East Harbor. Marine and residential development have highly altered both West and East Harbors, but Middle Harbor (within the State Park) still offers the visitor an excellent opportunity to view lush growth of vascular aquatic plants and the animals of a balanced marsh community.

Old Woman Creek

Old Woman Creek wetland occupies the lower estuarine portion of the stream. It is separated from Lake Erie by a narrow barrier beach at the stream mouth. The wetland is mostly non-wooded, with emergent and floating-leaf plants bordered by a mixed hardwood forest on the steep banks. Located east of Huron, Ohio near the southernmost point of the Great Lakes, this beautiful natural area was designated, in 1977, as the first National Estuarine Sanctuary on the Great Lakes. The sanctuary is operated by the Ohio Department of Natural Resources with support from the National Oceanic and Atmospheric Administration. A visitors' center and natural trails are open to the public. Portions of the sanctuary are reserved for the use of wetland researchers.

Within the Old Woman Creek wetland, four aquatic habitats can be found: (1) open water, (2) shoreline, (3) embayment marshes, and (4) mud flats. Common vascular aquatic plants occurring in the open water include yellow water lily (*Nelumbo lutea*), spatterdock (*Nuphar advena*), arrow arum (*Peltandra virginica*), coontail (*Ceratophyllum demersum*), pondweed (*Potamogeton* spp.), and duckweed (*Lemna minor*). The shoreline habitat features buttonbush (*Cephalanthus occidentalis*), rough leaf dogwood (*Cornus drummondi*), blue flag (*Iris versicolor*), and arrowhead (*Sagittaria latifolia*). Embayment marshes, which have been reduced in size due to high lake levels since 1972, are characterized by river bulrush (*Scirpus fluviatilis*), giant bur reed (*Sparganium eurycarpum*), cattail (*Typha latifolia*), and lizard's tail (*Saururus cernuus*). In mid-summer the mud flats are marked by marsh-mallow (*Hibiscus palustris*) and water smartweed (*Polygonum coccineum*).

Mentor Marsh

This wetland is primarily a swamp forest lying approximately 0.6 mi (1 km) inland from Lake Erie near Painesville, Ohio. This sinuous, 4.3 mi (7.2 km) long wetland owes its origin to Lake Erie shore erosion. The wetland lies in the former bed and flood plain of the Grand River. Several hundred years ago, as the lake shore gradually retreated landward under the pressure of wave attack, the loop nearest the shore eventually broke through, allowing the river to flow directly into Lake Erie near its present mouth at Fairport Harbor. With the full flow of water cut off, the remaining western portion of the river bed gradually filled with vegetation to form Mentor Marsh (Figure 5.57).

Mentor Marsh winds southwest from Headland Beach State Park to Mentor Harbor covering an area of 870 acres (3.5 km²). The natural lagoon at the west end (Mentor Harbor) has been dredged to form a marina and yacht club. Shipman Pond at the northeast end is one of the few open water reaches of the wetland; it lies within the State Park and is open to visitors. One of the finest bathing beaches on Lake Erie is located north of the pond where the lake cut the meander of the old river valley.

Presently, Mentor Marsh is dominated by cattails (*Typha angustifolia*, *T. latifolia*) and reed grass (*Phragmites communis*) and has low wooded banks. The swamp forest, composed of an elm-ash-maple community (*Ulmus rubra*, *Fraxinus americana*, *Acer rubrum*), has been reduced in size in the past few decades due to flooding and possibly effluents from brine wells and salt mine wastes.

Over 90 species of birds including the endangered bald eagle (*Haliaeetus leucocephalus*), sharp-shinned hawk (*Accipiter striatus*), and king rail (*Rallus elegans*), and 20 species of mammals have been observed in Mentor Marsh. The muskrat (*Ondatra zibethicus*) and short-tailed shrew (*Blarina brevicauda*) are the most common furbearers. The most abundant reptiles are the northern water snake (*Natrix s. sipedon*), snapping turtle (*Chelydra serpentina*), and midland painted turtle (*Chrysemys picta marginata*).

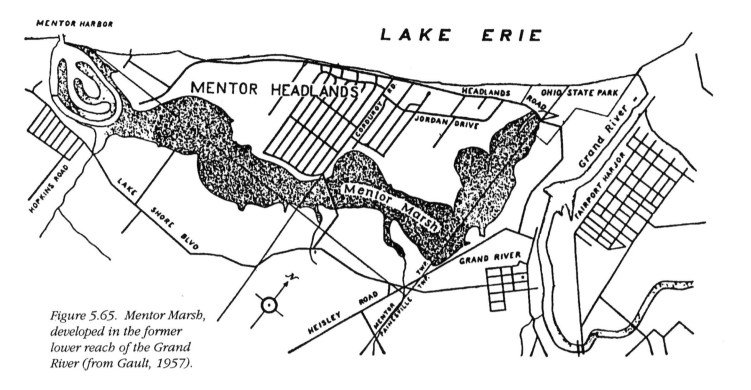

Figure 5.65. Mentor Marsh, developed in the former lower reach of the Grand River (from Gault, 1957).

Presque Isle Lagoons

Presque Isle peninsula is a hook-shaped sand spit that extends 6 mi (10 km) into Lake Erie offshore of the city of Erie, Pennsylvania. There are four major and several minor beach ridges or dunes extending east-west across the peninsula. They rise to an average height of 20 ft (6 m) above the lake; wetlands occupy the shallow depressions between these ridges. The complex interaction of waves and alongshore currents coupled with a progressive northeast growth of the spit have produced a clockwise rotation of ages for the wetland lagoons (successively younger ponds are continually being formed to the northeast of older lagoon ponds).

The major species composition of the wetlands vegetation on Presque Isle follows a successional pattern related to the age of the lagoons (Figure 5.52). As ponds are formed, cottonwood (*Populus deltoides*) and willows (*Salix* sp.) become established along the ridges which define the pond. Stonewort (*Chara* sp.) is the dominant aquatic species in this early stage. Within 3-5 years, the stoneworts are characteristic of the open water habitat, while narrow-leaved cattail (*Typha angustifolia*) is dominant among emergent vegetation. Within 10 years, the stoneworts are replaced by higher plants such as water milfoil (*Myriophyllum*) and coontail (*Ceratophyllum*). Floating-leaved plants generally do not appear for another 30-40 years. Major floating-leaved species include water shield (*Brasenia schreiberi*), pond weed (*Potamogeton* sp.), and yellow water lily (*Nuphar advena*). Major emergent species in addition to cattail include American bulrush (*Scirpus americanus*), soft-stem bulrush (*Scirpus validus*), rush (*Juncus* sp.), and spike rush (*Eleocharis* sp.). As filling of these ponds proceeds, more drought-tolerant species such as blue-joint grass (*Calamagrostis canadensis*) succeed the emergent vegetation. Ponds in very late stages of succession are characterized by an increasing encroachment by such terrestrial species as black oak (*Quercus velutina*), sugar maple (*Acer saccharum*), white pine (*Pinus strobus*) and wild cherry (*Prunus* sp.).

The Presque Isle wetlands are within Presque Isle State Park where recreational activities include hiking, picnicking, swimming, boating and fishing. This park is a popular location for observing migratory waterfowl. Misery Bay on Presque Isle was used by Commodore Oliver H. Perry during the War of 1812 as a base for building the American fleet which defeated the British near Put-in-Bay (September 10, 1813) for control of the Great Lakes.

Long Point

This point is the most massive accumulation of sand along the shore of Lake Erie. This 20 mi (32 km) long spit projects in an easterly direction for the north shore at the junction of the lake's central and eastern basins. Interestingly, it is being built out into the deepest part of the lake. Only a short distance from the tip, the lake reached its maximum depth of 210 ft (64 m). Long Point and nearby Turkey Point provide a sheltered environment in Long Point Bay which has fostered the development of magnificent wetlands. The formation of the Long Point peninsula itself, as a series of dune ridges and intervening lagoons, has also yielded a series of magnificent and varied marsh habitats. Long Point Provincial Park is located at the base of the peninsula. Northward, to the town of Port Rowan, the Ontario Ministry of Natural Resources manages an open marsh known as Long Point Crown Marsh. The marshes at the easterly end of the peninsula are privately owned by a hunting club.

Vegetation in the wetlands is highly variable and diverse, but relatively few of the species play major ecological roles. The emergent plants occur in mosaics of cattail, wild rice (*Zizania aquatica*), swamp loosestrife (*Decodon verticillatus*), water sedge (*Carex aquatilis*), or soft-stem bulrush, usually in monodominant stands of individual species. Major rooted aquatic plants with floating leaves are white water lily (*Nymphaea odorata*), spatterdock or yellow water lily and bullhead lily (*Nuphar variegatum*). The major submergent plants include water milfoil, pondweed (*Potamogeton* spp.), elodea (*Elodea*), coontail (*Ceratophyllum*), and water stargrass (*Heteranthera dubia*). All of these plants contribute to the ecological and visual vigor of the marshes.

Rondeau Bay

Rondeau Bay lies on the north shore of central Lake Erie between the town of Erieau and Rondeau Provincial Park. The bay is 6 mi (10 km) long, 3 mi (5 km) wide and fringed by extensive wetlands, particularly along its east shore. This shore is actually a peninsula, formed by a massive sandspit deposit. Over several thousand years of lake waves and currents have eroded bluffs to the east, transported the sandy material along the shore, and eventually deposited a series of parallel sand bars and intervening sloughs. The process has created one of the world's outstanding examples of a cuspate sand spit. The sandy shorelines provide habitat for sea rocket (*Caike edentula*) and clammyweed (*Polanisia dodecandra*). The swamp rose mallow (*Hibiscus palustris*) and yellow water lily are scattered throughout the cattail marshlands. In the damp forests of the sloughs, 18 species of orchids have been found, including the nodding pogonia (*Triphora trianthophora*), one of the rarest orchids in Canada. Other damp forest plants include wild yam root (*Dioscorea villosa*), yellow mandarin (*Disporum lanuginosum*), tall bellflower (*Campanula americana*), false mermaid (*Floerkea proserpina coides*), oswego tea (*Monarda didyma*), sugar maple (*Acer saccarium*), and American beech (*Fagus grandifolia*).

Rondeau is one of the best birdwatching spots in Ontario; 80% of all the species seen in the province have been recorded here. Hundreds of thousands of birds pass over the bay during their migration. The marshes and bay provide excellent locations to observe ducks, geese, swans, rails, bitterns, and herons in the spring and fall. Long before the white man came, Rondeau was well-known to the Indians for its waterfowl hunting. Today, the fall tradition is carried on in Rondeau Provincial Park at park-erected duck blinds in the marshes. Of the 323 bird species recorded for the peninsula, 124 nest here, including the rare prothonotary warbler (*Protonotaria citrea*).

Over 60 species of fish have been recorded for Rondeau Bay and the adjoining portion of Lake Erie. The most popular sport fish in the bay include yellow perch (*Perca flavescens*), largemouth bass (*Micropterus salmoides*), and sunfish (*Lepomis* spp.). Reptiles and amphibians are also plentiful—the spotted turtle (*Clemmys guttata*), Blanding's turtle (*Emydoidea blandingi*), spiny soft-shelled turtle (*Trionyx spiniferus*), and fox snake (*Elaphe vulpina*) are commonly seen in the marshes. The white-tailed deer (*Odocoileus virgianus*) is one of the most obvious of the 33 mammals inhabiting the area. A sizeable herd of deer live in Rondeau Provincial Park.

Point Pelee

Point Pelee is a massive sand spit on the north shore of Lake Erie that marks the division of the lake's western and central basins. The 5 mi (8 km) long spit is triangular in shape with an exceptionally sharp, narrow point projecting out into the lake. The spit has been formed by a convergence of alongshore currents, resulting in the deposition of sand eroded from the bluffs far to the east and west of the point. The sand bars deposited by these currents now enclose a cattail marsh of high quality. The entire spit and the 2,500 acre (10 km²) marsh lie within the boundaries of Point Pelee National Park. The park is surrounded by 14 mi (23 km) of sand and pebble beaches.

The terrain of Point Pelee is mostly marsh or woodland. The marsh contains six major open-water ponds. The largest (Big Pond) has a boardwalk nature trail constructed for the enjoyment of park visitors. Here, aquatic plants and sedges wage a constant battle with the open ponds, encroaching on them, filling the margins with a lush carpet of vegetation including cattails (*Typha* spp.), spatterdock (*Nuphar advena*), pickerel weed (*Pontederia cordata*), and marsh-mallow (*Hibiscus palustris*). Of the 600 plant species found on Point Pelee, the greatest variety can be seen along the woodland nature trail towards the southern end of the spit. Two major bird migration flyways overlap at Point Pelee. Each spring and autumn thousands of birds pass over the park. It is not uncommon for a single birdwatcher to tally more than 100 species during the height of the migration season. Of the 332 species recorded for the area, 90 remain to nest. Waterfowl and shorebirds are abundant in the marshes.

Fishing is permitted within the marsh. The most common species are sunfish (*Lepomis* spp.), yellow perch (*Perca flavescens*), northern pike (*Esox lucius*), largemouth bass (*Micropterus salmoides*), carp (*Cyprinus carpio*), and dogfish or bowfin (*Amia calva*).

Animals found nowhere else in Canada enjoy the mild climate of Point Pelee. The eastern mole (*Scalopus aquaticus*) burrows in sand dunes adjacent to the marsh ponds and the rust-brown fox squirrel (*Sciurus niger*) shares the shelter of the deciduous forest with the grey squirrel (*Sciurus carolinensis*). Raccoon (*Procyon lotor*) and mink (*Mustela vison*) can be found near the marshes where they feed on abundant creatures that thrive there. Muskrats (*Ondatra zibethicus*) build their community dwellings near the pond shores. At the edge of the forest other mammals include the eastern cottontail (*Sylvilagus floridanus*), white-tailed deer (*Odocoileus virginianus*), the white-footed mouse (*Peromyscus leucopus*), and the insectivorous, little brown bat (*Myotis lucifugus*).

Big Creek Wetlands

The wetlands at the mouth of Big Creek are located 12 mi (20 km) southeast of Amherstburg. The wetlands are largely within Holiday Beach Provincial Park and are administered by the Ontario Ministry of Natural Resources. The park, established in 1958, is green and shady with well-organized picnic grounds, camping sites and a pleasant sandy beach for summer basking. The marshland adjoining the park is a rewarding place for birdwatching (spring and fall) and waterfowl hunting (in season, late September to early December). The marsh within the park is designated as a waterfowl sanctuary while hunting is permitted in the adjacent wildlife management area. This is one of the best Canada goose (*Branta canadensis*) hunting areas in southern Ontario. During September and October, thousands of migrating hawks also congregate and move southwest along the north shore of Lake Erie. The hawks sometimes fly in "kettles," a cylindrical formation used by such species as broad-winged hawks (*Buteo platypterus*), turkey vultures (*Cathartes aura*), and red-tailed hawks (*Buteo jamaicensis*) in migration. Small mammals common to the area include muskrat (*Ondatra zibethicus*), raccoon (*Procyon lotor*), rabbit (*Sylvilagus floridanus*), and red fox (*Vulpes fulva*). A fishing pond constructed at the edge of Big Creek marsh is stocked each spring with trout. A boat launching ramp is located on Lake Erie at the west end of the bathing beach. Common fish species caught in the lake include walleye (*Stizostedion v. vitreum*), freshwater drum (*Aplodinotus grunniens*), and yellow perch (*Perca flavescens*).

References

APHA (American Public Health Association). Standard methods for examination of water and wastewater, 16th Edition. APHA, Washington, DC, 1268 pp. (1985).

Assel, R.A., F.H. Quinn, G.A. Leshkevich, and S.J. Bolsenga. Great Lakes ice atlas. NOAA, Great Lakes Environmental Research Laboratory, Ann Arbor, MI, 115 pp. (1983).

Bates, R.L., and J.A. Jackson. Glossary of geology, 2nd Edition. American Institute of Geology, Falls Church, VA, 749 pp. (1980).

Beeton, A.M. Changes in the environment and the biota of the Great Lakes. In *Eutrophication: Causes, Consequences, Correctives*. Printing and Publishing Office National Academy of Sciences, Washington, DC, 150-187 (1969).

Bird, J.M., and J.F. Dewey. Lithosphere plate-continental margin tectonics and the evolution of Appalachian orogen. Geological Society of America Bulletin 81:1031-60 (1970).

Bednarik, K.E. The muskrat in Ohio Lake Erie marshes. Ohio Department of Natural Resources, Wildlife Division, 67 pp. (1954).

Blanton, J.O., and A.R. Winklhofer. Circulation of hypolimnion water in the central basin of Lake Erie. Proceedings, 14th Conference, International Association for Great Lakes Research 14:788-798 (1971).

Blanton, J.O., and A.R. Winklhofer. Physical processes affecting the hypolimnion of the central basin of Lake Erie. In *Project Hypo*, N.M. Burns and C. Ross (Eds.). Canada Centre for Inland Waters Paper No. 6. U.S. EPA Technical Report TS-05-71-208-24, Burlington, Ontario, Canada, 9-38 (1972).

Bolsenga, S.J. River ice jams. Great Lakes Research Center, U.S. Lake Survey Research Report 5-5, U. S. Army Corps of Engineers, Detroit, MI 568 pp. (1968).

Bolsenga, S.J. Great Lakes snow depth probability charts and tables. U.S. Lake Survey Research Report 5-2, U.S. Army Corps of Engineers, Detroit, MI 40 pp (1967a).

Bolsenga, S.J. Snow depth probability in the Great Lakes basin. Proceedings, 10th Conference on Great Lakes Research, pp. 162-170 (1967b).

Bolsenga, S.J. Nearshore Great Lakes ice cover. *Cold Regions Science and Technology* 15:99-105 (1988a).

Bolsenga, S.J., G.M. Green, and K. Hinkel. Nearshore Great Lakes ice statistics. NOAA TM ERL GLERL-69 (PB89-100192/XAB), 42 pp. (1988b).

Brant, R.A., and C.E. Herdendorf. Delineation of Great Lakes estuaries. Proceedings, 15th Conference, International Association for Great Lakes Research 15:710-718 (1972).

Buck, M.W. In ponds and streams. Abingdon Press, Nashville, TN, 72 pp. Copyright renewal © 1983 by Margaret Waring Buck. Illustration used by permission of the Publisher, Abingdon Press (1955).

Burns, N.M. Erie the lake that survived. Rowman and Allanheld Publishing, Totowa, NJ, 320 pp. (1985).

Burns, N.M. and C. Ross (eds.). *Project Hypo*: An Intensive Study of Lake Erie Central Basin Hypolimnion and Related Surface Water Phenomena. Canada Centre for Inland Waters, Paper No. 6 and U.S. Environmental Protection Agency Technical Report TS-05-71-208-24, 182 pp. (1972).

Burt, W.H. Mammals of the Great Lakes region. University of Michigan Press, Ann Arbor, 246 pp. (1972).

Campbell, L.W. Birds of Lucas County. Toledo Museum Science Bulletin 1(1):1-225 (1940).

Campbell, L.W. The Lake Erie marshes in Ohio between Toledo and Port Clinton. Unpublished manuscript, 234 pp. (1982).

Carlson, R.E. (ed.). Shore Use and Erosion. Great Lakes Basin Commission Framework Study, Appendix 12, 111 pp. (1975).

Carman, J.E. The geological interpretation of scenic features in Ohio. *Ohio Journal of Science* 46(5):241-283. (1946).

Caskey, J.E. An investigation of the meteorological conditions associated with extreme wind tides on Lake Erie. *Monthly Weather Review* 90:39-47 (1962).

Chapman, L.J., and D.F. Putnam. The physiography of southern Ontario, Third Edition. Ontario Geological Survey, Special Volume 2, Ontario Ministry of Natural Resources, Ontario, Canada, 270 pp. (1984).

Coakley, J.P. Nearshore sediment studies in western Lake Erie. Proceedings, 15th Conference, International Association for Great Lakes Research 15:330-343 (1972).

Cole, G.A. Textbook of limnology, 3rd Edition. C.V. Mosby Co., St. Louis, MO, 401 pp. Reproduced by permission (1983).

Cooper, C.L., and C.E. Herdendorf. Resources of the Lake Erie Islands region. Ohio Department of Natural Resources, Water Division, 222 pp. (1977).

Cooper, G.P. Fish fauna and fishing of the Detroit River in the vicinity of Sugar and Stony Islands. Michigan Department of Natural Resources, Inssitute for Fisheries Research, Report No. 1350, Lansing, 37 pp. (1952).

Coordinating Committee on Great Lakes Basic Hydraulic and Hydrologic Data. Coordinated Great Lakes physical data. Detroit, MI and Cornwall, Ontario, Canada, 30 pp. (1977).

Crowe, R.B., G.A. McKay, and W.M. Baker. The tourist and outdoor recreation climate of Ontario, Volume 1: Objectives and definitions of seasons, 70 pp.; Volume 3: The winter season, 249 pp. Department of Fisheries and Environment, Atmospheric Environment Service (1977).

Dabberdt, W.F. Weather for outdoorsmen. Scirbner, New York, 240 pp. (1981).

Derecki, J.A. Evaporation from Lake Erie. NOAA TR ERL 342-GLERL 3. National Technical Information Service, Springfield, VA, 84 pp. (1975).

Derecki, J.A. Evaporation from Lake St. Clair. NOAA TM ERL GLERL-23. National Technical Information Service, Springfield, VA, 34 pp. (1978).

Dingman, J.S., and K.W. Bedford. The Lake Erie response to the 26 January 1978 cyclone. *Journal of Geophysical Reserach* 89(c4):6427-6445 (1984).

Dorr, J.A., and D. F. Eschman. Geology of Michigan. University of Michigan Press, Ann Arbor, 476 pp. (1970).

Duane, D.B. Character of the sediment load in the St. Clair River. Proceedings, 10th Conference, International Association for Great Lakes Research 10:115-132 (1969).

Dunbar, C.O. Geology, 2nd Edition. 500 pp. Copyright © 1949 by John Wiley and Sons, New York. Reprinted with permission. (1960).

Eagleman, J.R. Severe and unusual weather. Van Nos Reinhold, New York, 372 pp. (1983).

Edmondson, W.T. (ed.). Fresh-Water Biology. Second Edition, John Wiley & Sons, Inc., New York (1963).

Eichenlaub, V.L. Weather and climate of the Great Lakes region. University of Notre Dame Press, South Bend, IN, 335 pp. (1979). Illustrations reprinted by permission.

Fassett, N.C. A manual of aquatic plants. 403 pp. Copyright © Board of Regents of the University of Wisconsin System and the permission of the University of Wisconsin Press, Madison, WI. (1940).

Federal Water Pollution Control Administration. Lake Erie environmental summary 1963-1964. U.S. Department of the Interior, FWPCA, Great Lakes Region, 170 pp. (1968).

Feldmann, R.M., A.H. Coogan, and R.A. Heimlich. Field guide to southern Great Lakes. 214 pp. Copyright © 1977 Kendall/Hunt Publishng Company, Dubuque, IA, Reprinted with permission. (1977).

Fenneman, N.M. Physiography of eastern United States. McGraw-Hill, New York, 714 pp. (1938).

Fish, C.J. Limnological survey of eastern and central Lake Erie, 1928-1029. U.S. Fish and Wildlife Service Special Science Report Fisheries 334, 198 pp. (1960).

Flint, R.F. Glacial and quaternary geology. John Wiley and Sons, New York, 892 pp. (1971).

Forsyth, J.L., and D.R. Sparling. Geology of the Lake Erie Islands and adjacent shores. Michigan Basin Geological Society, 63 pp. (1971).

Foulds, D.M. Niagara River ice control. Proceedings, 24th Eastern Snow Conference, Niagara Falls, Ontario, Canada, 19 pp. (1967).

Gault, H.J. History of Mentor Headlands and vicinity, Lake County, Ohio. North Mentor Service Circle, Neal Printing Company, Fairport Harbor, OH, 52 pp. (1957).

Gedney, R.T., and W. Lick. Wind-driven currents in Lake Erie. *Journal of Geophysical Research* 77(15):2714-2723. Copyright by the American Geophysical Union (1972).

Geffen, A.M. A birdwatcher's guide to the eastern United States. Barron's, Woodbury, NY, 346 pp. (1978).

Goldthwait, R.P., G.W. White, and J.L. Forsyth. Glacial map of Ohio. U.S. Geological Survey, Miscellaneous Invest. Map I-316 (1961).

Goldthwait, R.P., A. Dreimanis, J.C. Forsyth, P.F. Karrow, and G.W. White. Pleistocene deposits of the Erie Lobe. In *The Quaternary of the United States,* H.E. Wright and D.G. Frey, (eds.). Princeton University Press, Princeton, NJ, 85-97. Copyright © 1965 by Princeton University Press. Reprinted/reproduced by permission of Princeton University Press (1965).

Goodwin, C.E. A bird finding guide to Ontario. University of Toronto Press, Toronto, Ontario, Canada, 248 pp. (1982).

Goodyear, C.D., T.A. Edsall, D.M. Dempsey, G.D. Moss, and P.E. Polanski. Atlas of the spawning and nursery areas of Great Lakes fishes, Volume 9: Lake Erie. U.S. Fish & Wildlife Service FWS/OBS-82/52, 192 pp. (1982).

Grabau, A.W. Niagara Falls and vicinity. Bulletin NY State Museum 45:37-54. (1901).

Grumblatt, J.L. Great Lakes water temperatures, 1966-75. NOAA TM ERL GLERL-11-1. National Technical Information Service, Springfield, VA, 127 pp. (1976).

Hamblin, P.F. Circulation and water movement in Lake Erie. Inland Waters Branch, Department of Energy, Mines, and Resources, Ottawa, Ontario Science Series No. 7, 49 pp. (1971).

Hamblin, P.F. Great Lakes storm surge of April 6, 1979. *Journal of Great Lakes Research* 5:312-315 (1979).

Hartley, R.P. Glacial lake stage in the Lake Erie basin. Ohio Department of Natural Resources, Division of Shore Erosion Manuscript Report, 25 pp. (1960).

Hartley, R.P. Bottom sediments in the island area of Lake Erie. Ohio Department of Natural Resources, Shore Erosion Division Technical Report 5, 79 pp. (1961).

Hartman, W.L. Effects of exploitation, environmental changes, and new species on the fish habitats and resources of Lake Erie. Great Lakes Fishery Commission Technical Report-22 (1973).

Herdendorf, C.E. Sedimentation studies in the south shore reef area of western Lake Erie. Proceedings, 11th Conference, International Association for Great Lakes Research, 11:188-205 (1968).

Herdendorf, C.E. Shoreline changes on Lakes Erie and Ontario with special reference to currents, sediment transport, and shore erosion. *Bulletin of the Buffalo Society of Natural Sciences* 25(3):43-76 (1975).

Herdendorf, C.E., and L.L. Braidech. Physical characteristics of the reef area of western Lake Erie. Ohio Department of Natural Resources, Division of Geological Survey Report Invest. 82, 90 pp. (1972).

Herdendorf, C.E., S.M. Hartley, and M.D. Barnes, (Eds.). Fish and wildlife resources of the Great Lakes coastal wetlands within the United States. Volume 1: Overview, Volume 2: Lake Ontario, Volume 3: Lake Erie, Volume 4: Lake Huron. U.S. Fish and Wildlife Service, Washington, DC, FWS/81/02-v1,v2,v3,v4 (1981).

Hobson, G.D., C.E. Herdendorf, and C.M.F. Lewis. High resolution reflection seismic survey in western Lake Erie. Proceedings, 12th Conference, International Association for Great Lakes Research 12:210-224 (1969).

Hotchkiss, N. Common marsh, underwater, and floating-leaved plants of the United States and Canada. Dover Publications, New York, 124 pp. (1972).

Hough, J.L. Geology of the Great Lakes. University of Illinois Press, Urbana, 313 pp. (1958).

Hough, J.L. The prehistoric Great Lakes of North America. *Amercan Scientist* 51:84-109 (1963).

Hubbard, G.D. Pre-cambrian in Ohio. *Ohio Journal of Science* 32:473-480 (1983).

Hunt, C.B. Natural regions of the United States and Canada. W.H. Freeman, San Francisco, CA, 725 pp. (1974).

Hunt, I.A. Winds, wind set-ups and seiches on Lake Erie. U.S. Lake Survey Research Report No. 1-2. U.S. Army Corps of Engineers, Detroit, MI, 58 pp. (1959).

Ibrahim., K.A., and J.A. McCorquodale. Finite element circulation model for Lake St. Clair. *Journal of Great Lakes Research* 11(3):208-222 (1985).

International Great Lakes Level Board. Regulation of Great Lakes water levels: Appendix D: Fish, Wildlife, and Recreation, 171 pp. (1973).

International Joint Commission. Great Lakes diversions and consumptive uses. International Joint Commission, Washington, DC and Ottawa, Ontario, Canada (1985).

Jacobs, C.A., J.P. Pandolfo, and E.J. Aubert. Characteristics of national data bouy systems: their impact on data use and measurement of natural phenomena. Travelers Research Center Report 7493-334, pp. 32-33 (1968).

Jaworski, E. and C.N. Raphael. Fish, wildlife, and recreational values of Michigan's coastal wetlands. Michigan Department of Natural Resources, Lansing, 209 pp. (1978).

Juday, C. The summer standing crop of plants and animals in four Wisconsin lakes. Transactions Wisconsin Academy Science, Arts, and Letters, 34:103-135 (1943).

Jennings, D.E. Peregrinating Presque Isle. *Carnegie Magazine* 4(6):171-175 (1930).

Kaatz, M.R. The black swamp: a study in historical geography. *Annals of the Association of American Geographers* 35(1):1-35 (1955).

Kemp, A.L., G.A. MacInnis, and N.S. Harper. Sedimentation rates and a revised sediment budget for Lake Erie. *Journal of Great Lakes Research* 3(3):221-233 (1977).

Kemp, A.L., R.L. Thomas, C.I. Dell, and J.M. Jaquet. Cultural impact on the geochemistry of sediments of Lake Erie. *Journal of the Fisheries Research Board of Canada* 33:440-462 (1976).

Kennett, J.P. Marine geology. Prentice-Hall, Englewood Cliffs, NJ, 813 pp. (1982).

Kessler, E. (ed.). Thunderstorms: A social, scientific, and technological documentary, Volume 1: The thunderstorm in human affairs. Environmental Research Laboratories, National Oceanic and Atmospheric Administration, Boulder, CO, 206 pp. (1981).

Klotts, E.B. The new field book of freshwater life. Putnam's Sons, New York, 398 pp. (1966).

Kormondy, E.J. Comparative ecology of sandspit ponds. *American Midland Naturalist* 82(1):28-61 (1969).

Kormondy, E.J. Concepts of ecology, 3rd Edition, 214 pp. Copyright © 1984 Prentice Hall, Inc., Englewood Cliffs, NJ. Reprinted by permission of Prentice Hall, Inc. (1984).

Kotsch, W.J. Weather for the mariner, 3rd Edition. Naval Institute Press, Annapolis, MD, 315 pp. (1983).

La Rocque, A., and M.F. Marple. Ohio fossils. Ohio Department of Natural Resources, Geological Survey Division Bulletin 54, 150 pp. (1955).

Langlois, T.H. Western end of Lake Erie and its ecology. J.W. Edwards Publishing, Ann Arbor, MI, 479 pp. (1954).

Leverett, F. and F.B. Taylor. The Pleistocene of Indiana and Michigan and the history of the Great Lakes. U.S. Geological Survey Mon. 53, 529 pp. (1915).

Lewis, T., and C.E. Herdendorf. Sedimentology of the Great Lakes. In *Limnology of Lakes and Embayments*, A. Pinsak, (ed.). Great Lakes Framework Study, Great Lakes Basin Commission (1974).

Lincoln, F.C. Migration of birds. U.S. Fish & Wildlife Service Circ. 16. 102 pp. (1950).

List, R.J. 1951. Smithsonian meteorological tables. The Smithsonian Institute, Washington, DC, 527 pp. (1951).

Lobeck, A.K. Geomorphology. McGraw Hill, New York, 731 pp. (1939).

Lowden, R.M. Vascular flora of Winous Point, Ottawa and Sandusky Counties, Ohio. *Ohio Journal of Science* 69:257-284 (1969).

Lundquist, J.B. A primer of limnology. University of Minnesota, Water Resources Research Center, Public Rep. Ser. No. 1., 27 pp. (1975).

Lucy, J.T., T. Rittern, and J. Larue. The Chesapeake: A boating guide to weather. Virginia Sea Grant Marine Advisory Services and National Weather Service, National Oceanic and Atmospheric Administration Educ. Series No. 25, 22 pp. (1977).

Marshall, J.H., and R.L. Stuckey. Aquatic vascular plants and their distribution in the Old Woman Creek Estuary, Erie County, Ohio. Center for Lake Erie Area Research, Ohio State University, Columbus, 53 pp. (1974).

McMurray, J., and M. Sillars. Weather for Great Lakes sailors. Commerical Weather Services, Flint, MI, 20 pp. (1980).

Melvin, R.W. A guide to Ohio outdoor education areas, 2nd Edition. Ohio Department of Natural Resources and Ohio Academy of Science (1974).

Mortimer, C.M. Lake Erie (1929-1978): Fifty years of physical limnology. *Journal of Great Lakes Research* 13(4):407-435 (1987).

National Climatic Center. Summary of synoptic meteorological observations for Great Lakes areas, Volume 1: Lake Ontario and Lake Erie. National Oceanic and Atmospheric Administration, 101 pp. (1975).

Nilsson, T. The Pleistocene: geology and life in the Quaternary ice age. Verlag, Stuttgart, 651 pp. (1983).

Odum, E.P. Fundamentals of ecology. Saunders Publishing, Philadelphia, PA, 574 pp. (1971).

Ohio Department of Natural Resources. Sand dredging areas in Lake Erie. Division of Shore Erosion Technical Report No. 5, 79 pp. (1960).

Ohio Department of Natural Resources. Ohio state parks, the visitor's guide. ODNR, Division of Parks and Wildlife, Columbus, 24 pp. (1982).

Olmstead, L.W. Report on ice jam - Niagara River 1955. U.S. Army Corps of Engineers, Buffalo, NY, 5 pp. (1955).

Panel on Niagara River Ice Boom Investigations, Water Science and Technology Board, Commission on Physical Science, Mathematics, and Resources National Research Council. The Lake Erie-Niagara River ice boom: Operation and impacts. National Academy Press, Washington, DC, 74 pp. (1983).

Pennak, R.W. Fresh-water invertebrates of the United States, 2nd Edition. 803 pp. Copyright © 1978 John Wiley & Sons, New York. Reprinted by permission of John Wiley and Sons, Inc. (1978).

Pepper, J.F., W. de Witt, and D.F. Demarest. Geology of the Bedford Shale and Berea Sandstone in the Appalachian basin. U.S. Geological Survey Prof. Paper 259 (1954).

Peterson, R.T. A field guide to the birds east of the Rockies. Houghton Mifflin, Boston, MA, 384 pp. (1980).

Pettingill, O.S. Ornithology in laboratory and field, 4th Edition. Burgess Publishing Company, Minneapolis, MN, 524 pp. (1970).

Phillips, D.W., and J.A. McCulloch. The climate of the Great Lakes basin. Climatological Study No. 20., Environment Canada, Atmospheric Environment, Toronto, Ontario, Canada, 40 pp. (1972).

Pincus, H.J. Engineering geology of the Ohio shoreline of Lake Erie. Ohio Department of Natural Resources, Shore Erosion Division, No. 7, Sheet G (1960).

Platzman, G.W. and D.B. Rao. The free oscillations of Lake Erie. In *Studies on Oceanography*, Hidaka volume, K. Yoshida (ed.). Tokyo University Press, Tokyo (1964).

Pond, C.R. The moderating effect of Lake Huron on shoreline temperatures. Canada Department of Transportation, Met. Branch, CIR-4016, TEC-514, 1964.

Pore, N.A., H.P. Perotti, and W.S. Richardson. Climatology of Lake Erie storm surges at Buffalo and Toledo. NOAA TM NWS TDL-54. Techniques Development Laboratory, Silver Spring, MD, 27 pp. (1975).

Pospichal, L.B. Preliminary management plan for St. Clair Flats Wildlife Area. Michigan Department of Natural Resources, Lansing, 17 pp. (1977).

Pratley, P.L. Collapse of Falls View bridge. *Engineering Journal* 21(8):375-381 (1938).

Prescott, G.W. How to know the aquatic plants. William C. Brown Company, Dubuque, IA, 171 pp. (1969).

Quinn, F.H. Quantitative dynamic mathematical models for Great Lakes research. Ph.D. dissertation, University of Michigan, Ann Arbor, 127 pp. (1971).

Quinn, F.H. Effects of ice retardation on Great Lakes water levels. Proceedings, 16th Conference, International Association for Great Lakes Research, 16:549-555 (1973).

Quinn, F.H., and B. Guerra. Current perspectives on the Lake Erie water balance. *Journal of Great Lakes Research* 12(2):109-116 (1986).

Quinn, F.H., and R.N. Kelley. Great Lakes monthly hydrologic data. NOAA Data Report ERL GLERL-26. National Technical Information Service, Springfield, VA, 79 pp. (1983).

Raphael, C.N., and E. Jaworski. The St. Clair River Delta, a unique lake delta. *Geographical Bulletin* 21(2):7-28 (1982).

Rawinski, T., R. Malecki, and L. Mudrak. A guide to plants commonly found in the freshwater wetlands of New York. Cornell University Department of Natural Resources, Ithaca, NY, 27 pp. (1979).

Rawson, D.S. Some physical and chemical factors in the metabolism of lakes. *Science* 10:9-26. Copyright © AAAS (1939).

Resio, D.T., and C.L. Vincent. Design wave information for the Great Lakes, Lake Erie. U.S. Army Engineer Waterways Experiment Station Technical Report H-76-1-1, 148 pp. (1976).

Richardson, W.S., and D.J. Schwab. Comparison and verification of dynamical and statistical Lake Erie storm surge forecasts. NOAA TM NWS TDL-69, Techniques Development Laboratory, Silver Spring, MD, 19 pp. (1979).

Rondy, D.R. Great Lakes ice cover. In *Limnology of Lakes and Embayments,* Great Lakes Basin Framework Study, Appendix 4: Section 5. Great Lakes Basin Commission, Ann Arbor, MI, 105-117 (1976).

Ross, H.H. Enchanting isles of Lake Erie. H.H. Ross Publication, Toledo, OH, 80 pp. (1949).

Ruffner, J.A., and F.E. Bair (eds.). The weather almanac, 2nd Edition. Gale Publishing, Detroit, MI, 728 pp. (1977).

Saylor, J.H., and G.S. Miller. Investigations of the currents and density structure of Lake Erie. NOAA TM ERL GLERL-49. National Technical Information Service, Springfield, VA, 80 pp. (1983).

Saylor, J.H., and G.S. Miller. Studies of lake-scale currents and temperature distributions. In *Technical Assessment Team Report on the 1978-79 Lake Erie Intensive Study*, D.E. Rathke (ed.). Ohio State University, Columbus, 39 pp. (1984).

Schaefer, V.J., and J.A. Day. A field guide to the atmosphere. Houghton Mifflin, Boston, MA, 359 pp. (1981).

Scharf, W.C., et al. Nesting and migration areas of birds of the U.S. Great Lakes (30 April to 23 August, 1976). 113 pp. and appendices (1979).

Schertzer, W.M., J.H. Saylor, F.M. Boyce, D.G. Robertson, and F. Rosa. Seasonal thermal cycle of Lake Erie. *Journal of Great Lakes Research* 13(4):468-486 (1987).

Schwab, D.J. Simulation and forecasting of Lake Erie storm surges. *Monthly Weather Review* 106:1476-1487 (1978).

Scott, S. (ed.). Field guide to the birds of North America. National Geographic Society, Washington, DC, 464 pp. (1983).

Shafiqur Rahman, K.H. Analysis of wind set-ups on Lake St. Clair. M.S. Thesis, University of Windsor, Department of Geography, Windsor, Ontario, Canada, 113 pp. (1974).

Sleator, F.E. Ice thickness and stratigraphy at nearshore locations on the Great Lakes. NOAA DR ERL GLERL-1-1, National Technical Information Service, Springfield, VA, 434 pp. (1978).

Sloane, E. Erie Sloane's almanac and weather forecaster. Duell, Sloan, and Pearce, New York, 168 pp. (1955).

Sly, P.G. Lake Erie and its basin. *Journal of the Fisheries Research Board of Canada* 33:355-370 (1976).

Spencer, J.W. Origin of the basins of the Great Lakes of America. *American Geologist* Feb:86-97 (1891).

Spencer, J.W. Relationship of the Great Lakes basin to the Niagara Limestone. *Bulletin of the Geological Society of America* 24:229-232 (1913).

Stansbery, D.H. The Unioninae (Mollusca, Pelecypoda, Naiadacea) of Fishery Bay, South Bass Island, Lake Erie. Ph.D. Dissertation, Ohio State University, Columbus, 216 pp. (1960).

Strahler, A.N. The earth sciences. Harper and Row, New York, 824 pp. (1971).

Stout, W., K. Ver Steeg, and G.F. Lamb. Geology of water in Ohio. Ohio Geological Survey Bulletin 44, 694 pp. (1943).

Strahler, A.N. The earth sciences. Harper and Row, New York, 824 pp. (1971).

Stuckey, R.L. The decline of lake plants. *Natural History* 87(7):66-69 (1978).

Sumich, J.L. An introduction to the biology of marine life, 3rd Edition, 359 pp. Copyright © 1976, 1980, 1984 William C. Brown Publishers, Dubuque, IA. All rights reserved. Reprinted by permission. (1984).

Terasmae J., and A. Dreimanis. Quaternary stratigraphy of southern Ontario. In *Quaternary Stratigraphy of North America*, W.C. Mahoney, (ed.). Dowden, Hutchinson and Ross, Stroudsburg, PA, 51-63 (1976).

Thomas, R.L., and J.M. Jaquet. Mercury in the surficial sediments of Lake Erie. *Journal of the Fisheries Research Board of Canada* 33:404-412 (1976).

Thomas, R.L., J.M. Jaquet, and A.L. Kemp. Surficial sediments of Lake Erie. *Journal of the Fisheries Research Board of Canada* 33:385-403 (1976).

Thomson, T. Birding in Ohio. Indiana University Press, Bloomington, 256 pp. (1983).

Thornbury, W.D. Regional geomorphology of the United States. 609 pp. Copyright © 1965 John Wiley and Sons, Inc. Reprinted by permission. (1965).

Trautman, M.B. Fishes of Ohio. 2nd Edition. Ohio State University Press, Columbus, 782 pp. (1981).

Verber, J.L. Bottom deposits of western Lake Erie. Ohio Department of Natural Resources, Shore Erosion Division Technical Report 4, 4 pp. (1957).

Verber, J.L. Current profiles to depth in Lake Michigan. Proceedings, 8th Conference, International Association for Great Lakes Research 8:364-371 (1965).

Verber, J.L. Inertial currents in the Great Lakes. Proceedings, 9th Conference, International Association for Great Lakes Research 9:375-379 (1966).

Verber, J.L., and D.H. Stansbery. Caves in the Lake Erie islands. *Ohio Journal of Science* 53(6):356-362 (1953).

Verduin, J. Changes in western Lake Erie during the period 1948-1962. *Verhandlugen Internationale Vereinigung Fur Theoretische und Angewandte Limnologie* 15:639-644 (1964).

Verduin, J. Man's influence on Lake Erie. *Ohio Journal of Science* 69(2):65-70 (1969).

Walters, C.J., T.L. Kovack, and C.E. Herdendorf. Mercury occurrence in sediment cores from western Lake Erie. *Ohio Journal of Science* 74(1):1-19 (1974).

Watts, A. Instant weather forecasting. Dodd, New York, 64 pp. (1978).

Webb, M.S. Surface temperatures of Lake Erie. *Water Resources Research* 10:199-210 (1974).

Welch, P.S. Limnology, 2nd Edition. McGraw-Hill, New York, 538 pp. (1952).

Wetzel, R.G. Limnology. W.B. Saunders Company, Philadelphia, PA, 743 pp. (1975).

Whelpey, D.A. Weather, water and boating. Arnell Maritime, Centerville, MD, 151 pp. (1961).

White, G.W. Pleistocene stratigraphy of northern Pennsylvania. Pennsylvania Geological Survey Report G55, 88 pp. (1969).

Wilson, J., and L.J. Walters. Sediment-water-biomass interactions of toxic metals in the western basin, Lake Erie. Center for Lake Erie Area Research Technical Report 96. Ohio State University, Columbus, 113 pp. (1978).

Wilson, J.W. and D.M. Pollock. Precipitation. In *IFYGL - The International Field Year for the Great Lakes*. Great Lakes Environmental Research Laboratory, Ann Arbor, MI, pp. 57-78 (1981).

Glossary

ABIOTIC	Without life; non-living component of the environment.
ADVECTION FOG	A fog formed by the slow passage of relatively warm, moist, and stable air over a cool surface, often associated with cool lake water in the spring
AIR MASS	A body of air in which horizontal gradients of temperature and humidity are relatively slight and which is separated from an adjacent body of air by a more or less sharply defined transition zone (front) in which the gradients are relatively sharp.
ALONGSHORE CURRENT	Littoral current; a current caused by the approach of waves to a coast at an angle, producing flow parallel to and near to the shore.
ALTOSTRATUS	Layered or sheet clouds, grayish or bluish color, fibrous or uniform in appearance that can totally cover the sky.
ANOXIC	Without oxygen; anaerobic.
ANTICLINE	A fold in rock strata which is convex upward and which contains a core of stratigraphically older rocks.
ANTICYCLONE	Atmospheric pressure distribution in which there is a high central pressure relative to the surroundings, resulting in clockwise winds spiraling away from the center (see HIGH).
AQUATIC ECOLOGY	The study of the relationships between aquatic organisms and their environment, including associated organisms (see LIMNOLOGY).
ARCH	A broad, gentle, anticlinal fold on a regional scale, often the result of basement rock doming (e.g. Cincinnati Arch).
ATMOSPHERE	Envelope of air which surrounds the earth, consisting principally of a mixture of gases (oxygen 21%, nitrogen 78%, and carbon dioxide 0.03%).
AUTOTROPH	An organism capable of manufacturing its own food from inorganic raw materials and energy (e.g. photosynthetic plants).
AVIFAUNA	Animals with the ability to fly, especially the birds of a given region.
BARRIER BEACH OR BAR	Long, narrow, sandy peninsulas, islands, or submerged bars lying parallel to shore and built up by the action of the waves, currents, and winds.

BASEMENT ROCK	The crust of the earth below sedimentary deposits; generally a complex of igneous and metamorphic rocks of Precambrian age.
BATHYMETRY	The measurement of underwater depths and the charting of the topography of lake bottoms.
BAYMOUTH BAR	A sedimentary bar, usually sand or gravel, extending partly or entirely across the mouth of a bar or cove.
BEACH BERM	A nearly horizontal part of the beach backshore formed by deposition of material from storm waves; some beaches have several berm terraces.
BEAUFORT SCALE	A numerical scale for estimating wind force ranging from 0 (calm) to 12 (hurricane).
BEDLOAD	The sediment material transported along the bottom of a stream or lake.
BENTHIC	Pertaining to the bottom of aquatic habitats and the organisms that inhabit the bottoms.
BENTHOS	Bottom-dwelling aquatic plants and animals.
BIOACCUMULATION	The build-up of a particular element or compound (often a toxic substance) to higher concentrations in successively higher trophic levels in the food web.
BIOMASS	The amount of living biological matter within a specified area or volume of water; often expressed as weight per unit area or volume.
BIOSPHERE	Portion of the earth occupied by the various forms of life.
BIOTIC	Living component of the environment; life.
BLOOMS	Dense algal growths that occur in nutrient-rich lakes.
BLUE-GREENS	Group of microscopic algae-like organisms which are related to bacteria and have the capacity to fix nitrogen from the atmosphere.
BOG	A wetland usually developing in a depression, often with poor drainage; generally characterized by extensive peat deposits, acidic water, floating sedge or sphagnum mats, and heath shrubs and coniferous trees.
BOUNDARY LAYER	That layer of a fluid (air or water) adjacent to a physical boundary in which the fluid motion is much affected by the boundary and has a mean velocity less than a free-flow value.

BRECCIA	A coarse-grained sedimentary rock composed of angular broken rock fragments held together by a fine-grained mineral cement.
CARNIVORE	An animal which preys on other animals.
CATCHMENT BASIN	Drainage basin; the tract of country that gathers precipitation and contributes it to a particular stream system or lake.
CIRROSTRATUS	Transparent clouds, whitish veil of fibrous or smooth appearance that generally produce a halo around the sun.
CIRRUS	Detached clouds in the form of white, delicate filaments or bands which have a fibrous appearance or silky sheen.
CLIMATE	Average weather conditions of a region throughout the seasons.
COASTAL GEOMORPHOLOGY	The study of the classification, description, origin, and development of coastal landforms.
COLD DOME	A closed center of low pressure resulting from the isolation of cold air at high levels from a main body of cold air.
COMPENSATION DEPTH	The depth at which primary production equals plant respiration; depth at which light is 1% of surface intensity.
CONSUMER	An organism that is unable to manufacture its food from nonliving matter, but is dependent on the energy stored in other living things; primary, secondary, and tertiary consumers constitute increasingly higher levels in the food chain.
CONSUMPTIVE USE	Water extracted from the lake, used largely in manufacturing, which is not returned to the lake via a waste water system or runoff.
CONTOUR	A line drawn on a map between all points of the same elevation (see ISOPLETH).
CONVECTION	The process of heated, moisture-laden air rising due to reduced density; at higher elevations the water vapor condenses to form clouds and eventually rain.
CORIOLIS EFFECT (or force)	The tendency, produced by the rotation of the earth, of particles in motion on the earth's surface to be deflected to the right in the Northern Hemisphere.

COVE	A small, sheltered recess in a coast, often containing a pocket beach, commonly found inside a larger embayment.
CREVASSES	A wide breach or crack in the bank or natural levee of a river (e.g. St. Clair River delta).
CUESTA	An asymmetrical ridge with a gentle slope on one side and a steep slope on the other, particularly with one face (dip slope) long and gentle and conforming with the dip of the resistant beds that form it, and the opposite face (scarp slope) steep or cliff-like and formed by the outcrop of the resistant rocks; the formation of the ridge is controlled by differential erosion of the gently inclined strata (see ESCARPMENT).
CUMULUS	Detached clouds, generally dense with sharp outlines that form rising mounds, domes, and towers which often resemble cauliflower and are brilliantly white where sunlit; their base is relatively dark and nearly horizontal.
CUSPATE SAND SPIT	See SPIT.
CYCLONE	Atmospheric pressure distribution in which there is a low central pressure relative to the surroundings, resulting in anticlockwise winds spiraling in toward the center (see LOW).
DECOMPOSER	An organism, usually microscopic, that breaks down organic matter and thus aids in recycling nutrients.
DELTA	The low, nearly flat, alluvial tract of land deposited at or near the mouth of a river, commonly forming a fan-shaped plain of considerable area enclosed and crossed by many distributaries of the main river, often extending beyond the general trend of the coast, and resulting from the accumulation of sand and finer sediment in a wider body of water (usually a sea or lake).
DETRITUS	Minute particles of the decaying remains of plants and animals.
DEW	Water vapor which has condensed on surfaces whose temperature has fallen (often by radiation cooling) below the dew-point of the surrounding air.
DEW-POINT	The temperature to which moist air must be cooled in order for it to be totally saturated with water vapor.
DIATOMS	Group of microscopic algae which have rigid cell walls composed of silica.

DIKE	An embankment of various materials to protect land from inundation by a lake or to control wetlands' water levels.
DISTRIBUTARY CHANNELS	A system of divergent streams flowing away from the main stream, and not returning to it, and in a delta or alluvial plain.
DIVERSION	Water directed into or out of one of the Great lakes (either in or out of Great Lakes Basin or between two lakes in the system) via artificial channels or canals (e.g. Welland Canal between Lake Erie and Lake Ontario).
DOLOMITE	A carbonate sedimentary rock of which more than 50% consists of the mineral dolomite ($CaMg(CO_3)^2$).
DOWNWELLING	The process by which surface waters move downwater in a lake.
DRAINAGE SYSTEM	A stream or lake, together with all other such streams and lakes that are tributary to it and by which a region is drained.
DRAWDOWN	Process of partially or completely dewatering a wetland with the use of pumps or other mechanical devices for the purpose of vegetation and wildlife management.
DUNE	Ridge of loose, wind-blown material, usually sand.
ECOLOGICAL NICHE	Ecological role of an organism in its ecosystem; its relationship to its biotic and abiotic environment.
ECOSYSTEM	Biotic community and the non-living environment functioning together as a system where exchanges of materials and energy between living things and their physical environment takes place.
ECOTONE	Biotic community and the nonliving environment functioning together as a system where exchanges of materials and energy between living things and their physical environment takes place.
EMERGENT VEGETATION	Various vascular aquatic plants usually rooted in shallow water and having most of their vegetative growth above water (e.g. cattails and bulrushes).
EPILIMNION	The upper, warmer, well-mixed, well-illuminated, nearly isothermal region or layer of a stratified lake.

EPILITHIC	Pertaining to algae growing on rock or stone surfaces.
EPINEUSTON	Organisms living on neuston at the water's surface.
EPIPELIC	Pertaining to algae and other flora growing on fine and/or organic sediments.
EPIPHYTIC	Pertaining to algae growing on macrophytic surfaces (large plants).
EPISAMMIC	Pertaining to algae growing on sand particles.
EPIZOIC	Pertaining to algae growing on surfaces of animals.
ERICACEOUS	Low, much-branched evergreen shrub.
ERRATIC	A rock fragment carried by glacial ice and deposited at some distance from the outcrop from which it was derived (e.g. granite boulders resting on limestone islands in Lake Erie).
ESCARPMENT	A long, continuous cliff or steep slope facing in one general direction which breaks the continuity of land by separating two level or gently sloping surfaces; generally an erosion feature marking the outcrop of a resistant layer or rock occurring in a series of gently dipping softer strata (e.g. the steep face of a cuesta).
EUTROPHICATION	The process by which a lake becomes rich in dissolved nutrients and deficient in oxygen, occurring either as a natural stage in lake or pond maturation or artificially induced by human activities (principally by the addition of fertilizers and organic wastes).
EUTROPHY	The state of a well-nourished productive lake which typically exhibits a hypolimnetic (bottom water) loss of oxygen.
FAUNA	Animal life of a particular region or community.
FEN	A waterlogged, spongy groundmass containing alkaline and decaying vegetation characterized by reeds which may develop into peat.
FETCH	The area or horizontal distance over which waves are generated by wind.
FILAMENTOUS	Pertaining to slender thread-like fibres (i.e. connected string of algae cells in *Cladophora*).

FLATS	Low-lying, exposed, flat land of a lake delta or of a lake bottom, composed of unconsolidated sediments (usually mud or sand).
FLOATING-LEAVED PLANTS	Rooted, herbaceous hydrophytes with some leaves floating on water surface (e.g. white water lily and floating pondweed).
FLOATING PLANTS	Non-anchored plants that float freely in the water or on the surface (e.g. duckweeds).
FOG	Obscurity in the lower layers of the atmosphere, which is caused by a suspension of water droplets or smoke particles (visibility less than 1 km).
FOOD CHAIN	Sequence of organisms, including producers (plants), herbivores (plant-eaters), and carnivores (meat-eaters), through which energy and materials move within an ecosystem; a series of organisms depending on one another for food.
FOOD WEB	A system of interlocking food chains in which energy and materials are passed through a series of plant-eating and animal-eating consumers.
FORAGE FISH	Fish species utilized as principal food sources for major sport and commercial fishes (e.g. gizzard shad and emerald shiner).
FORESHORE	The part of the shore lying between the crest of the beach berm and mean lake level; the beach face that is ordinarily traversed by the uprush and backwash of waves.
FORMATION	A persistent body of like bedrock, having easily recognizable boundaries that can be traced in the field and represented on a geologic map.
FRESHWATER ESTUARY	A semi-enclosed coastal body of water which has a free connection with the open lake; estuaries are strongly affected by wind tides and seiches, and they are mixing zones for lake water and tributaries from land drainage (e.g. drowned river mouths, coastal embayments, and lagoons behind barrier beaches).
FRONT	A sloping transitional zone separating two air masses of different temperature and density; a cold front is one in which movement is such that colder air is replacing warmer air and a warm front is the reverse situation.
FROST WEDGING	Process by which jointed rock is pried and dislodged by water freezing to ice, the resulting expansion thereby acts as a wedge.

GEODE — A hollow, subspherical body with its cavity partly filled with inward-projecting crystals.

GEOSTROPHIC WIND — The wind that results from a balance between pressure gradient forces and coriolis (earth rotation) forces and blows parallel to pressure isobars.

GLACIO-LACUSTRINE — Pertaining to, derived from, or deposited in glacial lakes; particularly deposits composed of material brought by meltwater streams flowing into lakes bordering a glacier.

GORGE — A narrow, deep valley with nearly vertical rocky walls.

GRAVEL — Size grade of coarse sediment particles larger than 2.0 mm or -1 phi units in diameter; includes granules, pebbles, cobbles, and boulders.

GREEN ALGAE — Group of mainly microscopic algae, both filamentous and single-celled, which have a high concentration of chlorophyll a.

GUST — A rapid short-lived increase in the strength of the wind relative to the mean strength obtained during a specified period.

GYRE — A large-scale, closed circulatory system that is larger than a whirlpool or eddy.

HABITAT — A place where a plant or animal species lives and grows; an organism's natural abode and immediate surroundings.

HAIL — Hard pellets of ice of various sizes and shapes, more or less transparent, which fall from cumulonimbus clouds and are often associated with thunderstorms.

HARBOR BREAKWATER — A man-made structure protecting a harbor, anchorage, or basin from waves

HEADLANDS — A high steep-faced promontory, often rocky, extending into a lake.

HEAT CAPACITY — The heat required to raise the temperature of a substance (e.g. water has the ability to absorb large quantities of heat without a great increase in its temperature).

HERPETOFAUNA — Animals belonging to the vertebrate classes Amphibia and Reptilia.

HERBIVORE — An animal adapted to feed on plants.

HETEROTROPH	An organism which is unable to synthesize its own food from inorganic substances and must utilize other organisms for nourishment (e.g. fish, birds, and mammals).
HIGH	A region of high atmospheric pressure.
HINGE LINE	A line or boundary between a stable region of the earth's crust and a region undergoing upward movement (see ISOSTATIC REBOUND).
HUMIDITY	The condition of the atmosphere in respect to its water vapor content (see RELATIVE HUMIDITY).
HYDROPHOBIC CUTICLE	Superficial covering that retards wetting in a water medium.
HYPONEUSTON	Community of aquatic organisms living at and under the water's surface film.
HYDROPHYTE	Any plant growing in water or on a substrate that is at least periodically saturated with water; aquatic plant.
HYDROSPHERE	Layer of water which covers 71% of the earth's surface, and forms the oceans, seas, lakes, and streams.
HYPOLIMNION	The poorly illuminated, colder, denser, lower region or layer of a stratified lake; overlies the profundal zone.
HURRICANE	Intense cyclones with wind speeds averaging over 64 knots, which typically originate over tropical seas.
IGNEOUS ROCK	Rock that solidified from molten material known as magma (e.g. granite, rhyolite, and basalt).
INERTIAL MOTION	Water movement or currents caused by the rotation of the earth (Coriolis effect) which tend to move horizontally in clockwise circular orbits.
INTERDISTRIBUTARY BAY	Embayment formed between two adjacent distributary channels and their levee deposits on the open water face of a delta.
ISOPLETH	A line drawn on a map or chart which connects points of equal value.
ISOSTATIC REBOUND	Adjustment (uplift) of the land surface covered by a continental glacier once the ice sheet has melted, removing the weight which had depressed the original surface.

ISOTHERMAL   Uniform or nearly uniform temperature conditions from surface to bottom in a lake.

JOINT   A fracture or parting in a rock surface, without displacement; joints usually occur in parallel, being produced by a common stress.

KEEN   A climatic comfort type intermediate between cool and cold conditions which is characterized by cutting or bitter weather.

KETTLE   A steep-sided, bowl-shaped depression of glacial deposits, often containing a lake or wetland, formed by the melting of a large, detached block of ice left behind by a retreating glacier, that had been wholly or partly buried in the glacial drift.

LACUSTRINE   Pertaining to, produced by, or formed in a lake (e.g. lacustrine sediment).

LAGOON   A shallow body of still water, normally separated from a larger body of water by a narrow barrier, but often possessing an inlet connection.

LAKE EFFECT SNOWFALL   Excessive snowfall resulting from wind blowing across the lake, picking up moisture, which is cooled and falls as snow on the lee side of the lake, particularly if there are upland areas adjacent to the coast.

LAKE SENESCENCE   The part of the developmental sequence of a lake when it is approaching extinction as the result of sediment infilling, erosion of the outlet, and filling by the remains of aquatic vegetation.

LAND/SEA (LAKE)   Local winds, caused by the unequal heating and cooling of adjacent
BREEZES   land and water surfaces under the influence of solar radiation by day and radiation to the sky at night, which produce a pressure gradient near the coast.

LANGMIR CELLS   Circular cells of vertical water movement created by wind blowing over the water surface; downward water movement leaves foam, debris, and plankton at the water surface in lines parallel to the direction of the wind.

LEEWARD   The direction toward which the wind is blowing; direction toward which waves are traveling.

LIMNOLOGY   The study of the physical, chemical, geological, meteorological, biological, and especially ecological conditions of lakes and other inland waters.

LIPOPROTEINS	Organic substances containing a combination of lipids (i.e. fats, oils, and waxes) and proteins (long-chain polymer of amino acids).
LITHOSPHERE	Solid crust of the earth; it projects through the hydrosphere to form the continents.
LITTORAL DRIFT	The sedimentary material moved in along the coast or littoral zone (shoreline to just beyond where waves break) by waves and alongshore currents.
LITTORAL ZONE	Referring to the marginal region of a body of water; the shallow, near-shore region often defined by the zone from zero depth to the outer edge of the rooted plants.
LOGARITHMIC SCALE	A graduated scale in which the intervals are governed by the power to which a base number must be raised to equal a given number.
LOW	A region of low atmospheric pressure.
MACROALGAE	Algal plants large enough, either as individuals or communities, to be readily visible without the aid of optical magnification.
MACROPHYTE	All macroscopic (visible without the aid of optical magnification) plants of lakes, streams, and wetlands; primarily vascular plants that are usually, but not always, rooted; can include large algae and mosses.
MARL	A calcareous ($CaCO_3$) clay sediment deposited in shallow, quiet waters.
MARSH	A wetland dominated by herbaceous or non-woody vegetation, often developing in shallow ponds or depressions, river margins, and estuaries; plants are often dominated by grasses and sedges.
MESOLIMNION	The central stratum or layer between the epilimnion and hypolimnion in a stratified lake; the region of the thermocline; metalimnion.
METALIMNION	See MESOLIMNION.
METAMORPHIC ROCK	Rock derived from pre-existing rock which has been chemically, mineralogically, and structurally altered by changes in temperature, pressure, and chemical environment (e.g. marble, gneiss, and schist).
METAPHYTON	Aggregates of algae found in the littoral zone which are often mixed with debris.

MICROALGAE	Algal plants that require optical magnification to be readily visible.
MODEL	One or more formulae which have been contrived by examining the variables in a natural process so that the process can be simulated by a mathematical expression.
MONODOMINANT	A situation where a vegetation region is controlled by a single species of plant (e.g. cattail marsh).
MORAINE	A ridge of unsorted, unstratified glacial drift (till), deposited by the direct action of glacial ice; terminal or end moraines represent static positions at the end of an ice advance or retreat; ground moraines are lower general deposits between the ridges.
MORPHOMETRY	The measurement of the form characteristics of lakes and their basins (e.g. area, depth, length, and volume).
NATURAL LEVEE	A long, low ridge of sand and silt built by a stream along the top of its banks during times of flood.
NEKTON	Large, actively swimming aquatic animals (e.g. fish).
NIMBOSTRATUS	Layered clouds, dark gray in appearance which more or less continuously render rain or snow.
NIMBUS	Rain clouds.
NICHE	See ECOLOGICAL NICHE.
NITROGEN FIXATION	The conversion of atmospheric nitrogen to a combined form by the metabolic processes of some blue-green algae and bacteria.
NEUSTON	Community of aquatic flora and fauna associated with the water's surface tension.
NODAL LINE	The line about which a seiche or standing wave oscillates and where there is little or no rise or fall in the water level but horizontal velocities are greatest.
NUTRIENTS	Chemical elements, organic compounds, or inorganic compounds used to promote growth (e.g. nitrogen and phosphorus).

OUTLET | The relatively narrow opening at the lower end of a lake through which water is discharged into an outflowing stream; elevation of the outlet controls elevation of the lake (see SILL AND SPILLWAY).

OLIGOTROPHY | The state of a poorly-nourished, unproductive lake which is commonly oxygen-rich and low in turbidity.

OROGRAPHY | In meteorology, used to signify the physical land features (e.g. hills or mountains) of a specific area.

OXIDATION | The combining of oxygen with a substance, or the process in which hydrogen is lost from a compound, or more generally, the loss of an electron from an element (e.g. iron rusting to iron oxide).

OZONE LAYER | Atmospheric layer of the triatomic form of oxygen (O_3) which reaches its maximum concentration about 12 to 15 miles (20 to 25 km) above the earth's surface; ozone is present in the high atmosphere as a result of photochemical processes (absorption of ultra-violet radiation by oxygen).

PALUDAL | Pertaining to a marsh or swamp.

PALUSTRINE | Pertaining to material growing or deposited in a marsh or wetland environment.

PEAT | An unconsolidated deposit of semicarbonized plant remains in a water saturated environment such as a bog or fen.

PERIPHYTON | Organisms attached to stems of aquatic plants or other submerged surfaces.

pH | A measure of the acidity or bacicity of a solution; negative $\log^{10}$ of hydrogen-ion activity in a solution (e.g. >7 base, <7 acid).

PHI UNITS SCALE | A logarithmic transformation of the Wentworth grade scale in which the negative logarithm to the base 2 of the particle diameter (in mm) is substituted for the diameter value.

PHOTIC ZONE | The portion of the lake where light intensity is sufficient to accommodate plant growth (1% of surface light or greater).

PHOTOSYNTHESIS | The process which takes place in green plants by which simple sugars are manufactured from CO_2, water, and mineral nutrients with the aid of chlorophyll within the plant cells in the presence of light.

PHYSIOGRAPHY	The description and origin of landforms.
PHYTOPLANKTON	Plant microorganisms, such as certain algae, floating in the water.
PLANKTON	Free-floating, usually minute, aquatic organisms (e.g. diatoms and copepods).
POIKILOTHERMIC	Pertaining to cold blooded organisms (e.g. fish) which have a body temperature that is the same as the surrounding water.
PRECIPITATION	In meteorology, any aqueous deposit, in liquid or solid form, derived from the atmosphere.
PRIMARY PRODUCTIVITY	Rate of photosynthetic carbon fixation by plants and bacteria forming the base of the food web (see PHOTOSYNTHESIS).
PRIMARY PRODUCER	An organism which is capable of manufacturing its own food from inorganic raw materials and energy (i.e. photosynthetic plants).
PROFUNDAL ZONE	Lake bottom offshore from the littoral zone.
PSAMMON	Organisms growing on or moving through sand.
QUADRANT	A quarter of a circle (arc of 90°).
QUARTILE	In statistics, the value of the boundary at the 25th, 50th, or 75th percentiles of a frequency distribution divided into four parts, each containing a quarter of the population.
RADIATION FOG	A fog which forms in low areas over land on nights with light winds, clear skies, and moist air.
RADIOCARBON DATING	A method of determining the age of organic material (in years) by measuring the concentration of carbon-14 remaining after degradation following the death of living material.
RECRUITMENT	In fish populations, the natural introduction of juveniles into the adult population.
RELATIVE HUMIDITY	Ratio of the amount of water vapor in the air to the amount (capacity) the air can hold at a specific temperature, expressed as a percentage.
RELICT CHANNEL	A long, narrow depression on the surface of a delta which was formerly occupied by a distributary channel.

RELIEF	The difference in elevation between the highest and lowest land surfaces in a particular region.
RESPIRATION	Life process by which plants and animals absorb oxygen and emit carbon dioxide.
RHEOTAXIS	Referring to the response of organisms to flow, particularly water current; an organism with a positive rheotaxis tendency would be attracted to flowing water.
RIP-RAP	A structure of large durable, irregular rock placed in water to prevent shore erosion, serve as a breakwater for a harbor, or protect a dike.
RIVERINE	Pertaining to or formed by a river.
ROOKERY	A group of nests or the breeding place of a colony of waterbirds (e.g. herons and egrets).
ROUGH FISH	Fish with low commercial or sport value.
RUNOFF	The water which flows on the land surface, via rivers and streams, from the watershed (drainage basin) to the lake.
SAND	Size grade of medium sediment particles between 0.0625 and 2.0 mm or 4 and -1 phi units in diameter.
SANDSTONE	A sedimentary rock consisting of cemented sand-sized grains, primarily quartz.
SEASONAL SUCCESSION	The progressive change in a biological community in response to changing climatic conditions throughout the year.
SECONDARY PRODUCTIVITY	The rate at which animals produce organic matter (e.g. zooplankton feeding on algae).
SEDIMENT	Fragmental material that originates from weathering of rock and is transported or deposited by air, water, or ice.
SEDIMENTATION	The process of forming or accumulating sediment in layers.
SEDIMENTARY ROCK	Rock resulting from the consolidation of loose sediment that has accumulated in layers (e.g. sandstone, limestone, and shale).

SEICHE | A period, rapid, and often violent fluctuation in water level within a lake or an embayment due to onshore or offshore winds and low barometric pressure; often results from a storm surge or wind setup.

SEISMIC MEASUREMENTS | A method of geophysical investigation which utilizes artificially induced or natural earth vibration to produce a graphic stratigraphic sequence of subsurface sediment and rock layers.

SHALE | A fine-grained sedimentary rock, formed by consolidation of silt, clay, or mud, which is thinly laminated (fissile).

SILL | A submarine ridge at a relatively shallow depth, separating a lake basin from its outlet stream and controlling the water level in the lake.

SILTSTONE | A sedimentary rock formed by consolidation of silt-sized particles, having the composition and texture of shale but lacking its fine laminations.

SINKHOLE | A circular depression formed by solutioning of limestone terrain.

SINUSOIDAL WAVE | A water wave which approximates the form of a sine curve.

SOLAR RADIATION | The transmission of energy by electromagnetic waves from the sun to the earth.

SOLSTICE | The time of maximum (summer) and minimum (winter) solar declination when the sun is farthest north or south of the equator.

SPECIES | A group of closely related individuals which can and normally do interbreed to produce fertile offspring.

SPILLWAY | A channel or outlet through which overflow water from a glacial lake is drained away.

SPIT | A point of land consisting of sand or gravel deposited by alongshore currents, having one end attached to the mainland and the other terminating in open water; cuspate sand spits are characterized by points which project toward the lake with intervening arcs that are cut into the beach.

SQUALL LINE | A belt of strong wind which rises suddenly, generally lasting several minutes, and dies away rapidly; they are frequently associated with rainshowers but are narrower than frontal zones and commonly precede cold fronts.

STEAM FOG — The formation of fog by rapid evaporation when cold air moves over warmer lake water.

STORM SURGE — An abnormal, sudden rise in lake level along the coast during a storm, caused primarily by onshore-wind stresses or less frequently by atmospheric pressure reduction, resulting in water piled up against the coast.

STRAIT — A relatively narrow waterway between two larger bodies of water.

STRATA — Layers of sedimentary rock.

STRATIFIED LAKE — A lake which has become horizontally layered, typically due to temperature or density differences (see EPILIMNION, HYPOLIMNION, MESOLIMNION and THERMOCLINE).

STRATIGRAPHIC SECTION — A diagram or description of the sequence of rock formations found in a given region.

STRATUS — Layered clouds, generally gray with a uniform base which may appear in the form of ragged patches.

SUBMERGENT VEGETATION — Various vascular aquatic plants usually rooted in shallow or moderate depth water while lying entirely beneath the water surface, except for the flowering parts of some species (e.g. wild celery and stoneworts).

SUBSTRATE — Base or foundation on which an organism lives (e.g. soil, vegetation debris, or lake sediment).

SUSPENDED LOAD — The sediment material moving in suspension in a fluid, being kept in the water column by the upward components of turbulent currents or by colloidal suspension.

SWAMP — A wetland dominated by woody plants, shrubs, and trees such as maple, cottonwood, and willow.

SWELL — Wind-generated waves that have traveled out of their generating area; waves are more regular, longer period, and having flatter crests than waves within their fetch area.

SYNOPTIC CHART — A chart showing the distribution of meteorological conditions over a wide region at the same moment.

TAXON — A named group of organisms of any rank (i.e. species, family, or class); plural taxa.

THERMAL CONDUCTION   The process of heat transfer from regions of high to low temperatures by molecular impact, without transfer of matter itself.

THERMAL STRATIFICATION   Layering of lake water into a warm surface layer (epilimnion) and a cold bottom layer (hypolimnion) separated by a thin transition zone (thermocline), generally initiated by spring heating and terminated by fall cooling.

THERMOCLINE   A subsurface zone in a lake of rapid temperature change with depth.

THUNDERSTORM   Sudden electrical discharges, manifested by lightning flashes and a sharp rumbling sound, normally associated with cumulonimbus clouds and heavy rainfall and frequently accompanied by hail.

TOPOGRAPHY   Configuration of a land surface, including its relief and position of its natural and man-made features.

TORNADO   A violent cyclonic whirl, averaging a few hundred feet in diameter and with intense vertical updrafts capable of lifting heavy objects into the air.

TRANSGRESSIVE BEACH   A beach deposited during the advance or encroachment of water over land (e.g. rising lake level).

TRANSPARENCY   The capacity of a medium (e.g. air or water) to allow radiation, particularly light, to pass.

TRANSPIRATION   The loss of water as vapor from a plant.

TROPHIC LEVEL   The position of an organism or species in a food chain.

TROPOPAUSE   The atmospheric boundary between the troposphere and the stratosphere.

TROPOSPHERE   The lower layer of the atmosphere, extending from the earth's surface to the tropopause, a thickness of about 7 miles (12 km) over the Great Lakes.

TURBIDITY   A condition of opaqueness or reduced clarity of lake water caused by suspended sediment and/or plankton.

TURNOVER

A period (usually in the fall or spring) when a lake has uniform vertical temperature permitting vertical convective circulation or mixing to take place; such conditions result in the destratification of a lake (see STRATIFIED LAKE).

ULTRA-VIOLET RADIATION

Electromagnetic radiation from the sun in the approximate wavelength range from 100 to 400 nanometers (nm), which is largely screened from the earth's surface by various photo-chemical reactions in the high atmosphere.

UPWELLING

The process by which water rises from the lake bottom to a higher depth.

VASCULAR

Pertaining to higher plants which have an internal conduit system for conveying fluids to various parts of the plant.

VISIBILITY

The greatest distance at which an object of specified characteristics can be seen and identified with the unaided eye.

VORTEX

A whirling mass of air or water, particularly one in the form of a visible column or spiral (e.g. a tornado) or one in which a force of suction operates (e.g. a whirlpool).

WARM MONOMICTIC LAKE

Lake with one period of annual mixing; circulation occurs during the winter months (because of only partial ice cover) and thermal stratification during the summer.

WATER BUDGET

An accounting of the inflow to, outflow from, and storage in a hydrologic unit, such as a drainage basin, lake, reservoir, or wetland; the relationship between evaporation, precipitation, runoff and the change in water storage.

WATERSHED

Drainage basin; the region drained, by or contributing water to a stream, lake, or other body of water.

WATER VAPOR

Water in a gaseous form.

WATERWAY

River, channel, canal, or other navigable body of water used for travel or transport (e.g. St. Clair River and Detroit River are connecting waterways between Lake Erie and Lake Huron).

WAVE CLIMATE

A description of the average or typical wave condition of a given region.

WAVE HEIGHT	The vertical distance between a wave crest and the preceding wave trough; significant wave height is the average height of the one-third highest waves of a given group (this value approximates the wave height estimate of a human observer).
WAVELENGTH	The distance between corresponding points (e.g. crests) of two successive periodic waves in the direction of propagation.
WAVE PERIOD	The time, in seconds, required for a wave crest to traverse a distance equal to one wavelength.
WEATHER	Temporal conditions of the atmosphere as described by various meteorological phenomena, including atmospheric pressure, temperature, humidity, precipitation, cloudiness, and wind speed and direction.
WENTWORTH GRADE SCALE	Size scale for sediment particles based on grain-size in mm (see CLAY, SILT, SAND, GRAVEL, and PHI UNIT SCALE).
WETLANDS	Lands where saturation with water is the dominant factor determining the nature of soil development and the types of plant and animal communities in the soil and on its surface.
WIND ROSE	A diagram showing, for a specific location and period, the frequencies of winds blowing from the main points of a compass for specified speed ranges.
WHIRLPOOL	A body of water moving rapidly in a circular path of small radius, produced by a current's passage through an angular or irregular channel.
WHITE ICE	Ice formed by freezing of lake water to a thickness of 12 to 27.5 inches (30 to 70 cm).
WIND CHILL INDEX	The combined effect of temperature and wind velocity on exposed skin expressed in terms of the temperature alone.
WIND SETUP	Wind tide or storm surge; the difference in water levels on the windward (toward the wind) side and leeward (away from the wind) side of a lake caused by wind stresses on the surface of the water.
WINDWARD	The direction from which the wind is blowing.
ZOOPLANKTON	Animal microorganisms, such as small crustacean (e.g. water fleas and copepods) rotifers, and protozoans, floating in the water.

Index

Dr. Stanley J. Bolsenga is the Assistant to the Director and a Research Hydrologist with the Great Lakes Environmental Research Laboratory in Ann Arbor, Michigan. His current research endeavors lie in the fields of ice and snow, under-ice ecology, bioclimatology, and climatic change. He earned his Ph.D. and M.S. degrees from the University of Michigan and his Bachelors degree from the University of Colorado. As a Research Geologist for the Cold Regions Research and Engineering Laboratory in Hanover, New Hampshire, he conducted research on lake ice, micrometeorology, photo-electric photometry, snow drifting control, and weather modification in Greenland and Alaska. Dr. Bolsenga has published over 70 scientific papers and authored two books. As a member of the National Academy of Sciences, Committee for the International Hydrological Decade, he served as the U.S. Coordinator for a large-scale, U.S.-Canadian research program from 1968-71.

Dr. Herdendorf is Professor Emeritus of Limnology and Oceanography at The Ohio State University. He is a certified professional geologist and a certified fisheries scientist. For over 30 years he has conducted research on the Great Lakes, specializing in wetland ecology, coastal geomorphology, eutrophication processes, fish habitat restoration, and offshore mineral resources. He served for 11 years as Geologist and Lake Erie Section Head of the Ohio Department of Natural Resources, Division of Shore Erosion and Geological Survey. He has been on The Ohio State University faculty for 20 years and has served as the first Director of the Center for Lake Erie Area Research (CLEAR) and the Ohio Sea Grant College Program and the seventh Director of the Franz Theodore Stone Laboratory at Put-in-Bay on Lake Erie. Dr. Herdendorf received his B.S. and M.S. degrees from Ohio University in Athens, Ohio and his Ph.D. from The Ohio State University. Dr. Herdendorf has authored hundreds of technical reports and scientific papers. One of his recent works is a chapter on the distribution of the world's large lakes in *Large Lakes: Ecological Structure and Function.*

TITLES IN THE GREAT LAKES BOOK SERIES

Freshwater Fury: Yarns and Reminiscences of the Greatest Storm in Inland Navigation, by Frank Barcus, 1986 (reprint)

Call It North Country: The Story of Upper Michigan, by John Bartlow Martin, 1986 (reprint)

The Land of the Crooked Tree, by U. P. Hedrick, 1986 (reprint)

Michigan Place Names, by Walter Romig, 1986 (reprint)

Luke Karamazov, by Conrad Hilberry, 1987

The Late, Great Lakes: An Environmental History, by William Ashworth, 1987 (reprint)

Great Pages of Michigan History from the Detroit Free Press, 1987

Waiting for the Morning Train: An American Boyhood, by Bruce Catton, 1987 (reprint)

Michigan Voices: Our State's History in the Words of the People Who Lived it, compiled and edited by Joe Grimm, 1987

Danny and the Boys, Being Some Legends of Hungry Hollow, by Robert Traver, 1987 (reprint)

Hanging On, or How to Get through a Depression and Enjoy Life, by Edmund G. Love, 1987 (reprint)

The Situation in Flushing, by Edmund G. Love, 1987 (reprint)

A Small Bequest, by Edmund G. Love, 1987 (reprint)

The Saginaw Paul Bunyan, by James Stevens, 1987 (reprint)

The Ambassador Bridge: A Monument to Progress, by Philip P. Mason, 1988

Let the Drum Beat: A History of the Detroit Light Guard, by Stanley D. Solvick, 1988

An Afternoon in Waterloo Park, by Gerald Dumas, 1988 (reprint)

Contemporary Michigan Poetry: Poems from the Third Coast, edited by Michael Delp, Conrad Hilberry, and Herbert Scott, 1988

Over the Graves of Horses, by Michael Delp, 1988

Wolf in Sheep's Clothing: The Search for a Child Killer, by Tommy McIntyre, 1988

Copper-Toed Boots, by Marguerite de Angeli, 1989 (reprint)

Detroit Images: Photographs of the Renaissance City, edited by John J. Bukowczyk and Douglas Aikenhead, with Peter Slavcheff, 1989

Hangdog Reef: Poems Sailing the Great Lakes, by Stephen Tudor, 1989

Detroit: City of Race and Class Violence, revised edition, by B. J. Widick, 1989

Deep Woods Frontier: A History of Logging in Northern Michigan, by Theodore J. Karamanski, 1989

Orvie, The Dictator of Dearborn, by David L. Good, 1989

Seasons of Grace: A History of the Catholic Archdiocese of Detroit, by Leslie Woodcock Tentler, 1990

The Pottery of John Foster: Form and Meaning, by Gordon and Elizabeth Orear, 1990

The Diary of Bishop Frederic Baraga: First Bishop of Marquette, Michigan, edited by Regis M. Walling and Rev. N. Daniel Rupp, 1990

Walnut Pickles and Watermelon Cake: A Century of Michigan Cooking, by Larry B. Massie and Priscilla Massie, 1990

The Making of Michigan, 1820-1860: A Pioneer Anthology, edited by Justin L. Kestenbaum, 1990

America's Favorite Homes: A Guide to Popular Early Twentieth-Century Homes, by Robert Schweitzer and Michael W. R. Davis, 1990

Beyond the Model T: The Other Ventures of Henry Ford, by Ford R. Bryan, 1990

Life after the Line, by Josie Kearns, 1990

Michigan Lumbertowns: Lumbermen and Laborers in Saginaw, Bay City, and Muskegon, 1870-1905, by Jeremy W. Kilar, 1990

Detroit Kids Catalog: The Hometown Tourist, by Ellyce Field, 1990

Waiting for the News, by Leo Litwak, 1990 (reprint)

Detroit Perspectives, edited by Wilma Wood Henrickson, 1991

Life on the Great Lakes: A Wheelsman's Story, by Fred W. Dutton, edited by William Donohue Ellis, 1991

Copper Country Journal: The Diary of Schoolmaster Henry Hobart, 1863-1864, by Henry Hobart, edited by Philip P. Mason, 1991

John Jacob Astor: Business and Finance in the Early Republic, by John Denis Haeger, 1991

Survival and Regeneration: Detroit's American Indian Community, by Edmund J. Danziger, Jr., 1991

Steamboats and Sailors of the Great Lakes, by Mark L. Thompson, 1991

Cobb Would Have Caught It: The Golden Years of Baseball in Detroit, by Richard Bak, 1991

Michigan in Literature, by Clarence Andrews, 1992

Under the Influence of Water: Poems, Essays, and Stories, by Michael Delp, 1992

The Country Kitchen, by Della T. Lutes, 1992 (reprint)

The Making of a Mining District: Keweenaw Native Copper 1500-1870, by David J. Krause, 1992

Kids Catalog of Michigan Adventures, by Ellyce Field, 1993

Henry's Lieutenants, by Ford R. Bryan, 1993

Historic Highway Bridges of Michigan, by Charles K. Hyde, 1993

Lake Erie and Lake St. Clair Handbook, edited by Stanley J. Bolsenga and Charles E. Herdendorf, 1993.